Acclaim for

"Chief Doris Sumner's memoir, *Life at Camp*, is essential—if not required—reading for anyone/everyone interested in a military career and deserves to know certain minuscule facts—that don't easily come to light—which contribute mightily to the quality of the experience one might have. Chief Sumner's provocative story unpacks what often feels like never ending transgressions toward women soldiers—and unabashedly reveals the reality of male privilege—within the National Guard. This is a needed to be told tale of one relentlessly brave woman's journey, moral courage, intestinal fortitude, and professional outrage. It's a tale of the allies she acquires along the way; and those pseudo allies, who often posture authentically, as such, while their actions, or lack thereof—are more akin to white lies—in terms of their true feelings about a level playing field between women and men.

"As a result of not wanting to lose their unearned privilege their white lies eventually morph into alibis for not doing the right thing, which consistently become bye-byes said by countless women departing. Warriors, who far too often had their once-upon-a-time dreams crushed, simply because of their devalued gendered reality, and audacity to expect equality. So, who should read *Life at Camp*, an unpretentious memoir that provides a behind-the-scene glimpse of the sexism and sexual harassment that is somehow illogically ignored/dismissed by the sanctioned military classism (hierarchies) that abounds in most—if not all—military camps?

"Women interested in a military career must read this book. Men interested in transcending their socialization must read this book. Men who desire to be courageous in varied contexts, men who dare to be brave enough to transcend the good old boys' network must read this book. Men interested in making this world a better place for the women in their lives (daughters, romantic partners, spouses, mothers, friends, colleagues) must read this book. And of course, people with an inherent sense of fair play would also benefit from reading this compelling story."

— Dr. J.W. Wiley, Author; Diversity Consultant

"This book was fascinating and educational. I believe reading it will help to resolve pain in others, as writing it was probably therapeutic for you. Starting with naïveté that evolved into crusading, your real life struggles turned into lessons shared through your strength and tenacity to help others. Your Paragraph 1, Chapter 1 grabs the reader. Throughout the book you include uncensored powerful messages that 'you can do it, you can overcome.'

"Sexism is still a very real problem in society. As is alcoholism. Both of which you have the energy and persistence to fight. Alcohol impacts every U.S. family. Sexism could negatively influence more than half the world's population. In person, and in your book narrative, you demonstrated the courage and passion to do the right thing, not just the easy thing. Not everyone experiences blatant sexual harassment but many have experienced or witnessed the impact of sexism. Your message was NOT lost. Your lessons are appropriate for any leader in an environment with 'non-traditional roles' for women, military or civilian.

"I believe you and the National Guard have the same ultimate goals:

"1. Prevention of the sexism, bias, and prejudice that cause assault, harassment, and career speedbumps/roadblocks.

"2. Sense of security and closure for accusers and accountability with penance for the accused.

"You reinforced many lessons in your book, some of which you initially taught me several years ago when we served in the JDEC together. I enjoyed learning the very appropriate terms 'mansplain' and 'Bureaucratic Harassment'".

"A fantastic book. Every state and national JDEC member should read it. New (and old) TAGs should read it. It could serve as a training aid or continuity book for SEEMs, EEOs, and others. Others paved a path before us, you have PLOWED a path for others. It was obvious when speaking with you in person years ago, and in reading this memoir, that your time as EEO manager was not only a journey, it became your calling.

"YOUR SERVICE DEFINITELY MATTERED. And your lessons still resonate to the hundreds you briefed and spoke with over the years. Great work all around!"

— Dr. Kimberly Baumann, former National Guard Bureau Northeast Region Joint Diversity Executive Council Chairperson

"As an MST survivor, and an unwittingly assimilated successful soldier across a 15 year career, I was thoroughly impressed by the scope of this book.

"My own passion in training and developing talent was cut short due to sexism in the military. While Doris's book at times was a difficult read, due to my own personal experiences with sexism, it ultimately is a story of tremendous courage in fighting for those who may have lost the will to fight. There is just so much to unpack here, like the contents of the invisible backpack that Doris equates to the baggage soldiers carry when their stories of suffering and mistreatment through sexism are downplayed and often become a double edged sword for the victim.

"I myself, like Doris prior to taking the job as the Equal Opportunity Manager for the State of Vermont, didn't recognize my incredible ability to assimilate into an organization changing myself to fit the dominant culture. This failure to see the reality can be a subtle, unconscious bias even toward ourselves, because to admit assimilation in some way takes away from the uniqueness of our ability to rise through the ranks, when so few women do.

"The male dominated power structure has a similar unconscious bias—it is the 'like me bias,' it is the gravitational pull we feel toward similar people. As Doris describes, it is apparent in the hiring and developing talent practices, as much as the disciplinary practices. I believe many leaders of the Vermont National Guard and other military units do believe they are doing the right thing, but the reason they so boldly oppose oversight is that, even though they don't believe they are unconsciously biased, they at the same time are smart enough to know oversight will arbitrarily remove any blinders. I could relate to each story of sexism, there were so many common trench holes, and Doris keeps you captivated through her incredible ability to write with such pure emotion about the struggles of fighting for a cause she could not ignore. Her tenacity throughout the years yielded national attention, and yet her bosses continued to dismiss her strategic ideas of changing the culture through gender equality accountability.

"Doris frames the problem statement so clearly in this memoir. She breaks down how the organization created the problem, and then how its obvious dysfunctional response to that problem is a barrier to top talent. The military cannot police itself, as she states it—you cannot write your own report card and at the same time claim transparency.

"Commanders all the way to the top hide between the articles of the UCMJ. They are uniquely able to pick and choose which articles to apply and which soldiers to hold accountable. Doris proves time and time again through the years how the system is able to manipulate the results of any attempt at accountability and blatantly shut her down and silence her over and over again, right up to and even after her 36-year career with 13 years as the equal employment manager.

"You would think an organization that touts mission ready top talent would see the value in her continued service and expertise in the subject matter. Certainly 4-star generals on a national level did see her value, yet the 1- and 2-star generals somehow missed this and even manipulated and reprimanded her for her tenacious efforts.

"I felt the great sense of loss for all the talent that left the organization solely because of this issue. It's clear to see, if it were void of sexism and followed its own declared process, this could be a highly effective organization with the most talented pool of warriors available.

"The solution is laid out with gender equality accountability as a requirement, because the military cannot continue to police itself. It is an organization made up of people who have brains, therefore there is and always will be bias.

"I feel honored to know Doris, I am impressed with her tenacity and commitment to writing this book, and with her belief in the cause and her tribute to the future soldiers of America!"

— CINDY MARIE KINGSLEY,
VETERAN, ARMY NATIONAL GUARD

LIFE AT CAMP

Combating the Sexism We Tolerate,
and Why the Military Should Take the Lead

LIFE AT CAMP

Combating the Sexism We Tolerate,
and Why the Military Should Take the Lead

A memoir by
DORIS J. SUMNER
Chief Warrant Officer Four
Vermont Army National Guard (Retired)

empowering gender opportunities

Life at Camp

First Edition October 2023

All rights reserved. No part of this publication may be reproduced, stored in a retrieval system, or transmitted in any form, without the written prior permission of the author, except for the use of brief excerpts in reviews or for publicity for author events.

This is a memoir of my early years and my experience in the active duty Army and Vermont Army National Guard. Quotes or conversations have been reconstructed from memory to the best of my ability. Certain names and identifying details of characters in the book have been changed to protect the privacy of the individuals involved. Often, authentic aspects of the sexual offense violations I describe have been purposely mixed to protect identities. The incidents were written attentively to highlight the harsh reality victims found themselves in. The purpose of relaying these events is to lift the voices of the many survivors who never officially reported, yet carried the weight of Military Sexual Trauma and the unfortunate reality of sexism.

Copyright © 2023 by Doris J. Sumner

Book cover and interior design by Carrie Cook
Author photo by Joanna Key

The text of this book was set in Adobe Garamond.

Published in the United States of America by
Empowering Gender Opportunities, LLC Milton, Vermont 05468

ISBN: 979-8-9878149-1-8
Library of Congress Control Number: 2023907187

Printed in the United States of America

For information, permissions, and appearances, please visit
www.itsallaboutego.com, or Facebook at:
Empowering Gender Opportunities, LLC

DEDICATION

The trudge I endured to find where I fit in life is dedicated to my mother, and all the strong, competent, courageous, funny, talented, sweet, emotional, authentic women I encountered along the way. May you find your solace.

For men who attempted to reject assimilation when it did not feel right, and to those who never could, may you move out in peace.

To my father and brothers who did not survive alcoholism, I love you.

To my sweet granddaughter Rayya, who sparked my activism to make the world a better place for you and others.

AUTHOR'S NOTE
Relating to the National Guard Culture
★ ★ ★

In my memoir, I describe my experiences as a service member in the National Guard (NG) of a small state. Readers may relate the State National Guard to be like a branch of a national company. Each branch has a chief executive officer (CEO). The CEO equivalent in each State's National Guard is The Adjutant General (TAG), a military 2-star general officer in charge of the operations within their State. The headquarters of a business administers the policies focused on the overarching company's mission, though each State (or branch of a company) may have independent missions. The headquarters for the National Guard is called the National Guard Bureau (NGB), with the main office located in Arlington, Virginia.

In the military, the acronyms, titles, and hierarchal structure can be daunting to someone who has no background in this type of system. I encourage you to trust in the story. Behind a first sergeant (1SG), commander (Cmdr) or the acronyms TAG, SEEM, Director Joint Staff (DJS) is a human being with the great qualities and defects any character in a story can have. *[For future references see Diagram 4 Acronyms and Terms Table.]*

I was advised to keep the military jargon out of the memoir because it can be overwhelmingly complicated. I compromised by keeping some of the jargon and describing the hierarchal status in an attempt to highlight what a big deal the National Guard is to our American culture. The National Guard operations are integrated into every community across our country. The National Guard warriors are your local doctors, clerks, mechanics, school teachers, and neighbors.

I included footnotes and diagrams as applicable for those interested in understanding the massive Department of Defense (DoD) structure and how national policies impact hometown National Guard members in profound ways. There is also a resource page on my website annotating links to websites, reports, and articles I used to formulate my perspectives. If you can understand to some degree, where your hometown Guard fits in the scheme of our nation's national defense, you can better hold them accountable to do the job they have been entrusted to do.

Additionally, reading about sexual harassment, sexual trauma, and humiliations of oppression can be triggering. I encourage anyone disturbed by the cultural issues described in *Life at Camp* to seek help and support. I maintain a resource page on my Empowering Gender Opportunities, LLC (EGO), website at www.itsallaboutego.com/resources. Please take care of you so you may be empowered to live a purpose filled life.

CONTENTS

Prologue	1
Chapter 1: Chilled Out	3
Chapter 2: Unpacking the Power Dynamics	11
Chapter 3: Do I Like to Fight?	23
Chapter 4: The Road to Camp	35
Chapter 5: Life at Camp	51
Chapter 6: Growing Up at Camp	61
Chapter 7: What is Equal Opportunity?	79
Chapter 8: Not as Simple as Black and White	89
Chapter 9: Stumbling Through EO	105
Chapter 10: The Good Old Boys' Club	117
Chapter 11: Processing Powerlessly	135
Chapter 12: What About a Women's Program?	149
Chapter 13: On a Mission	169
Chapter 14: What Culture Needs to Transformed?	189
Chapter 15: Transforming the Task Force	207
Chapter 16: The Highs and Lows of the Enduring Battles	221
Chapter 17: The Power of Command	237

CHAPTER 18: Keeping Up the Fight - Here or There	253
CHAPTER 19: Keeping Up the Fight - Field Duty	265
CHAPTER 20: Enlightenment Growing Dim	279
CHAPTER 21: Fighting the Naysayers	297
CHAPTER 22: Behind the Scenes	313
CHAPTER 23: Moving On	333
CHAPTER 24: Going National	347
CHAPTER 25: Let's Get Real	365
CHAPTER 26: Right on the Money	383
CHAPTER 27: Final Year at Camp	401
CHAPTER 28: Go Fuck Yourself	413
CHAPTER 29: The Issue with Isms	429
CHAPTER 30: VTDigger's Dig	449
CHAPTER 31: We are Not Perfect	463
CHAPTER 32: The Final Blows	487
CHAPTER 33: Not Letting Go	507
CHAPTER 34: Keep Fighting	525
CHAPTER 35: God's Taps	545
CHAPTER 36: Putting the Plow Down	561

DIAGRAM 1: Full time Force Structure
        vs. Drill status Structure   573

DIAGRAM 2A: Air Chain of Command and EO Process   574

DIAGRAM 2B: Army Chain of Command and EO Process   575

DIAGRAM 3A: Air Force Rank   576

DIAGRAM 3B: Army Rank   577

DIAGRAM 4: Acronyms and Terms Table   578

ADDENDUM: RECOMMENDATIONS TO COMBAT SEXISM
        IN THE NATIONAL GUARD   591

ACKNOWLEDGMENTS   599

PROLOGUE

At the age of 18, I joined the United States Army to be a truck driver. My mother approved the three year tour as a good way to gain experience toward eventually driving for United Parcel Service. She accepted that I would not take any job that required me to wear a skirt. I pretended to support her idea, but really, I wanted to be a Smokey and the Bandit character and purchase a semi. Decades later, I was the State Equal Employment Manager (SEEM) processing discrimination cases for the Vermont National Guard (VTNG). All of my cases involved sexual harassment against women. I asked myself, why would good patriots commit such horrid acts against their comrades? Why aren't leaders committed to preventing these events from happening? Unconsciously trying to find my purpose, I made it my mission to combat sexism. The subsequent journey was humiliating, heart wrenching, and seemingly an impossible task, yet I persisted. There are many stories which will never be told. This memoir is my offering for anyone willing to take up arms with me and crush the phenomenon of sex-based offenses in our United States military and the world.

CHAPTER 1

Chilled Out

★ ★ ★

"Do you want to snuggle?"

The young female soldier on her first annual training (A.T.) event lay in her combat shelter tent and responded to the text from her team leader, "No thanks."

The leader texted that he could take her back to the barracks for a shower, if she wanted. She responded again, "No thanks."

It had been a long hot day, and it would be another one tomorrow. Her team members were settling into their own shelters for the night. They were spread out along the wood line, dark and quiet. She lay in fear that her leader would show up, unzip, and enter her tent.

The following morning, how ready was she for the new day? Unit leaders and fellow team members, unaware of her circumstances, may have judged her impaired performance, but it was the team leader's text that disrupted their unit's synergy.

The National Guard soldier who reported this incident was appointed to an extra duty position as an Equal Opportunity Leader (EOL). She told me the simple text

LIFE AT CAMP

sent by a team leader to a new recruit had created a big problem for that soldier.

I was on the very same base, but I experienced a completely different evening. I lay on my cot in a barren room in the barracks for what was called the "White Cell." A White Cell takes care of administrative needs during exercises, so the brigade itself can focus on training.

I had my own personal bathroom, a locked door, and no fear impacting the comfort my cot provided me for the night.

The Vermont National Guard 86th Infantry Brigade Combat Team (IBCT—my team) *[For future references see Diagram 4 Acronyms and Terms Table.]* was taking part in what's called an XCTC—the Army National Guard's Exportable Combat Training Capability program. It's a field training exercise designed to certify platoon proficiency within a brigade.

XCTC offers Guard soldiers an experience similar to what they'd receive at a combat training center, but the training is held at their home station, or a regional center, minimizing logistical cost and the time Guard members spend away from homes and jobs.

This event took place at Fort Drum, New York. Vermont Guard personnel knew the base well and had prepared at length for the exercises. Soldiers from several states would participate in the XCTC, and the Vermont Guard's Garrison Support Brigade functioned as the event's White Cell.

I was invited by the Garrison Support Brigade to help

with a VIP team that took care of senior officers and local government officials who would visit the base and watch the live exercises. We had to wear tactical gear, which always made me feel powerful despite no weapon on me.

In addition to my duties with the VIP team, I used my time onsite to connect with colleagues helping me build the VTNG Women's Program. We were developing strategies for a task force to reduce sexual assaults. Our task force (TF) commander was an outstanding leader who actively engaged with our team to enhance gender equality as a means to change a sexist culture—a culture that we believe gives predators camouflage, enabling them to probe for opportunities and take advantage of soldiers.

When the XCTC was over, I rode home from summer camp on a bus with a crew of support soldiers from my unit. We beamed with delight, looking forward to sleeping in our own comfy beds back home. I left Fort Drum feeling good and confident about my participation at camp, but I was ignorant of the painful experiences some service members had endured—more of them, I am sure, than I would ever know about.

In my office back at base Camp, I reviewed a sexual harassment report filed by one of the units that had just returned from training. I'd read enough statements about sexual harassment to recognize someone practicing "anxiety management." The incident report is a matter-of-fact statement of what happened. Victims of these offenses are not documenting the impact of the emotional toll the incident had on them. Yet, I could often read between the lines, the distraught fear and shame. Documenting the story knowing many people will read it, is no simple task and is enough to deter reporting at all. But that is what the system required.

Reporting an incident is even more wrenching when you're describing a sexual offense. You worry about the effect, and ask yourself: Who am I reporting to? Who else will they tell? Will they judge me? Did I cause this to happen? Most importantly, you wonder if having the courage to report will result in some form of justice. Will it improve your professional setting? Or will it reflect badly on you and damage your career?

Most likely, the first time an incident happens to a service member, they don't consider all these factors. But when incidents are repeated, and they've experienced the aftermath, they will weigh these concerns. Under such circumstances, most soldiers opt out of making an official report, and thus, sex-based offenses are known to be highly underreported.

During my 13 year tenure as the VTNG SEEM, our program received around seven incident reports of sexual harassment a year. Those that come into the system begin as "informal" statements made on a form that's submitted to the Equal Opportunity (EO) program. More often, though, an incident is handled verbally between the service member and a leader in the unit, and is never documented at all.

I only processed two cases that started as an informal statement and were elevated to formal, with one being later rescinded. Predominantly, these informal submissions to the EO process were for sexual harassment.

The seven submissions a year in Vermont came in through the Army and the Air Guard, which accounted for approximately 3,400 service members. One may consider seven cases a year as an acceptable number, however for a force of people who primarily serve one weekend per month, and two weeks a year, the math works out to one reported sexual harassment offense every fifth duty day.

And many sex-based offenses—just as painful, humiliating, and oppressive—are never reported. Often, service members who don't officially report situations never seek a solution. The offenses are shrugged off as part of the culture. Seasoned veterans too often absorb the reality—reporting is not worth the trouble.

I was the collector of these heart wrenching reports. But it was the response to them that haunted me and the service members who dutifully reported them, following the guidance given to them by their superiors. They were told that, somehow, reporting would restore justice and prevent sexual harassment in the future. EO instructions affirm the commander's policy: We will hold violators of sexual harassment accountable.

Not so in reality.

Life at Camp

This system became increasingly painful for me as, over the course of my career, I witnessed the incremental stress and ultimate regret of women who reported sexual harassment or assault. There is little anonymity when a report is submitted. As word gets around, unit members take sides, they spread rumors, and they too often shame the person who has disrupted business by making a charge. Each time a woman came to me or to one of my EOLs, they had different measures prompting them to report. Very few left satisfied.

Reprisal is a subtle foe. It's a force working against you, often unrecognizable at first. You can feel the cold, yet it is hard to describe the act of coldness. Your next performance evaluation may be minimized, or you're denied schools you requested, or assignments you'd hoped for. You lose opportunities to attain awards that would give you increased points for promotion. Or you may notice you're not receiving timely information to perform your duties, or your time off request are denied.

Service members often confront such disappointments for legitimate reasons. But survivors who have reported incidents have the added weight of doubt: Is my failure to advance because I reported him?

In a small hometown Guard, loyalty runs deep and long. The young soldier who reported the inappropriate text invitation to snuggle may not have pondered, "If I report that my team leader texted this, what does my future look like?" As a young woman on her first A.T. summer camp, would she even think about reprisal? Was she aware it's an issue?

The soldier who received that text told a friend, and the friend encouraged her to tell the unit EOL. From there, the story would progress through the system: the EOL would inform the unit first sergeant (1SG), who would inform the company commander. Most likely the battalion Command Sergeant Major (CSM) would be told, since the incident involved an enlisted soldier. Then the brigade Equal Opportunity Advisor (EOA) would receive the report and conduct an informal inquiry. During the inquiry, the EOA would ask the alleged offender, and any other witnesses, what they knew about the incident. *[See Diagrams 2A and 2B: Chains of Command and EO Process]*

Each one of these service members has buddies they whisper to about the case. Already, a host of people in the ranks know about the embarrassing text. Stories begin to proliferate. The culture goes to work, and only she could feel the chill.

CHAPTER 2
UNPACKING THE POWER DYNAMICS
★ ★ ★

VETERANS UNDERSTAND THE POWER DIFFERENCE between a company commander and a brigade commander. Many nonmilitary citizens understand a general officer has more power than a captain, but these are not the critical power differentials I'm talking about here. It's the cultural power that I found most military leaders I engaged with tended to dismiss. Perhaps unconsciously or unintentionally, they did not buy into the need for more feminine power to improve the organization's effectiveness.

Cultural power is determined by the size and strength of a group that influences social power—a group that maintains control over prevailing norms and rules and can enforce individual adherence to the dominant culture voluntarily or involuntarily.

The United States National Guard was established in 1636—the precursor to our standing military services. Three-hundred and twelve years later women became official members of the military. Although women served in varying capacities prior to 1948—such as the Army and Navy Nurse Corps, Women's Army Auxiliary Corps, or in the Marine Corps Women's Reserve—they were not officially part of the Department of Defense (DoD). There is a long history of established norms entrenched in *androcentrism* before anyone had to seriously deal with women in uniform in the United States.

I had to look up the meaning of the word androcentrism when I was in my 50s, far into my career as an EO Manager. Androcentrism: a noun meaning dominated by or emphasizing masculine interests through a masculine point of view. The definition astonished me. I never considered how true the word characterized the institution I had worked in for more than 20 years. Men created the first U.S. militias and set up foundations for managing the citizens who would fill the ranks.

In 1948, three years after the end of World War II, President Harry S. Truman signed the Women's Armed Services Integration Act into law, officially allowing women to serve as full, permanent members of all branches of the armed forces.

This law was not a guarantee of equal opportunity. The act actually restricted the number of women who could serve to only 2% of each branch, and also limited how many women could become officers. Additionally, service women could be automatically discharged if they became pregnant, and they were not allowed to command men or serve in combat positions.

It was not until 1967 when Public Law 90-130 authorized the enlistment of women into the National Guard, and it took over a decade to build up a small number of women serving in the National Guard. In 1978, the Army Guard had approximately 3% female representation and many states, including Vermont, were just beginning to recruit women into various positions. I was 15 years old in 1978, and I had no comprehension of any limits on what I could do with my life or where I could go because of my gender.

Although women have a long history of supporting the military, they remain culturally underrepresented among our forces. Across the services, the percentage of women has remained essentially stagnant for the last several decades, ranging between 15-22%. Less than 10% (of the entire force) are in senior ranking positions.

Thus, the dominating point of view remains masculine.[1]

A 1994 U.S. armed forces policy entitled, "Direct Ground Combat Exclusion Rule," also known as "Combat Exclusion Policy," stated that women shall be excluded from assignments to units below the brigade level whose primary mission is to engage in direct combat on the ground. The policy remained in effect until it was repealed in 2013.[2]

In 1998, a General Accounting Office report stated that such policies were instituted on the rationale that there was no

---

[1] https://download.militaryonesource.mil/12038/MOS/Reports/2020-demographics-report.pdf
[2] https://military-history.fandom.com/wiki/Combat_Exclusion_Policy#cite_note-1

Life at Camp

military need for women in ground combat positions because an adequate number of men were available. The report cites transcripts of a 1994 press briefing in which DoD officials stated their belief that including women in such combat units "would not contribute to the readiness and effectiveness of those units," citing physical strength, stamina, and privacy issues as obstacles.

Although women were not supposed to be in positions that engaged in direct combat, thousands of women interacted directly with the enemy during Operations Iraqi and Enduring Freedom. Women may not have held military orders assigning them to a combat unit, or their service number may not have lined up in an authorized position, yet many women were temporarily attached to direct combat units slipping in through bureaucratic loopholes.

These women performed admirably, and yet, because they were not officially assigned to combat positions, these experiences negatively affected their career trajectories. They lost out on pay, benefits, awards, and recognition as combat vets.

All of this inequality is well documented not only in recent campaigns, but in decades of reports on women in the service. It is the power core of an organization which sets the overall culture, and the power core of our U.S. military has remained culturally consistent. And androcentric.

In the year 2000, the overall percentage of women in the

DoD was 14.6%. Twenty years later, the rate is 17.2%. The representation rate for women only increased by 2.6% and the rate of men decreased by 2.6%.

Such data appears to be compatible with veterans' and citizens' nostalgic fondness for the past even as they cheer on "how far we have come." When I look at the numbers, I become as frustrated as a suffragette who sought the vote for women.

How can the androcentric culture change unless we include more women, and how can we get more women into an androcentric culture? Some may even ask, "What's wrong with the androcentric culture?"

When I was growing up, I never gave a thought to how my girlishness might prevent me from doing…anything. It was not until I was 40 years old, had been in the Army for more than 22 years, and had landed a job as the State Equal Opportunity Manager (SEEM) for my home State National Guard that I consciously recognized disparate status between the genders in uniform. As the disparity became clear to me, I wanted to diminish the gender status gap for reasons I didn't even know, yet.

The United States military and our hometown Guard unit members deserve unwavering respect, yet this should not excuse an absence of accountability for achieving the diversity we tout as a positive trait in America.

At 4th of July parades, neighbors cheer on the National

Guard (NG), yet many people never question how it operates. In my job as the SEEM, I saw the cost of this operation. The dominant culture often oppresses the benefits of diversity we are protecting as patriots of the United States military. Sexism negatively impacts more women than men, but men as well.

The NG is a reserve component of the United States armed forces. Its Air Force and Army formations are predominantly made up of local citizens joining to serve one weekend a month and two weeks a year. The Air Force, Army, Navy, Coast Guard, and Marine Reserve members have similar service time commitments, yet are in separate components of the DoD. The NG differs from the active duty services in that your reporting unit is in your home state, often near your hometown where you have generational history and connections.

Although each state, territory or district has their own history, all NG units operate under the Armed Service Component of the Air Force or the Army and the National Guard Bureau (NGB). Regulations, policies, and command structures set up a unifying culture.

The National Guard can deploy or mobilize for both federal and domestic missions. There are approximately 443,543 Guard personnel authorized to serve across the 50 states, three United States territories, and the District of Columbia.

In the wake of the War of 1812, the federal government attempted to standardize training and laws that govern mobilization for militia organizations throughout the United States. As a result, state governors no longer exercised direct command with military rank, but each state appointed a State Adjutant General referred to as the TAG. The TAGs report directly to the governor and serve as commander of the state's militia.

Each state has a specific mission assigned by the U.S. Army and U.S. Air Force, typically based on the sizes and types of units the state has maintained or gained throughout history. Vermont National Guard's history dates back to the 1700s, when many settlers relied on the militia for protection as they formed their communities. Early in the 1770s, the militia took on a more organized structure and formalized its name: the *Green Mountain Boys*. Ethan Allen was appointed as a colonel and several locations around the state were named after him.

The first Vermont brigade or "old brigade" was an infantry brigade in the Union Army dating to the American Revolutionary War. The second Vermont brigade was an infantry brigade in the Union Army of the Potomac during the American Civil War. Subsequent reorganizations of the National Guard resulted in the 86th Armored Brigade, which had been a separate organization, becoming part of the 50th Armor Division, then the 26th Infantry Division, and later the 42nd Infantry Division. These are all Army foundation units from which the Vermont National Guard was built.

LIFE AT CAMP

The name Green Mountain Boys is proudly painted in giant letters on the Air National Guard (VTANG) hangar that faces the runway at the Burlington, Vermont, International Airport. The most notable recognition for Vermont Guard highlights its 158th Fighter Wing's response to the attack on 9/11, and the Wing's numerous deployments in support of the war in Afghanistan.

Vermont is recognized for having the first female TAG in the history of the Natonal Guard. Vermont Air Guard female TAG, Martha T. Rainville, Lieutenant Colonel, was elected by the Legislature in 1997, and although discussions about dropping the word Boys came up, the new TAG did not see a need to change the historic and proud moniker.

When you ask a Vermont Guard member why they continue to use the term Boys, the majority say it is historic and despite the male pronoun, it includes women, too.

There have been other names in our society that became politically or socially unacceptable, however any consideration to stop using the Green Mountain Boys has never gained enough support to make for substantive public or even private debate, so the name remains.

The Vermont National Guard—with approximately 3,400 personnel assigned—is considered a small sized Guard. Units of the VTNG consist of the Green Mountain Boys centuries-old infantry, cavalry, and armor, and Vermont's Air Guard flew missions during 9/11, and now is home to a new generation of jet fighters, the F-35 Raptor.

A majority of Vermont's 86th Brigade enlisted positions are combat arms occupations, consisting of units with less than 4% of their contingents being women during their long, proud historic tenure. This representation range differs somewhat between units, with few units having any feminine cultural power.

One third of Vermont Guard personnel work as full time employees in varying employment statuses to ensure that weekend warriors can hit the ground running when they report for drill weekend duty, or deployments. *[See Diagram 1; Full Time vs. Drill Status]* Notably, the percentage of women in these full time support roles is slightly higher than the rate of women who drill one weekend a month. Yet the powerful positions that command the full time force and structurally support the Guard's military mission are predominately filled with men.

Unpacking this power dynamic means considering how the culture is dominated by or emphasizes masculine interests through a masculine point of view. This does not negate the positive influence of the Vermont National Guard having installed the first female TAG in the country, or disparage other successful service women who took the road less traveled upon. But, in Vermont, I recognized a micropattern of a macroculture.

Through my EO training, I became familiar with the terms racism, sexism, ableism, and other forms of illegal discrimination. More and more sexism became the predominant issue for the conflicts I managed in the EO realm of the Vermont Guard.

Although sexism is prejudice or discrimination based on one's sex or gender, it primarily affects women and girls, because without power, discrimination has a weakening impact. Women and girls historically have had less power.

It took a few years in the job for me to recognize that all of the power was in the androcentric culture and that bothered me immensely. Therefore, that short text, "Do you want to snuggle?" meant much more to me than most, because I recognized the power the sender was stealing from the female soldier recipient.

The young female recruit making her way to Fort Drum for her first A.T. event may not have grasped the enormity of the culture she would need to acclimate to.

Years ago, I was a small town tomboy who wanted to learn to drive trucks. Years after I joined the Army, I found myself in the Vermont National Guard as a personnel management specialist. At the age of 41, I landed a full time job in the Human Resources Office (HRO), EO section. I had two elementary school aged kids, and was married to a combat veteran in the Vermont Infantry Brigade. After working 16 years in the Human Resource Office (HRO) I took on the role of SEEM.

Doris J. Sumner

Prior to this job, I never considered sexism as a problem within the military.

I was about to find out all about it.

CHAPTER 3

DO I LIKE TO FIGHT?

★ ★ ★

WHILE I WAS WORKING AS VERMONT'S SEEM DURING the workweek, I also held the weekend military position as the Vermont National Guard (VTNG) Headquarters Equal Opportunity Officer. I was often invited to serve as an adjunct instructor for the EO courses at the Defense Equal Opportunity Management Institute (DEOMI).

I enjoyed working with fellow EO managers from around the country. It was exciting to meet 80 or more service members hungry to learn how to be advocates of a just process and become change agents within their state. The school house where we worked sat on the edge of the Banana River at Cape Canaveral in Cocoa Beach, Florida. It was not a bad gig.

Six months before I was to retire from the military and my full time job working for the Vermont National Guard (VTNG), I served for the last time as an adjunct instructor. I enjoyed bantering with a colleague, a Army field artillery lieutenant colonel (ret), who had taken a job as a SEEM. Now a civilian with senior status, he enjoyed engaging his National

Guard leaders without the intimidation of career roadblocks. He had been an Inspector General (IG) and clearly understood the Uniform Code of Military Justice (UCMJ). Through our connections in the EO world, we supported each other's efforts to improve discrimination case processing, and the management of directives from the NGB. The officer was a fun, energetic teammate and a great ally. I was chair of the Equal Employment Management Advisory Council (EEMAC), the National Committee for EO Managers from each state and territory. Allies were important.

I sought his input often, and the time together was a great opportunity to strategize on several key initiatives we worked on with NGB. We had many excitable conversations about cases and how we approached our state leaders in resolution efforts. The EO community in the Guard is small. Often, SEEMs had no support staff. Most of the EO representatives were assigned in collateral duty status, meaning the service member had their primary position, and the job as EO representative was extra duty. The turnover rate was high.

The network of SEEMs across the country became an invaluable source of support and strategizing for all of us. On conference calls, meetings, and training events, we exchanged and validated the challenges we had to deal with while advocating a process we did not own. Most EO cases across the Guard were about sexual harassment, with race-based cases a close second. The sexism and command climate around the good old boys' club was a constant roadblock to improving synergy within all of our commands. Many of us expressed our frustration with leaders whose egos and biases often impeded fair processing or accountability.

As I conveyed my frustrations, challenges, expectations, and defeats, my EO partner there was entertained and impressed at my tenacity. He would say, "You sure have guts, Chief," or "You sure give it to them in Vermont."

On the final evening of our time at Cocoa Beach, as I vented about another disheartening outcome, he said, "You know what I get when I listen to your stories? You like to fight."

I responded passionately. "No, I don't like to fight, but I will fight. I must fight when I see injustice, and when I know how harmful sexism is to a person's core."

I was born in a small New England town in the early 1960s, the fifth of six kids. My parents were not rich, but they had enough to pay the bills and feed us. Back then, you played outside and made your own toys. We lived next to our cousins, similar in age. Life was barefoot, brooks, and fireflies.

We had two boys in our house and two boys next door. They were the minority, but they seemed to take up the air around our yard. My oldest brother was the epitome of pride for my dad, a straight A student who liked to fish, hunt, and help build stuff. My oldest male cousin was a strikingly handsome teen with a chiseled body and firm jaw. They were the gold standard of the bunch.

Life at Camp

The younger boys tried to find their place but struggled. The younger male cousin became a "thick" bully. He didn't like the word chubby. My younger brother was a scrawny follower who had talent—he could draw and loved music—but nobody paid attention to such things, so they remained suppressed.

The seven girls in our two families maneuvered between the boys to find our place. That's when I decided I wanted to be a boy. I cut my hair short and refused to wear those pantsuit outfits my mother made on her sewing machine. I liked playing in the sandpile with the boys' matchbox cars, and I loved the tree houses my brother built, or the rafts he constructed of milk jugs and wood pallets.

After eighth grade graduation from our small country school, kids from our town went on to high schools scattered among a number of surrounding towns. I went to a very large high school where I hardly knew a soul. Any confidence I may have had quickly faded. Looking for a place to land, I found a few smokers to bond with down by the bridge. Fearless Friday keg parties at night fueled enough confidence in me to endure moving to each of the area's three high schools over the course of the next four years.

During those early years living in the country with large families and small town connections, sexual abuse was often present but not discussed. The first time a boy touched me, it was a kid from my own family. He came at night to my bed and quietly put his hands under my pajamas. What did a girl's skin feel like? I moved the hand away; it came back. I moved the hand away again, and he left.

I arose the next morning and jumped into the normal day's routine. I dressed, made my bed, ate cereal, rinsed my bowl, and ran to the bus stop. I don't think I looked at my night visitor any differently.

Then it happened again, and I don't know why I did not scream or punch him this time. I just lay there. I was nine or ten at the time and he was 12 or 13. After several quiet minutes of exploring, he would go away. This happened a few times.

One day all the kids were bored, sitting around a picnic table. My bully of a cousin said out loud, "Hey cousin, are you going to let me touch you like you let him?" I felt shock and shame. The silent moment stretched out on the air until one of us kids threw a ball, and we scattered like flies.

I told my mother about all this. I found her alone with the laundry and nervously told her he was visiting me at night and touching me. She did not stop folding clothes or look at me as she said, "Tell him to stop it."

I recall defensively describing how I wake up and he is already there, I told her I shooed him away, but he comes back. Still concentrating on the laundry, she said, "Put some bottles in front of the door so you can hear him come in, then he will not come in." I remember putting Budweiser beer bottles in front of the door where I slept with my younger sister. Perhaps my mother took some action I didn't know about, but I don't remember ever hearing the bottles tip over, and he didn't bother me again.

My mom and dad often had alcohol fueled fights that we kids could never make sense of as we listened from the top of the stairs. My brothers and I would side with our dad and criticize my mother's defiance. Why wouldn't she just shut up? She left Dad a few times, but she'd eventually come back.

One night when I was around 13 and my mother was staying away, my dad was crying and calling my name. I woke up and went to his bedroom. He described his heartbreak over Mom leaving and asked me to sit on the bed. He asked me to rub his belly and then took my hand and tried to get me to rub him lower. I yanked my hand away, and he excused me saying, "Go back to bed."

I remember feeling pain, but I wasn't sure where to place it.

Soon after this, my mother and father divorced. The boys went with Dad and my little sister and I went with Mom. Our two older sisters were now with their own husbands. Our cousins' family broke up too, so all of us scattered, breaking up the tribe and leaving that piece of land on the country road that held our memories.

My first serious boyfriend was 18 years old, and

though I was just 16, he seemed like an old man to me. A rebellious teenager refusing to follow my mother's rules, I moved into my boyfriend's family home.

For two years, we had a tumultuous relationship that included alcohol, abuse, and threats of violence. Breaking away from him was a long process that cemented my twisted tendency to form codependent attachments, not to mention firmly establishing my own alcoholism.

I would often lie with my boyfriend and dream of getting away, of owning my own house and having friends who envied my single, free spirited life. In reality, I was stuck. When I tried to break up with him, he became violent and threatened anyone I tried to run to for safety or support. I found myself controlled and manipulated to stay in a life I did not want.

I finally broke free of him. I only had a few close girlfriends at that time, and I always felt like I was a problem, the one who ruined parties, the one who couldn't take off with the girls, couldn't go to concerts. At my high school graduation, I walked up the middle aisle to my spot on the stage and my ex-boyfriend's sister tripped me as I walked past her. I steadied myself and crossed the stage to receive my diploma. I resolved at that moment never to let anyone control me again.

After graduation, a friend and I spent summer nights partying at local bars and considering our options. I had no focus or discipline. My mother worked for an employment

Life at Camp

agency and found me temporary jobs. She wanted me to be a secretary or settle into something along those lines, but I totally rejected any sort of professional setting where I would have to dress like a girl.

I quit jobs often, discouraging my mother. Toward the end of that summer, a high school friend and I signed on at the local fair. I worked in the "Dime Game" booth where I was not afraid to grab a microphone and shout at the passersby, "If you have some time, throw in the dime. Win the big teddy bear, and she'll follow you anywhere!"

I made up rhymes and kept my mouth going, drawing in customers. The owner loved me. At one point I looked up to see my mom and her partner watching me with big grins on their faces. Were they proud of me? Had I found my talent? The last night of the fair, the owner offered my friend and me a chance to travel with the carnival down the East Coast to Miami. We could sleep in his camper and he would pay us. Fearless, and with nothing else planned, we both said, "Hell yeah!" We woke my mother up, and I started grabbing clothes while she made us sandwiches for the road. I suppose I worried my mother sick, but I'd stopped surprising her, for sure.

The carny gig was just as it sounds. Scary people and nice people all mixed up like a group of distant travelers. They put me in the front seat of a box truck with a guy who had a reputation for falling asleep while driving. The boss told me to keep talking (since I was good at it) to keep the driver awake.

The guy would pretend to fall asleep every time I stopped talking, just to mess with me. I enjoyed sitting way up high in the cab of the truck looking out at the traffic. I begged to drive, but they never let me.

After we did a couple small town fairs, the boss informed us he would be taking a month off when we reached Miami. We would be on our own for a while, but when he got back from his fishing trip, he'd hire us back to work the game booth he'd set up on the Miami strip.

My friend and I fought over what we'd do. I wanted to buy a bus ticket back to Vermont and she wanted to go to Miami and wait it out. She was certain we could find jobs and live on the beach for a few weeks. I won the argument; the carnival crew dropped us off at a bus station in North Carolina with our two green garbage bags full of clothes and we headed back home.

Afterward, we wound up back in our hometown with not much to do. We continued our nightly barhopping. One of those nights, we met an Army recruiter out having a drink. He set up an Armed Services Vocational Aptitude Battery test for us, and I remember having to get up at four a.m. taking the test very hung over.

The sergeant 1st class (SFC/E-7) was a tall, ugly old dude to me, but to my mother he was a handsome, official man of the

Army. She gave him unwavering trust. He showed my friend and me scary videotapes of drill sergeants screaming at new recruits and asked us if we could handle getting yelled at.

I said, "Sure," but my friend said, "No way."

I found it ironic that she was not afraid of being jobless and homeless in Miami, but she was afraid to have a bunk, a job, and get yelled at.

Over the next couple of months, I met with the sergeant to do the paperwork for signing up, and he always showed up with my favorite beer. We spent time in bars playing pool, and I supposed he was giving me soldierly advice, but more often, he tried to get me to make out with him. The ride home was always filled with anxiety, as I wondered if I could hold him off long enough to get back to my mom's trailer.

Before leaving for Army basic training, I was sent to take a medical physical at the New Hampshire Military Entry Point Station (MEPS) where I'd have to spend the night in a hotel room. I remember feeling grown-up and ready to find the world. I couldn't wait to be rid of the recruiting sergeant, and I hadn't the heart to tell my mom what a real drunk and creep he was.

A month later, on December 27, 1981, my mom brought me to a local bus station with one small military green bag my older sister bought me. I remember the short packing list the recruiter gave me, and I didn't waver from it. I recall traveling throughout the night and having trouble sleeping on

Doris J. Sumner

the stinky, creepy Gray Line Bus, but I smoked my Marlboros as comfort and hugged my cool Army green bag.

CHAPTER 4

THE ROAD TO CAMP

★ ★ ★

Basic training was easy for me, yet looking back, I realize I was an empty vessel, ready for conformity. I was one of many young kids being shuffled into a massive system to transform lost teens into regimental adults, ready to give their life for the United States of America. A couple months in—on a freezing evening with icy winds blowing through the torn plastic in the watchtower I was told to patrol—I asked myself, "What am I doing?"

Looking out over the blackness, I tried to see any movement in the truck depot we were guarding. I wore my All-Purpose Lightweight Carrying Equipment (ALICE) with a canteen of water and empty ammunition pouches. I held an M16 assault rifle with an empty magazine in the chamber. Tired, hungry, clueless, I waved to my battle buddy over in the gate shack who had the comfort of a light bulb, and I wondered what she was thinking. I thought about my little sister and how she would cry right about now, "I want to go home." But leaving was not an option. I would have to trudge on and make something of this Army life.

Life at Camp

My score on the test I took to qualify for the Army was not a high one and that limited the options I was given for occupations. Recruiters tried to get me to be an administrative clerk, but I opted to be a truck driver. The military occupational code that identified a truck driver at that time was *64 Charlie*, and I took a lot of pride in my new identity.

Basic Training was at Fort Dix, New Jersey, and so was the Advanced Individual training school for the 64 Charlie truck drivers. After my eight weeks of basic training, I arrived down the block to the new building and right away I had to drop to do push ups for not having a cover (hat) on my head.

I did well on my physical fitness (P.T.) test back in basic training, and somehow the drill sergeant knew this about me. He mentioned my outstanding P.T. score and gave me extra push ups, chastising me for being such a success.

"You are so strong aren't you, why don't you drop and give me 100 push ups Private Show Off!" After I was completely exhausted, he excused me. Throughout my 36 year career, I often forgot my cover, probably to spite the lesson he tried to teach me.

I graduated from truck driving school with many male drinking buddies, my alcoholism taking hold of my choices—who I hung out with and what I did in my spare time. I arrived at my first duty station at Aberdeen Proving Ground (APG) in Maryland in May, 1982. I was assigned to Alpha

Company, but they had to bed me in the Headquarters and Headquarters Company (HHC) where most of the women stationed at APG lived. Alpha Company was 99% men: mechanics, infantrymen, scouts, artillery, tankers, and truck drivers. The two other women in Alpha were married and lived in base housing.

The taxi that brought me to the base, dropped me off near some World War II wooden barracks on a Sunday afternoon. I reported to the staff duty officer and nervously saluted. He said, "Chill out, I'm cool. I'll show you to the barracks." I took my duffle bag and found my bunk in a large open bay on the second floor of the barracks.

One latrine with two toilets and two showers and 50 neatly made empty cots. Everyone was out and about on this beautiful day. These were temporary barracks on the outskirts of the busy base while new construction for HHC was being completed. I would eventually live in the new brick housing for HHC that was constructed right next to my unit of assignment.

That first warm Sunday was the longest Sunday of my military career. I just laid there with no cigarettes, no beer, and no idea what tomorrow would bring.

I somehow found the chow hall and met up with my fellow truck drivers, who welcomed me to the unit with cheers and playful teasing between each other. My section sergeant was a female staff sergeant. At the time, she was probably mid-30s,

Life at Camp

but she seemed very old and timid to me so I judged her. How could she be a staff sergeant? How could she be in charge of anything?

I made instant friends with a guy named Damon from Ohio. He was in the tanker section, but he came over to introduce himself. Damon was beaming with confidence and making plans for the barracks crew to get pizza, play pool, drink some beer, and meet me, but that never happened. Suddenly, a specialist whisked me away and said I was to report to the commander of Alpha Company. We took a jeep from the work area known as "behind the fence," because you had to have special security to go there. The jeep driver took me to the company area.

I walked in and saluted a short redheaded captain standing behind his desk. The commander saluted back, ordered at ease, and then dismissed the specialist. Inviting me to sit down, he told me to relax. He was talkative and cheery and asked me questions but didn't pause long enough for me to answer. Before I knew it, we had plans to meet up for dinner and he was going to show me what a great town Baltimore was. I went back behind the fence, a bit dazed and confused. They brought me to several places for in processing then, and the day went by too quickly.

I waited nervously outside the barracks hoping the commander would not show up, but he did right on time. I got in his car and I was uncomfortable until he handed me a beer. Beer was always my calming juice. We drove to the city and I had no interest in anything he talked about, but I was polite. I was anxious to make it back to my bunk. I was a country girl, and I don't believe I had ever been to a fancy restaurant before.

We were seated on the dock by the water, and I pretended to understand the menu. He ordered for me—the best seafood platter in Baltimore he said, and he promised I'd love it if I tried it. I hated how he kept talking and eating and drinking wine, but I kept drinking my beer.

When I tried the crab plate, the server must have recognized my taste buds rejecting a food I would never come to appreciate. She was easygoing, slouching back, and asked, "You want a cheeseburger instead?" I nodded yes.

This redheaded old Army captain kept chatting away. He said something about moving soon, that he needed to stop by his apartment for something. I had never been so far away from the comforts of my hometown, without access to people who knew me or knew my family. I felt intimidated, but the buzz diminished my judgment or fear of being harmed. After arriving at his apartment that was full of boxes everywhere, I was suddenly lying on the bare mattress and he was on top of me and taking off his button up shirt. I surrendered to whatever was going to get me through the night and back to my bunk.

Almost four decades have gone by, and I can still remember

that he was the first man I ever touched who had hair on his back, lots of it, and I was as uncomfortable as I had ever been, even being drunk.

He dropped me off at the World War II barracks and asked if I wanted to go out again. I remember saying, "I don't think I am your type." What an emotional tool to use—transferring the compliment to him. I wasn't his type, rather than he wasn't my type.

Today I know that was sexual assault, but at that time, I thought it was survival. I was conforming to the circumstances. I was a girl from a small town finding her world and navigating the places I found, some with fight and some with surrender. I thought I was in control.

The next day, I met up with Damon and my section crew. They asked me where I had gone. When I told the guys about events of the night before, they showed brotherly concern with no judgment. They all agreed the commander was a jerk and only had days left before ending his term in service. No one suggested reporting him to anyone, but they seemed to take on a protective attitude toward me. I felt good. During my time in Aberdeen, I did not have any close women friends; all of my best friends were men.

As it was, I belonged to this small band of brothers from Alpha Company. We called each other by our last names or by nicknames, like Speedy, Coon-dog, Kid, Killer, or Beauregard. I was Rickert. We were all under 23 years old, and we loved to drink beer and listen to AC/DC, Van Halen, Phil Collins, and Aerosmith. We played beer drinking games and complained about our supervisors. My brothers insisted I get their approval before going out on a date, and most of the time, it was not OK because they did not approve of my date choices.

During an unguarded weekend, I said yes to a playboy from the infantry section, and we ended up dating for over a year. He was one of those bad boys—a terrible soldier, undisciplined. He went to the city on weekends and we all suspected he was into buying, selling, and doing drugs. This was not part of our scene—alcohol was our high—and my buddies tried to tell me I was being used. I ignored their heartfelt warnings because I did not feel worthy of love from a good guy, despite them telling me I deserved better.

My alcoholism was getting worse. All of us were drinking hard every chance we got. One weekend while partying with my crew, I almost died in a car crash after a night of drinking at a club called Billy's. I was riding in the back seat of a small Volkswagen Jetta with the veteran we called Killer. Despite being done with his term of service, Killer had moved outside the base and enjoyed partying with us. Our driver crashed the car into a telephone pole, and Killer and I had to be pulled out after the rescue crew sawed the small car in half. The driver and front seat passenger walked away untouched. Killer was badly hurt, but he recovered. I woke up in the hospital with a stitched up ear, bruised ribs, and a collapsed lung.

My Alpha Company buddies surrounded my bed, showing me the picture of our crash in the local Aberdeen newspaper. They told me the sordid details of a night that was a blackout to me. I asked someone to bring me some beer in the hospital when I learned I'd be laid up for several more days. When our first sergeant (1SG) heard I'd asked for the beer, he ordered me to a mandatory class on alcoholism. He was a recovering alcoholic, and he let us all know how bad our drinking was. I remember joking with my buddies that he was jealous because he couldn't drink anymore.

I partied hard during off hours but I was always a good worker. Prior to the crash, my name was at the top of the driver board. I had racked up the most miles on the various types of test vehicles that we drove behind the fence, where testing was done prior to the military contracting purchases. I was out of work for a month recovering from the accident before another driver surpassed my mileage record.

When I returned to the shop, the crew held a small welcome back ceremony for me. The female section sergeant gave me a homemade certificate that read, "Certificate of Achievement for PVT Doris Rickert for leading the driver board only to lose it after 30 days for two for one night at Billy's." So often during my drinking days, I didn't see what I was losing, and only chuckled at what I thought I was winning.

I fought all the time with the undisciplined soldier who was my boyfriend for that one year. Then on a wild, drunken trip home, I met a man who would become my first husband. Wayne was a popular athlete, a man's man. The ultimate buddy, friendly, funny, and loving. He was in the process of joining the Regular Army. After I returned to Aberdeen, he visited my mother often and told her he was going to marry her daughter. He left Vermont and was stationed in Texas. We wrote to each other for six months before he asked me to be his wife. I was flattered that this nice guy I had only met one night was so fascinated with me. When I told my mother I was getting married, she said, "Don't you ever cheat on him. He will be devastated."

Somehow, she knew I was not as in love with Wayne, but I was in love with the idea of someone nice loving me. Before he flew to his new assignment in Germany, we flew home to one of those '80s weddings with a big white wedding dress, bridesmaids, grooms, fancy cake, and kegs of beer.

It was lonely being married but not having my spouse around. I didn't fit in with the married couples, and I didn't fit in any longer with the single guys either. Damon and the crew moved on—I was no longer their little sister to protect.

I did not fit in anywhere.

I wrote Wayne letters and drank my beer. After completing two years and ten months at Aberdeen base, I'd solidified

LIFE AT CAMP

my alcoholism, drinking daily. In December 1984, I left for Germany to join my husband.

I arrived boasting that I would remain loyal to Budweiser beer. Before leaving the terminal, Wayne and his buddies bought me a German beer at McDonalds. For most of the 14 months we spent in Germany, we had many fun times as a young married couple. We went to music concerts, joined volksmarching clubs, and enjoyed many drinking festivals, including Oktoberfest, in our small village. At times, I would run into some of the men from my tour in APG, and it felt good to be remembered. I did not like being a housewife or being dependent on Wayne for money. I made friends with several beer drinking wives who had babies to take care of. I had no interest or desire to be a mom, but it was fun to watch them with the little ones and get to leave when the kids were cranky.

I often felt discontent with my life. I wanted to go back home and get away from the Army life. Wayne liked the Army, but he agreed to get out and join a hometown Guard unit. The move home was a geographical improvement for me, but I took my emptiness and discontented self with me.

Back in our hometown, I was a terrible wife. My husband went to drill with his National Guard unit, only to find I had partied all weekend while he was gone. I ended up cheating on him with an old high school flame who'd never held a torch for me. Wayne wanted to work things out, but I knew I didn't love him.

My mother wasn't surprised when I came back home. Wayne had never wanted me to join the Army National Guard whenever I inquired about it. He wanted a stay at home wife with kids, and I think he accepted that he had not chosen well.

Days after I left him, I looked up the number for the Vermont National Guard and talked to a recruiter. I moved into an apartment I shared with a roommate in a small Vermont city and got a job working at a jogging bra company. The owners and crew were mostly women. I told amazing embellished Army stories, which impressed them. They liked my confidence and strong work ethic when I showed up for work. Often, though, I showed up hung over or just missed work altogether. In denial of my disease, I felt powerful—single, independent, and fearless.

I did not impress the National Guard recruiter with my three years of active duty as a truck driver or my time in Germany as the spouse of an infantryman. He insisted I join as a clerk in the Personnel Service Company (PSC). I had no knowledge to fall back on, or any friends to ask about his directive, so I signed on the dotted line, feeling proud to be in uniform again, with a bit of an in your face attitude toward my ex-husband.

The PSC included a lot of female soldiers, but all the non-commissioned officers (NCOs) were males. The 1SG, the full time Readiness NCO, the supply guy, even the head clerk was male. But our company commander was female, and this impressed me. The female lieutenants in the units were super supportive leaders. I found the drinking bunch and quickly fit right in.

The Guard was just one weekend a month, but I was excited to have a group of women friends. I can't remember if I quit or was fired from the jogging bra company, but I know I was still a drifter, and I hopped from one job to another thanks to my mom's connections at the employment services company where she still worked.

Surrendering to her daughter's interest, she sent me to a construction site in the city where a crew was tearing down an old three story building. I walked up with confidence and was hired instantly. They gave me a crowbar, and I spent several weeks on the job. The men were impressed with how I ripped down walls and climbed on the rafters to rip off the roof.

We threw the scrap lumber into a big dump truck. When it was full, one of the guys jumped in and took it to the nearby city dump. One day I was up in the back of the dump truck leveling the load, high above the everyday cars that passed by on their way to offices or nearby college campuses. A car full of "boys" heckled at me and asked if I'd like to manhandle them. I gave them the middle finger and yelled, "Fuck off and get a real job!" My crew all laughed. I was proud of my ability to be crass to blend in with my environment but I was always searching for a new place to be.

After work, we would go to a local bar, play pool, and drink beer. I asked the boss if I could drive the dump truck, since I was a truck driver in the Army. Some of the guys teased me about it and took bets on whether I could do it without hitting cars along the city streets. The next day, I jumped into the driver's seat of the truck with flashbacks of my road trip with the carnival crew. I had a co-driver, and we made our way to the city dump. I backed up the truck, handled the levers, and dumped the load with no problems. At the bar that night, the boss said I had a new job as a dump truck driver. But they were soon disappointed when this drifter moved on.

One of my best friends in my new Army National Guard unit was Lisa. She had joined up with her two sisters and a few girlfriends from their hometown. Many of them worked full time at the base, Camp Johnson. I had never heard of the National Guard in high school.

I remember Army, Air Force, even Marine, and Navy commercials, but I never paid attention. I don't remember National Guard commercials. When I met that Army recruiter, he never told my high school friend and me about a National Guard option.

The first time I drove onto Camp Johnson, I felt competent. My three years of active duty at the Aberdeen base and the

Life at Camp

time in Germany gave me a basic understanding of an Army base and its culture.

Now, I was between jobs, and Lisa asked me to stop by and apply for a full time job on base. I suddenly felt intimidated walking into a sturdy brick building with USPFO above the door. The acronym stood for the United States Property and Fiscal Office.

I felt out of place wearing jeans, seeing all the military personnel in their dress uniforms. There were desks and typewriters, metal filing cabinets, and telephones with blinking lights. Everyone seemed very busy moving among desks with folders, or talking on phones.

My friend Lisa looked and spoke so professional in this setting, compared to our unit area or the drinking bars we visited after drill. I was respectful as I spoke to the colonel, who was unassuming and eager to have me accept a job at the USPFO. I was hired on the spot to operate the switchboard, not because of any credentials, but based on Lisa's recommendation. I did not want to let her down.

They hired me on January 4, 1987 and I was employed there until my retirement, March 29, 2019. Lisa was my age, but she was way more mature than I was. She had this important job, a home, a steady boyfriend, and a young son. She took me under her wing, mentored me, and most of all empowered me to develop as a Human Resources Specialist.

Although I had taken typing as a freshman in high school,

I had no clue how to place my hands on a typewriter now. It was Lisa who gave me the confidence that I could be successful, too. I am forever grateful for her sister solidarity. She is in heaven now, and I hope she's raising her fist in support of the woman I became.

Although I joined the National Guard with my truck driver occupation code, I needed to qualify for the military position I was assigned to in the Personnel Service Company. The Guard sent me to Army AIT for the administration occupation and I earned my credentials. I had a new identity.

For the first time in many years, my mother was proud of me, but I think she was more relieved that I had a steady job. Driving into Camp to go to work, in my dress uniform, and sitting at a desk with the switchboard blinking before me, I welled with pride in myself.

CHAPTER 5
LIFE AT CAMP
★ ★ ★

The Camp switchboard was a great place to start a career for a hometown National Guard member. You learn ranks, names, and positions quickly. Lisa was always available to give me the scoop on certain people, since she'd been in the Guard more than six years by the time I arrived, several of those years as a full time National Guard employee.

There are two cultures in the Guard. One is the drill weekend culture, where Army members reported to units at armories throughout the state at unit locations and Air Guard members reported to the Air Base, called the Wing. The other group of National Guard members are called full timers. The majority of the Vermont Army National Guard full timers worked on the main base at Camp Johnson, with a few full timers working in the unit armories around the state. The Wing had many full timers working to maintain the aircraft and Air National Guard operations.

One of the most intimidating females in the building I was assigned to was an older woman, with the rank of

Life at Camp

chief warrant officer four (CW4). That's the rank I would eventually retire at. She had been at Camp Johnson and in the job in the contracting office for many years. She was one of those old soldiers who smiled little, who only used enough words to get her message across. I didn't have reasons to converse with her much, other than transfer calls to her, and she was always curt.

The switchboard person had to stay an extra half hour after everyone else left. At four o'clock, the building emptied out except for me. At five past four, the Chief would come back carrying a small grocery bag and go back to her office. She was usually still in there when I left.

One day, she stopped to chat with me, and it surprised me how friendly she was. I am not sure what I revealed at the time, but after that day, whenever she returned to the building after-hours, she'd stop at the switchboard and hand me a cold 16-ounce Miller Lite. She'd wink and take her bag back to her office.

I was making progress professionally, but I was still a mess personally.

Lisa and the girls from my company became my new drinking crew, and I had several fair weather boyfriends for the first couple of years I was in the Guard. The mission of our Personnel Service Company (PSC) was to visit the units out in the field, set up our typewriters, and help the soldiers update their personnel records. We filled out their life insurance, health insurance, and death benefit forms. I became an expert typist on the many carbon copy forms.

We enjoyed being off the main Camp and out at the armories with the soldiers. The men in charge of our company would try to look busy, but we made fun of how they didn't fool us. We assumed they spent their time gossiping with the unit leaders and whatever it was they were interested in. We organized unit information and coordinated with unit clerks to maintain as many records as possible. We flirted with soldiers and gossiped about our encounters, too. After long Saturdays, we would go out and party, have some fun, just to get up and do it all over again on Sunday.

During the week, the office was more of a professional setting, although from time to time, several of us would go to lunch, have a beer, and then never return to work that day. Many coworkers or old timers encouraged me to apply for other internal jobs and move off the switchboard. After a year, I gained enough confidence to apply for something else. Lisa was always my confidence booster.

I applied and got a job at the Camp's HRO. In 1987 the title of the office was the Support Personnel Management Office (SPMO). The new position was a promotion and the office was in another building, away from the switchboard and Lisa.

At the management office, I worked for an Air Force sergeant who was very serious about the job. When he, John, interviewed me, he asked if I smoked cigarettes. I remember lying and saying no. When I moved to my new area, I sat right next to him. John was an excellent teacher and he gave me meaningful work to do that built my skills. He put walls around his work section in the open bay area of the office, trying to create a smoke free zone. In those days, everyone smoked right at their desk, and overflowing ashtrays sat on the top of the gray metal filing cabinets.

The inside walls of our World War II era building were tinted with cigarette smoke. In one corner of the open area was a lamp with a bright pink shade, several house plants, a kitty calendar, and pretty pink decorations.

This is where I met Patty. The way she wore her Army dress uniform, made her look like a Hollywood actress. Her makeup was perfect, and her hair swept up in a twisted bun, pinned neatly. Puffing away and typing fiercely, she popped up like a toy top the first time I said hello. Patty already knew who I was, and she told me she was excited to have me in the building.

"If you want to smoke, come over to my desk," she said. For the first week, I snuck over when John was away from the office. One day he said, "You don't have to hide smoking from me. As long as you don't smoke near me, I don't care."

Patty and I became close friends and drinking buddies, too. After another of my boyfriend breakups, Patty helped me get an apartment close to Camp, near hers. It was a one bedroom, and it was all mine. Now I had a great job, I lived close to work, I was single, had lots of friends, but I still felt empty.

Drinking daily now, I went to bed when I was too drunk to drink anymore.

When we had family parties during this period, our personal connection was beer and gossip. My dad was a free spirit pool playing carpenter who moved around the towns, never settling down. My mother still worked for the employment service and her interest in and approval of our careers was meaningful to us. None of us graduated from college. My oldest brother was in the active duty Air Force, and whenever he came home, he got the hero's welcome from my mom. She made his favorite dishes and gushed over his tall, athletic, professional stature.

One of my older sisters was serious about her career. She worked full time and was a single mom, attending college part time. I often sought her advice about dating and work situations. After another of my breakups from a boyfriend who was abusive, I met her for lunch, and she was glowing.

"Who is he?" I asked. She'd met a construction worker at the local deli, and she was gushing over him. In our eyes, it was movie romantic.

He had a brother, and it was not long before she and the guy set me up to meet the brother. We met for lunch, and he was like a script straight out of Hollywood. A cocky, loner, troubled, lost guy with big brown eyes and shaggy unkempt hair. The kicker in this Lifetime movie with a twist—he was a single dad living in a beat up old trailer just on the other side of Camp. I bit, hook, line, and sinker, in spite of my sister's warning: "You can't drink around him. He's an alcoholic."

Why would a hard partying single girl date a non drinking single dad? My friends tried to warn me to get off the road I was on, but I jumped in. One of the first drunks we had together, he told me about Alcoholics Anonymous (A.A.). He was wearing an ankle bracelet at the time, after a recent arrest for beating up his brother. His sad story just drew me in more.

His son was about nine years old, a kid with sweet marble brown eyes and hair that matched his dad's. He didn't trust any woman his dad brought home. His biological mother didn't visit him much; she had two daughters in a new marriage. I felt sad for this boy who hung on to the only parent he had.

I believed I differed from those other chicks, and I worked to prove to this boy that I cared. I moved in with them and began to fix up their life. When I cleaned the trailer, I found beer cans in the cupboards and inside broken panels in the walls. I remember thinking, "What did I get myself into?"

For the first time as an adult, I was going to bed early and not spending my time in bars. Helping this guy and his son made me feel good.

I took an extra job at a quick stop store right next to the trailer park we lived in and bought my first brand new vehicle—a black Toyota pickup truck that I loved and was so proud to drive. I had splurged for the personalized license with F.I.D.O. on it, which stood for Fuck It Drive On. I realized now that was a way to hide my inferiority complex.

My boyfriend was on parole, so he couldn't drink and was mandated to go to A.A. meetings. The first meeting I went to with him was one of the largest in the area. Cigarette smoke formed a huge gray cloud floating above the recovering drunks sitting in metal chairs facing a stage. A wooden podium had a sign hanging on it: "One Day at a Time;" people passed by with coffee cups in hand, and I sat in the back of the room and cried listening to men talk about their indiscretions.

I was amazed. Quitting drinking was to support my boyfriend and impress his son.

A year passed. We fought a lot, and turned to alcohol for the solution to pain, frustration, or not knowing what else to do. I was a soldier and a full time federal technician in the Army Guard. I was in my early twenties and dating a man with a son. I went to A.A. meetings. My friends tried to convince me I was not an alcoholic, telling me how sad my life was becoming. Something inside of me triggered the old message: Don't let anyone tell me what to do.

My boss was patient with my excuses, calling in sick, showing up late, or not being able to focus. The older men in

LIFE AT CAMP

the office told me I had potential to be an outstanding member of the team. It was a compliment, but also a suggestion—be outstanding. When I focused, I performed well at my job and during soldier development training. I made sergeant rank, and was proud.

After I got my new job with John and Patty, I was transferred from the PSC to the Camp headquarters company, titled Joint Force Headquarters (JFHQ). Just after I transferred, the personnel service unit was mobilized to Fort Drum, New York, to support Desert Storm. I sat on the hood of my Toyota pickup and waved goodbye to Lisa and the girls as their unit convoy rolled out of Camp and served on a deployment I would miss out on.

The JFHQ was in the main building on Camp Johnson and my full time job at the SPMO, where I worked (Monday through Friday) was in a small building on the corner of the base. Many service members worked full time in one area, but conducted their military duty in a completely different location. Not so for me, I worked and conducted my drill weekend in the same office. But for two short assignments out of the Joint Force unit, I spent the rest of my military career (29 years) there and I spent the rest of my federal career (a total of 32 years) in the SPMO, which became the HRO. Of course, this pleased my mom!

Unknowingly, I anchored myself to Camp Johnson. As a child growing up, I hated moving every year to another school, another home, and a new neighborhood to get used to. I found a place to grow up, there at Camp Johnson, and the work had just begun.

CHAPTER 6
GROWING UP AT CAMP
★ ★ ★

Over the year with my boyfriend and his son in the trailer, we had short spurts of sobriety and nice moments together. I finally hit bottom, though, with using alcohol as a solution to my personal problems.

I was working days as a soldier and nights at the local fair, the same fair I worked at when I shouted at people to throw their dime in and take a chance.

This time I was in a food stand called Chicken Licken. I always kept a beer under the counter to sip on. After work on August 30, 1989, I stumbled out to my truck in the pitch black field beside the fair. I got in and drove my precious Toyota pickup home in a drunken stupor. On the way, I picked up a hitchhiker, and although my boyfriend's trailer was only miles from the fair, I drove her to her own home out of town. She was drunk, too.

On the way, although I was drunk, I told her all about A.A. and how sobriety was the way to go. When I got back to the trailer with a six pack in hand, I snuck in the back way to avoid waking my boyfriend's son. The back door of the trailer was missing a step, so I had to jump up to reach the door handle, and jump up again to roll inside. I placed the beer inside the hall and was just rolling over when the hall light flicked on. The boy stood there in his Ninja Turtle pajamas, staring at me with those big brown eyes. Disgusted, he shut the light off and went back to his room. I will never forget that face.

I like to think those eyes got me sober, because I never drank again.

The next morning dawned hot. I was hungover with one of those headaches that feel like your brain is swelling right out of your skull. Patty came over and woke me up.

"You're late. Get your ass to work."

I dragged myself to the office to find the team out back surrounding a picnic table. They had muffins and coffee and were singing "Happy Birthday" to an older civilian lady. I snuck up to the group and hoped I wouldn't pass out and fall on the ground. I remember looking upward despite the pain and whispering, "God, help me. I am an alcoholic."

After surviving the day, I had what I felt was a miraculous awakening. I stopped pouring alcohol in me, and I started to feel great. As the days rolled by, I felt better physically and spiritually. I was going to work every day and even working on physical fitness, as policy permitted National Guard full time employees the benefit of exercising on base during work hours.

I married the boyfriend who introduced me to A.A. and became a stepmom to his son. We moved out of the beaten up trailer and into a home.

My job was going better, too. The old timers in the personnel office encouraged me to take a computer course, saying computers were the future, so I took a class at the local college in Microsoft DOS. Younger people may not recall the term *DOS* (Disc Operating System). I was learning how computer programs function and to be an administrator for our office needs. It was the first of many new technological skills as computers became an indispensable tool for personnel management.

My boss at Camp was an outstanding teacher. I respected him as my first real supervisor who taught me how to do the job right, how to manage personnel records and take care of clients. My self-esteem grew. I was selected for a new job as the Data Base Systems Manager, an important move for me. I got the job because I'd taken the DOS course, and I was now a sober person showing up for work. The job was intimidating, but I rolled up my Army sleeves and learned as much as I could. It was new to all of us because, for the first time, the personnel office had computers.

Our office eventually moved out of that old World War II building and into more modern quarters across Camp. We each had our own office with carpet on the floor, and we even had an office kitchen. One corner of the building held the mysterious data processing center filled with humming machines and lots of flashing lights.

In military style, we switched acronyms as the official title of our section became known as the Human Resources Office (HRO). Over the next 14 years, I would grow into an established HR specialist. For the first seven years, I was the Data Base Systems Manager, a highly technical job, often overseeing rapid changes in the system. For a lot of the time, it was just me and the computer, detached from other human beings. Perhaps this was a good thing, because early in my sobriety, I had a lot of internal work to do learning how to be part of a team and how to be a partner to anyone.

I never really liked the technical world, but I was fearful of change, so I stuck it out. I finally worked up enough esteem to make a move, and after seven years in data management, I became the HRO training manager, processing employees' requests for training to help them do their federal jobs. This was separate from the military training branch, which develops warrior and leadership skills. In my post, I sent federal civilian technicians to train on new equipment and take supervisory classes.

In the personnel office, we were always serving two combined cultures. Though we were "civilians" (Monday through Friday) we wore our military uniforms. We had our civilian jobs and we also had our military weekend jobs. The two worlds mingled throughout the organization, with separate regulations, policies, and hierarchy systems. Often, your rank and military position surpassed any civilian status.

I could feel a sense of excitement as my personality was more attuned to doing the satisfying work in training. One of the first classes I took for my new job involved the Myers-Briggs Type Indicator (MBTI), a personality measuring system. Learning that I was an Extraverted, Intuitive, Feeling, Judger (ENFJ)—an outgoing "people person" who liked to get things done and keep things orderly—made all the sense in the world to me, and that personal understanding would be the saving grace for future relationships.

I remained sober, but my marriage ended in divorce when my husband couldn't accept sobriety. I said goodbye to the boy, who was in middle school. It was hard. He had loved me, and he hugged me tight. Being a stepmom to him taught me how unconditional love works, and about being dedicated and committed to someone other than yourself. I am forever grateful to this boy who forced me to grow up. His father loved him, but too often the disease stole the selflessness of good parenting away. The disease would take him, confirming A.A. warnings: Drunks get sober, institutionalized, or die.

After a couple years of dating while sober, I hit an emotional bottom regarding my relationships with men. I bemoaned the pattern of my dating behavior—why could I not find intimacy; why did I attract men who were emotionally unavailable; why did I jump into relationships with men I didn't even like?

Life at Camp

I disliked the inferiority complex that came with intimate relations.

The story of meeting Phil—who was a mature, nonalcoholic, emotionally available man—and becoming his wife and the mother of our two children could go into another book about men and relationships. Of all things, I went out with Phil the first time hoping to make another boyfriend jealous. We went line dancing and had a great time. He'd been in the service and was discharged during a downsizing of the active duty. His story made me think perhaps he couldn't cut the military, but I found out he was nothing like I had expected. Over time, his love became the anchor I needed to become a true partner.

Information from the MBTI made sense to me, because Phil is an Introverted, Sensing, Thinking, Judger (ISTJ). Our personalities are complete opposites except for our militant need for structure and uniformity. The structure the military gave me saved my life.

Phil was born with a need for structure. My husband is a good man, a great patriot, and about as meticulous of facts, purpose, and having a place for everything as a person can be. He is a lifelong mechanic and comes from a very structured life with a strong work ethic. He grew up in the same town, went to the same school system until joining the Army. I don't think he ever quit anything.

The first few dates with Phil were weird as I found myself

with a polite, selfless man. I dated kind and selfless men before, but because I always wanted to control, I didn't recognize this as a valuable trait.

We both love country music, football, and being soldiers. We enjoy the same sense of humor, although he uses sarcastic ribbing more than I. My recovery team of women approved of Phil. I had some fears and self-consciousness about dating a good guy. Was I good enough? I was uncomfortable with Phil's authentic kindness. It took me time to trust him.

Very early in our relationship, we were pregnant. My fears and thoughts of running away from a good thing were intense. This was a true crossroads for me, emotionally and spiritually. I did not need a man; he did not need me. I did not want to control him, and he didn't want to be controlled. We admired our differences and felt confident we could care for a child no matter how we meshed.

After our daughter, Joanna, was born, we married. My mother held Joanna, and women from my recovery group walked me down the aisle. Our vows were, "As long as it be thy will."

We've stayed together and we've done the emotional work to be selfless partners. Over the decades together, we raised two children and now have a beautiful granddaughter and two super step-grandchildren.

Phil and I were the dual military couple. He was in the combat brigade and I was at Headquarters. He would often

LIFE AT CAMP

taunt me about how easy we had it at Headquarters, or how I wasn't in the "real" Army.

Life was moving along well. Joanna was born when I was 32. My rank at the time was staff sergeant, and I had about 12 years of service combined between the active duty Army and the Army National Guard. Phil had 12 years of active duty Army and had been in the Vermont Guard for about two years.

My six years of sobriety continued to serve me well. The job in the HRO was fun. I developed great relationships with professionals who mentored me to be a solid program manager. Reaching out for help and mentorship to improve my competency now came easy.

Phil and I didn't have wordy arguments about the way the National Guard operated. My drill weekends at headquarters were never a strain. Supportive bosses and good friends made life at Camp Johnson easy. Phil worked for a civilian truck service and was a military shop mechanic on drill weekends. We focused on our firstborn, our wedding, our secondborn, and fixing up our home.

I put myself on a military path to achieve the next rank, sergeant first class (SFC/E7), and I gave no thought to possible gender barriers, nor did I think my options for professional development might have been greater if I'd joined the Guard as a truck driver.

Sobriety had given me confidence. I adopted the attitude

that I'd be the best I could be. My intention was to rise to the rank of sergeant major (SGM), but it was daunting to realize that room for promotion under my current circumstances was sliver thin. Promotion often required a job to go along with it, and my career path didn't include a lot of slots for sergeant majors. One of my coworkers held the rank of warrant officer. I had seen and heard of warrant officers before, but I never considered how a person went about becoming one.

Commissioned officers such as lieutenants, captains, and so forth must have a college degree and attend officer training. Their positions are more authoritative and supervisory than specialists in a field. Warrant officers, on the other hand, are subject experts. The qualification to become a warrant officer is based on experience in a particular occupation as an enlisted member. Some warrant officer specialties are administrative, logistical, mechanical, even Special Forces. Many warrant officers specializing in avionics are recruited from the civilian population.

My experience in Human Resources as an enlisted soldier qualified me for an administrative warrant officer field.

Changing rank structure and aiming at warrant officer status instead of SGM required tenacity, confidence, and a bit of grit, happening as it did when I was 38 years old. Giving up my dream of being a SGM was hard. And to become a warrant officer, I had to start from the bottom to complete all the professional development training needed to ascend through the warrant grades. Leaving my two toddlers for a month to attend training was challenging. The mental grit I needed just to sign up was harder than getting through the actual Warrant Officer Basic Course (WOBC).

Talk of getting through WOBC is always hellish, and those who go through it are proud of surviving and not quitting. Older warrant officers would talk about it like a scene from *An Officer and a Gentlemen,* the Richard Gere movie that put *washing out* high on a candidate's list of things to fear. Stories of students quitting stoked my insecurity. The good news was, the course lasted just 30 days for Guard personnel. I chanted, "It is only 30 days."

My WOBC was held at Fort Rucker, Alabama, February 2001. The class of 60 included eight females. None of us quit, but eight from the male side left during the first week. The drill instructors (DIs) were tough as nails and would taunt us with: "Go back home. The Army needs more NCOs."

I wasn't aware of gender disparity during this training. We were all held to the same standards when completing leadership tasks and passing our academic classes. In environments where physical performance was a focus, bias came in the form of picking on the weak, male or female. For this training, I had enough warnings and advice to remember: "This will not last forever. They're trying to see how tough we are, and I can do anything for 30 days."

After the first hot run in the Alabama heat, where DIs

relentlessly hounded us, several men lost discipline and yelled back at the DIs. As we stood there panting and letting the sweat run down our faces, the lead DI told us to look to our left. "You see those losers doing the duffle bag drag back to their units? They don't belong here. Do you?"

Part of me wondered if they were actors just set up to motivate us. I couldn't believe I outlasted anyone.

I was never an athlete, with all my drinking and smoking, but those addictions were behind me, and now I found myself in the best shape of my life. I was still not the fastest or toughest woman by any means, but I was the only woman in my class to max out the Army Physical Fitness Test (APFT).[3]

During the graduation ceremony, I was recognized for my APFT score, and at the graduation social, my fellow male graduates poked fun at me.

"I can't believe the slowest member of our team gets a P.T. award! Well, women only have to do ten push-ups for 100 points, right? And they get an hour to run the two miles. Ha ha ha."

But the taunts weren't accurate. Each branch of the military has intentionally designed APFT calculations to measure strength and endurance with varying standards based on gender and age. Although the original purpose for testing was to ensure combat readiness, the tests have evolved to measure a service person's general physical fitness. Military

---

[3] https://usarmybasic.com/army-physical-fitness/apft

Life at Camp

Occupational Specialty (MOS) service schools test a warrior's ability to do the actual job they will be assigned to. We weren't educated on the sex differences of body composition, muscular strength, and cardiorespiratory endurance between the sexes. These sex differences didn't mean an individual was unable to accomplish certain combat-related jobs, but the different standards for the APFT still fueled a belief in women's inferiority to men.

I shrugged it off, thinking to myself, "You are assholes." That sort of bantering might uplift and motivate men, but for women, it chipped away at our confidence, feeding our fear that we were never good enough. I was super proud of becoming a warrant officer. My ego took another hit when I had to temporarily take off the rank and put the enlisted staff sergeant stripes back on. For almost eight months, the Army had to maneuver around Human Resources to find a warrant officer slot for me to move into.

On September 11, 2001, my husband and I came home from work and turned on the television. Our two young children ignored our worried faces as we stared at the news unveiling the horrific terrorist attacks on our nation.

At Camp the next day, security was extreme, and the mood somber. A new little guard shack had been quickly built and placed at the entrance to the Camp. It looked like an ice shanty fishermen would put on a frozen lake. Military police soldiers held mirrors to look under our cars, and they checked everyone's identification, even if they knew us. In HRO, we kept the TV on in the conference room, and we'd pop in throughout the day, talking with comrades about what America would or should do next. Life was suddenly much more serious.

The organization finally detailed me to a warrant position in the Federal Auditor Section. They appointed me as a warrant officer one (WO1) on Joanna's birthday, October 20 in 2001. My husband was in a cast after ankle surgery, but he insisted on hobbling up after the promotion pinning to salute me.

I always aimed for the top rank I could achieve. I kept a three by five card inside my desk drawer outlining the timeline I would follow to become a chief warrant officer five (CW5). I would be 55 by the time I was eligible for CW5 in the Warrant Officer Corps.

Camp life was very different after 9/11. The security shacks became permanent structures, and a Joint Operations Center (JOC) was added to manage base security. Prior to 9/11, Camp Johnson was open to the public and traffic drove right through the base. I was still in JFHQ working full time as the training manager for technicians, and spending drill weekends in the auditor warrant slot, wearing my warrant office bar, doing nothing.

The Guard hired my husband as a civilian federal technician, and he worked in a maintenance shop (Monday

Life at Camp

through Friday) at Camp Johnson, which supported all Army Guard vehicles. His drill weekends were busy, as Vermont's long tradition as an armor brigade transitioned to an Infantry Brigade Combat Team (IBCT).

The mission realignment challenges didn't affect my own life much, but my unit in the JFHQ had ramped up operational strategies to ensure soldier readiness, preparing for deployments that came along more regularly now. This meant heightened attention to personnel records, medical records, legal documents, and security clearances. Operational training plans needed to be adjusted to fit new timelines and meet deployment notices.

The Vermont Guard saw numerous active-duty deployments in support of the wars in Iraq and Afghanistan. Unfortunately, we lost some service members and our Family Readiness Programs became a hub of increased activity.

With the added security missions, the HRO had to move once again, this time to the main building on base, and we all crammed into open bay spaces on the second floor. I developed my managerial skills and made important connections with other professionals at Camp. People always like the manager who approves sending them on business trips or to attend trainings. That person was me. Our budget was ample to meet the training requirements, and approvals came easy.

From my view, the Guard became a force more respected

now. Service members felt increased pride and unity, knowing we mattered a great deal to the country's security efforts. Recruiters in the Air and Army Guard were busy with citizens' newly-piqued interest in serving.

In the summer of 2004, my boss gave me an extra assignment as the State Diversity Coordinator. I didn't even know what that meant, but I went along with two men to a national diversity conference in Chicago, Illinois. Dr. Samuel Betances was the keynote speaker, and every word mesmerized us. His educational and gripping perspectives on embracing diversity filled the three of us with hope and spunk as we drafted a state diversity plan to submit to our leaders back home.

But as we settled back into our full time jobs and weekend duties in Vermont, the term *diversity* went to the back burner, even though it was gaining traction at the NGB. From time to time, top leaders would poke one of us to brief them on our plan to build a state diversity program for the Guard. We would create a PowerPoint, but the event always seemed to get kicked down the road.

Still, learning to function as State Diversity Coordinator, I started to take note of equal opportunity as it related to establishing and maintaining member diversity.

My boss at the time was a female Air Force lieutenant colonel. I liked the way she engaged with every person in HRO. She was the type of colonel who put her name on the kitchen cleanup roster with the rest of us, and she spoke to the janitor the same way she spoke to the general. She was the first female HRO in the history of our Camp, but I still didn't take note of any barriers she might have broken to get there.

The lieutenant colonel supported the work I recommended in my training management job to incorporate more workshops aimed at *soft skill* management. Soft skill training included how to effectively lead a team, coaching methods, mediation skills, and counseling employees (not warriors). These skills were different from the military's transactional leadership, known as the *telling* style of leadership, which focuses on structure, results, rewards, and penalties.

In civilian status, supervisors had to consider the rights of employees that often were not a part of the military culture. The Civilian Labor Relations Specialist in the HRO had a challenging job chipping away at the egos of military supervisors who could not order a civilian to do something. I set up volunteer training sessions to explore alternate management styles and quickly learned most service members didn't like any sort of training categorized as *soft*.

Just outside the big bay office area that I shared with a few other Human Resources specialists was an empty private office (prime real estate on our small base Camp) intended for a SEEM. One day I talked to my boss about taking the SEEM job (and about moving into that empty private office), since the duties aligned with my extra assignment as State Diversity Coordinator.

She was excited to find out I was interested, saying it would be a great fit with my team building skills. It wasn't an immediate promotion (civilian) promotion, but I'd get an upgrade, if I could incorporate community outreach into the Equal Opportunity program. As I began my career as the SEEM and Diversity Manager, I still had blinders on regarding all the kinds of bias that were at play. I wasn't yet taking note of bias that other women had to overcome to attain their positions. Personally, any pain I had endured from previous sexual abuse, assault or harassment had been neatly tucked away in my imaginary backpack.

In November 2004, I became the Vermont State Equal Employment Manager, and I felt pretty giddy as I slid my nameplate on the door of my new office.

CHAPTER 7
WHAT IS EQUAL OPPORTUNITY?
★ ★ ★

I began my new job as the Vermont National Guard State Equal Employment Manager. The full time federal position (Monday through Friday) had been vacant for over a year. With a big grin and key in hand, I was excited to have my own office. While the space had been considered empty, it somehow became a closet for various items other HRO managers decluttered from their own cramped offices. I overlooked the mess as I beamed out the window facing toward Vermont's Green Mountains. Mount Mansfield's blanket of white glistened for me.

I didn't know it at the time, but years later when I read the statement, "Do you want to snuggle?" and other statements like them, they landed in the same place where I had already stashed my own pain. It took time for me to face it, but the humiliations that were reported to me in this job sparked an intense need to resolve a pain for others that I recognized in myself, as well.

I am an extrovert and my thoughts become words, often hastily. Speaking without consideration is how many discrimination cases begin. As an advocate of a fair equal opportunity process, I had to quickly learn to consider my own words. Growing up with five siblings and five cousins next door, I had become somewhat of a competitive talker, therefore, I had to learn to actively listen, too. The first year in my new position catapulted me into a world I had never contemplated, given my privilege of circumstance. I had not recognized nor experienced so blatantly the unfair or impartial treatment based on my race, color, national origin, religion, sex, age, or any disability. I hadn't even considered how others may have experienced discrimination. These challenges never occurred to me. This is the privilege I would later come to fully appreciate.

As I sorted through the boxes, binders, folders, and mail in my new office, I tried to categorize things into topics. The first few weeks were mind boggling, but I had this energy to uncover every nook and cranny of the office and figure this job out A.S.A.P.

2004 was coming to an end. It was significant that while I was energized to learn a new and challenging job, my husband, Phil, was deploying to Kuwait with Task Force Green Mountain. We had two children, an eight year old daughter, Joanna, and a six year old son, Troy. Troy had special education and psychological needs, later diagnosed on the Autism Spectrum. I managed all this with exuberant energy.

I was basically a single mother while Phil was deployed. I welcomed the help of my family, friends, and the Guard's Family Program services. My female boss recognized my anxieties and I almost broke down to cry one day when she said, "Doris, I don't want you to ever feel rushed getting here in the morning. If the kids aren't being cooperative or you forget something and have to run back home, don't panic. Just get here when you get here." Her emotional intelligence to sense my stress relieved much pressure. I was rarely ever late.

I found all sorts of information in the office that I'd need for my new job. The position required oversight of Vermont's military EO program, both the Air and the Army. There were military EO regulations for both. My prominent duties required management of the civilians who worked full time for the VTNG. These employees were called federal technicians and I found a stack of federal Equal Employment Opportunity (EEO) regulations. There was an array of diversity references coming from the NGB. I found dated Affirmative Action Plans (AAPs) for the military and the civilian workforce. I never heard of such plans despite having 17 years of working for the Guard and most of it working in the HRO staff who maintained those plans.

I continued discovering programs, policies, and processes that boggled my mind. I found cases of program guides for an E-mentoring program. I heard of mentorship before but never witnessed any systematic mentoring happening. I scratched my head. The guides assisted units in conducting climate assessments. I remember taking these surveys every year but I never considered why or what happened to the answers we submitted. There was an array of annual reports required to be distributed to a variety of entities—NGB, the Equal Employment Opportunity Commission (EEOC), or service specific program directorates.

My head was spinning. I'm a visual person, so I posted flip charts on the wall, lined up colored folders on the credenza, and filled a yellow legal pad with my to-do list.

In my new office, the mailbox was overflowing. I found an unopened copy of a notice from the NGB's Equal Opportunity Office (NGB-EO), addressed to the TAG. The letter thanked the TAG for volunteering to be one of the first states to receive an in person program evaluation from the national EO office. The evaluation visit was scheduled in eight months.

I thought this was important, so I took it to my boss. She confirmed with the TAG that, yes, we were going to have representatives from NGB-EO come to Vermont to evaluate our EO program. We had eight months to get our pre-inspections completed and put a visit plan in place.

One way to quickly indoctrinate oneself into a program is to have a national entity come to see how your program operates. I had rummaged through enough piles by then to know—we were not operating at all. I was thrown into the deep end of the pool. To stay above water, I'd have to learn to swim here, learn my job, and also get ready for the visit.

In my previous position as the full time training manager, I had gotten to know many of the important players on base, enjoyed great relationships as the person who approved people's business trips and organized travel for training sessions. In the military, we use the acronym TDY—temporary duty travel. There was a time when the term *boondoggle* was often associated with TDYs, and the person who facilitated the travel got the credit for allowing the trips. I only approved trips per regulation, but I earned a lot of gratitude around Camp for my professional and expedient processing of people's travel arrangements.

The first woman who came to me as a client in the EO office brought a complaint to be resolved. She was a sergeant, a seasoned enlisted maintenance administrator, who had been around the block long enough to be a bit cynical, but she relished her expertise to handle the bullshit. I hadn't even read a regulation yet, nor could I find the definition for sexual harassment, but I was frightfully concerned by her allegations against the maintenance officer who supervised her.

I knew the maintenance officer named in this administrator's complaint. I'd interacted with his team for years, sending his mechanics to new equipment training. He was the "old soldier" colonel, who barked as needed but could change his tone and speak like a favorite uncle when he wanted to. When the aggrieved sergeant described working conditions, she allegedly had to endure and frantically asked me to fix the problem, I felt sweat run down my back.

As it turned out, she didn't file an official complaint and she ended up retiring out of the military. But through our engagements, she gave me an astonishing view of the culture of our organization outside of my bubble. She described the vast status gap between men and women in the military maintenance arena. I remember being shocked at the behavior she described. I hadn't experienced, or at least recognized, such blatant acts of everyday sexism. The sergeant described being ordered to get coffee and run personal errands, and being told flat out that women didn't belong in the military. She said she was blocked from pursuing greater responsibility within her job. She described being cursed at, including the word *bitch*, and having to hear a constant barrage of breast jokes.

When she chose not to file an official complaint, I sighed in relief that I didn't have to process a charge against the maintenance officer. Shamefully, I was relieved, because I liked him. In the job, though, I was gaining knowledge and passion as I strategized how to stand up this perennially flatlined program I'd been put in charge of. I needed to figure out how to update and activate discrimination prevention plans that hung in the filing cabinets, a bit dusty.

Striving for the top with my extraverted can-do style, and considering the promotion promised if I incorporated community outreach, I set out to make important connections. The looming evaluation visit dictated urgency. The first section I sought to collaborate with was the Army Recruiting and Retention Battalion (RRB). Early in my career, I turned down a job in RRB, opting for a promotion within the HRO. I felt confident if I was to establish any community outreach, recruiting was the place to make my connections.

I confidently walked into the recruiting unit area, but I suddenly felt like I had a purple face. The men—who appeared to loiter around the unit area with nothing in particular to do—set piercing eyes on me as I reached out my hand to introduce myself to the kindest face I could find in the room.

"Hello, I'm Chief Sumner from the Equal Opportunity office." Silence and a limp hand met mine. The SGM stared at me as if wondering, "What are you introducing yourself to me for?"

He didn't invite me to sit down or to accompany him to a private area for a chat, so the onlookers listened in as I attempted to cheerfully talk about how EO was an important aspect of recruiting and retention, and how I'd like to see what community outreach events their team attended.

It was a short, uncomfortable one-way conversation.

Life at Camp

The SGM thanked me and said he'd discuss this with the commander and get back to me.

I didn't hear from the recruiting SGM or the recruiting commander. Within a few hours, I did receive an email from the colonel in charge of personnel *(entitled the J1 Section)*, who oversees RRB. He was the first of many antagonists I would battle.

His curt email stated that any coordination between the EO program and recruiters would remain focused on pursuing the female market. He made sure to convey that Vermont is the whitest state in the nation demographically, and any attempt to increase diversity for the sake of affirmative action or *political correctness* would not be supported. He wanted any collaboration and sharing of recourses between our offices to focus on return on investment. He ended with, "Let's work on the female market."

I'd spent the past five months boning up on manuals, reports, and policies. I was drafting action plans to organize the EO office and prioritize tasks. This email was a complete shot to my ego and put me off-balance. Why would the recruiters feel defensive about community outreach? Had I said something wrong? I don't even remember mentioning race, or even the word *female*.

My boss encouraged me to press on and find other ways to engage with underrepresented groups in the community.

Doris J. Sumner

CHAPTER 8
NOT AS SIMPLE AS BLACK AND WHITE
★ ★ ★

So, that's how talking to the recruiters went. According to regulations, the organization should have a soldier assigned as the Army Military EO Officer. I learned a new acronym, HREO for Human Resources Equal Opportunity Officer. I set out to find the soldier. I met a cheery full bird colonel who worked full time for the Guard as the State Surgeon assigned to the Medical Detachment. He told me he used to be the HREO but only in a part-time collateral duty status. He handed the duty off to a junior chief warrant officer in personnel.

Later, I would recognize the nonchalant way he perceived the EO job. At that time, I still wasn't attuned to realize the full impact of how EO was not taken seriously. I came to realize, most Guard members in Vermont did not consider there was disparate treatment based on anything other than competence. Military people like to tout the one standard for all and believe we can operate absent any bias or ego. Equal Opportunity was for racists and Vermonters couldn't be racist, we lived in the whitest state in the nation. Therefore, the

EO program was given little thought. The consideration of sexual harassment as an EO issue was a blind spot and sexual harassment was downplayed at every level.

The colonel referred me to the chief, who was a superstar Human Resources (HR) specialist. He was a weekend soldier, meaning he didn't work full time for the Guard. He had a full time civilian Post Office job and attended military drill weekends at the JFHQ, where he worked in the primary military personnel directorate *(entitled the J1 Section)*. We were in the same unit and same section, but amazingly, I hadn't met him before. My drill weekends *[See Diagram 1; Full Time vs. Drill Status]* were sitting in the Auditor Section.

I found out senior leaders assigned the chief the Equal Opportunity job of HREO as a "collateral" or additional duty, just like they had the full bird colonel. Collateral duty was like extra duty, not your primary job on your drill weekend. But they invested a lot of time and money sending him to the Defense Equal Opportunity Management Institute (DEOMI), for 30 days of training to become certified for this extra duty.

When I introduced myself, he raved about EO, and he was excited to have a teammate. But as I outlined a training plan to prepare a program for the approaching evaluation visit, the chief said, "I'll have to get this approved through my boss."

My next battle ensued. I tried to get the HREO aspect up to speed, according to regulations. The EO regs spelled out the required staffing in black and white: *HREO assignment will not be a collateral or part-time duty.*

The program required one Equal Opportunity Advisor (EOA) with officer rank of major (04) or lieutenant colonel (05), plus one Advisor with enlisted rank of master sergeant (E8) or sergeant major (E9). *[See Diagram 3A Army Rank]*

Titles of these positions varied by state, and some documents used different terms for the roles, but these two EO positions—both at the officer and the enlisted level—needed to be senior ranks, ensuring that the individuals working in the posts had years of service experience to manage the programs and effectively advocate for EO with senior ranking leaders in other specialties.

The junior chief explained that he was told his primary duty was managing J1 Section, not EO. His boss was the colonel in charge of the J1 Section—the same colonel who sent me the fiery email about RRB priorities.

I was a junior warrant officer, too, but based on the regulation, I dared to challenge the J1 colonel's decree. I went to his (very intimidating) office with the regulation in my hand. Referring to the staffing section, I requested that we establish compliance.

He was not pleasant as he explained, "The chief is mine. He works in J1. That is his priority, as we conduct soldier readiness for mobilizations. If he isn't busy, he can assist you. However, you are the full time State Equal Employment Manager, and you will be responsible for any Human Resources Equal Opportunity duties."

I just gulped, saluted, and walked out.

The chief was a valuable asset to me, nonetheless, since he was the only qualified Equal Opportunity officer in the Vermont National Guard, having attended the certification school in Florida. According to regulations, if any member wishes to file a military discrimination case, only a graduate of the EO Management Institute could process the case. I wasn't certified yet to handle military cases, and I wasn't yet a qualified Equal Employment Officer able to conduct discrimination case management for the full time federal technicians. I wanted to be in staffing compliance with a full time HREO to do these things, but I would have to take what I could get, even if the position remained part time.

I was gaining a thick skin by now as my positive, cheery training manager glow turned into the person who seemed to anger people, someone to be avoided.

When I talked to my boss about the HREO position, she did a little research and told me the requirements for the EO branch in Vermont had been moved to other sections by the leaders who do that sort of thing. As with any business, Human Resources management requires strategic planning to maximize the quantity and skill sets of your labor force. Both my boss and I grumbled over the decision to move Equal Opportunity assets.

We mimicked the decision makers: "We can use these senior grades in more important sections. Vermont is 98% white, and we don't have EO issues here." They considered EO officers would be like Maytag salesmen, sitting around with nothing to do. There was no consideration of disparate treatment based on race, and certainly not gender.

My boss told me she would bring the staffing issue to the leaders who held the reins, and she'd work to get the authorizations back. In the interim, I would be the HREO on drill weekends despite not meeting the grade requirement. I moved out of the Auditor Section and drilled at the same office I worked at Monday through Friday. When I retired in 2019, the Vermont Guard's staffing was still not compliant.

According to regulations, the HREO was to have direct access to the TAG. Despite my appointment, my junior grade and lack of a supportive network landed me a few officers down the access chain of command, with no direct connection to the TAG. I had to use my leadership chain to communicate case information and wait for feedback.

When there were military EO incidents of discrimination, or federal technician EEO issues, I had to report first to my direct supervisor, the HRO, or Human Resources Officer. The HRO would inform the Director Joint Staff (Chief of Staff for Air and Army Programs). That director would either inform the Assistant Adjutant General (AAG) for the Air or Army depending on the Service-specific issue. Then, depending on the urgency, case information would be presented to the TAG. If the case involved enlisted, the State Command Sergeant Major or Wing Command Chief Master Sergeant were notified. Layers of leaders between me and the TAG can be seen in *Diagram 2; Chain of Command and EO Process*.

Like a kid's game of gossip telephone, the transfer of information along this path tended to dilute or alter what I naively thought would make its way to the top. In hindsight, gender bias too often altered the way the information was presented and affected sensitive decision making all along the way.

Vermont's liberal reputation did not exclude us from sexism. In February 1997, Vermont Air National Guard Lieutenant Colonel Martha T. Rainville defeated Major General Donald Edwards in a high profile reelection bid. Major General Edwards held the TAG post for 16 years; rejection of the *old sexist* Guard fueled much of Rainville's momentum.

General Rainville became the first woman in U.S. history to serve as head of a State's National Guard.

I was just beginning my career as the training manager in the HRO at the time of the election. I remember being proud and elated for our state's recognition, but I didn't yet consider how noteworthy the election was, nor did I pay attention to the cultural struggles involved. When I moved into the SEEM job, General Rainville was the TAG. I wish

I had challenged those chain of command barriers so I could have reported directly to her.

But, as 2005 ended and I was gaining credibility as both SEEM and the State's Diversity Manager, General Rainville was ending her tour as TAG and embarking on a run for Congress. I had minimal opportunity for engagement with the General during my first year. She retired in April 2006, before I had my feet under me and could accept myself as a key staff officer.

Eight months after I found the memo about an upcoming inspection in the messy office of an all but nonexistent program, the Vermont program evaluation happened. The NGB-EO officials cited Vermont as the most successful visit NGB-EO had done. In fact, they were so impressed by my pre-visit checklist and the way I organized the evaluation visit for the team, they requested that I share my preparation procedure for the inspection at a national training event with SEEMs from across the country. Thus, I received the first of many accolades and awards for my work in Equal Opportunity and Diversity.

Still, Vermont's evaluation had highlighted what we were lacking regarding EO Program Management. It was almost pleasant, fueling a resentment seed, to read how the RRB was identified as the most egregious of violators.

I attended the SEEM orientation training and other qualifying courses during the year, and made myself known to NGB-EO directorates and other national leaders for Equal Opportunity and Diversity. The NGB team members who performed the evaluation visit would come to be great mentors and friends to me.

I had no inhibitions in calling other SEEMs to learn as much as I could while developing my plan for the evaluation. I impressed Bureau professionals with my passion and a *roll up my sleeves* kind of grit to tackle the job. These seasoned social activists told me they admired my passion, but I still remember them making empathetic eye contact with each other as I enthusiastically declared my EO action plans.

I dove in and conducted a few Equal Opportunity trainings, receiving the much deserved karma for not paying attention the past 25 years. Service members who attended my trainings resented the topic, or they were indifferent, as I had once been. The training facilitation skills I thought I had learned while serving as training manager did not work. My glow waned.

I hadn't found any formal discrimination cases in the piles of paper that cluttered my office when I arrived. All I had were book smarts about cases and how to process them when a young, bright eyed woman came to my office with serious concerns about being sexually harassed.

Looking back now, I wish I had been a more seasoned manager when she came to me. With more experience, I believe I could have served her better. Yet even today, the military's response to sexual harassment is hampered by a negative bias that continues to affect everyone.

They had put me in charge of a process to address issues regarding disparate treatment based on race, color, religion, ethnicity, and sex. My job also included the federal EEO issues regarding disabilities and age, and it now includes sexual orientation and genetic information. Yet, the leaders themselves didn't believe disparate treatment happened based on personal bias. All of these were and are sensitive life changing issues, and my lack of understanding and experience was impactful.

It was 2006, and I did not know about decades of issues the military had dealt with regarding sexual harassment. The Tailhook and the Aberdeen Scandals were never my concern. I didn't know about the integration battle for women coming into the military. Here I was a chief warrant officer, 43 years old, 25 years in the service, who had personally experienced sexual assault and harassment, but I tucked all this deep in my imaginary backpack. My everyday reality—my mindset—did not connect my experiences as relevant to my ability to do well in the Guard. In A.A., we joked at times, ignorance is bliss. On this journey, I incrementally recognized the privilege of my past ignorance.

As the young woman described her situation, I realized how serious this event was. Her previous supervisor was a general who resolved a reported discipline issue with her;

however, a male colleague was unhappy and took matters into his own hands. The offenses alleged against the male colleague were sexual harassment. The case included several administrative complications, including both military and civilian components involving the victim, the offender, witnesses, and responsible leaders. I could never disclose case details, but the response from the leaders I interacted with, pulled back the curtain. I could see the playbook regarding how the androcentric leadership dealt with allegations of sexual harassment.

For the first time, I had to interact with the JFHQ Judge Advocate General (JAG). The JAG is legal counsel for a military unit. I had never worked for or with an attorney before. You hear stories and jokes about what coldhearted jerks lawyers can be, and until you engage with an attorney, you don't know what to expect. I was intimidated.

He was not the opposer, but I found myself very opposed to everything that came out of him concerning this case. Through correspondence, I sensed our agency's disdain for the aggrieved (the woman filing the case), and I couldn't understand why. Although I had started the informal military and civilian processes, the JAG took charge and left me out of the loop regarding the complaint. Due to the level needed to adjudicate the case, based on the offenses and the ranks/positions of those involved, the administrative process was elevated to a formal EO case. I did not have enough experience to challenge any processes. I researched and made phone calls to the NGB-EO, and was somewhat of a nuisance, not liking the answers I got.

One of the NGB-EO program people who had taken me under their wings sternly reminded me that as EO program managers; "We have no power or authority to resolve the case or administer accountability. We are advocates of a process." My job was to shephard a case through the system, but I had no say in the outcome. That was a hard pill to swallow.

I wanted to stay on top of how the case progressed. I emailed the JAG my questions, and I'm certain my emotional discomfort came across, based on my lack of experience. One day, the JAG responded rudely to my email, but he cc'd my boss and other top leaders on the response. He tore into my lack of competency and told me to stand-down until given administrative instructions.

I remember yelling about it to my boss. Although she was always a comforting leader and mentor, she gave me the command, "At ease!"

But she gave me permission to meet with the JAG to clear up what she termed a lack of clear role expectations between the JAG and my position as the SEEM.

In person, I saluted the JAG and stood at parade rest while I made my case that he had not respected my role. He softened and asked me to sit. Then he told me stories of many sex-based cases he'd prosecuted in the city he'd lived in. He assured me that he understood the cultural problem that gave rise to sexual harassment in the military. He reiterated what the program manager at the NGB-EO said. Our role was to be advisors only. Commanders have the authority to make decisions in these cases, regardless of our approval.

This has been at the heart of advocates who support the Military Justice Improvement and Increasing Prevention Act of 2021 (MJIIPA 2021).[4] The purpose of the bill is to reform the disposition of charges for certain offenses under the UCMJ. This would establish procedures taking some power away from commanders and placing the decision onto a third-party official. Supporters believe this will increase the prevention of sexual assaults and other crimes in the military. Over and over again, testimony throughout the decades confirm the reluctance of survivors to come forward and report due to the bias and inherent conflicts of interest posed by the military chain of command's sole decision making power over whether cases move forward to a trial. Yet, the predatory behaviors of gender bias and sexual harassment are undermined by the same bias.

I engaged with the JAG. We discussed and outlined an operating guide to develop a working relationship. Referring

---

[4] www.congress.gov/bill/117th-congress/senate-bill/1520/all-info

to my Myers-Briggs training, I accepted that the JAG's legal recommendations were based on facts, whereas I made many decisions based on how I felt about a situation. The JAG referred to the point made by the NGB-EO program manager about advocating the process. He said, "Print that quote and paste it where you can see it every day."

When I was ready to leave, he stopped me and said, "Chief, I never had anyone give me such respectful pushback, especially a CW2. Respect."

The compliment reminded me of the grade requirements for my position as Joint Force Headquarters HREO—a person of rank and experience, able to interact on a solid footing with those at the highest levels of the organization. I went to my office and taped a sign at the top of my monitor: "I AM AN ADVOCATE OF THE PROCESS."

It would not be the last time I thought about that statement and its implications.

The woman's case was elevated to my first and only formal civilian discrimination case. I worked late nights to support the JAG. The NGB-EO regarded this case as one of the most troublesome they worked on and empathized with me. "If you had to learn about EEO processing, this is the case to learn from." We processed the case in a timely fashion. I had to coordinate with a court reporter and send out notices to testify to numerous Guard members. I managed to detach from my personal viewpoints and emotions and do my job. The JAG provided me with great mentorship and professional praise for my work.

In the end, her sexual harassment claim was substantiated, yet both the offended and offender were reprimanded in some way. I do not know what disciplinary actions were taken against the two officers involved in the case, however, I never saw them on Camp Johnson again. Rumors from soldiers floated around the Camp and I recognized the harsher judgments against the female, for what the warriors were deeming as so inappropriate rather than the male who arrogantly brought her private affairs out to others. It was a shock to me that a person coming forward to file a complaint could end up being disciplined. Lesson learned.

Doris J. Sumner

CHAPTER 9
Stumbling Through EO
★ ★ ★

The previous case—the one I cut my teeth on—and subsequent admonishments to several members of the Guard brought heightened attention to the Equal Opportunity program. With AG Martha T. Rainville's retirement, the disposition of the case was done by a new TAG, Michael Dubie.

Major General Dubie previously served as a fighter jet pilot. The General was friendly, and he always made deliberate eye contact with the troops.

Our Guard members had been on many deployments by this time, and we had grieved painful personnel losses. Plans were underway to build a memorial to fallen heroes. Veterans returning to Vermont brought their war zone intensity back with them. Old armored units had transitioned to infantry and cavalry units, and the 86 Armor Brigade turned in its Abrams tanks, ending its armor designation after almost 43 years of history. The culture of the Vermont Guard was shifting from a weekend warrior mentality to an infantry mentality of preparing for war.

Life at Camp

By now, 2007, I was qualified to process cases, after attending the DEOMI in Florida. I bugged brigade commanders to staff our EO positions in accordance with regulatory guidance, and I used the NGB's Program Evaluation Feedback Report to gain compliance. The process was tough; the military is socialized to downplay soft prevention programs that look to future problems, always focused on the urgent now. The Guard was training for war and members often indicated their impatience with EO and diversity training requirements.

The Civil Rights Act of 1964 is the founding law that prohibits employment discrimination on the basis of race, color, national origin, religion, and sex (now including gender identity, sexual orientation, and pregnancy). Amendments to discrimination laws have added age, disability, and genetic information to the protected statuses, as well as protections against retaliation for filing a case. These policies and regulations governing EO set up the means by which organizations should respond to illegal discrimination, prevent occurrences from happening, and hold persons accountable when violations do happen.

The military is somewhat permitted to discriminately select on the basis of age, disability, or physical fitness when assessing a member's ability to perform military duties, which often take place in harsh environments, including combat zones.

In the National Guard, when a service member alleges to

a leader that discrimination has occurred, this is called an *incident*. Leaders in the lowest ranks may attempt to come to a resolution informally, without creating a record.

When an incident is recorded on an official form and signed by the service member, it is called a *case*. The case begins with an informal status, and the lowest level commander involved attempts to remedy the situation in accordance with regulatory guidance. The commander conducts a fact-finding inquiry to determine whether discrimination occurred. If an incident is substantiated, the commander decides on a "make whole" remedy intended to restore the service member to the status they would hold if discrimination had not occurred. The commander also has the power to hold violators accountable, in accordance with the UCMJ.

If the service member is unsatisfied with the commander's remedy, they can elevate the case to formal. A service member cannot appeal on the basis of a commander's punishment or no punishment of the offender, they can only appeal if dissatisfied with the "make whole" remedy. The next higher level commander may then use the previous inquiry, or a new and more thorough investigation may take place, including taking sworn statements to determine whether discrimination occurred. The new commander then presents a "make whole" remedy to the complainant. The highest level for appeals of a National Guard military EO discrimination case rests with the TAG. The EO process is an administrative procedure used by the military and not a criminal procedure. If you don't think the investigation was impartial or the "make whole" remedy satisfactory, there is nowhere else to go. Some service members seek out the Inspector General's (IG) office. Their oversight rests on following procedures; you can follow procedures and still be quite biased. The IG office has no power or authority over the procedures. They investigate and make a report to the TAG. The IG is another completely separate process; in the interim, while an investigation is underway, you are still a warrior expected to perform. These processes can take many months, sometimes over a year. I witnessed many clients withdraw or accept the outcomes with complete regret for reporting.

The complaint process is completely different for federal technicians, who fall under Equal Employment Opportunity Commission (EEOC) regulations. These were handled in our offices as well, but the cases might be appealed to Federal District Courts and higher. The majority of federal technicians in the National Guard are also military members. The two processes, and the variations in statuses of the complainants or the alleged offenders, can complicate "make whole" remedies and can impact strategies to prevent reprisal against complainants.

I managed both types of programs, working under the supervision of the HRO. I was a junior warrant officer with one collateral duty person to assist me in managing the VTNG's EO program for our 3,400 Guard members.

Incident reports or cases presented to my office were predominantly from women who had been sexually harassed. During my tenure, I never processed a case for any other type of discrimination.

Generally, the team processed about seven incidents or cases per year, some military, some civilian, but predominantly military.

The education and advocacy had brought incidents to light. By the nature of the cases, I became acutely aware of the disparate treatment women received and the socialization process used to survive—assimilate and accommodate the existing power dynamic. I had done it. Many of the incidents included use of offensive terms or a lack of professionalism. Often, it was not the initial act that infuriated a female Guard member, but the response from authority when they attempted to hold someone accountable for this behavior.

I remember an older woman who had prior National Guard service. She rejoined after 9/11 to help the Guard out. She sat in my office completely disgusted about her time at a mobilization site, and she vented to me as a friend. The boys she was serving with—she called them boys—were *disgusting*, and they drew inappropriate sexist pictures on the guard shack. When she complained, it got worse for her. She said no one took her seriously, and she regretted joining again; "I am too old for this shit," she said. Venting sessions occurred in my office often. We may have strategized a way to counter the offense, considered officially reporting, but often, women felt relief just being heard and opted to put the pain of surrender in their imaginary backpack and carry on.

The chief warrant officer working with me in EO part time had mastered his ability to appease commanders, who felt EO was a nuisance. Chief was always feeding their egos. "I work at the pleasure of the Command." He was an excellent mediator, though, and together we resolved all of our cases during the informal stages.

Merriam-Webster defines *resolve* as *to deal with successfully, clear up, to find an answer to.* In a far distant retrospect, I see we did not successfully clear up these issues of sexual harassment at all. Our actions taken to close the informal process were Band-Aids to cover the wound, perhaps comfort the wounded, and camouflage the problem. Our interventions were better than nothing, and perhaps we shifted perspective for a few members, preventing further harm. We felt like we were doing good. But were we?

As time went on, I gained credibility in the New England States, identified as Region 1, (There were 7 NG regions across the U.S.) and I was selected as a representative for Region 1 to the NGB Joint Diversity Executive Council (JDEC). My colleagues who attended the initial diversity conference resigned from their collateral duty assignments, but I was all in. I published Vermont's first Strategic Diversity Plan. I got busy building the program, and set up a meeting to recruit council members. I diverted from the typical detached military writing style and included feeling words as I attempted to entice employees in the Vermont federal workforce to come talk about diversity and Special Emphasis Programs (SEP).[4] The federal government instituted SEPs to remove barriers for underrepresented groups that were subjected to discrimination in the workforce. Even then, I knew the topic was unappealing. Of the 900 full time employees, less than half even read emails, only eight showed up for the first meeting. My expectations were always too high, yet the small group of activists who showed up inspired me greatly.

We entitled this group of volunteers; focused on the special emphasis programs, the Cultural Diversity Enhancement Team (CDET). Later, the NGB would formalize diversity councils with the title Joint Diversity Executive Councils (JDEC).

I also joined a local diversity business council off base and interacted with community diversity programs operating at the University of Vermont and other college campuses close to the base. My boss in the HRO respected the community outreach I brought to the job and promoted me to the maximum grade for my federal technician position, GS-12 level. My civilian and military workforce cultures often clashing, I was considered senior level as a civilian but I was

---

[4] https://usda.gov/oascr/special-emphasis-programs#:~:text=Special%20Emphasis%20Programs%20(SEP)%20were,strengthened%20by%20two%20Executive%20Orders.

Life at Camp

still a junior warrant officer. I enjoyed the diversity aspects of my job tremendously.

Despite being warned by the colonel about interfering with recruiting missions, I became friendly with the recruiters. In my first year on the job, the recruiters helped me to coordinate a women's exhibit right in the middle of downtown Burlington during an Air Show. I interviewed Vermont National Guard female combat Veterans and displayed pictures from their service in war. I dressed up the tent area with plants and ribbons to attract more people than only those drawn in by military vehicles or fighter jets. I bonded with my sister Veterans and felt totally energized about my new job.

I expanded my team of allies through the diversity council and staffing brigade EOAs. The Brigade (86 IBCT) appointed an EOA, and we became great teammates as we strengthened the brigade's program, knowing they would need certified EOLs at the mobilization station before their next deployment.

One of the first sexual harassment cases we processed in the brigade reemphasized the risk to warriors when reporting insidious behavior, or trying to achieve any kind of "make whole" remedy for wounded warriors.

The unit was conducting A.T. at the VTNG Ethan Allen Firing Range. For A.T., Guard members spend two weeks training together, increasing readiness for their unit's mission. The range is spread out massively over the mountains of Jericho, Vermont. It has several billeting areas, a dining facility, warehouses, and numerous target ranges for a variety of weapons.

The incident in question happened miles out on the range, far from headquarters. The female involved was alone, with no communication facility, and no transportation to leave the scene.

Although the soldier later reported the incident to the unit's EOL, the incident she alleged was actually criminal behavior under the UCMJ, Article 134, Indecent Conduct. The incident was not sexual assault. According to military regulations, when criminal behavior is reported, EO processes must stop, and the unit commander is notified.

Although the commander was notified of this event, and top leaders consulted with the JAG, the EO team continued to process the allegation as an informal sexual harassment case, conducting a fact-finding inquiry and taking informal statements. The unit leadership conveyed their opinions to the brigade EOA, saying the young woman was not credible and had violated a dress code policy. They were basically saying she brought the offense on herself.

When my EO team met her, she was dust covered and exhausted. A.T. at the range could be grueling, with long days, dusty trails, and organized chaos. She did not want to report the incident, but after telling her husband (a fellow soldier who

Life at Camp

was on the range in another unit), he demanded she notify the unit's first sergeant (1SG).

We listened as the young soldier tearfully described the incident to us. The offender made lewd physical gestures offering himself to her sexually. She described being horrified. We asked her what she needed. She wanted to go home. We explained we would talk to command and the unit's EOL would keep her informed. We had genuine concerns about the alleged offender.

We learned that unit leaders called the Vermont State Police, but the female did not want to press charges, and none were filed. The EOA brought the case file to me and we talked over lunch. He was furious over the commander's decision to keep both soldiers at the A.T. site.

The unit command team drafted a counseling statement for the female. She had taken off her outer camouflage jacket and put a road guard vest over her T-shirt when she was stationed at the guard shack. The offender said this caused him to become attracted to her. Command determined that she'd been out of uniform and needed to be counseled.

My EOA told me about conversations unit leaders were having. They were heavily biased against the female, and another commander bragged about the offender's top gun abilities. They also speculated that she'd reported the incident because she feared her husband would find out what happened and think badly of her.

We reminded each other of our frustrating powerlessness as "advocates of a process" we did not own. We could only advise, and then we had to let go.

After a commander's inquiry, the commander issued a code violation against the offender, he lost one rank. The following year, we learned they promoted the soldier back to his original rank.

These types of outcomes fueled the EO unit's annual climate assessments, filled with comments about favoritism. It wasn't only men who benefitted from favoritism; it was largely dependent on who liked you, but there were more men to like. The favoritism was not rooted in men's sheer outnumbering of women, the favoritism was rooted in assimilating.

This had been one of the first serious EO cases in the brigade. My EOA and I felt horrible. Somehow, we felt responsible for the awful way the case ended, and we resolved to do better, not really knowing how.

Typical attitudes around reports of sexual harassment revealed a pattern of denial and distrust. The system almost seemed to console the offender. This affected leaders' decision making. My team and I dealt with these cases repeatedly, often surrendering to the mess, left unresolved. Command's response rarely improved actual conditions for anyone. It was like playing Whac-A-Mole. The victim regretted reporting, and the offender remained defensive, and it would happen again, and again, nothing changed.

CHAPTER 10
THE GOOD OLD BOY CLUB
★ ★ ★

Hearing about the good old boy club may trigger an array of emotional responses from defiance to defeat and indifference. The term refers to a network of male connections with close ties of loyalty and mutual support, typically excluding females. What is wrong with a male dominated operating culture? Perhaps it is the club effect. In many organizations, clubs or alliances can run deep. Equal Opportunity laws, policies, and the appreciation of diversity can weaken that below the surface, exclusionary power system.

The good old boys' club in the military, and especially the National Guard, remains strong. Evidence of the powerful network gleams in every EO demographic report, and it's counter to the mission of EO. These strong alliances of support may not be intended to harm. Perhaps it's just human to help a friend you know and trust. You feel confident of their abilities, so you advocate for them. It took me too long to recognize the entrenched gender bias that impeded efforts to weaken the club's hold on power, but more importantly, made it difficult to promote equal respect for the genders.

LIFE AT CAMP

Most of our discrimination and harassment cases were resolved informally, but this pattern required emotional energy and patient persistence to be able to satisfy the aggrieved while ego feeding commanders. As I marked each sexual harassment case file informally closed, I shook my head and asked myself why.

Some of the allegations were made against service persons I knew and held in high regard. As for the ones I didn't know, they certainly looked the part of a professional warrior, often with certificates of honor and earned challenge coins adorning their workspace.

Why would a professional service person behave in such an undignified manner?

I hadn't given much thought to Vermont having the first female TAG in National Guard history, nor to any other female "first." The only female HRO who was appointed during my tenure was hastily reassigned out of the position to clear the spot for one of the good old boys. I didn't recognize it at the time, but through the course of the following year, such maneuvering became painfully clear.

The reassigned HRO had been my boss. She filed a gender discrimination case, and although a mediator was flown in from out of state, the agency failed to reach a resolution and she withdrew her complaint. She completed her final months in the Guard in a less prominent position and retired. Her personnel file gleamed with a long history of selfless service and impeccable performance ratings, yet she never made the rank of full-bird colonel. We were friends, so I attempted to remain in touch with her. Though she respected me greatly, she asked me to stop corresponding, because she did not want to think about the National Guard.

Her case and many others fueled my conviction that I had to combat the sexism everybody seemed to accept. Though gender discrimination cases were rarely filed, most of the sexual harassment cases that came to me stemmed from a basic lack of respect for anything feminine or out of the status quo.

The number of women leaving the Guard without the opportunity to explore and employ their full talents, skills, and capabilities was all so devastating, so sad to me. They didn't fit the masculine mold, they didn't play the game, or they never had the privilege of powerful mentors who would help them navigate the gates to power. Many of them just got tired. I had a picture of my former boss at her farewell luncheon, and I kept it in my drawer beneath the pens and notepads, noticing it from time to time and resolving to keep going. She was another woman underutilized, undercut, undervalued, and the agency didn't blink an eye at the loss.

The lieutenant colonel who was put into the HRO position in her stead swooped in like a new sheriff in town, his ego bulging out like the chest on a rooster. I knew him from having approved travel orders for him and his buddies, who went on what many whispered were boondoggles. His deputy was one of those buddies, and it was shameful how they giggled like schoolboys as they disparaged the previous boss's leadership style, constantly remarking at "what a mess she made."

I was defiantly defensive about her when speaking to the deputy. I had worked with him for years, and I was disappointed at how he immediately sucked up to the new boss. He barked about how our previous boss was never prepared for meetings and looked foolish flipping through reports when she was speaking to the TAG. I asked why she wasn't prepared, if he was her deputy? I asked why her supervisor didn't mentor her during performance reviews? I came to know why. She was the anomaly—she did not fit the mold, and there was no mentor willing to help her, nor a leader who would recognize her worth.

At one of my gender diversity trainings, I attempted to convey the challenges women faced standing in front of a roomful of men. I talked about the audience scrutinizing a woman's looks, or honing in on every word to find error, or ignoring the content of her presentation from a lack of respect.

I got pushback from the kind men in the room who took the time to attend these optional training sessions.

A friend of mine stated with absolute assurance, "Doris, I don't think that's true. Regardless who is presenting, I listen to what they have to say."

Maybe he did, but he didn't convince me. I attended many

male dominated staff meetings, and they all sounded dutifully the same. If one attempted to be funny or take a different stand, there was a defiant silence that quelled creativity. Anyone seeking success in the organization knew the ticket: assimilation.

The new boss flat out told me he was not a fan of affirmative action when I sought his signature on some annual reports. He let me know any "foolish" diversity emails would need his approval before being sent out. He told me, "Nobody reads them."

I went to my office and cried, then I put the grudge in my backpack and carried on.

To be clear, each and every incident of sexual harassment my team and I processed was sensitive and difficult. There was no black and white way to process these cases. I always felt a bit incompetent to be the person responsible to help survivors find a "make whole" remedy for the damage these offenses caused.

In 2009, I had not even considered the possibility that a proven warrior would come to me and describe a sexual assault and ask where she should seek redress. I was not trained to deal with the impact that trauma has on individuals. I don't believe the woman who filed the complaint used the term *assault*, either. She said, "He put his hands on my breast." I was unprepared to hear an allegation of such importance. At the time, I never saw myself as a victim of sexual assault or even a survivor of sex-based trauma. I had packed any pain from those past events away, not conscious of the impact such offenses had on me.

The DoD now has a single point of authority for its sexual assault policy. The Sexual Assault Prevention and Response Office (SAPRO)[5] provides oversight to ensure compliance with DoD policies. This program was initiated in April of 2004 after a Joint Task Force released a report on sexual assault[6]. There were challenges for the National Guard to meet the requirements.

Resources and authorities for part-time military/civilian National Guard personnel were very different from the military's active component resources. The Service Components for the Air Force and Army were required to ensure a Sexual Assault Response Coordinator (SARC) and a Victim Advocate (VA) be available to respond to incidents of sexual assault. No additional resources were allocated to the National Guard to hire personnel to serve in these positions.

Consistent training for the Guard's SARCs was delayed due to issues with reporting options, such as restricted reporting,[7] which meant confidentially reporting the crime to specifically identified individuals without triggering an

---

[5] https://www.sapr.mils

[6] https://www.sapr.mil/public/docs/reports/task-force-report-for-care-of-victims-of-sa-2004.pdf

[7] https://sapr.mil/restricted-reporting

official investigative process or notification to command. Another reporting option is unrestricted,[8] where the victim desires an official investigation whereby the command is notified. This also qualifies the victim to receive healthcare, victim advocacy, and legal services. These processes are very different between active duty and National Guard military and civilian statuses.

There were also delays in service members qualifying for line of duty service benefits[9] involving eligibility for healthcare benefits under military healthcare programs. A Guard member is not covered for health care benefits after drill weekend, so if they needed medical care from a sexual assault, the Guard Medical Command would have to issue a line of duty order for the member to get benefits. These processes required extra time to work out and ensure confidentiality. The Guard didn't begin to hire SARCs to handle its member complaints until November 2008, and Vermont did not have a SARC in place until 2010.

The female officer alleging a fellow service person touched her breast provided me with the details of the alleged offense. She came to me in my capacity as the subject matter expert (SME), and she was simultaneously aghast that she was describing herself a victim. I recall her stating she had

---

[8] https://sapr.mil/unrestricted-reporting

[9] https://www.tricare-west.com/content/hnfs/home/tw/prov/auth/lod.html

never imagined someone doing this, and she was in shock. She confessed to having listened for two decades to training programs on the prevention of sexual harassment, yet she was unprepared to respond to this offense in lesson plan fashion.

Early military training described sexual harassment as verbal, and even physical, such as caressing or rubbing a person's shoulder. The canned training always focused on sexual harassment as a quid pro quo type of offense, like there was no other way to sexually harass a person. In accordance with policy, service personnel were to report incidents within 180 days.

The Guard member who was allegedly touched inappropriately had put the event in her backpack for almost a year before coming to me. She finally reached her limit for absorbing what she alleged was his retaliation after she failed to reciprocate the advance and immediately communicated to him her rejection of such behavior. She alleged two of his buddies had engaged in creating a hostile environment for her, as well, in good old boys' club fashion.

No employees in the HRO, myself included, had any training in how to respond to survivors of sexual assault. I did not know the critical responsibility sexual assault response coordinators had, nor how our initial tone, words, body language, and actions can impact survivors forever. I was proud of my street experience dealing with sexual harassments, yet I had no professional experience responding to sexual assaults. I knew this was serious, and my inexperience with such events was a factor in some poor decisions, although today I'm not sure what else I could have done.

It was a travesty, one case among thousands of others in which survivors sought justice in the United States military. It demonstrated the very reason why the DoD created a task force to look into military sexual assaults and how they are handled. This was years before the documentary *The Invisible War* was released, in May 2013, revealing the continued practice of the good old boys' network policing itself.[10]

The woman typed out her statement detailing the long, painful year she had endured since the alleged offense happened. She named several offenders, and I recognized them all. As I took her statement, I remained stoic, glancing at the sign on my computer: "I'M AN ADVOCATE OF THE PROCESS," although silently I wanted to scream.

When she revealed the officer who sexually assaulted her, and the others who she alleged created a hostile work environment, my world changed because I had professional engagements with the offenders she named. I was dismayed and fraught with anxiety. I thought the first sexual harassment case I worked on had changed me, but I quickly realized that all the sex-based offenses were changing me.

---

[10] https://www.itvs.org/films/invisible-war/

Life at Camp

There are substantial legal, psychological, and emotional differences between sexual harassment and sexual assault. According to military regulations, sexual harassment is defined as a form of gender discrimination that includes unwelcome sexual advances, requests for sexual favors, and other verbal and/or physical conduct of a sexual nature between the same or opposite genders, including the following conditions:

(1) Submission to, or rejection of, such conduct is made explicitly or implicitly a term or condition of a person's job, pay or career.

(2) Submission to, or rejection of, such conduct by a person is used as a basis for career or employment decisions affecting that person.

(3) Such conduct has the purpose or effect of unreasonably interfering with an individual's work performance or creates an intimidating, hostile or offensive working environment.

(4) Any person in a supervisory or command position who uses or condones implicit or explicit sexual behavior to control, influence or affect the career, pay or job of personnel is engaging in sexual harassment. Similarly, anyone who makes deliberate or repeated unwelcome verbal comments, gestures or physical contact of a sexual nature is engaging in sexual harassment.

I was familiar with sexual harassment's definition. Although physical contact was included within the definition, I had never dealt with this conduct.

The definition of sexual assault is intentional sexual contact characterized by use of force, physical threat and/or abuse of authority, when the victim does not or cannot consent. Sexual assault can occur without regard to gender, spousal relationship or age of the victim.

Regardless of where a sex-based offense lands on the spectrum of harm, the damage is irreversible, the impact forever imprinted on the individual's identity.

I had my own imprints.

The only thing this warrior wanted as a resolution to her case was for the Guard's senior leaders to know what happened and know the type of person this officer was. He was in an important position with promotion opportunities and she wanted the senior leaders to consider this information. She wanted to stop the hostile work environment she alleged had continued for over a year. After taking her statement and assuring her I would contact the TAG and legal officers, I waited just long enough for her to be out of the building before I rushed to the JAG's office.

The JAG office itself was intimidating—you knew only serious business was going on inside. I went to the legal officer, handed over an informal EO discrimination form with the "informal" box checked and the survivor's signature at the bottom.

I recognized instant alarm from the JAG, who said, "Come with me."

We went to the TAG's office. I was hyper aware of every reaction, and I saw sincerity in the General's eyes as he spoke to his JAG.

The TAG said, "Let's appoint an investigative officer and look into this right away."

As the JAG and I walked out of the TAG's office, we passed the accused officer in question. He looked surprised but did not stop us. I went back to my office, and within a minute, he was in my doorway.

"What's up?" he asked.

"You will have to ask the JAG; I can't talk to you about it," I said.

His faced crinkled, and he said, "Is it about me?"

I said, "Go see the JAG."

I had been working in the HRO for 11 years, and my fellow colleagues knew me well. After all, I am an ENFJ, the extraverted feeler personality type, according to Myers Briggs Personality Indicator. I had many authentic professional friends, but I could tell no one about this heavy situation. The only one I felt safe and legitimate to talk to was the part-time Equal Opportunity chief. I called him and I could feel the seriousness between us.

The date of the offense was the first of many challenging issues with the case. According to regulations, military personnel have 180 days to submit a discrimination claim. The initial offense alleged was thirteen months ago. Yet the woman described a subsequent hostile environment that continued throughout the year, and the last straw for her was an incident that happened more recently.

The agency wanted to reject the discrimination claim. Subsequently, I defended the nexus between the original offense and the hostile working environment claims, which did fall within the 180 day window. I knew a criminal offense had no such time limits on reporting, and my personal alarms were pinging—did they just want to reject her entire claim?

I was overwhelmed by the seriousness of this case put in my hands. It involved generals, senior officers, sexual assault. Questions whirled in my head: How could I work unemotionally knowing a senior officer was under investigation for sexual assault? How was I going to interact professionally with the witnesses she described as "schoolyard bullies"?

Based on my own sense of urgency and lack of experience, I typed a recommendation, in my capacity as SEEM, and I addressed it to the Director Joint Staff (DJS). I did not have enough confidence to send it directly to the TAG, although regulations specifically directed that SEEMs have direct access to the head of the agency.

In my letter, I recommended the officer's removal from the current full time position he was in, so myself and the alleged victim would not have to engage with him during the investigation. I mistakenly used the word "remove" versus "temporarily reassign," and hastily emailed the memo bypassing my own boss in the HRO.

In the Guard, the DJS is similar to a Chief of Staff. The general officer manages the full time employees of the Air and Army Guard. Despite each of the component services maintaining a military position labeled Chief of Staff, the person in that slot only works on drill weekends. So, the DJS is the focal point for all issues related to both the Air and Army Guard members, and often to those of both military and civilian status.

My junior grade, and possibly my lack of field duty assignments, provided me an unsophisticated perspective regarding the power of a DJS. Perhaps I was naïve thinking I could bypass my boss and address my recommendation letter directly to the DJS about the alleged offender.

I did not seek approval from my immediate supervisor before sending a memorandum directly to the DJS, although in hindsight, I should have sent the memorandum directly to the TAG. The DJS was identified as a witness in the complainant's statement. This was one of those poor decisions I made.

The DJS called me in. He was very tall and had a commanding voice. He did not intimidate me, though. I knew him well and had the fearlessness of ignorance regarding any impact he could have on my career. He had attended many of my cultural events, and he supported our EO and Diversity efforts. I'd submitted many reports through him, and we had conversed on policies.

When I arrived for the meeting, he told me my recommendation to remove the officer from their position was out of line. I asked how I could appear to be neutral, as the advocate of the process, and still have to converse with this officer and many of the witnesses mentioned in the complaint, while I managed the EO and Diversity program?

The DJS said, "You will report to me. I will let the officer know."

It was an emotional time, and I glared at the sticker on my monitor often. "I AM AN ADVOCATE OF A PROCESS." I felt very alone and emotionally distraught realizing warriors could create such damage internally.

We were handling this incident absent any formal Sexual Assault Prevention and Response Program (SAPRO) to guide our actions. The victim did not want to contact law enforcement. The JAG recommended a formal investigation called a 15-6. The investigation would provide the commander with facts and sworn statements to ensure, if the allegations were substantiated, that the commander could take military action. The EO process was only an administrative procedure to "make whole" the complainant. The term haunted me—it meant that, if substantiated, an attempt would be made to create the status and career circumstances the aggrieved would have reached, if the discrimination had not taken place.

Life at Camp

It didn't deal with what consequences the perpetrator would face.

Other complications existed with the case, because the aggrieved, the alleged offender, and witnesses all worked for our agency under different employment statuses, working full and part time, as federal technicians or in Active Guard Reserve (AGR). Reported events happened during the week as well as on weekend drill.

The JAG called me in to meet the agency's appointed investigating officer who held the rank of a colonel. I knew this high-ranking officer, too. The person did not want the job, claiming his son could suffer reprisals, since the kid served in a unit with one of the alleged offenders. In the Guard, there are many members related or connected through multiple generations, and it is hard to avoid a possible conflict of interest. The JAG dismissed the investigating officer's concern. I remember feeling wary of the decision to choose this person for the 15-6 Investigative Officer. I asked myself how this colonel was qualified to investigate a complicated case involving alleged sexual assault? He had 30 days to submit a report.

Although the DoD SAPRO has coalesced into an inclusive organization of resources, all of these well intentioned strategies have not diminished the continued cultural problem that propagates sexism. Victims of sexual assault in all military branches report these crimes to a well established response team. The SAPR.mil website has an impressive amount of research and strategies, yet very little to do with the androcentric, sexist culture fueling offenses and sabotaging responses. Sexual assault claims in the military continue to rise.[11]

---

[11] https://www.defense.gov/News/Releases/Release/Article/3376241/department-of-defense-releases-fiscal-year-2022-annual-report-on-sexual-assault/

CHAPTER 11

PROCESSING POWERLESSLY

★ ★ ★

During the processing of the recent sexual harassment case, one of the Generals identified as another witness called me to his office. I frantically called the JAG, and excitedly ranted about how inappropriate it was for me to go talk to him, yet he was a General ordering me to his office.

The advice given by the JAG saved my career. The JAG Officer was sharp and loud as the words interrupted my emotional tirade; "Calm down Chief, calm down right now. I want you to take a deep breath. You will go to the General's office and you need to take your emotions out of this case. Your recommendation is sound, but you must remember who is in command. You are the subject matter expert they seek for guidance. Listen to his concerns, lean forward and listen well; then you need to talk calmly, without your hands waving and your voice getting loud. You need to talk low and slow, so low and slow he has to lean in to hear you. You got it?"

I was sweating and nervous as I reported to the General. I never dealt with him before, and I did not know him at all. He was an older man, bald and rugged looking. He had the respect of many since he had been a former brigade commander.

The General had me sit in the chair in front of his desk. He was loud and emotional and I think waved a hand or two. I remained stoic. He said, "I saw your memorandum; we will not remove an officer for an allegation. This is a conflict between two officers. You need to resolve the conflict. Why do you think the officer would be so stupid to do this in a business setting? You believe her, don't you, because she is a woman? How can anyone know what went on in that room but the two officers there? You need to get these two together and settle this now."

I could barely breathe saying very low and slow; "Respectfully, Sir, that is not the way the EO process works." Before I finished speaking, he yelled; "You're not doing your job. If you can't do the job, I will do it. I will settle this situation."

Again, very low and slow, I said; "Sir, respectfully, you cannot process the resolution because you are a witness in the case."

He reacted; "What do you mean by that?"

I informed him he was identified by the aggrieved as a person with information pertaining to her allegations. His face got beet red, and he yelled some more about how he was going to do the job I was not doing and he ordered me out.

I left the room very flustered and shaking. I made it to my office, shut the door, and cried. This was hard stuff. I called a female mentor who was a lieutenant colonel; she held the same job in another state. Her support was calm and smart. She had dealt with generals and colonels for many years. She had the street smarts and confidence to maneuver within these battlegrounds. I felt weak. She recommended I contact the TAG directly, after all, the regulation dictated the HREO have direct access to the TAG. He was out of the country but she told me; "Email him now."

I wish I had saved the email because it was the most professional and succinct email I ever sent. I swear my God typed it for me as I was in an anxiety blackout. The subject was entitled, "Urgent," and I detailed how a General planned to call the alleged offender and the aggrieved to mediate a resolution. I explained how several of his top officers were witnesses in the case since they had been contacted just after the original incident occurred. I explained about how re-victimizing the aggrieved would be retaliatory and ill-advised for the agency. Within a minute, the TAG out of the country responded; "Got it."

I hadn't caught my breath before the woman who filed the case called me extremely upset about how the General called her and wanted her and the alleged offender to meet. She flatly declined and asked me what the hell was going on. I apologized and told her the TAG had been informed about the request and she will not have to meet with the alleged offender. I hung up and went for a long run.

The voices in my head did not subside for many miles.

"What is going to happen to the officer who allegedly sexually assaulted the woman?" Yes, I did believe her allegations. "What is the 15-6 investigation going to reveal? What does a resolution look like in this case? How can the incident be proven when they were behind closed doors with no witnesses?" Not telling my coworkers what was going on was stressing me out. All of my programs and administrative processes were doubly painful and slow, as I had to wait for the DJS to review them before I did anything. I did not attend normal staff meetings, and I avoided the witnesses she named. Dodging any engagement with them wasn't hard since an internal resentment grew inside of me before I ever saw the lengthy, internal detailed report of investigation.

This was my fifth year as the VTNG SEEM. I accomplished a lot to build a structurally sound EO program. I had earned a solid reputation as a SME. Unit commanders called me when they wanted advice on handling situations. For the first time in the history of the Vermont EO Program, each one of the brigades had a trained EOA who worked for the brigade commander. Now, the senior power intimidated me. My powerlessness hurt and I had concerns about an angry General stripping me of everything I had worked for.

Many areas of my life were strengthening. I was still active in my recovery from alcoholism with ten years of sobriety. Along with my military duties as the HREO, I also attended my warrant officer professional development training and was a warrant officer level 3. I was a federal technician serving as the SEEM and State Diversity Coordinator, and as the Region 1 representative to the NGB Joint Diversity Executive Council (JDEC). I made many trips to regional council meetings and the NGB expanding my network.

I was not calling myself a feminist nor did I even know about the suffragette plight, but, the culmination of my recovery as a codependent alcoholic, the sexual harassment cases I processed, and the layers of learning about social justice, civil rights, and disparate treatment was changing my heart. This female officer's allegations against a senior male officer were very serious and sensitive. Only through hindsight can I reflect on my then-naiveté and my own bias. I thought an investigation would validate her claim and an appropriate action would be taken; that is as far as I got with my thoughts in the beginning.

The JAG and I agreed to process the informal discrimination EO case alleging sexual harassment. The 15-6 investigation was looking into the allegation she made that the accused put his hands on her breast, a clear sexual assault violation. The report of investigation would need sworn testimony if the claim was true and the commander wanted to use any military action against the alleged offender.

They assigned a female lieutenant colonel as the EO Inquiry Officer. She would use many of the 15-6 investigative documents and testimonies to complete her discrimination inquiry and make recommendations to "make whole" the aggrieved. The regulations touted; accountability for substantiated misconduct is solely at the discretion of the commander to restore good order and discipline and prevent future misconduct.

The 15-6 investigating officer revealed to me a pattern of inappropriate behavior was emerging about the officer. Within the 30 days of the initial investigation, the investigating officer requested an extension because he wanted to interview witnesses from a midwestern National Guard State where Vermont often had joint training events. The investigator received approval to travel to the midwestern unit. This alarmed me and my bias of an outcome grew. I was still baffled at what, "whole" looked like for the aggrieved and especially wondered what accountability looked like for the offender.

The EO inquiry officer and the 15-6 investigating officer completed their reports within 60 days, and they both substantiated the claims. The 15-6 investigating officer recommended action against the offender. The EO inquiry officer recommended the acceptance of the resolution offer contained on the discrimination form. To be made-whole, the aggrieved requested a statement be read to the current senior leaders of the guard as a means to expose the officer's bad behavior. She requested the top leaders receive additional prevention of sexual harassment training as if this could open their eyes to the kind of leaders camouflaging themselves among warriors with integrity. The aggrieved officer thought by telling several top leaders after the incident happened, they would protect her and have her back, but she felt abandoned by the club leaders. All of the good old boys' club networking came out in a hometown paper years later when the DJS put in a bid to be the next TAG.[12] As I read the article, I shook my head knowing how little the public knows of the operating system. The Guard may accomplish great things, but the cost of managing sexism was all so devastating to me.

The TAG returned from his overseas trip and he called me and the JAG to his office. On his desk, were the 15-6 investigative binder and the EO inquiry binder. The General looked tired and distressed. He acknowledged he read every page of both reports and he received my concerns over the top generals as witnesses. Speaking with sincerity and making eye contact with each of us, he said, "I read every word, and I am disgusted, embarrassed, disappointed, and angry. I want to fire all three of these guys."

He looked at the JAG, and said, "I expect you will tell me what I can do." Somehow the discussion came up about the generals being aware of the offense, which was a *crime*. Although in my discussions, no one was saying the word crime. Initially I was naïve over the seriousness of the offense,

---

[12] https://www.sevendaysvt.com/vermont/how-anonymous-claims-ended-a-generals-bid-to-lead-the-vermont-guard/Content?oid=2242750

however I kept referring to the Army Regulation 600-20, citing; "when commanders become apprised of complaints or accusations against military personnel, commanders will be expected to inquire into the matter and attempt a resolution. All complaints will be acknowledged and/or documented in writing."

The TAG's face reddened and his voice heightened with a bit of anger, claiming we didn't have an official sexual assault program in place then. I did not respond, even though the regulation was in place with clear directives to investigate complaints and accusations. I noticed the Generals putting the responsibility on the aggrieved victim, referring to how they had asked her then if she wanted to file a complaint and she said no. Insinuating since she didn't want to file a complaint, they were void of the responsibility to look into the allegation, claiming they were accommodating her wishes. This reasoning disheartened me; I put it into my backpack of other emotions. We were excused from the Adjutant General's office.

Soon after, the TAG was set to meet with the aggrieved and she asked me to attend. The TAG, JAG, the female officer, and I sat in the General's office. We all seemed nervous and were extra polite as we took our seats and nervously found a place for our hands. This Adjutant General is a kind man, and I still tear up when I remember how he respected her this day. He said, "First, I want you to know how sorry I am that you had to experience this situation. I respect you as one of my premier officers, and it pains me to think of what you have gone through. I knew your father as also an outstanding officer who served our Guard. I read every detail of the reports and I have spoken at length with my team. I want to honor your request to have extra training focused on sexual harassment for our senior leaders and I will work with Chief to get some quality training." He nodded at me. "I will also schedule the Army Equal Opportunity Officer to take part in the next Army Senior Leader Council (ASLC) meeting and we will notify them of this substantiated report." The woman looked peaceful as she nodded and thanked the General. He continued, "You have put in your resignation papers. I don't want you to leave. What can we do?"

She said, "I put in my papers to resign from the full time AGR status for other reasons." He made an offer for her to remain in the Guard, but she seemed settled on her exit.

I left her a voicemail after the meeting. I can't remember what I said, but I kept the response she sent in an email: "I just wanted to drop you a line and say thank you for all of your time, effort, thoughts and emotion throughout this process. I received your voicemail from today and your words were so meaningful to me and came at the perfect time.

I think today was a little anticlimactic for me, but I have faith that when we (you, the legal officer, and all involved) look back on this day and the closing of this chapter we will all feel that justice has been served. I hope the final resolution brings peace to your job and that you feel more confident and supported and validated in all the hard work you do for the EO process and the VTARNG."

Despite my recommendation as the SEEM to reassign the offending officer, he remained in his high level position. Over the next few weeks, the senior leaders kept me in the dark about how the agency planned to admonish the officer for his substantiated offense. I was well aware it was a substantiated sexual assault, and the lack of urgency frustrated me. I hated the sign on my computer, "I AM AN ADVOCATE OF THE PROCESS."

Myself, the aggrieved, the offender, and witnesses still continued on with the business interactions of a small hometown Guard with work to be done.

The aggrieved had crafted the sentence she wanted read at the ASLC as part of her EO resolution. The ASLC was approaching. We determined the part time chief was best suited to attend the council meeting and read the EO statement which disclosed that the named individual sexually harassed a female officer. My defective expectation management made me think the group of men in the room would be horrified one of their leaders sexually harassed a female officer, not officially aware of the assault investigation.

I remember the warm spring evening; I was at an A.A. meeting which began at 7:00 p.m. and the ASLC meeting at Camp was on my mind. I got a call from the Chief ten minutes past seven and I stepped outside. Chief told me the DJS opened the meeting and introduced him saying, "The Chief has to read this statement as part of an EO resolution agreement. Go ahead, Chief." Chief read the prepared statement. He said it was silent for a quick second before the brigade commander said, "We are preparing for war; we can't afford senior leaders to have extra training on sexual harassment without interrupting the current training plan. How is this going to work?" The DJS said, "Chief is in the brigade now and he will work it out without interfering with warrior readiness training." There were no other comments. The Chief was excused. As he was telling me this, I cried. We talked about their aloof response and conceded they surely got the details from the DJS after the Chief left. I was disappointed, not livid, relinquishing my powerlessness.

As the Vermont Guard was preparing for a major deployment to Afghanistan, many guard members from the JFHQ and other brigades were reassigned to the 86th IBCT as part of the deployment readiness. One day the woman who filed the case came to my office very agitated and told me she just found out they reassigned the officer in her case to the IBCT and he would deploy to Afghanistan. She said, "that's just great, let's make him a war hero. They are rewarding him for the offense." The officer was not on the original list to be transferred to the brigade. I let her know I did not have any information regarding the disposition of the report. I was frustrated over how the command was handling the case, but I was powerless. This was the kind of venting SEEMs engaged in, because we could not discuss with coworkers.

Seasoned EO managers and staff members at the NGB validated my discontent, but it always came back to our powerlessness. We were advocates of the process with no say in the adjudication. I felt hypocritical during my trainings where I encouraged warriors to report all offenses and allow the process to hold violators accountable. It became very clear to me the process was a group of biased leaders protecting their guys, their statuses, their egos. I formed an opinion fogging my neutrality; I concluded those leaders thought, if he was stupid enough to do this thing, it made them look bad since they had been applauding him during his entire career. They couldn't come out and admonish him because he was one of them. This opinion sank deep with my resentment toward the offender, the senior officers who did not investigate, and the buddies who hounded the aggrieved female officer for a year like schoolyard bullies.

The aggrieved officer requested another meeting with the TAG and asked me to be at the meeting. The JAG attended, and it was the same group who a month earlier had what we thought was closure. This time, the TAG looked as agitated as the woman. The lawyer and myself sat silent. She explained her frustration over the time passing that the offender was still the officer in charge of personnel policy affecting her program.

She described the agony of sitting in staff meetings with the three men who tormented her with harassment over the past year and how they continued the pompous passive aggressive comments. She acknowledged her time in service (resignation date) was fast approaching, however did not feel satisfied the response to the substantiated allegation was to send him off to war along with other culpable offenders. She said, "I feel stripped of any resolution you thought you were providing me."

The General was agitated and slapped his hand on the table saying, "What do you expect me to do? Our legal team is preparing actions of accountability. I don't know what you want from me, I have done all I can do." This time around, I felt disheartened by his demeanor toward her. Something shifted; he no longer saw the officer who assaulted her as any less of an officer who needed to be fired for what the report revealed. The TAG only seemed bothered that he was being asked to hold these men accountable. He even stated his anxiety of preparing the Guard for war, all the trips he had been on, and he said, "I am exhausted." The woman stood, we all stood, and she walked out of the TAG's office.

I found her in my office and she vented her frustration on the process. I most likely validated her assessment. In her previous email, she hoped I would feel more confident and supported.

She left, and the disappointment remained with me.

CHAPTER 12
WHAT ABOUT A WOMEN'S PROGRAM?
★ ★ ★

I WAS AWARE OF THE WHISPERS REGARDING THE RECENT case, all framed differently depending on who was whispering. The offender, associated senior officials, and witnesses were all going to war. Major shifts in power happened, and an expected realignment of personnel.

The Brigade Combat Team's (86 IBCT) upcoming deployment to Afghanistan touched every aspect of the National Guard, and everyone contributed to ensure a successful send off. My husband, friends, and colleagues were among those deploying. They would spend a month at Camp Atterbury, Indiana, conducting readiness training prior to their deployment overseas. Tensions escalated within the force, and the public was anxious about sending beloved Vermonters to war.

I almost went to war with them.

The 86 IBCT had a personnel readiness shortfall. Some brigade soldiers had personal, medical, or legal issues that disqualified them as deployable, so they transferred some JFHQ and other Vermont soldiers to fill in. I transferred into

LIFE AT CAMP

the 86 IBCT in September 2009, for a short time before being released back to JFHQ at Camp. This tour in the brigade was the first time I'd been in another unit since 1990.

My husband was a 1SG in the 86 IBCT. He managed a support company, and he'd been developing his soldiers for more than a year with pre-combat training exercises. The size of the Vermont brigade was about 1,500 soldiers. There were 14 married couples the brigade commander would interview to determine who would go and who would stay, based on what was best for the Army.

Reporting to our new unit, my EO chief and I, along with other JFHQ soldiers, had cultural shock when we reported to the armory and took part in training events. The first thing we caught was the use of the word *fuck*. Other jokes and words alarmed us, too.

We joked amongst ourselves, "You can tell who's an outsider every time a brigade soldier swears, and we jerk our head to see what's going on."

The command climate at JFHQ was a professional setting. It's not like we never used cuss words, but if we swore at the office, it was a big deal. Here in the brigade, vulgarity was the accepted language. We adjusted to fit in and prove our comradery, while also speaking up as EO activists, putting us in the spotlight as outsiders.

I had always been a terrible marksman. I had no desire to shoot a weapon other than the once a year qualification required by the National Guard. Since I became a warrant officer in 2001, my qualification weapon was a 9 mm pistol. We had 40 rounds to hit at least 23 targets to qualify. I failed every year in the first rotation, and I would reshoot two or three times to achieve a minimal qualifying score. As an officer, the points I received in weapons qualification didn't affect my performance rating, although shooting *expert* always positively flashes that report—expert—to any performance evaluator. You could be a minimalist regarding your occupation, but when an evaluator sees an expert marksmanship badge on your record, everything shines brighter.

Weapons qualification for all brigade soldiers would be with the M4 carbine rifle, a variant of the M16A2 assault rifle. My second drill in the brigade was a chilly Vermont October weekend and weapons qualification day. I was aggravated and annoyed, not looking forward to failing among my new colleagues. I paid attention as the operations range sergeant gave us a class on the M4. The next day, we jumped on buses with our All-Purpose Lightweight Individual Carrying Equipment (ALICE) gear. I felt sort of badass and confident just wearing that. Nothing else about me changed, yet I felt more powerful.

You could tell who had worn the gear before. They knew how to adjust the various items for maximum comfort and efficiency. The new soldiers had straps hanging, and belts were too low or too high. The experienced soldiers had their backpacks filled with the right stuff to improve their training.

Life at Camp

Things like rain gear, extra rags, pipe cleaners, gun oil, and they had inserts for their eye protection, or special earplugs instead of the cheap foam plugs handed out on the line.

I had my lunch and cell phone in my bag.

I spent extra time on the zero qualification range in an attempt to improve my sight picture, stance, and trigger control. I meagerly zeroed my weapon, not really hitting the bullets in a tight group but good enough to be sent to the qualifying range. You had to hop on a bus to be driven to the range farther up Jericho Mountain.

The site was a stretch of bunkers at least a quarter mile long. I reported to the Range Control Officer, who gave me a scorecard and assigned me a shooting pit. I walked to my lane, met the Safety Sergeant, and waited to hear, "Commence Fire."

I failed by many rounds. The safety sergeant gave me some advice about trigger control, breathing, and sight picture. I shrugged and walked back to range control tower and got in line to shoot again. Sometimes, I'd have to wait several rotations before being given another scorecard, and I'd make the slow march to the next humiliation station.

Each time I went to shoot again, it seemed like the Safety Sergeants—who were also sharpshooters—would be even more competitive, seeing if they could be the one to coach me to success. After I spent the 40 rounds, the tower would announce the lane number over the loudspeaker, and we'd hear a "Pass" or "No Go." It was demoralizing each time they announced my lane number with a big loud "No Go."

I did not qualify with the M4. I think it was six times through, when, at the end of a long bitter day, I stepped on to the return bus. One of my comrades said, "I got to hand it to you, Chief. You have some tenacity to keep trying. You don't have to qualify. You're an officer. It won't affect anything." I shrugged, embarrassed and ashamed.

Monday morning, I was in my SEEM office and got a call from the brigade commander. He spoke very casually, informing me the brigade would take my husband, on the deployment, and I was released back to JFHQ.

I half joking asked, "Does this have anything to do with my rifle non skills?"

He laughed and said, "Oh, not at all!"

The send-off for the 86 IBCT took place out of the Gutterson Fieldhouse at the University of Vermont in early January 2010. Phil left at 0400 in the morning, and I woke the kids up to give him sleepy goodbye kisses. I had a friend drive me over later to attend the ceremony, unsure if I would find him among the thousands of people for one more hug, but I did. He looked a bit sad among the sea of soldiers as I blew him a last kiss.

I was better prepared as a mother, soldier, and sober alcoholic during this deployment than I had been when he deployed to Kuwait in 2005. We also had more contact

Life at Camp

through cell phone and email to Kabul during this deployment. Phil expressed no concerns for safety, although his team was a transportation company going outside the Green Zone on daily missions.

Our children were 12 and 14, and I needed every 12 step tool available to manage life at home without Phil. Our son, Troy, joined the football team, and our daughter, Joanna, was detaching from me to be her own independent woman. Joanna found my counsel repulsive.

The short tour away from JFHQ gave me a new perspective and respect for the culture that brigade soldiers endured. I would have been proud to deploy with them and serve the commander as his EOA. But I know the best decision was taking my husband, who brought 109 service support soldiers to Afghanistan and back safely. Nine years later, at his retirement, my husband said that mission—Task Force Long Trail in Kabul, Afghanistan, 2010—was the highlight of his career. Some of his troops were there at the ceremony confirming that he was among the best 1SGs they had served with.

Personnel changes included a new boss for me at Camp. He was a senior leader who had been at the ASLC meeting when the EO statement was read regarding the sexual harassment case. He knew the full facts surrounding the case, and sympathized with the emotional strain I endured processing it, and being alone with it all. It felt good to have an honest conversation with a high-ranking member of the Guard who seemed to understand my alarm.

Vermont had now established a Sexual Assault Response Coordinator (SARC) federal position within the HRO. Although the DoD SAPRO was initiated in 2004, the National Guard was just now—in 2009—establishing an official program and staffing a program manager.

The SARC position was filled by a title 32 federal technician (working Monday through Friday), managing reported sexual assault cases, and developing prevention strategies for the military and federal workforces.

Back at Camp, with a large part of our Guard deployed, things seemed quiet. We had a new HRO, and a new Director Joint Staff (DJS). The new SARC arrived. I loved her immediately. She was a young mother, married to a fellow soldier, and they had just transitioned to the Guard after serving in the active duty Army.

She was the ultimate professional, a competent emergency room nurse who had served in Baghdad. She took this federal technician job as an opportunity to continue to serve full time for the military, yet remain in her home state and raise her children. Her office was right next to mine.

I watched in amazement as she confidently created important networks. She coordinated resources to stand up her office and help her tackle the important work of responding to victims of sexual assault. It was a relief to have her there.

Life at Camp

We became close allies and talked over the business of preventing sex-based offenses. She looked over EO case files along with the unit climate assessments we had on file. These assessments reflected only a small portion of the Air and Army Guard because response rates and consistent management were lacking.

Our new SARC was alarmed at what she reviewed. The EO case files made her gasp. She pointed out red flags, inappropriate behavior, and trends that I naïvely accepted as the way the Guard operates. Her experience in a war zone, her active duty tours, and her nursing profession were the opposite of the managed chaos she was coming to understand as Guard culture.

The SARC highlighted how the culture contributed to an increased risk for offenses. She explained how those with tendencies to commit violations (predators) look for cultures where they can camouflage themselves among good people and not stand out so much. Fitting in, falling in line, assimilation is a military pastime. This sort of management may have benefits for handling the masses, but simultaneously it provided cover to those with less integrity. If you can't take a dirty joke, you best not join the service.

She pointed out the probing techniques that twisted service members use to identify and isolate a victim, then attack. She highlighted several places within the report of the previous investigation where this occurred. These factors weren't taken into consideration as part of the disposition of that case. I was in shock and acutely aware of how little I knew and how much we as an agency missed.

Her assessment of some of the pilot call signs for the F-16 Fighter pilots at the Air Guard took me by surprise. She was astonished no one ever requested they be changed. In the historic testosterone laden world of military aviation, call signs for pilots are a tradition. As barriers fall, what was once an edgy call sign was now being seen as offensive. I never even considered this to be a contributing factor to the command climate. Call signs like Maverick, Goose, or Apollo all gleam with pride. However, signs like ALF (Annoying Little Fuck) or CAT (aka pussy) have more of a teasing purpose.

The new SARC was respected, and she had the confidence and status to talk directly to the TAG or other senior staff officers. They listened to her, and I was impressed when she told me a few pilot call signs were being retired based on her recommendation. I followed her lead like a dutiful soldier. She recommended we reenergize the VTNG Federal Women's Program to analyze the culture for women in the Guard and create recommendations to deter acts of sexual harassment and gender bias from occurring.

I was eating well and running longer, getting in the best shape of my life. I was handling being a single mom, and my husband in Afghanistan. Although I missed him a great deal, professionally I was in my prime. I felt like I was on a mountaintop, empowered to change the world. It had taken me five years of training, networking, managing, and processing cases. I heard over and over again the challenges for women operating in the masculine arena. I was all in for facilitating change.

We began monthly meetings with two other women who had volunteered to be Federal Women's Program managers (FWP). These collateral duty assignments were extra duty, and most of the time the managers for Special Emphasis (SEP) groups used their time to coordinate a monthly observance corresponding with their program. For example, the Black, Hispanic, Disabilities, Asian program managers would arrange an art exhibit, movie showing, educational brief, or a dance. They invited members of the force to take part in it, and then chalk it up as a cross cultural event.

Camp Johnson was the headquarters for the Vermont Air and Army National Guard, and the Air Base was a mile away. The Army Aviation Support Facility (AASF) was in between the two bases. The Ethan Allen Firing Range was about 15 miles away, with several units headquartered there, like the Mountain Warfare School. Between these four main training locations, over 500 full time Guard members worked, yet our events at base would bring in merely five, ten, or 15 of the same employees to experience diversity events.

When I began my job as SEEM, I was motivated to work on the Federal Women's Program within the VTNG.

I remembered the colonel of the J1 section who sent me the stern email after I visited the RRB, when he directed me to focus on the female market. I coordinated a women's picture exhibit at the 2006 Air Show and at subsequent fairs. I produced a picture slide show honoring Vermont woman in combat, and facilitated several Women's History Months, with gallery timelines, special guest speakers, and workshops related to the role of women in the military. My diversity council and I received many accolades over the years for our operation, but we were not reaching the bulk of the force or recognizing any cultural impact for our work.

I was active with the local FWP a subset of the national Federally Employed Women's (FEW) Program, but I could see they were focused on the federal working climate more than the field duty that women of the Guard were being challenged in. Women were approximately 40% of the federal technician workforce (outside the Guard), and many of the issues the women programs focused on involved navigating in a professional administrative setting.

I formed the VTNG Women's Program, focused on improving the unit level experience for women in the Guard. Our mission statement: "Enhance readiness by increasing the representation of competent women in all grades and occupations. Develop an exchange of ideas and information to promote cross cultural harmony and team synergy."

We asked to hold an all-female workshop to synchronize

the issues and forge recommendations to effect real cultural changes in the Guard. Our team recruited a large group of volunteers to help coordinate the workshop focused on issues for women in the military. During the year the 86 IBCT was in Afghanistan, we conducted assessments from women at home station and among Vermont women who deployed. The TAG endorsed our workshop solicitation letter with authentic curiosity and a commitment to remedy conditions that perpetuated sexist attitudes and inappropriate behaviors.

Our team began developing the format, theme, location, and logistics, as well as workshop content based on assessment information. We came up with four major themes: mentorship, work life balance, family support, and career progression. We coordinated with SMEs within our organization who could lead these discussions and facilitate effective solution sessions. It was a lot of sister energy, and we were gaining momentum and heart with the support of the TAG and his senior staff.

The 86 IBCT returned in December 2010, and spirits were high. The community had a very Merry Christmas, and my little family was a foursome once more.

My EO team returned pleased with the job they had accomplished. They let me know they'd witnessed much of the same favoritism for those in the *inclusion zone*. Leaders in the 86 IBCT personnel section counseled my EO chief to get out of EO. He wanted to be promoted to a CW5 position in the JFHQ, and competition for that selection would require him working in personnel. I questioned why EO was not recognized as personnel, but I was powerless. EO remained a one person team at JFHQ.

During the deployment, a promotion packet was submitted for the senior officer who had the substantiated sexual harassment case on file. Senior leaders all heard the statement that was made in the ASLC, yet they still recommended him for the promotion. There was some gossipy chatter about how deployed leaders attempted to step over our home base process and get him the promotion. Through my personal connections, I knew that the aggrieved woman—who'd since resigned from the National Guard— was aware of the attempt by some leaders to promote him. It was another blow to the "make whole" notion, even though the promotion was finally denied. The size of our small guard, and its connections, caught the maneuver and stopped it. Since my retirement, though, he could have received a promotion without me ever knowing.

As troops returned to Camp, I avoided those involved in that substantiated case processed before they left. I had put it all in my backpack as a huge resentment. Over the year they were gone, I continued to process sexual harassment cases, resolving them informally, owning my powerlessness, yet managing expectations for myself and the clients who came to me.

About three years after returning from Afghanistan, the offender in the before-mentioned sexual assault case spoke to me. He happened to be the only employee to show up for a special training I coordinated as part of my job. After about ten minutes with no one else showing up, I said, "Sir, I will give you credit for attending." He asked, "Can I talk to you?" I was nervous, but I said, "Sure." He told me Jesus Christ had saved him. Then he followed his saving grace with telling me some people file discrimination cases to retaliate against people, and I should always take that into consideration. It made my stomach turn, because when he began with the Jesus revelation, I had a slight bit of hope he'd gained some humility. I wasn't expecting a confession, but, I thought, maybe he'd offer an apology for letting the organization down. He may have found Jesus, but he didn't sound a wee bit humble to me. After he walked out of the room, I felt my resentment leave me, and compassion replaced it. I felt sad that he could not take accountability for the awful pain he had caused.

During 2011, we continued preparing for the first ever all-female women's workshop. My team of women warriors, and some men warriors, engaged our plan to improve conditions for women and deter sex-based offenses from occurring. Our special logo and theme energized us—"Realizing Our Potential." We worked with recruiters to make special T-shirts and planned to have an empowerment walk/run at the end of the one day workshop.

I contacted the first female TAG of the National Guard, Major General (Retired) Martha T. Rainville, to be a keynote speaker. A woman named Mary who was the CEO from a local power company and a command chief master sergeant (CCMSgt) from the NGB volunteered their time to the lineup.

Based on our surveys, we developed four breakout sessions. Each group was to develop recommendations based on their discussions. A squad of women who had been part of a female engagement team in combat provided a powerful presentation about their experience in Afghanistan. We invited combat experienced warriors for a question and answer session. We felt powerful, hopeful.

It had been a long road to get to this moment. The DJS during this time was the former personnel chief. He was the officer who had emailed me to focus on the female market. He was the colonel who would not give me a full time asset to support EO staffing authorizations. Although the TAG supported the workshop, the DJS told me, "I will direct no one to attend the women's workshop. If you want attendance, it will be voluntary only." These scrimmages were relentless, but did not deter me.

To gain interest and confirm registrations, I asked the Family Support Program to have a space at post deployment yellow ribbon events.[13] I set up my women's exhibit picture

---

[13] https://www.yellowribbon.mil/cms/about-us/

collages and displayed loads of demographic statistics around us. I asked CSM's for five minutes at the podium to show one slide. The slide featured the four major brigades in the Vermont Army Guard with the number of females assigned and the number of females registered. In military fashion, green, amber, and red colors showed the status of each brigade registration. It became a competition for the leaders to have their brigade greener than green.

Women who had deployed and knew me came up, saying they detested my dedication to such an event. They hated "women's events," and many still do. I defended our plan, stating we must come together to gain a true feminine voice for change.

They argued with me. They claimed the workshop was taking women back in time, separating them and giving men a reason to see women as different. These were women who were seriously trying to fit in and assimilate to the culture. That was their ticket for success, and I was tearing it up. I was now labeled a feminist, and I was unaware this was an insult.

Some commanders ordered some of the female troops to attend the event, and they heard sarcastic chattering from their comrades: "You all go ahead and cluck like chickens. Us men will remain at drill and the get the real work done."

Despite such resistance, more than 70% of women in the Vermont Guard attended the September 2011 workshop, and the energy was undeniable.

At our closing ceremony, the line up of senior leaders in the front row was one of the proudest sights of my career. All of the generals and senior enlisted were there, the only men in the room. We had a special guest from the Senegal Armed Services. General Rainville sat with the them in the front row, and I couldn't help but feel a big "YES" in my heart.

All of them were leaning forward with genuine enthusiasm. I received an Army Commendation Medal, and all the women cheered with authentic support.

After the workshop, a dedicated group organized feedback cards into categories and formulated recommendations for change. 21 recommendations contributed to a lengthy After-Action Report submitted to our TAG.

The work we conducted solidified a band of sisters dedicated to the aim of gender equality. We made a short video all cheering, "Women Power!"

A short time after the Military Women's Workshop (MWW), the TAG held an officer's call. Every officer in the Vermont Guard would listen in person or through a teleconference line. The SARC and I were sitting in the same room as the TAG. It was a crowded room of senior officers with very few women.

In his opening remarks, he boasted about the women's workshop and held up the 21 recommendations, announcing, "We will do these things and we will make the culture better for everyone in the Guard."

We had our SARC in place and we had our game plan to deter sex-based offenses. The SARC and I suppressed our excitement as we gave each other an imaginary high five.

I never felt that close to victory again.

Doris J. Sumner

CHAPTER 13
ON A MISSION
★ ★ ★

THE SARC AND I CONSIDERED THE MILITARY Women's Workshop (MWW) and the endorsed 21 recommendations as a success measure helping to counteract sexism. We entitled our team the VTNG Military Women's Program (VTNG MWP). These were the employees holding the collateral duty positions under the VTNG FWP. After the workshop, our team continued to engage and keep the momentum going.

I took the #1 recommendation—provide breastfeeding stations—and began developing the policy and working with the construction facility management office to get it done. This should not have been so hard or taken so long to happen. When you are in the trenches making a difference, you don't have time to consider, "Why was this never done before?"

Knowing the need is not enough. Those in power must understand and embrace the need, or it is too easy to ignore. When the voices of women are few, it does not make this need less urgent. Requests from nursing mothers occurred over the years, but they were sporadic, individual, and incremental in need. It took 350 women in a workshop to make enough noise. Having the list endorsed by the TAG gave me leverage to move a policy, but I also had to work with facility managers. The complexities of finding, designing, and funding nursing rooms took resilience and time. If the MWP did not press the facility office, our priority placement for scheduling the renovations moved down the list. All the work took 18 months from the time of the Workshop. The day they sent the email out announcing just two permanent spaces for the entire VTNG, many women cheered.

Nursing mothers now may not appreciate the intensity of effort that was needed to gain what is available to them today. Perhaps women of my generation did not appreciate enough the resilience and intensity of effort it took to join the ranks at all.

The facility management office incorporated nursing rooms in all new armory construction from then on. In the interim, the policy dictated that commanders build temporary spaces to accommodate nursing mothers. Women had been using restrooms, their cars, or closets. The policy made it clear that the dedicated space had to be near the training area and not in the latrines.

The military's effectiveness depends on service members following orders, policies, and protocols. If leaders do not understand the need or benefit of a rule, they are more likely to refrain from enforcing that guidance. Some may refuse to believe warriors ignore policies or regulations. After all, the business of the military is serious, policies are orders, and orders must be obeyed.

I learned the three general orders all the way back in basic training;

1. I will guard everything within the limits of my post and quit my post only when properly relieved.
2. I will obey my special orders and perform all of my duties in a military manner.
3. I will report violations of my special orders, emergencies, and anything not covered in my instructions, to the commander of the relief.

Despite the orders being drilled into all of us, I operated in a culture where an array of violations occurred daily, and though reports of infractions occurred, that did not nullify reprisal. We may have cheered the two nursing rooms, but leaders embracing the policy enough to create them in existing facilities, and to build more, would be a distant realization. A year after the policy was declared, we were holding several meetings with the State CSM's to highlight continuing cultural barriers for women.

A young mother solidified the ongoing sexism impeding the culture. This is the story she told the room: "I would routinely show up for drill and have to find a place to pump breast milk to feed my young son. Sometimes it would be in the closet, in the car, or in a bathroom where someone else was taking a shit. Sometimes I would bring the breast milk to the refrigerator and get childishly taunted by men saying 'Eeew!' I would respond, 'This is food for my child.' At one drill, I was dramatic—being fed up—and I entered the orderly room and asked aloud, 'Where am I going to pump my breast this weekend?' A mid-level non-commissioned officer (NCO) in the room of several staff members said, 'If I have to accommodate you pumping your breast, then you will have to accommodate a place for me to jack off.'"

There were about two dozen women and a male State CSM in the room listening to this story. My cofacilitator and I witnessed their stunned faces as the group paused. Then someone said, "Did you report it?" The woman who told the story angrily reacted, "No I did not report it. The fucking leaders were in the room. They just told him to shut up and laughed it off. I took my breast pump and went to the latrine." The CSM spoke up and said, "I would have locked him up." Before he could complete his thought, my anger controlled my vocal cords, and I said, "Well, your NCOs did not lock him up, and that is the problem. This shit is happening in every armory around the state."

The room broke into chatter, as women described what they would have done, but the young woman interrupted and continued her story. "I've been in the Army a while, and I can take the crap. But sometimes, I get sick of the childish bullshit. I went home and told my dad I want to get out. I am sick of the Army. My dad is a pragmatic man, and he said to me, 'No you are not, and you are going to deal with it.' I have a full time job and benefits with the Army. I have a son, and I am a single mom, so guess what? I'm going to deal with it. But I shouldn't have to."

The CSM was disturbed, and of course he wanted to know who said what she reported. We all agreed, the only response to the CSM punishing the soldier would mean more retaliation for the young mother. He told us he planned to tell the story at the next CSM council and reinforce the nursing policy. That day was like many others during my career as the SEEM and Diversity Manager. It was a powerful moment, and I planted it in my heart with the myriad other powerful moments.

The MWP and I took our list of 21 recommendations under our arms and scattered about. One officer was an experienced strategic planner, and she brought the Vermont National Guard State Strategic Plan to me, very passionately saying, "Here is where we begin. We need to hold them accountable for growth rate."

I had been in the job for seven years and had never been involved in strategic planning meetings. Intermingled in our 21 recommendations was the need to evaluate the statuses of women in the Guard. We could not ensure inclusivity in hiring practices (#12), if we could not show the disparity as it existed. Our EO reports showed gender representation overall, but now we needed to look more critically at where and how women were serving. Within the strategic planning document, there were few entry lines of measurement regarding race and gender. The document producers had included columns for fiscal years, with objectives to increase representation by ½ to 1% each year. Nothing too bold or outside a normal progression of growth.

Our MWP proposed changes to the Vermont State Strategic Plan. We understood, numbers mean accountability. In addition to the overall percentage of gender, we needed the representation of women in the officer and NCO leadership positions as well. This was the beginning of what would become a separate and distinct Gender Report. It would take two years from the date of the Military Women's Workshop to attain an approved analysis format that reflected gender representation in the Vermont Air and Army Guard.

In each edition, the data pointed to the culture as the barrier to the growth rate for women. The leaders would ask us to include another mode of measurement, rejecting our analysis. The senior leaders continued asserting that the disparity in the growth rate was due to positions not being available for women, or women just didn't want to join the military. They proposed what they considered reasonable conclusions for the underrepresentation. For instance, the Combat Exclusion

Rule enacted in 1994 barred women from combat positions. Since the Army Guard *manpower* document in Vermont was primarily combat, there were fewer opportunities for women to join and move up in rank. Yet, the data showed that in brigades where all positions were available to women, women were still underrepresented in command.

The Air Guard had excuses too—it was a flying unit, with fighter jets to maintain, they asserted. There had always been a lack of women interested in becoming fighter pilots. Most of the positions on the flight line were maintenance, and women just were not interested in those occupations. Despite no official policy barring women from these occupations, little was done to entice women to join the units. Their reasoning that women were not interested always satisfied any Affirmative Action push. An increase in gender diversity was just not possible.

In 2013, the VTARNG's overall representation of women was 13%, and five years later in 2018, it was 14%. The VTANG's overall female representation was 18% in 2013, and 19% in 2018. The repeal of the Combat Exclusion Policy expanded opportunities for women, yet the lack of a creative means to capitalize on this was obvious. The standard operating system remained in place. In my recovery circles, we loved to remember the colloquial definition of insanity, doing the same thing over and over and expecting different results, or the short version: nothing changes, if nothing changes.

When I consider the exhaustive activities pursued to increase the numbers, and the massive failure, it still haunts me.[14]

Members of MWP were determined to pursue our list of 21 recommendations with whatever effort we could. My relationships with my counterparts around the National Guard were strengthening. I sought to align Vermont's efforts with whatever NGB might be doing nationwide. My pursuit of knowledge was exhilarating, but I often realized how little I knew of actual women's history. I read about activities of the Defense Advisory Committee on Women in the Services (DACOWITS).[15] How had I missed knowing about this organization for eight years? Despite always putting in the effort to fill the collateral duty position of the VTNG FWP, the workshops, trainings and networking in the Federally Employed Women's (FEW) Program did not address the same challenges women in uniform faced. The FEW was a powerful national network of women seeking to equalize opportunities, yet they had their challenges with gender bias. I remained connected to the Vermont Chapter of the Federal Women's Program, and I attended annual conferences and facilitated several workshops over the years. They selected me as Woman of the Year for the local chapter of the FWP, and I received the National

---

[14] https://legislature.vermont.gov/Documents/2020/WorkGroups/House%20General/Military%20Affairs/National%20Guard/W-Steven%20Cray-Vemont%20National%20Guard%20-%20Military%20Women%27s%20Program%20Annual%20Gender%20Report%20-%202018-1-22-2019.pdf

[15] https://dacowits.defense.gov/

Guard Award for the Federally Employed Women in 2012.

Connections with local diversity initiatives for Vermont businesses, universities, and colleges were part of my outreach. These enrichment efforts and networks broadened my understanding of the vast gender disparity throughout our society, and I witnessed the longstanding feminist energy that improved professional opportunities and the workplace climate for women. Yet, my observations over the years reflected powerful women moving in the opposite direction on a moving walkway. A lot of energy is expended, and just when you think you are getting ahead, the belt moves faster, and you're thrust backwards. The process never remained consistent long enough to reach true equality.

The years after my mountaintop high felt like this moving walkway. We saw more sexual harassment and sexual assault cases, and there was the constant thought, "Something's got to give."

My good friend, the SARC, resigned her position and returned to nursing. I cried, thinking I would never find another ally like her. It felt like the world had rescued her off the island, but it had abandoned me. I was left to carry on alone. She assured me the new SARC was the right person for the job. I only had a few lonely weeks before I smiled again, realizing how right she had been.

A very young junior officer stepped into the job. Her personality did not fit the traditional military recruit. She admitted she disliked the idea of a patriarchal militia run by old white men. Joining the military for the benefits had been her ticket out of poverty, and it was a means for her to earn a degree in sociology.

She was direct when she told me she was queer. I had never met anyone who identified as queer. I didn't know how to respond because I didn't even know what it meant. She politely told me the word is used to describe individuals who don't identify as straight and/or cisgender. Merriam-Webster defines as, "of, or relating to, or being a person whose gender identity corresponds with the sex the person had or was identified as having at birth".

I remember asking if she was OK with my fight for women's rights? She said of course, and she explained to me that her issue was with society's binary options regarding gender identity and sexual orientation. She shared with me some of the social problems she studied. She described her view of the blatant discrimination happening toward people who didn't assimilate to the majority identity narrative. Over the course of our time together, we became very close allies. I learned more about social justice from this woman in her 20s than I have ever learned anywhere or from anyone else.

As 2012 began, the VTNG members were clear about the Sexual Assault Prevention and Response (SAPRO) Program being a priority. The training was always well attended, campaign posters were up, and the SARC held the monthly command meetings to synchronize prevention, advocacy, and adjudication efforts regarding sexual assaults.

The SARC was extremely busy.

I was not privy to sensitive facts regarding each of the cases, however I participated in the monthly status meetings. Vermont Guard personnel were being sexually assaulted by guard members, and now, some were officially reporting it. Those survivors were receiving improved advocacy and care. There were also survivors who reported assaults from previous years, naming offenders not in the military. Perhaps a service person was experiencing trauma from a sexual assault or abuse that happened as a child, reporting to the SARC gave them an opportunity to be linked up with advocacy groups in the area. This was the commitment the military made for survivors to receive help. Trained Victim Advocates (VA) within the force were assigned to survivors.. Each survivor might seek something different—medical evaluations, adjudication, validation.

As of 2020, the average number of sexual assaults by service members against service members in the Vermont Guard was three assaults per year.[16] National reports claim the odds of a woman experiencing a sexual assault in the DoD was 6.2%, and it was 0.7% for men. In 96% of cases, the alleged offender was a man.

---

[16] https://vt.public.ng.mil/Portals/19/FY21SAPR.pdf

Nearly one in four of all women experienced an "unhealthy climate" because of sexual harassment. About 16% of women faced an "unhealthy climate" because of gender discrimination. Underreporting is estimated at 76%, and 64% are retaliated against for reporting at all.[17]

These numbers were not getting better, and the system was not changing the culture that perpetuates sexism. But I did not see the dismal future; I was in the thick of my persistence, and determined to make a difference.

I got animated any time I spoke about strategies to prevent sexual harassment from even occurring. I recall the JAG, with an air of benevolence, telling me to let go of the idea that we could prevent sexual harassment. It was always going to be a part of the culture. The JAG stated I should focus more on the case processing. I was offended, and naïvely defiant.

I recognized a degree of ignorance regarding the topics of special emphasis, gender equality, and sexual harassment and assault when I engaged with members of the Guard. I had been very ignorant myself before landing the EO and SEEM jobs and was learning how knowledge could impact change. In the Army, there was specific Sexual Harassment/Assault Response and Prevention (SHARP) program training. These trainings often received more attendance and attention than any other prevention trainings. My team chose to intertwine

---

[17] https://sapr.mil/reports

EO and diversity into the SHARP training as a means to highlight how the culture contributed to the prevalence of problems. These three topics were listed as mandatory trainings (among many others) in accordance with the state training plan.

Our team created a facilitation guide to formalize, synchronize, and save time by cross training the topics, helping to increase the number of service members trained in all three required subjects. Diversity training was #11 on our list from the MWW. We predominantly focused on gender diversity, though we often expanded our conversations to other forms of diversity. We justified the focus, claiming gender crosses all forms of diversity and an understanding of the feminine perspective would help leaders disseminate and support policies enticing women to join, stay, and thrive in the military.

The format allowed facilitators to use small group interactive discussions to cover the required training topics. We wanted to create a safe space for warriors to exchange their challenges and ask questions related to counteracting negative behaviors within group settings. Most of us were not professionally trained or prepared to manage these conversations. We felt the brunt of denial, defiance, and insult from service members who did not sign up to *get real*, or to reveal sensitive vulnerabilities. The warriors had a right to give pushback, because our good idea was a work in progress, and emotional safety controls were not always in place. These were sensitive and personal perspectives, almost like asking a group to talk about religion or politics.

We found people often considered sexual assault as only rape. The military definition is "Intentional sexual contact characterized by the use of force, threats, intimidation, or abuse of authority, or when the victim does not or cannot consent." The term includes a broad category of sexual offenses comprising the following specific UCMJ offenses: rape, sexual assault, aggravated sexual contact, abusive sexual contact, forcible sodomy (forced oral or anal sex), or attempts to commit these offenses.

Regardless of where in the definition the assault occurred, facts and research bear out the immense negative impact of experiences. Every incident is personal, painful, subjective, and complicated by each person's perspective.

Sexual assault in the military was nothing new, but new attention was being drawn to the issue, in part because of *The Invisible War*. Men and women told heart wrenching stories of survival, and a common theme was the lack of leadership in preventing occurrences, validating the reality of occurrences, and holding offenders accountable. Some survivors featured in the documentary told how they ended up being punished by the UCMJ and terminated from the service, while their offenders carried on with their careers.

The stories from the documentary made good patriots angry, and new policies arose to help survivors. The lingering thought—why are men disrespecting women in such vile ways?—was at the heart of the emotional turmoil I struggled with. I saw a lack of respect for anything feminine, and everything about the military was slanted masculine. I knew men were victims, too.

According to the Veterans Administration, sexual violence remains pervasive to this day in 2023. In 2018, 20,500 service members were sexually assaulted or raped, including 13,000 women and 7,500 men. Each one of those is a life disrupted in a devastating way because a person loved their country, was a patriot, and wanted to serve. Yet their individual pain was just another wave landing ashore. The sea keeps churning, but the waves and the sea have an effect. Land erodes, crumbles, and disappears just as MST survivors do.

National numbers were a problem I could not grasp completely. The numbers from my own state hit me emotionally. Despite having VAs in place— people who had empathy and a commitment to ensure care— the cultural retaliation against those who report was always present. Reporting an atrocity appeared to be perceived in the ranks, and even among some leaders, as a kink in the flow of action needed to accomplish the military's mission. Whether it was a sexual assault, gender discrimination, or sexual harassment, a report stopped the day. What I witnessed was that reports were bothersome to leaders,

Life at Camp

presenting another personnel problem they had to deal with. They often met the incident details with skepticism. Gender bias permeated much of the process.

Most commanders regarded the individual acts that happened under their command as individual problems, not grasping the totality. Often a commander's response depended on the offender's status within the Guard. There was always disparate treatment, regardless of the severity of the offense. The commander focused on the power they had to discipline or not. Their priority was on getting back to business, not on solving the problem. Yet as an analyst of the totality, I knew it would happen again, to someone else, somewhere else. I wanted to stop the waves. These were hard realities to accept.

There were times a commander would overreact to an allegation, expressing outrage at a lesser offense. I would internally shrug, thinking the reaction sort of overkill, but grateful that they cared. These moments and others fueled my optimism and confidence that our efforts were making a difference. There were many scrimmages I could describe that took all of our tenacity, resilience, and will to peck away at what we thought was changing a culture.

In March 2013, the Senate Armed Services Subcommittee on Personnel held a hearing on sexual assault in the military.[18]

---

[18] www.senate.gov/isvp/?auto_play=false&comm=armed&filename=armed031313&poster=https://www.armed-services.senate.gov/assets/images/video-poster.png&stt=

National news regarding sexism in the military, and Vermont's sensational story regarding senior officers not taking sexual assaults seriously, heightened the intensity during the election of a new TAG for our state.

The case regarding the sexual assault before we had the SAPRO kept demanding our attention. An article, "Farnham Drops Bid to Lead Vermont Guard, Citing Anonymous Complaint" by *Paul Heintz Seven Days*, January 28, 2013 reported on one of the candidates in the running to be the next TAG.[19] He was dropping his bid after an anonymous letter was sent to representatives in the Vermont Legislature, which in Vermont is the body that names the Adjutant General. The letter claimed Vermont Guard leaders did not take the sexual assault seriously from the accuser. The accuser further asserted this behavior toward the case was substantiated by internal investigations. The TAG candidate said the allegations were not true, but he thought the distraction was not helpful in selecting a new leader.

A Guard spokesperson said that, despite the anonymous letter, the agency would not look into the matter further, because the incident had been investigated, adjudicated, and closed. A representative from the Burlington Legislative District, Chittenden 2, Jean O'Sullivan, had been trying to get an accounting from the Vermont Guard regarding the

---
[19] https://www.sevendaysvt.com/OffMessage/archives/2013/01/28/farnham-drops-bid-to-lead-vermont-guard-citing-anonymous-complaint

number of sexual assaults reported annually. She wanted to know how big the problem might be, and what the Guard was doing about it. She drafted legislation requiring the Guard to divulge the number of sexual assault cases each year to the Legislature. In several articles published when the bill was passed, Representative O'Sullivan validated what our MWP had sought through our Gender Report—when you see numbers, the issue becomes real.

A law passed in 2013 mandated an annual Legislative review—Vermont Statutes Annotated, Title 20 § 427 (20 V.S.A. § 427).[20] The Statute, was entitled "Sexual Assault and Harassment Report." It required the TAG and IG make a report to the General Assembly on January 15, 2014, and annually thereafter, regarding complaints of sexual assault and sexual harassment involving members of the Vermont National Guard.

Local press articles quoted the new TAG, Major General (Maj Gen) Steven Cray and Representative O'Sullivan as being pleased with the bill. The Representative was quoted saying she believed the anonymous letter "helped tremendously" to turn the bill into law.[21]

Solution strategies were growing. The SARC, the MWP, and now the accountability bill. These promoted our sense of optimism.

---

[20] https://legislature.vermont.gov/statutes/section/20/023/00427

[21] www.sevendaysvt.com/vermont/how-anonymous-claims-ended-a-generals-bid-to-lead-the-vermont-guard/Content?oid=2242750

Doris J. Sumner

CHAPTER 14
WHAT CULTURE NEEDS TO BE TRANSFORMED?

★ ★ ★

When I joined the Vermont Army National Guard in 1986, the 158th Fighter Wing of the Vermont Air National Guard (VTANG—we pronounced V-Tang) was just receiving the F-16 Fighting Falcon. The fighter aircraft was the best the Air Force offered, and the Green Mountain Boys had earned the honor to fly it. Among other recognitions, the unit received the Air Force Outstanding Unit Award for its response to the September 11 attacks.

Since becoming federally recognized in August 1946, one year before the official birth of the U.S. Air Force, the VTANG has flown more than eight different bomber and fighter aircraft types. In 2019, with over three decades of successful flying operations in the F-16, the unit began transitioning to the F-35A Lightning II. This is another proud milestone for the VTANG in their 70+ year history.[22]

At Camp Johnson, one mile from the VTANG Wing, my first boss in the HRO was an Air Guard sergeant. While

---

[22] https://www.158fw.ang.af.mil/history/#:~:text=The%20Vermont%20Air%20National%20%20Guard,the%20historic%20P-51%20Mustang

listening to their planes fly over Camp Johnson over the years, I worked very closely with the Air Guard members. They always impressed me with their dress blues—even their casual class-b appeared superior to the old Army dress green uniform. Air Guard personnel seemed to have a more professional demeanor and were visibly proud of their overall unit.

In the Army, brigades, battalions, and companies were spread out around the state. Pride seemed to be centered more about one's individual unit than the overall Army Guard. The Army aviation unit, located on the Burlington International Airport runway, had its own esprit de corps, different from the Infantry (86 IBCT), the 124th Regimental Training Institute, or the Mountain Warfare School. Each Army unit had a specific mission, but the VTANG 158th Fighter Wing was primarily in one location and had one mission: get aircraft in the air. Everything centered on the aircraft and the talented pilots who flew them.

It was not until 1971 that the VTANG first began to recruit women. In 2019, women made up approximately 19% of the Air Guard, yet there were no women flying fighter jets for the VTANG. In 1994, 2nd Lieutenant Michelle Rocco was the first pilot for the VTANG she flew C-26 support aircraft. In 2019, the 158th Fighter Wing selected 1st Lieutenant Kelsey Flannery to fly the F-35 for Vermont. In 2022, after completing her training, she was in the air making history.

When the SARC suggested some of the Air Guard pilot call signs were sexist, I was flabbergasted. I never linked some of the routine terms used in and around the Vermont Guard as sexist in any way. As time went on, I started to notice the words service personnel used. Suddenly, they leapt off pages and out of emails at me. Over the years, I developed a habit of intense scrutiny over the operating culture. Each sexual harassment case I worked revealed an entrenched masculine lifestyle the military protected, and words were the foundation it stood on.

Early in my tenure as Equal Opportunity Manager, the Air Guard asked me to mediate an EO resolution at a detachment located on another base between an Air Guard junior enlisted woman and her supervisor, a senior enlisted male. The detachment commander scheduled me to fly down from Burlington in a small jet and I was giddy sharing the flight with a full-bird colonel who was taking a business trip to the location.

I flew back, disappointed with my failure to reach a resolution agreement in the case. What I gained from the trip was sorrow for the woman who had to work under conditions she had to cope with. My privilege of circumstance was to be at a Camp in our JFHQ, working at the highest levels in our State National Guard. Service members in my area rarely used the f--- or b---- words. Our JFHQ staffers treated the warriors who sought our administrative support as clients and not joes (military slang for soldiers) who had no other options for customer service. Unfortunately, women in field units were often isolated. Although there were some great, supportive units who embraced differences, there were also units who were less than inviting.

The woman in the case I was asked to mediate had filed a sexual harassment case despite being months from ending her term in service to leave and start a civilian career. She alleged that she had received a letter of reprimand, unfairly, for not being where she was supposed to be. She claimed the chief master sergeant (CMsgt) in charge did not like her because she did not *fit in* and was always calling her out in staff meetings. The accuser said she had great experiences in other units but was having a hard time in this unit where there were few female colleagues. She tried to keep her head down and just survive the tour. She wanted the reprimand stricken from her record before ending her time in service. She was emotional as she provided me her story. She did not want to transition out feeling so unwanted and underappreciated.

I remember pleading with her very nice commander that withdrawing the reprimand was a reasonable request, given that the woman would be ending her time in the Air Guard in two months. It seemed reasonable to send her off feeling good about her service, since her job performance was commendable with no other disciplinary strikes against her. My informal inquiry recognized the disparate treatment she received. Her coming and going was closely scrutinized, and although no one would admit it was due to her gender, she felt the disparity.

I could find no one who would admit that they would occasionally skip out on duty to get a haircut or run an errand. No one ever said a chief had followed them (or had them followed), to verify their status. She alleged that she was followed, which was intensely unfair to her. Her direct supervisor was a young enlisted man unwilling to back her up and confirm she had received permission to run an errand. The commander politely gave me his confident push back, saying it was a principle of his duties to enforce behavior standards. He concluded she had been deceitful regarding her duty, therefore must get the letter of reprimand.

I returned with the image of her disappointed and hopeless face on my mind. She was adamant there was a bias against her. Was I wrong to believe her? I felt disappointed and hopeless as well. I had a few Air Guard friends with whom to converse about the case and about my failure to convince the commander to withdraw the letter. These conversations validated the reality that women continually received disparate treatment for administrative violations versus the slack men received based on who they knew. It became apparent to me that intertwined relationships were fundamental to a person's failure or success. I realized everybody in the Air Guard knew everybody else, and everyone held opinions about others' credibility. Despite the reality that those I spoke to had high respect for this commander, they made it clear he would never take her side and undermine his male chief supporting the young enlisted male supervisor.

As an EO officer, I could not encourage anyone to file a formal complaint that would spark an investigation and perhaps reveal the disparate treatment, which was very hard to prove. I was the advocate of a process, there to be a neutral processer. I came to understand that, even if more clients demanded investigations, it still did not "make whole" their situation.

My cynicism grew. The process too often went like this: a commander appointed an investigating officer, and before the case was closed, isolation and hostility toward the client increased. The crew of bros would implicitly defend the offender. This all had a chilling effect, dissuading anyone else from making the mistake of reporting.

The Wing had its own military EO program and a strong mindset to keep things on their side of the Winooski River. They kept me out of the loop on their discrimination conflicts, which happened occasionally and were informally resolved. The call for help from the detachment was rare, because it involved a full time employee, and my full time job dictated that I tended to the issue. They rarely called on me again. Through the years, Air Guard friends would tell me an experience with a sexual harassment case and act as if I must have known about it because of my position, but I didn't. I developed relationships with a few Wing EO Officers who, over time, shared the same view about bias being problematic in too many cases. New EO Officers were appalled at my jaded negativity about EO.

I was busy building my Cultural Diversity Enhancement Team (CDET). Like many military acronyms, we used them like words, pronouncing our diversity team as C-Det. At times, I would chuckle about service members who ducked into bathrooms when they saw me coming, knowing I was looking for volunteers. I had an exhausting quirk for sending loads of emails with high hopes that someone out there enjoyed my lengthy explanations about why diversity was important.

In Vermont, minority communities were under 5% of the population, so anything we did on that score was an anomaly, typically regarding food, music, art, or education. Our target audience for all our EO work was comprised of the 900 full timers running the Air Base and Camp Johnson. Emails and flyers made it to the outlying armories in the state, but often the traditional drilling members outside of Chittenden County, where Camp Johnson is located, did not know what a C-DET was.

Even so, I was building national recognition as a leader in the Guard EO and diversity community. I received local and national awards. We published one of the first state diversity plans across the country. I was gaining respect, credibility, and street smarts.

The backdrop to all this diversity flurry was a continuous flow of sexual harassment cases, which were informally resolved through the delicate balance of working with commanders and our clients who had experienced the disrespect. Somehow the team of EO staff could often attain resolutions without the client elevating the process to a formal complaint. The military JAG advised commanders to conduct investigations for more serious cases, and investigations were carried out in conjunction with the informal EO process. If any allegation proved to violate the UCMJ, the commander could choose to discipline or not.

There was a standing directive derived from our certification training and national guidance: resolve at the lowest level possible. This may sound good in theory—who wouldn't want to resolve quickly, with as little pain and time as possible? Early in my career, that was my aim. Yet, resolving at the lowest level—typically meaning *locally*—meant those in charge locally were spearheading the resolution. From my lens, their motive was to end the conflict happening on their watch, not solve the issue.

After the infamous 2011 Military Women's Workshop, I focused more on gender equality as a means to improve the overall climate of the force. I assumed my superiors supported the strategies I presented. My analysis always highlighted the correlation between the representation level of women and the prevalence of sex-based offenses.

One of my teammates from the MWP was assigned weekend drill duties at the Air Staff Headquarters located at Camp Johnson. I visited her office and vented to her on the many challenges I faced processing cases that reeked with gender bias.

I went on about the lack of leader engagement in the mandated EO training. In order to get any face time, we had to integrate EO and diversity into the Sexual Harassment/Assault Response and Prevention Program (SHARP) that warriors attended more out of compliance with regulation then any desire to prevent the problem from occurring. A majority of comments on our training feedback forms demonstrated overwhelming ignorance, denial, and childish pouting about the mandate for training at all. Of course, we had respectful, professional warriors who added value to our training events, yet, never enough to gain core buy in.

Program managers and VAs, who met face to face with the wounded, understood the cost of such indifference. We were hoping for a hero to appear.

Brigadier General (Brig Gen), (his rank at the time) Steven Cray was one of the candidates running to be our new TAG. He had been a strong supporter of the diversity council, CDET, and the Military Women's Program.

While I was visiting with my friend at the Air Staff HQ,

the General popped his head into the office and said, "If I get elected, would you both be willing to be on my task force to eradicate sexual assaults from our force?" We each took a silent gasp and nodded, sure.

I complained about the drudgery of defending diversity initiatives in the unit and the difficulty getting mid-level commanders' participation, but I always had polite support from the very top. This sort of engagement gave me hope and always kept me pushing the topic, despite the many nasty comments written in unit climate assessments or on training feedback forms.

I felt confident General Cray could be the person in power who would finally take the issue of the sexist culture seriously. Our team was giddy with anticipation and happy about the hard work we'd been doing.

Lawmakers grilled the TAG candidates and pressed them on how they planned to mitigate sexual harassment and sexual assault from the force. General Cray's authentic and knowledgeable strategies got him the job in March 2013.

The tempo at Camp changes quickly when the power shifts—policy updates, staff changes, and a new seriousness from people who refrain from slacking so they can make a good impression on the new leaders. A week had not passed when the new Assistant Adjutant General came to my office and began to discuss the task force General Cray wanted to stand up to eradicate sexual assaults.

Brigadier General Michael Heston was a great Assistant Adjutant General, a former State Trooper and brigade commander. I'd never met him before, but he treated me with respectful seriousness, given the subject. General Heston directed me to gather a team for a meeting to draft a mission statement and a task list. My head went buzzing straight back to the force of women who helped to orchestrate the successful 2011 Military Women's Workshop. I called my allies and let them know the general was not joking. We had to stand up a task force.

We met with General Heston in the windowless office conference room. The room felt dark despite the florescent lights hovering above. The General had little direction for us. We enthusiastically discussed the Military Women's Workshop 21 recommendations and tasks of that sort. General Heston didn't see a connection. He firmly reminded us that the crux of our mission was to prevent sexual assaults from happening on their watch. He was adamant that we forge the fix with this task force. The conversations between the General and the MWP activist was intense. Did he not see a connection between increasing respect for women, their contribution to the force, and reducing sexual assaults against them? Did the lights go out, I wondered?

It took many meetings and a varied cast of characters to come up with the name and purpose for our task force. The name we chose was Cultural Transformation Task Force. (TF)

General Heston didn't like it at all, but we defended the name, claiming the purpose demanded a fundamental change. The documented purpose for our special task was "to increase the operational effectiveness of the VTNG by cultivating and committing to an organizational climate of equality and professional respect."

We heard many complaints through our allies about the name of the TF, especially from the Air Guard senior leadership, some even spewing their grievance to us directly. Leaders were downright angry at the name Cultural Transformation Task Force. The chatter around Camp regarded the word *transformation*. We were told some senior leaders seemed appalled because they did not believe there was anything to transform. Transformation threatened egos. They tried to push General Heston, and even the TAG, to change the task force name. General Cray and General Heston defended the name. I wished we could have heard what they said.

Warriors feed off pride. Gloating was appetizing stuff. Criticism seemed like a bland, strict diet. Our cynicism grew. A few of us smirked, "Of course, there's nothing to transform. All is great from your white, high-ranking, privileged command post. What is there to change about the Green Mountain Boys?" Supportive leaders encouraged us to communicate the TF purpose broadly and often, to educate the force on why a change was needed. This was not easy to do when unit training NCOs scoffed at carving out time for diversity training.

We made posters, magnetic door strips, mouse pads, and banners, all with the big letters: DIGNITY and RESPECT. The TF mission statement was published, and marketing posters went up. We published a procedure guide with our specific goals and objectives detailed. We split the TF into three major areas, each one focused on Air and Army Guard strategies:

- Sexual Assault Prevention
- Gender Equality initiatives
- Non-Traditional Roles (NTR)

Some of the TF council members didn't like the term *non-traditional role*. They objected, seeing it as suggesting occupations women were not supposed to be in. The focus was intended to look at occupations where women were extremely underrepresented, and to shed light on why and how to attract more women into those roles—roles like fighter pilot and command sergeant major or command chief master sergeant. (CSM/CCM). The title remained and the need was real.

There was an urgency to stand up the TF, while simultaneously, I was still trying to grow the diversity team. I had recruited many volunteers to fill the EO and Special Emphasis Program Manager (SEPM) extra-duty positions who attended the quarterly diversity meetings. Many of them took on extra duty as CDET Representatives and posted information on the dedicated diversity boards that we mounted at the Wing and at different armories throughout the state. They also helped coordinate the diversity venues. Finding additional volunteers to fill the roles for the TF would be challenging. I gained a few members to add to the long list of volunteers already supporting EO and Diversity.

Major General Cray called for the first Cultural Transformation Task Force meeting, including the highest-ranking senior officers of the VTNG. General Heston and the Assistant Adjutant General Air, including their chiefs of staff were there. Army brigade and battalion commanders, and Air Wing and group commanders attended. The State CSM and the Wing CCM. The entire leadership audience was male.

General Cray was direct, honest, and clear. He said something along the lines of, "We must do everything we can to prevent sexual assaults from happening in our force. The damage is irreparable. I have put this TF together, and General Heston will lead it. I expect your full cooperation with any directives coming from the TF."

Each focus group briefed the meeting on their individual mission and on the initial strategy for the tasks that needed to be accomplished. When a female engineer captain talked about the function of the NTRs subcommittee for Army service women, she made clear the urgency for a cultural transformation. This captain had a stellar reputation as a no no-nonsense, impeccably competent, tough as nails officer. She was the first female to command the historic 131st Engineer Company of the VTNG. I worked with her on a sexual harassment case that happened within her unit. I got to know her even better while she was an active volunteer for the MWW team.

When her small frame stood up and her soft voice spoke, always making eye contact with her audience, people leaned in. She told those at the meeting that she considered herself pretty tough and competitive, but someone she knew was even tougher. Her friend had joined the Army and deployed to combat. Something happened to her on deployment, and she came back broken. The captain said it took several years before her friend opened up to her about what happened.

She'd been raped by a fellow member of her combat unit. As I listened, I got that lump in my throat, and I had to breathe slowly, softly, or I would have broken out in tears. You could have heard a pin drop in the room.

The captain continued to talk about how her friend almost committed suicide the night of the rape, but just shoved the pain deep within the imaginary backpack so many survivors carry. The captain explained how her friend had wanted to reject being a victim. She was tough, smart, and armed in full battle gear when the predator struck. The humming sound of generators had disguised any cries for help she may have let out. The captain ended by saying, "Whatever you can do to prevent that, do it."

My team left the meeting profoundly moved and with a great deal of hope that we were on an actual path for change. How could that tragedy not inspire a genuine commitment for change? The solution strategies were growing. But our hope would rapidly dissipate, and it took continued grit, resilience, and the General's assurance that we were making a difference, to keep us trying.

Doris J. Sumner

CHAPTER 15
Transforming the Task Force

★ ★ ★

The task force met each quarter in between the Cultural Diversity Enhancement Team (CDET) meetings. The Director Joint Staff (DJS) was at the CDET and the TF meetings. It was challenging to measure any degree of effectiveness for the list of events we accomplished in either council. How do you measure the effectiveness of gender diversity training? Was an increase in reporting sexual assault a positive trend? Assignment of women to the combat arms would not necessarily reflect success, and we were a long way off from counting women in the infantry.

During a diversity training, I was discussing the new TF focused on combating sexual assaults in our force. The combat commanders who attended the diversity training, complained the TF committee was made up of only women. They rightfully pointed out there was a lack of diversity involved in solving the problem of sexual assaults in the military. Of course, we agreed, but attaining a gender diverse group of volunteers for the TF had proven to be a challenge. After the diversity training, a few men joined our committee. The men's perspective within the sub-groups became invaluable to us.

In early TF meetings, the senior leaders, such as the brigade or battalion commanders and the Wing or Vice Wing Commander, attended. As the TF quarterly meetings continued, the commanders became too busy, and appointed junior ranking unit representatives to sit in. It felt insulting to watch the minimal effort shown from the commands. The men on the TF witnessed our challenges of maintaining momentum.

At each meeting the unit TF representative would provide, 'check the block' standard answers the TF Commander or the DJS would accept. The appointed representatives knew how to baffle the leaders with bullshit, and I had a hard time not rolling my eyes. Whenever I presented about the gender equality efforts under the Military Women's Program, I felt like I was talking to deaf ears. I saw few active listening signs from the unit representatives. This deepened my insecurities regarding my ability to communicate, what I strongly suspected as the crux of the problem regarding sexual assaults happening in the military.

From time to time, the TF Commander would provide an assertive order to accomplish a specific goal. Unit leaders would attempt to rally, yet the enthusiasm would fade. Ordinary unit readiness training took precedence and the TF became secondary. There were some *cultural transformation* accomplishments and good people trying to be a part of the solution. I believed the general officers wanted deliverables and were counting on the TF members to make it happen. Field commanders and leaders down the line showed little buy in that eradicating sexual assaults through these efforts was the solution.

The SARC and I would need a venting destress session after each TF meeting or major event. We felt powerless to hold the units accountable for the culture change needed. It exasperated us that those with legitimate power could not ignite the real passion and commitment to rigorously tackle the excellent strategies on the docket. There was always an excuse, a roadblock, red tape, or time which inhibited the TF mission. We experienced no decrease in the number of reported incidents of sexual harassment or sexual assault cases. The biased responses to reporting sexism continued. The culture was not transforming.

In 2013, a comprehensive campaign aimed at helping National Guard units combat sexual assault was launched by the NGB. According to official reports, in Fiscal Year 2012, there were 201 incidents of sexual harassments reported within the National Guard. Based on data extrapolated from an anonymous survey of service members by the Defense Management Data Center, experts believe the actual number could be as high as 4,500. "Sexual assault is a global problem," said James Thompson, SAPRO program management analyst.[23] Regardless if the number was 201 or 4,500, it was unacceptable to me. A rolling boil was always within me; why aren't more people ticked off?

Although there was some legitimate, professional training for the sexual assault program, more often than not, service members complained about the redundant overkill on a subject they felt they didn't need to be lectured on.

Instead of one cohesive joint Air-Army program, the Wing had to follow the Air National Guard's separate national program in response to sexual assault, entitled Sexual Assault Prevention and Response Program (SAPR). Because the Vermont Air National Guard members drilled primarily in one location, all on the same weekend, coordinating their required training had fewer challenges than the Army, though credentialing staff for the program had plenty.

Feedback from the SAPR/SHARP training detailed a sense of disdain for the topic and claimed the instruction was a waste of time. Even at the highest level, I witnessed the junior ranking SARC berated by high-ranking commanders regardless of her tone, the data, or the multiple ways she attempted to engage the audience in the seriousness of prevalence regarding sexual trauma for military members.

---

[23] https://www.nationalguard.mil/News/Article/574738/national-guard-bureau-launches-broad-campaign-against-sexual-assault

The EO training was neglected by the force for decades, and now, it was increasingly cast aside to conduct the real important training everyone was ignoring.

Our CDET and the TF accepted the fact that unit members were not prioritizing any diversity or special emphasis awareness gatherings. Vermont Air and Army Guard leaders acknowledged the sexual assault mandatory training was the priority. However, the connections to gender equality and appreciation of cultural differences were not appreciated or understood. Despite strategic efforts by the CDET & the TF, the lack of understanding ties to SAPR/SHARP training and the cultural ignorance were counterproductive.

The NGB gave specific guidance related to preparing Vermont's combat arms units for accepting women into legitimate positions. As part of the TF, the SARC and I asked the combat commanders if we could schedule the special training at the battalions during the next drill. The infantry and cavalry battalion commanders rejected our offer and said, "we got this." We provided them our outline for small group interactive discussions, using the probing questions drawing on the recent surveys conducted about female integration.

After the training, we met with the commanders to ask about how it went. They told us the infantry commander spoke to the cavalry men and the cavalry commander spoke to the infantrymen. Both of them appeared proud of this inventive strategy, thinking the message would come across as more serious. Our frown lines deepened.

The commanders did not use our outline at all. They were outside on the rifle ranges, spread out in resting positions, and each commander spoke to their entire battalion as a group to save time. Each battalion had hundreds of soldiers. They told us with macho pride, "There were a few who weren't getting with the program, but they will." The commanders felt they had adequately provided the required sexual assault prevention training to prepare the cultural acceptance of women into the Vermont combat arms battalions.

Exasperated and frustrated, the SARC and I recognized the unconscious ignorance of the men serving in all male units. Even after officially allowing women to serve in combat arms units, men were not competing with women for dominance or authority: they had it. Still in 2023, losing anything to a woman can still be considered, emasculating. Women who succeeded professionally had their battle scars scrutinized.

Years ago, one Vermont woman served in a position for Vermont's Field Artillery Battalion. This violated the 1993 Combat Exclusion Policy ground. Her assignment in the artillery battalion caused red flag errors in the personnel system due to the sex code. Regardless, she remained on the professional track. The female soldier served as a company commander and then progressed to the rank of lieutenant colonel. She handled sexism through her determined competency and take no punches attitude. She had the respect of superiors, comrades, and subordinates, but not without sacrifice. She worked at Camp Johnson as a full time federal technician in logistics, which also had few females. I knew her when she was a 2nd lieutenant and we remained casual friends along the way.

I regretfully did not recruit her for the 2011 workshop or the TF, but now, as a senior female officer, I was feeling grateful for our longtime friendship. When she was promoted to lieutenant colonel, I took her to lunch and pleaded with her not to forget the storms of scrutiny she endured. She always loved talking about her command time and the success she experienced navigating among the boys. She promised me she understood the work I was doing was necessary and had her backpack full of unnecessary experiences because she was female. The officer had an unpretentious sense of humor. Her words and gestures were strategic. You had to carefully listen to catch her amusement at being in on her own joke.

This female senior leader was unpretentiously intelligent and thus experienced the competitive nature of men not enjoying being outsmarted. As a battalion commander in the 86 IBCT, she regularly was the only woman in the room. During one of the leader meetings, she was contributing to the fundamental calculations of operational readiness. The brigade commander made a comment, sternly speaking, he said, calling her by her first name, "Mary, you don't have to be the smartest person in the room."

That example of sexism never made it past the ears of the senior leaders I told. My boss laughed and said the commander was joking. Yet every female I told recognized instantly, the superiority complex. Consciously or unconsciously, the men loved to chip away at our confidence.

With the 2013 repeal of the Combat Exclusion Rule, women could attend military occupational specialty schools that had been only afforded to men. These trained female soldiers would come back and be competitive members of units where some men had never served with women before. There was evidence to base our concern on the type of environment women would need to assimilate into just to survive, and this alarm didn't even include being sexually assaulted.

When I was at Fort Drum during the VTNG training exercises, the White Cell commander held a safety meeting for the staff. There was a lot of diversity among the staff, and most were of mid-level to senior grade. During one of the first meetings the commander cautioned everyone on the prevention of sexual assault. Maybe it was the news cycle or the conversing of the TF, but he was sincere in his messaging of safety. Part of his brief included, "I don't want any females walking alone, you must have a battle buddy with you if you are walking about after dark." I made eye contact with several women TF council members who were in the room and we avoided showing our disturbance about the messaging. After the meeting we discussed if we should say something to the general. We respected him immensely and did not want to seem overly sensitive to what we knew was him trying to mitigate risk. We asked if we could talk to him after the building got quiet.

When we explained the statement was sexist by requesting only females walk with a battle buddy, insinuating only women were vulnerable, his face dropped. He was very disappointed in himself for making the statement. It was refreshing to provide feedback about sexism without the leader becoming defensive. He asked, "What should I have said?" We said, "Leave out 'female.'"

The next evening at the status meeting, without hesitation, the general provided the safety brief, leaving the word female out. Then he pressed on to the business at hand. Eyes facing front, we just smiled on the inside.

I spent that summer A.T. on the VIP team escorting officials around Fort Drum. One stop our team made was at the infantry outpost. This was a company size element hunkered down with their individual combat shelters scattered in the wood lines. We stopped our Humvee when we recognized a commander along the road. He was a friendly captain who invited us out of the vehicle to chat. We talked to him about the TF and integrating women into infantry occupations. He supported female integration, yet offered chummy banter of the problems he could see happening for some duration.

The infantry captain spoke directly to me when he said, "Chief, most men in the infantry are not opposed to women, as long as they can do the job. The problem is we are pigs. We like to hang our junk out and scratch our ass. We use foul language and like to joke around. When women are in the area, we can't do that, so we feel like we are losing something. You're going to get some EO cases. Most guys are going to behave, but many will slip up and get into trouble. It's going to take a while to create a new culture."

The combat engineer captain I was with responded that they better get their act together sooner than later. The Military VIPs always recognized our engineer captain's Sapper tab. Someone who is qualified as a combat engineer and completed a Sapper Leader course wears a Sapper tab. There were very few VTNG soldiers wearing such a prestigious badge. General officers were always super impressed when speaking with the female combat engineer captain. The high-ranking officials often looked past us like we had no purpose to be there with the captain and we had a hard time injecting ourselves into the conversations.

These responses revealed to me how important outward identity can be. The VIPs did not know if I was a bad-ass competent soldier with medals adorning my *love-me* wall. All they could see was an old warrant officer with no combat patch standing next to a combat engineer captain. I loved being on her team, however I had flashbacks to high school days when as a flat chested tomboy, guys overlooked me and swarmed over my busty best friend. Some would joke, "Here come the hung and the breastless," spinning the daytime soap opera show, *The Young and the Restless*.

This experience at Fort Drum made me grateful I was an administrative warrant in the JFHQ. I had no desire to be a combat soldier. My set of skills were not with a rifle or toughing it out in the field. It gave me more respect for women in line units like the captain. My respect deepened for women who were out there operating in a tough environment and dealing with being the anomaly. I gained greater appreciation for all the soldiers who did these tough things in a training environment to be prepared for combat. I could only imagine combat because I had never been. My husband and many of my friends had. I imagined, on the plane to a combat zone, you reflect on all the lessons you have learned and are ready to use them. I also knew personal issues, your socialization strategies, your biases, and character defects come along for the tour too.

I gained some understanding why the soft skill training or TF strategies were such a nuisance for most service members. They were busy getting the job done with little time to regroup, rest or even reflect on the day. The weekend drills and summer camps flew by and often ended with a long list of things to do next time.

Doris J. Sumner

CHAPTER 16
THE HIGHS AND LOWS OF THE ENDURING BATTLES
★ ★ ★

An important task among the Military Women's Workshop 21 recommendations was authentically analyzing the representation of women and where they were assigned in the Vermont National Guard. The Military Women's Workshop team submitted specific targets for the VTNG Military Strategic Plan. We set annual goals for gender diversity overall, as well as in leadership positions and new occupations available to women since the repeal of the Combat Exclusion Policy. If women would *just naturally* enter the military and develop into those positions, why did the status gap remain, since women make up 51% of the population?

As attention turned to the role of women in the military, and access to positions for women expanded—including in combat—those in the DoD who kept track of such things seemed satisfied with the growth rate of women's representation. Yet, I was not. I believe all people are of equal worth in the task of securing our national defense, and I did not see female representation growing at a rate that showed respect for their value, or for the military's ability to recruit and retain them.

Two years after the 21 recommendations were endorsed by the TAG, we finalized a detailed Gender Report. We insisted the report be presented to the Joint Senior Leadership Council (JSLC) of the Vermont Guard. The JSLC is made up of the general officers, brigade and Wing commanders, the Army command chief warrant officer (CCWO), the State CSM and the Wing CCM. During my 13-year tenure, these posts were filled by all men, except for one female chief CCWO who served for two years on the council during the latter part of my tenure.

The Air Guard federal women's program manager and I nervously prepared a comprehensive Gender Report PowerPoint for the JSLC. During our first presentation, the senior officials were polite as they admitted some shock regarding the scarcity of females in command positions. They began to provide a rationale for the underrepresentation other than the sexism conclusion that was highlighted in our executive summary.

Each year in my job, I gave standard EO reports to the TAG that showed no increase in ethnic, racial, or gender diversity in the commander column. The general was sincere when he said he understood the racial disparity, given the recruiting pool in Vermont, but he asked me, "Where are the females?"

I took his question to heart. The organization had few

females in leadership positions. The DJS kept waving off a formal presentation of the data in the Gender Report during those two years since the 21 recommendations had been endorsed. The DJS kept asking us to include additional comparatives until the document was 48 pages of every conceivable gender comparison. The Report measured the representation of women in multiple statuses. We examined the representation of women in drill status and we also looked at the women working in federal status. We categorized by officer, enlisted, warrant officer, occupation, and command level. The MWP utilized demographics, case data, training, and event feedback forms, as well as our own experiences out and about talking to service men and women to develop our analysis of the gender gap.

In the Report, we listed secondary reasons for the gender gap—suggesting it was due to a lack of interest in joining, based on historic narratives that the military was a man's job. We listed the pregnancy and family care falsehoods that women couldn't be in the military and remain engaged moms. We recognized institutional barriers based on sexist policies that kept women from *officially* serving in combat and attaining the awards, decorations, and special assignments that increased their career opportunities. We detailed the lack of networking and mentoring women received for various reasons that contributed to their underrepresentation in positions of authority, including that men were reluctant to mentor women, fearing the perception of sexual harassment occurring, or of actual claims being lodged. There were plenty of reasons for the underrepresentation of women and the stagnation of progress.

Our bold proclamation within the Gender Report was that the primary reason was the culture itself. This was not an original summation on our part, as several national studies over the years concluded that military culture was not conducive to engendering dignity and respect for minorities among the troops. Our small town VTNG Gender Report described the same culture. This culture continued to be ignored, downplayed, or accepted by men and women as *military life*.

Examples of sexism played out to me daily. I was kicked out of my blissful ignorance when I took the job. I was now a member at the Army JFHQ where 90% of members in the unit had been in the service a decade or more. Each year we received a mandatory review of policies through countless hours of boring PowerPoint presentations. Most were told by stoic presenters never swaying far from a predictable format. One mid-level officer in the line up the year before I retired, decided to take a risk for his presentation on operational security, a risk management process that prevents sensitive information from getting into the wrong hands. He first showed a bunch of historic videos of brave men fighting in war, including some awful images of prisoners of war. He talked about the Geneva Convention rules for warfare, and switched the video to something more modern. We all sat around on metal folding chairs in a large open bay of the armory. As soon as the new video began, the mood in the room shifted. I could hear chattering as the video music turned to some sort of romance tune. A gray bearded man, dressed in a dark velvet suit to indicate his wealth, had two young scantily dressed women clinging to him. He was giving them a talk about "keeping your valuables safe."

Just before the operational security briefing, the commander had introduced the new SARC—who happened to be male— to the unit. The commander stated, "We don't need a briefing on this subject, right? We all know not to be stupid." The SARC sat down. As the sexist video played now, I leaned over to one of my EOAs and said, "Am I the only one who sees how improper and sexist this video is? The SARC isn't even rejecting the video." She shook her head and mumbled a line from a beloved Army song, "and the Army goes rolling along."

I was tired of the Army. I thought back to the courage it took to get on a bus bound for basic training at Fort Dix on a freezing cold day after Christmas. I thought about the band of brothers who had cheered me on in Aberdeen, when I was a truck driver and received the top driver rating. I second guessed myself now, who am I to change the Army? Fit in or get out was the path of least resistance.

The DoD is still documenting these stats: one in 16 women, and one in 143 men, are expected to experience sexual assault within the military, according to a RAND Corporation study released in 2021.[24] There was never a shortage of data on the prevalence of sex- based offenses, just not much narrative on why. One of the references we used in our Gender Report was a Secretary of the Army report on sexual harassment. It was documented at the Pentagon in September 1997, after the Secretary ordered a review based on the Aberdeen Proving Ground military base scandal.[25] It was the biggest sex scandal in Army history, in which women recruits at the Army Ordnance Center were harassed, assaulted, and raped by their drill staff. Among the conclusions and recommendations in the short report, it stated: "We are firmly convinced that leadership is the fundamental issue. Passive leadership has allowed sexual harassment to persist; active leadership can bring about change to eradicate it."

This simple statement said so much yet no one seemed to get it.

Our MWP told the senior leaders why a high prevalence of sex-based offenses existed in the military. But the excuses persisted. Too often the fallback attitude remained, this was something to accept and manage, not eradicate.

---

[24] https://www.rand.org/pubs/research_reports/RRA1318-1.html

[25] https://www.washingtonpost.com/wp-srv/local/longterm/library/aberdeen/aber3.htm

The TAG said he appreciated our hard work, and he wanted us to continue with our data collection. Each year, the data did not change much, and our recommendations were mixed in with a host of TF strategies, all being managed with minimal buy in by those who held the cultural power. The initial politeness regarding our reports wore off, and the defensive posture that started showing up at annual reviews of the Gender Report was infuriating. We could always count on the CSM of the Vermont Army Guard touting the fair Enlisted Personnel Management System (EPMS). Promotions were all based on points, they told us. You get the points; you get the promotion. The CSMs did not want to hear about bias in acquiring points.

The Air Guard could brag about their higher percentage of women, especially women E-9's, the top enlisted. They didn't want to talk about having few female commanders, or acknowledge that the top enlisted women weren't being selected for supervisory positions. They defended their fighter pilot recruitment program despite never having a female fighter pilot in the unit's 70 year history. The Wing loved to tell the story about selecting a pilot and sending her off to school, where she married a fellow student and never returned to service in Vermont. This happened with the male pilots too, but we only heard about the one female who did this.

During the briefings, the senior leaders often ticked off their explanations and excuses for low numbers. They loved telling stories of noble women they served with or bragging about Vermont having the first female TAG. Regardless, the problem statement was always the same: women were underrepresented in all grades and occupations for the Air and Army Guard. The stated goal was to increase their numbers, but an answer to the question "Why increase the number of women?" was never fully understood by the all male senior leaders. The value of gender diversity was as baffling to them as the idea that their culture needed to transform, or why *Green Mountain Boys* was considered sexist.

Our aim had become laser focused—to highlight how sexism was a deterrent to women joining the force, excelling in the ranks, and attaining command positions. We attempted to point out that, with a male majority in command, they set the climate. And the male majority climate in general perpetuated sexist attitudes (masculine, better than feminine), and this attitude that women were second class people contributed to the rate of sex-based offenses. To help reduce sex-based offenses, more women were needed in command positions, which would help to eradicate sexism in the culture. This problem statement became as simple to me as Alice Paul's idea that "Equal rights is the right direction."

In 2014, a local on-line media outlet, *VTDigger* published a story about the first annual report from the VTNG to the Legislature based on a law passed in 2013 mandating an annual legislative review of sexual assault and harassment complaints involving members of the Vermont National Guard.[26] Prior to this, information was not made public. In the article, a Vermont Representative Jean O'Sullivan, who supported the bill, said she was pleased and that she believed the report covered the intent of the law, providing the information the Legislature was looking for. I was part of the team that produced the sexual harassment portion of the report. I went through the painful process of scrutinizing the data with the JAG and staff from the Public Affairs Office (PAO). They wanted to comply with the requirement without opening the report to negative interpretations that could dampen local patriotism. We dutifully presented the report to the House members, not spending time discussing the nuances of the cases.

Shortly after the first annual report was submitted to the Legislature, I saw Rep O'Sullivan working at the Employer Support for the Guard Reserve (ESGR) table in the Green Mountain Armory drill hall. I introduced myself and gave her my elevator speech regarding the problem statement about changing the culture that I'd been voicing to anyone who would listen. Jean was friendly and interested in the work I talked about. She was busy, so we exchanged emails. Within a week, we met for lunch. I was uncertain if this violated any protocol, but I felt emboldened to be bold.

At lunch, I told Jean the current bill, § 427, did not help

---

[26] https://vtdigger.org/2014/01/30/vermont-national-guard-reports-six-sexual-assaults-one-year-span/

to minimize the sex-based offenses. I applauded the SAPRO. I applauded the bill giving the public an opportunity to reflect on the number of offenses occurring within the Guard. I agreed the Legislative Report on Sexual Harassment and Sexual Assault provided oversight to ensure the Guard had a legitimate program staffed and was serving survivors of sex-based offenses. My concern was the lack of transparency showing why a high prevalence of sex-based offenses continued or how the cases were completed and closed.

My honesty flabbergasted her, as I conveyed the true sexist culture women experienced in the Guard. Jean had worked in the financial industry, as well as being involved in a host of other male majority occupations, committees, and councils. She had no problem recognizing the sexism women shoulder. She asked if I would meet with other representatives and help them draft a bill that would achieve more accountability to combat the sexism, we knew was a problem.

I met with two other representatives who were just as astonished, saddened, and inspired to do more. If we were to change the androcentric responses to sex-based offenses, which were predominantly reported by women, then we needed more women in the power core. I described the enormous risk survivors took just to report violations. It was a bro culture, so even if their leaders took them seriously, reporting tagged you as a troublemaker. The system trapped women in a sometimes-hostile culture they had to assimilate into and keep the status-quo, if they expected to survive. Being Superwoman was the expectation, if you wanted to thrive.

I saw the totality of the culture. Individually, there were outstanding leaders, units, and teams working with the professional spirit which kept drawing recruits. When you are accepted, the comradery can be exhilarating and devastating when you are the outcast.

I handed the representatives a note given to me from a Military Sexual Trauma (MST) survivor that read: "I was successful because I didn't speak up. I didn't speak up because I wanted to be successful. I was going to be successful. To be successful, I had to wear the armor. I put the pain in my backpack and I carry the weight."

I gave the representatives the Gender Report and told them about the lack of urgency VTNG leaders showed regarding the proposals we kept printing. I told them about the lack of leader engagement regarding gender diversity training or the Lean In sessions we kept doing. Lean Ins were small group interactive discussions based on Sheryl Sandberg's book, *Lean In: Women, Work and the Will to Lead*.[27] Sheryl Sandberg was the former Meta Platforms Chief Operation Officer. She resigned from COO position at Meta Platforms in August 2022.

Our MWP began these monthly sessions with a handful of

---

[27] https://leanin.org

the same employees. We talked about gender related challenges within the organization. Men and women contributed to solution orientated discussions. It gave us hope, but it was a pebble on the beach that the waves often took back out to sea. I left the meeting with the representatives feeling flat, not sure what other drums I could bang.

In late January, I headed to Montpelier, Vermont, to testify with my colleagues and our TAG on the fifth Legislative Report on Sexual Harassment and Sexual Assault. There were two sexual assaults against members of the VTNG by members of the organization, and we reported four sexual harassment cases. Although the Legislators received the Report prior to the testimony, it had become routine for our team to present our talking points, then answer inquiries from representatives who wanted a better understanding of the cases. I don't think they knew what to ask or understood the underlying issues of the events we reported.

I never felt the Guard leaders wanted to be dishonest, however, I watched their trepidation as they drafted talking points. I was not free to express my frustrations about the culture that our MWP had surmised creates an opening for minor violations, a culture that gives true predators places to hide and strike. The Guard had been treating these incidents as unfortunate acts by careless men, rather than as a cultural issue created by a tolerance for sexism. I was a soldier, an employee, and a program manager. I was proud of many efforts we had accomplished, but it also frustrated me that those with power did not feel like I did.

After we testified, Rep O'Sullivan walked through the room where we were socializing amongst lawmakers. She handed me a piece of paper and said, "Here is your legacy." I opened the paper in the coatroom and read a draft bill requiring the TAG and IG to submit an annual report on gender equity in the VTNG, detailing the Guard's efforts and programs to recruit, retain, and promote women to senior noncommissioned officers, warrant officers, and commissioned officers. I was the one flabbergasted now, in a good way.

I considered all of the women I watched leave Camp, wanting never to be reminded of the place they had given their all. Could this bill be the foundation for the change we had been working toward? I knew nothing about getting a bill passed, or how laws provided the controls for change. I was naïvely hopeful that my tenacity had elevated the problem beyond the confines of the Guard, but I had no expectations.

In early February, the TAG sent me a copy of an email sent to all the Vermont senior leaders. The draft bill that I received in my hand a week before was attached. The general said the bill would get traction in the Legislature, and he wanted me to confirm that we were tracking all the requirements already in the Gender Report.

Jean had heard me, and she formulated accountability in the

form of a bill. Now these strategies were gaining momentum. I was grateful. Responding to the general's email, I asked if anyone understood the purpose of the new bill? I was asking if anyone could see the connection between the number of sex-based offenses and the representation of women in command positions? When I got no response to my questions, I had my answer.

I was resolved to surrender any hope that these leaders would understand, as long as results were possible. I was reminded of wise advice I'd received from a pastor about my husband. I wanted Phil to have faith along with his dutiful act of attending church with our young children. The pastor said, "He is in the place where change can happen. Let go."

Doris J. Sumner

CHAPTER 17
THE POWER OF COMMAND
★ ★ ★

HOME LIFE AND SOBRIETY HAD BEEN A TRUDGE OVER THE time my husband reacclimated to family life after his deployment. Our kids were teens, and they were emotionally struggling as they sought to gain their own identities. I had not realized how difficult it was for the kids to spend that year without their dad. Phil and I questioned our parenting techniques and struggled to meet in the middle. Life during this time brought me the most highs and lows I had ever known.

Despite the grueling battles at work, my team and I felt empowered having top leadership supporting the TF and the CDET. With the nursing room accommodations in place, our Gender Report format completed, and an annual briefing for senior leaders on the rotation, our small group of women involved in the MWP felt like suffragettes. We expected and accepted that it would be a long haul.

Our next priority was to address the lack of senior enlisted women in the Army Guard. Enlisted personnel make up 70% of the force. They start out as privates (E-1), increasing in rank and responsibility up to SGM (E-9). The National Guard promoted its first ever female SGM in 1985, coincidentally, she was a member of the Vermont Guard. She filled a CSM slot in the unit at the Ethan Allen Training Site in Jericho. This was the second prestigious *first* for Vermont promoting women.

Being a SGM in the Army is a big deal. You are generally a subject matter expert within your occupation, and are managing specific programs or supervising the enlisted soldiers within your unit area. In 2020, the Vermont Guard had promoted only its sixth female SGM in a span of 35 years.

Becoming a CSM is when you are put into a specific position with command authority. This provides you with the power to influence policy and command the culture. After the first female was promoted to CSM in 1985, she held the position only for a short time before leaving the Vermont Guard. No other women held a position of CSM in Vermont until 2020.

The Vermont Guard had ten CSM positions. They were generally in each brigade, battalion, school house unit, headquarters unit, and at the top was the State CSM. The State CSM works at headquarters for the TAG and oversees the entire enlisted force. Plenty of men rotated through those slots, with the ability to influence the entire command climate.

I knew if we were going to change the culture of the

Guard, I would have to take the road less traveled, so I began engaging with those ten male CSM's in Vermont. I remember my trepidation, assuming my strategies would not be welcomed, thinking back to the chill I received when I cheerfully walked into the VTNG Recruiting and Retention Battalion (RRB).

I first met the State CSM at the Fort Drum exercises. About a week into the training, he was standing over a few of us in the chow hall. His belly was full with a hot breakfast, and he stood before us with his clean field gear on, ready to jump into a Humvee. He was on his way back to the tactical zone, the field duty area, to do whatever it is CSM's do. Before leaving, he told us how some soldiers were complaining about the directive not to use their military camping cots. Instead, they were directed to sleep on the ground. His face welled with pride, and he began bragging. Back in his day, they had no cots or cell phones. He described one female at our training site telling him the cots were right next to her in the tent, and she didn't see the purpose of bringing the item if they weren't going to use them. He had a big grin on his face, telling us his response. "It makes you tougher. Toughen up soldier." He grinned and walked away.

None of us nodded agreement with his tactic. We glanced at each other with a disgusted "UUGGH." I imagined the young soldier he told to toughen up giving him an imaginary finger as he walked away from her.

Life at Camp

That was the attitude I had in my day—questioning ridiculous, unexplainable Army directives. I said out loud to my colleagues, "Imagine what a difference he could have made by instead saying, 'It is uncomfortable. I didn't like it myself back in the day. Hang in there.'"

I didn't forget his smug attitude, and perhaps my bias found him smug at every interaction thereafter. I supposed it to be natural to pass on what had worked for you and what you thought made you tough. But this ideology troubled me; just because it worked for you, doesn't mean it worked for all, and especially a new generation.

I found many CSM's were determined to use the tactics they were brought up on, as a mark of their loyalty to the Army. Old timers loved to brag how tough they had it and how weak and lazy the young recruits were. It bothered me they never considered the socialization of that youth was in their hands.

I emailed the CSM a request to attend the next Vermont Guard CSM's council to brief them on gender issues. I tried to arrange a townhall type meeting, with a group of Army enlisted females on hand to discuss integration barriers. The responses from him were always forms of procrastination. Maybe I didn't insist enough because of my disdain for him. An entire year went by, and our MWP never met with the CSM council. When the crusty old CSM retired, I sighed with relief, but I knew it cost us a year.

The next State CSM was fit for a movie role as a good old boy. He always had a wad of tobacco in his cheek and a spit can in hand. His head and hands were tanned, the way they were supposed to be on outdoorsmen. He was short and stocky, and he had the raspy voice of an old Vermonter. He was an infantryman, but he cleaned up nice, wearing the dress uniform and high gloss shoes as he decorated his staff office at Camp Johnson.

This new CSM was more responsive to our MWP, and I worked with him for more than five years. At my retirement ceremony, he admitted we didn't see the Army through the same lens, but he proclaimed respect for my passion to make a difference. I did not like his tone, his ego, his playbook, or the strategies he used to achieve his goals, but I respected his passion for the Army. I believe he thought he was doing an outstanding job for the force. The problem for me was, he was doing an outstanding job focused on his boys.

After months of struggling with schedules, we had our very first enlisted council meeting with the new State CSM. I invited about ten women to attend, telling the CSM we wanted him to hear from junior women in the Guard. We told him gender issues were affecting the way women were treated within the ranks, minimizing opportunities for women to excel. His face crinkled, but he agreed to the meeting.

The SARC and I were ready to take notes and forge an action plan and bust down the obstacles for female enlisted.

Each of the women expressed their frustrations operating in a male dominated environment, not seeing a level playing field. Younger enlisted women described feeling like interlopers, and how important it was to forge friendships with the guys. These same women claimed that being friends was a tightrope, depending on how you managed it. Someone was always ready to label you either the *slut* or the *bitch*. The women admitted their personal goal was to fit in and prove themselves just as tough as any guy. They knew from the first meeting with a recruiter that they were joining an organization that was less than 14% female. Most of them ended up serving with only one or two females in a squad, platoon, or company.

That first meeting with the State CSM was painful, but useful. We felt confident that we'd selected women who would be fearlessly honest and unconcerned about reprisal. When the CSM came into the small room, he took up the air, and I could feel the women stiffen. Because I regularly worked at JFHQ with many senior staff enlisted, as well as officers, I took for granted my ease at seeing them as just another coworker with rank. But service members who drill one weekend a month in outlying units seldom saw high-ranking officials outside of their company/squadron command. Most of them didn't have daily interactions with Army CSM's or Air command chief master sergeants, the most senior of the enlisted ranks. When they saw senior officials, they had been conditioned to use professional military courtesy, as directed in the hierarchy structure of the military. Making a good impression is important in a smalltown Guard, because people will remember you.

The CSM took his seat at the head of the table in a ready posture. I think he was expecting highly pitched bitching, but instead, we followed our script and turned to the first enlisted woman to share what she had to say to us. If I had been watching a video, I would have sought the volume knob. Where was her voice? She spoke low and timid, sharing how some guys avoided her, and how they were unwilling to mentor her. The SARC and I made eye contact. "Oh, shit."

The next young specialist bragged about how she didn't take shit from the guys. But, she exclaimed, it was fucking exhausting.

The rest of the meeting consisted of mild discussions about the male culture, and the unintimidated enlisted leader had an answer or recommendation for every situation. He gleamed with importance and satisfaction. He bragged about the fairness of the EPMS, and he said that women only need earn the points to be equally qualified for promotion.

The meeting could not end fast enough. I was disappointed in the women who were intimidated, but I was more disappointed with myself. I walked the few steps to my private office, shut the door, and cried. I could get so frustrated with myself. Every time I had the opportunity to highlight the real problem, it seemed I failed. My self-pity party did not last long, though, because the CSM knocked on my door.

He tried to mansplain to me what the real problem is concerning the underrepresentation of women in the enlisted force. He believed if women just volunteered to join the infantry units, or requested special assignments such as first sergeant (1SG) or platoon sergeant positions, there would be no underrepresentation. He went into great detail about how the promotion system works (like I didn't know). I had just enough energy to give him some pushback. I woman-explained to him—the points soldiers can earn to increase their opportunities for promotion are based upon how they are mentored, coached, supported, and treated, all of which are affected by gender bias.

There are hundreds of stories I have told men in senior military positions in my attempt to help them understand the cultural barriers that hold women back. One female in the meeting that day had not provided the example she told me earlier. I thought it might be a simple enough example to get through to the CSM. So, I told him how she explained it to me:

"I had a terrible headache at drill, so I went up to the first sergeant and asked if he had an aspirin. He said, 'No, but I can run you to the store.' I said sure. We were walking across the armory, and a bunch of the guys were standing around. The first sergeant yells over to them, 'Ya'll don't talk about us while we're gone.' They all laughed, but it mortified me. This was a combat arms cavalry unit. I was one of two women in the unit, and I was trying to earn respect. I was seeking to get a full time job in the unit. This one comment erased what I had worked so hard to build." I further explained to the CSM that, even if they hired her for the full time position, many of those guys might perceive it as a quid pro quo sort of deal. Although women did not need a scene like this one for guys to think that. Sexism was ever present.

When she told me the story, I heard her pain, humiliation, exasperation, disgust, and irritation. When I told the CSM, the leader of all enlisted, he chuckled and said, "I probably have said dumb shit like that before." He admitted to seeing the problem, but was quick to add, "She should have spoken up and called him an asshole," I shook my head. What kind of recommendation is that? I kept on talking, explaining that she wanted to get a job, and the 1SG was the selecting official, so she couldn't make a fool out of him in front of his subordinates. All she could do was suck it up, put it into her imaginary backpack, compounding her headache.

I told him so many women don't even recognize this as sexism, but it is, and it deters inclusion and objectifies females. The 1SG in this story took away her power. He made her out to be something he could go have fun with, just so his boys could laugh. To him, it was just a joke, just him being funny, but it was another humiliation for her.

I told the CSM that women get tired, constantly combating sexism along with competing with the men. I must have felt like I was getting through to him as I continued making my case, "This is why we had the Women's Workshop, the MWP, and why we need these forums," I said. "We need women to understand where their energy is being drained."

He said to me, "If they don't know it, why would we want to tell them?"

It was an exhausting conversation that ended with him telling me gleefully to schedule another council meeting and bring more women in.

He said, "I want to help them. I want women in combat. In fact, find me a squad of women who want to be infantry, and I will mentor them myself. I will prepare a squad of women, and then we'll send them to the 11 Bravo Infantry school as soon as it opens up."

After he left my office, I'm certain I vented to the SARC and went for another long run. I looked forward to my runs. They were slow, steady, and they were getting longer, so I could calm my emotions. I could run a ten minute mile for an hour and I was proud of that. I turned up the country music on my headset and tried not to think.

A common chorus in the service has it that, because men had to run faster and do more push-ups for the traditional Army Physical Fitness Test (APFT), women were getting a break in the standards. APFT assessments were categorized by gender and age. A young male between ages 17 to 21 had to run two miles in 13 minutes to achieve the max score of 100 points. A young female received 100 points for running the two miles in 15 minutes and 36 seconds.

Regardless of the biology validating the differences between the sexes, the disparate scoring always fueled a sense of male superiority. Young females desperate to prove their worthiness struggled to perform at the same level as the men, believing the male standards were about combat readiness. The APFT was never about combat readiness, it was about fitness for our age and gender, but you could not convince these soldiers. Despite their rigorous efforts, often the women had to go beyond the 100-point score to get equal respect as a warrior combat ready. To pass, a soldier only had to achieve a score of 60 points in each category; the two mile run, sit-ups and push-ups. Some females experienced injuries for the goals they set to prove themselves, delaying career progression.

When Secretary of Defense Leon Panetta announced on January 24, 2013, that the 1994 Direct Ground Combat Exclusion Rule[28] was to be rescinded, this opened up 237,000 positions across the services to women. The urgency to ensure that the APFT focused on combat readiness intensified. Many of us feminists felt the sting of the double standard.

---
[28] https://www.npr.org/sections/thetwo-way/2013/01/23/170093351/panetta-is-lifting-ban-on-women-in-combat-roles

Life at Camp

For decades, when men only were in the combat arms units or occupations, they only needed to pass the APFT to be considered combat ready, yet now that women could join in combat occupations, the Army wanted to validate readiness with a new assessment. Therefore, a new Army Combat Fitness Test was developed.[29]

We knew overweight, out of shape infantrymen had existed and affected readiness for as long as the Army had infantry. Now, the question of readiness was serious, because feminine was part of the equation. These sorts of enlightenments along the way fueled my ambition for gender equality.

Our Cultural Transformation Task Force and MWP focused efforts on helping to safely transition women into the combat arms units of the VTNG. Our TAG was serious about transforming the culture to ensure a sexual assault did not happen under his command.

It still astonishes me that the most revered units in the Army or Marines were the very units in which commanders feared for the safety of women from sexual assault. Weren't these your elites? Along with my pride for the military, I carried this sense of annoyance over the problem. How could such an esteemed entity continue to maintain this pattern of sexism? I watched, year after year, report after report, headline after headline, military academy scandal after scandal. It reminded

---
[29] https://www.army.mil/acft/

me of the A.A. reality often spoken of at meetings: "I couldn't fix the problem with my problem mind."

In my pursuit of the cultural change needed, I acknowledged that men were also survivors of sex-based trauma. Although I was often negatively labeled as a fanatic feminist, only focused on women rights, I attempted to show how all service members were affected by sexism. Defining the problem became my Kryptonite. I claimed sexism remained because men were the majority in the power core. These men didn't want to hear that greater gender diversity would help solve the problem. I was taking the problem to the problem.

I vented to my allies about the need for a cultural change, and wondering how to accomplish it was the daunting task I allowed to keep me up at night. Some of my A.A. friends warned me about the obsession getting out of control. They reminded me lovingly of the powerful Serenity Prayer:

> God, Grant me the serenity,
> to accept the things I cannot change,
> the courage to change the things I can,
> and the wisdom to know the difference.

The military was failing to embrace the full potential of its human resources because of sexism. This was more certain to me than any other fact of my job. Determined, I thought I could convince, rally, or excite enough allies to raise consciousness about the problem and propel a revolution.

I would continue to engage with the CSM's for the next five years. Every conversation was hard and felt senseless. I would often vent how I wanted to stick a fork in my eye, as it would probably have been less painful than explaining gender bias to another man.

Doris J. Sumner

CHAPTER 18

KEEPING UP THE FIGHT - HERE OR THERE

★ ★ ★

The Vermont Air Guard was preparing for their annual training (A.T.). Specific training is conducted during the two weeks to certify a unit's readiness for deployments. The Wing Equal Opportunity office would use the time at A.T. to provide the required annual EO and prevention of sexual harassment training. Half of the 158th Fighter Wing would travel to the Combat Readiness Training Center in Alpena, Michigan, that year for training camp. It was a big deal to have a dedicated airstrip and the entire base for all the specialized training.

Although I completed my A.T. at Fort Drum, the Wing EO officer requested I augment her staff during the Wing A.T. She was part of the MWP and the TF, and she hoped we could use our small group facilitation guide to lead the training in Alpena. I was thrilled to get orders for Alpena. The Air Guard trip was different from any Army summer camps I attended, or from what I knew of my husband's field days. The first pleasant surprise was the transportation mode: groups of us would fly on a C-130. I was the only Army

LIFE AT CAMP

Guard soldier among the 500 Air Guard service members on the base flight line waiting for our ride. Once aboard, the pilots invited me to sit between them during takeoff. It was a thrill.

The training site was a remote military base, minimally staffed with locals awaiting our arrival. The Green Mountain Boys descended onto the property and quickly established operational momentum. At the first full unit assembly, the Wing Commander notified everyone of a sexual assault training stand-down ordered by the Chief of Staff of the U.S. Air Force. Our group locked eyes anxiously.

A training stand-down is an organized cessation of normal duties until a specific training is accomplished. None of us in EO were trained in the specialized field of sexual assault prevention. We were uncertain who would run the training, although we expected to be involved. We were convinced of the connection between the culture of sexism, EO, and the spectrum of harm from sex-based offenses.

The Wing Commander appointed the Wing EO officer as the Officer-In-Charge (OIC) of the training stand-down. The Wing didn't have a trained SARC but it did have several trained VA's for the SAPR. There was no specialized certification to conduct the training, however, a VA, mental health professional, or pastoral staff was required in each training session to ensure support for MST survivors or other persons who may have become triggered by the topic.

The mathematical problem of organizing small group sessions for 500 Air Guard personnel—with limited time, space, and trainers—baffled me, however the OIC assigned two person teams and handed the outline to us. A 17-page guide provided direction. The first line of the guide quoted General Mark A. Welsh III, the Chief of Staff of the Air Force: "We must drive sexual assault from our ranks."

Facilitators were to create an environment that engaged all learners in the room. A tall order, given the dismissiveness we'd experienced at A.T. training sessions we were already doing. In order to fulfill the Air Guard's SAPR requirement, facilitators had to read a full page disclaimer and, at a minimum, ensure they covered the boldfaced text elements that appeared in the guide. Despite the sensitivity of the topic, the script was unemotional as it led the facilitator through key discussion points. The first question was: "Do you know to whom you can report sexual harassment or assault, if you or a fellow service member experience such treatment?"

They focused most bullet points on the response to being sexually assaulted. We were to review the reporting options, such as reporting confidentially without triggering an investigation *(restricted)*, or reporting to ensure command notification and an official investigation *(unrestricted)*. We were to cover who to report to if a service member wanted to receive the physical, emotional, and mental support available.

We explained the VA's role and other staffing requirements for the program. The only sexual assault prevention bullets involved a few bystander intervention strategies. Those included actions a person could take if they fear a sexual assault might happen, and how to intervene.

After most of the crew left, our small EO team began protesting the issued guide. We insisted our facilitation guide would be more effective. After all, the mission was to drive sexual assault from our ranks. We clamored, this stand-down was another *check the box* strategy, with no effect on cultural issues that make sex-based offenses more probable in the first place.

We proposed distributing a short handout with the administrative need-to-know items on it and instead, use our own facilitation guide for small group discussions. With approval from the Wing Commander, we held our first session with the senior leaders, who were all men. Our plan to brief them using our guide was risky, since we hadn't had time to break through egos denying sexism. Only the Wing Commander and Wing command chief had heard of our Gender Report. We pushed the tables to the side and arranged the chairs in a big circle. I was nervous. I didn't know these senior leaders as well as I knew Army senior leaders. The Wing Commander came into the room first, and his unpleasant facial expression revealed his disdain for the circle.

He sat in the farthest seat and faced across the circle to the doors, his arms crooked on each side, ensuring everyone knew where the head of the room was located.

The meeting began, and I watched the OIC assert command of the space. She followed the script, setting the training objective and providing protocols for anyone triggered by the topics to find support. The mandated topics were covered with the detachment handout we passed to each participant. Then she explained the research done that supported the idea that a sexist culture allows offenders to embark on a spectrum of harm from sex-based offenses, often unimpeded. She presented the idea of early intervention to change the culture and disrupt the spectrum of harm. She opened up the conversation for sharing about sexism or gender bias, inviting anyone to talk about what they may have witnessed or experienced.

Tense silence, until the Wing Commander spoke. He was self-assured and assertive as he related a story about mentoring strong women he served with, talking about how mentoring is very important. One of our team members was a female lieutenant colonel. She chose to inject the idea of disparate treatment of females into the discussion, talking about a lack of mentors throughout her career. She explained that males in positions to mentor females worry about their wives or their male colleagues suspecting that the relationship is other than professional. She challenged the leaders to support mentorship by shutting down rumors and rewarding men who mentor women.

Somehow, the opportunity came for me to speak up, and I did not plan on telling the story of my sexual assault, but I did. I gave the details about my first company commander asking me out to dinner under the guise of showing Baltimore to the Vermont girl. I confessed to drinking a lot and going to his apartment with him, because he said he had to pick up something. I continued with the defenseless way I allowed sexual intercourse with him, and how he dropped me off at my barracks. Then I said to the room: "Is this sexual assault?"

The room was silent.

I looked at the faces of these men, who were all looking at me. Their eyes seemed to seek an answer, and then a few quietly said, "Yes."

I said, "Yes, it is." I added that these situations are still happening.

We began talking about consent and other sexual harassment and sexual assault issues. The engagement and energy around the circle intensified, as several leaders gave their opinions on the problem of sexual harassment or sexual assault within the military. It got very uncomfortable for several people, and we witnessed the changes in body language.

We had completed less than an hour of the 120 minutes, when the commander said, "Let's stop right now. This is not how we are going to facilitate this stand-down. We are going to end this session." And he motioned for the OIC to follow him out of the room, saying sharply to us, "Dismissed."

When she returned, she was flushed. She said it was the most intense meeting she had ever had with a commanding officer. We were directed to use the 17 page original guide and not waiver. We were told a senior leader would sit in on each training session to ensure that conversations did not get offtrack. I was leading a group in a small room. A full-bird colonel came in a few minutes late. He sat down and let me know he was the senior leader assigned to my session. The female Wing Chaplain was among us, serving as the required support person for anyone who might feel vulnerable or triggered. I obediently followed the script, yet the conversations about sex-based offenses naturally flowed.

One of the male NCOs said, "When all this SAPR stuff started being required, I thought it was ridiculous. I said, this is not a problem for us. Then I went around to every woman friend I had and asked them if they had ever experienced sexual harassment. Not one of them said no."

A mid-level female NCO spoke up. "I was sexually harassed constantly by a coworker, and I complained to my supervisor.

You know what he told me? 'Just ignore him, and don't be alone with him.'" Another young female described in detail some of the sexist remarks she put up with working in maintenance, and how reporting them only earned her a dose of reprisal.

Suddenly, the senior officer broke in. "I can't remain silent, as I sit here in shock. I am disgusted and angry. Why am I not hearing about this? This is wrong."

An NCO replied, "Respectfully, Sir, there are buffers between what happens at the work centers and what gets to you. All you hear is it's all good, Sir, because they don't want to look bad."

Some of the language was very raw, and a few times people hesitated and apologized to the Chaplain. She fervently encouraged the sharing. The consensus among the group recognized a need to have more such discussions. They believed in supporting early intervention to prevent the sexism from continuing. The rest of our group's time together was one of the best exchanges of support I ever facilitated.

After the group left, the senior officer faced me and said, "We need to keep the format like this—let airmen freely talk. I am shocked this much is going on without me knowing, but I am going to support the fix." I believed he understood we could not have conversations about sexual harassment or sexual assault absent emotions. The old saying was, "If the military wanted you to have emotions, they would have issued you them." It's so much easier to control the masses—just don't feel.

The OIC notified us that we could conduct the small group sessions using our internal facilitation guide, and senior leaders would not be in the room. We had four groups doing three sessions per day to get through all 500 members at Camp. Hundreds of Air Guard personnel were exposed to the sensitive topics of sexual harassment, sexual assault, gender discrimination, and all the experiences along the spectrum. The watercooler talk was welcomed by those seeking authenticity, and avoided by those who wanted to steer clear of the topic all together.

By the end of the first day, our team was emotionally exhausted. We talked about some of our challenges managing tension, sensitivity, survivors, and deniers. There was always a mix of these people in each group. The rank and age diversity, was particularly challenging. Group guidelines encouraged everyone to speak freely, stripping the power to use *at ease*! Our facilitators handled this freewheeling aspect with professionalism and confidence. We all believed the conversations were helpful in highlighting how bias shows up, how it makes a person feel, and how we can be supportive team players in calling it out.

After the first evening, the OIC was called to the commander's office. The Wing Commander expressed concern over the command climate. He felt there was too much pain, too many converging ideas regarding the SAPR program. He had concerns about the facilitation format and

Life at Camp

the techniques used by the facilitators. He didn't have faith in her plan. She reaffirmed her confidence in the format and the painful process. She restated that the training stand-down is intended as the beginning of a culture change. Change is painful, she stressed. She told us he said, reluctantly, "Carry on. Just get the job done."

That evening, there was a party at a base bar called the River Cove. We were feeling giddy. We had some goofy, paper Hawaiian themed sunglasses, and we put them on and took selfies, posting, "EO going covert to the River Cove." Hundreds of Air Guard members were already there drinking, playing horseshoes, feasting on barbecue chicken, and mingling when we arrived. We sat down with one of the commanders who loved his cold beer. My Air Guard team knew him well, and they shared laughs about summer camps past. The commander got drunk, and my team convinced him to go back to his barracks before something happened. This all seemed normal to them, but I had never seen a senior officer drunk around his troops before.

Our team dispersed around the party and enjoyed the lighthearted banter, as some would jokingly say, "Shhh, be quiet. EO in the space!" Private conversations always validated those who did not benefit from the boys' club and the sexist culture women had to manage, but the open conversations were a buzz. Some Guard members conveyed their appreciation for bringing up a sensitive problem.

The week flew by in a flurry of emotions, conversations, and stress. We were on the flight line in our groups for the trip back home when a small jet pulled up. It surprised me when the OIC said, "This is for us." I was with a small group of officers. We flew back on the jet, serviced by the D.C. National Guard. What a week we had experienced. We understood better now the message from *The Invisible War* and the enormity of the battles we would face, if we intended to help the TAG combat sexual assault within the force. At base Camp, or on these A.T.s, we marched on with our mission. We felt like we had accomplished something in Alpena, but just like Fort Drum, later I would learn, our experience was very different from that of others who were there.

When we landed, my Air Guard officer friends grabbed their civilian luggage, and I swooped up my od green duffle bag. They wheeled and I did the duffle bag drag, all of us headed back to our lives at Camp.

CHAPTER 19
KEEPING UP THE FIGHT - FIELD DUTY
★ ★ ★

SHORTLY AFTER MY TRIP WITH THE AIR GUARD, I WAS informed I would be reassigned from the JFHQ unit to a small detachment of the Recruiting and Retention Battalion (RRB). This was a change in my military assignment, not affecting my full time job as the SEEM.

Other than the short stint with the 86 IBCT, I had been in the JFHQ for 23 years. The command team thought an opportunity outside of HQ would be good for my career. I scratched my head, considering I was now a 50 year old CW4. I didn't fear grunt drills, hiking, or bunking in the woods, but somehow, I thought my time to serve in line units had passed.

I was a Human Resources (HR) specialist, so my drill weekends focused on those administrative missions. My HR skills had to count for something; I was contributing to the overall mission of the VTNG. I often received passive shame from people, though. To them, I wasn't a real soldier. My husband was a real soldier. He had deployed to combat several times. His drill weekends focused on combat skills training, and his two weeks each year always involved sleeping on the range.

The only place or unit that would accept an old administrative warrant officer was the Recruit Sustainment Program (RSP). My insecurities fueled my suspicion that someone didn't think I knew what I was talking about regarding Guard culture, since I wasn't ever in the real units. The personnel officers created the position of executive officer (XO) for me, which wasn't even on the unit manpower document. The RSP was a new type of unit to the Guard, where recruits would spend one weekend a month learning about Army culture, expectations, marching movements, and physical development before they shipped to ten weeks of basic training. Their time in this unit depended upon their ship date and passing the different phases.

The RSP had a cadre of staff who developed a curriculum and facilitated training. Each weekend the RSP had close to 100 brand new soldiers at different phases of the process. They considered your first weekend the red phase, when you didn't even have a uniform or a haircut yet. Soldiers would progress through the phases, generally monthly, as they moved closer to their ship date. When they returned from basic training, they would continue drilling in the RSP until they left for their Military Occupational Specialty (MOS) service school. They held a ceremony when a trained soldier was ready to drill with their unit of assignment.

Each weekend was very different for the recruits, but was like Groundhog Day for the staff. Red phase instructors conducted the same classes for all the new recruits. White, blue, green, and gold phases were the same each weekend. The RSP support staff provided gear, food, training materials, medical support, and the administrative coordination needed to ensure recruits were ready to succeed at basic training and beyond.

I spent a year in the RSP, and I consider it one of the best years of my 36 year career. I had fun teammates to work with, and I was around young people excited to be soldiers. I explained to my boss that, when I left JFHQ and the EO officer job, there'd be a vacancy that needed to be filled. I'd be busy with the RSP, and I wondered who would run the weekend Army EO Program. I was adamant they fill the Army EO Program position I was vacating for the RSP.

My boss said they'd advertise the vacancy. In the prior eight years, I consistently fought for proper-ranking soldiers to fill the two EO staffing positions, but as the DJS said to me early on, "You can do it." The thought was not lost on me that the personnel officers could create a new position just for me in RSP, but they resisted filling these two positions, to the detriment of a healthy organizational climate.

On my first weekend in the RSP, I met the commander and CSM of the Recruiting and Retention Battalion. They came out to our drilling location and welcomed me and our new

1SG. He was not new to recruiting, but this was his first drill as the RSP 1SG. The kind RSP commander told me, "Just mull around and observe this drill, so you can understand how things work here."

As the small staff drank coffee and discussed the business of the weekend, I noted the new 1SG used the word *fuck* a lot. It was not offensive to me, and the way he used it seemed to help express his direct approach to getting things done.

At this point in my EO and diversity manager job, I was very keen on language. I had met and was working with a professor from New York, Dr. J.W. Wiley. A Black man, originally from Los Angeles, president of his own diversity education and consulting firm, a published author, Chief Diversity Officer for a N.Y. University. He was a fraternity brother of the new Wing EO Officer. The Wing EO Officer suspected I would appreciate Dr. Wiley's work, and our TF team had been building a new training series for our diversity program based on Dr. Wiley's theory of Leadership Moments.

J.W. had a masterful approach to engaging with people who were oppressing others, often unconsciously. He used the phrase "stepping into leadership moments" as those moments when we found the courage to confront bias or flat out discrimination. He encouraged all leaders (and everyone was a leader) to enlighten and lift people up and stop the oppression. Often, he demonstrated this by being inquisitive. His tone always de-escalated defensiveness and encouraged a more considerate conflict.

J.W. shared many examples of his techniques with us, and I couldn't wait to read his book, *The Nigger in You: Challenging Dysfunctional Language, Engaging Leadership* that I brought with me on my first day in the RSP. I carefully shielded the provocative title from the staff. As I sat in the staff office, the word fuck stuck out like a lightning bolt in conversations all around me, along with *gay*, *queer*, *bitch*, and *faggot*. I didn't hear these words during the morning coffee, but I heard all of them my first weekend in the RSP. I was a 50 year old warrant officer, and I was still anxious about fitting in here. I was an EO officer, but I refrained from entering into the leadership moments I was teaching about. I considered the insecurities a young gay person might have to cope with, and I felt a tinge of shame for not being more proactive about engaging on the use of these terms. All of this deepened my understanding of the issues and obstacles involved in changing a culture.

By the end of the weekend, I felt comfortable enough to say to the 1SG, "I got to tell you, I have heard no one say the word fuck as often as you do." He apologized, but I didn't insist he stop using the word. I was comfortable with the idea that it did not cause a climate of unprofessionalism, though my mentor Dr. Wiley would one day ask me why.

The next drill weekend, I met a new commander for the RSP.

Life at Camp

I didn't like his vibe. He never made eye contact with me, and he provided no guidance for how I was to serve as his XO. I just hung around, asking the staff if there was anything I could do. I enjoyed watching the recruits' activities, but was eager to be useful. I read everything available about the RSP—what an XO's job was, what basic training was like in 2014 versus back in 1981 when I attended. I also continued doing EO work on my laptop while the cadre did their thing, since the EO position back at headquarters was still vacant.

I found a useful job in the RSP red phase as co-instructor for the SHARP, working with a woman who had been a great friend and ally of mine for years. We incorporated the EO and diversity portion of the program, so I could provide these brand new troops with the organization's vision of inclusion. I felt excited again.

From the beginning, the 1SG and I had conversations about our perspectives on the military. He was a former Marine, battle experienced, and his job was to promote the patriotic privilege of serving in the Army. I was an old administrative warrant officer focused on feminism and how we need to combat sexism. Our binoculars saw different formations, but these exchanges were always respectful, and our mutual curiosity about each other's perspective was refreshing. All of it was carried on with a bit of good humor, and the playful use of the F word.

The 1SG was curious about the diversity trainings we

conducted based on Dr. Wiley's book. He asked me to give the staff a class after the troops were put to bed. I did not recognize that some of my teammates were irritated. I was too excited that a leader *wanted* a diversity class. I had little experience with Dr. Wiley's concepts, but I stepped into the leadership moment. I don't remember what I taught, or all of the examples I used, but I remember a wall of resistance from several of the guys. In fact, the use of the word "guys" was an intense part of the dialogue during the evening's training.

I had adopted Dr. Wiley's stance that "The cavalier use of 'the guys' aimed at women is another version of stereotypical inclusion." J.W. wrote,

> "Women and all the uniqueness they bring to bear are erased when they are categorized as just 'one of the boys,' or 'you guys.' Of course, the use of 'you guys' is often so casual that it has no conscious overtones. However, no conscious intent for its usage makes it no less dysfunctional. Can anyone be certain that the use of 'you guys' doesn't contribute to a subconscious elevation of men over women, especially when contrasted to the lack of usage of the phrase 'you girls' toward a group of men or mixed-gender groups?"

This enlightenment was a perfect example of how words matter. I caught myself when I used *you guys* and trained my brain to strike the term from my vocabulary, unless, of course,

I was talking to a group of men. I found courage at times to step into those leadership moments, when I could casually and respectfully enlighten others on the use of dysfunctional terms. As J.W. reminded me, "You don't have to be the diversity police. Just find your moments."

During the staff training, the 1SG and a few of the unit members welcomed the enlightenment, but there was some rejection from the cadre to the thought of striking the use of *you guys*. We used the term constantly in society, but especially in the RSP. I witnessed them rolling their eyes, and their foreheads furrowed as passionate dialogue about the issue only lengthened the training time. My surprise at this pushback was a fresh round of internal insecurity for me.

The females in the room connected with the examples of unconscious bias and added a few of their own. The 1SG was supportive, and almost defensive, with any "but" or "what about" objections coming from the guys who had never considered male privilege before this. Afterward, the ladies and I huddled in the female barracks for the night. I listened to their lively enlightenment. They spoke about their challenges, frustrations, and some traumatic experiences they carried in their imaginary backpacks so they could keep moving along. We kept our voices down to keep the content of our discussion from the anxious young female recruits, who were excited at the prospect of their future in the Army. I did not know until much later that a few of those guys did not like me one bit, and they let the 1SG know they thought the training was a waste of time.

At the next drill, the RSP sexual assault VA came to me a bit hyped-up about a situation. She told me a young female private had come out of a room with her male platoon sergeant, and she was in tears. The VA checked in with the private, who explained that she'd been sharing some upsetting things about family matters with her sergeant, but she was better now. The VA spoke to the 1SG and advised a policy be developed to ensure cadre were not alone in a room with female recruits. Although it was an incident of professional counseling, the circumstance put both soldiers in a risky situation. The VA told me the 1SG went nuts on her and rejected her counsel. He said soldiers are fucking soldiers, and platoon sergeants need to talk to their recruits in private from time to time.

He said, "We don't need no fucking policy."

The VA was upset. "He says I am being too dramatic about the situation," she said, and she asked me to talk to the 1SG. The 1SG was hyped-up as well about the idea of a sexual assault risk on his watch. I could see the intensity on his face. He wanted everyone under his command to be safe. What I respected about him was his ability to soften and listen, even when I was intense myself. Validating his point, I explained that the platoon sergeant could have the best intentions, but he is still a decade older and 100 pounds heavier than the female recruit, and he has a penis. I had to be blunt and provided him with the awful statistics regarding sexual assault in the military. I reminded him of the TAG's directive to support the SHARP, and how an updated policy to protect recruits and cadre would benefit everyone. 1SG was an outstanding leader. He went to the commander and recommended the policy, then he defended it when the "but" or "what about" objections came up.

Each month at the traditional graduation ceremony for RSP soldiers, the unit invited a special guest to provide a motivating speech and welcome the new soldiers to the Vermont Guard family. An infantry captain and current company commander stepped up in front of about 14 gold phase soldiers, with at least seven females in the class. Three of the females in the front row were officer candidates. They would become commanders, like the guest who stood before them. The captain's speech was full of the same old references to glory. and reminders to be tough no matter what. As he spoke, the phrase *you guys* was used constantly, and I made eye contact with the cadre sergeant who had introduced him. We grinned for a moment. The captain kept using male pronouns and said *you guys* so consistently that I had to look away. The 1SG was next to me and nudged me to look at his notepad. He had marked the number of times the captain used *you guys*. I chuckled with lighthearted amusement, but a leadership moment was nudging me.

After the ceremony, I followed the infantry captain to the exit hall. I asked if I could speak to him. He had a kind face and intense eyes, but changed after I began speaking. I was the XO of the RSP, I was a CW4, and I worked full time running the TAG's EO and Diversity Program, as well as managing the Cultural Transformation Task Force. That should have been a big deal. I first thanked the captain for giving such sound advice and motivational reminders to the new troops. Then I asked if he knew about the TAG's TF and the diversity training the Guard was facilitating. He nodded blankly. I told him how we were emphasizing inclusive terms, and especially trying to recognize that women serve, too. I told him he consistently used male pronouns when talking about first sergeants, supply sergeants, and commanders, and that he'd used the term *you guys* many, many times. I reminded him the class had three female officer candidates right in the front row.

Feeling confident I could inspire him, I told the story about his brother, a full bird colonel and brigade commander, who recently addressed the troops and stated, "I will not use *you guys*, because I recognize we have great female warriors among us." I told the captain that the women in the formation were impressed and felt valued by their commander's intentional inclusion. The captain nodded and said, "Thank you" and left. I told the 1SG and the RSP commander what I'd said to the captain. The 1SG said, "Good, you should have.

Life at Camp

I get using a few *you guys*, but he was terrible. I counted 23 times in a 15 minute talk." The commander just nodded.

The next workday, the RSP 1SG called me and told me that the infantry captain paid him a visit, and he was steaming mad. He didn't appreciate me judging his speech, and he yelled at the 1SG, claiming he had been doing him a favor by speaking to the troops. The 1SG told me he pushed back, saying, "If you have a problem with the CW4, you need to go talk to her. She was right to confront you. We have female recruits who need to be recognized." This relay of the encounter reminded me once again, most people didn't like those leadership moments. I believed the 1SG, and it made me respect him all the more. Years later, I heard the infantry officer gained a reputation as an inclusive leader.

As my year anniversary in the RSP approached, I requested to be transferred back to the JFHQ. I'd completed my field duty to satisfy the command team, despite their failure to use their influence to fill the weekend EO position during my time at RSP. I felt torn, because I loved drilling with the RSP. Many times, I posted on Facebook that these weekends were the best times of my career. I enjoyed being part of the team and meeting the new young recruits who were brimming with anticipation at becoming a soldier. Yet, there was so much work for me in EO, diversity, and the TF.

The RRB was full of people selling the dream, not like at JFHQ, which included a mix of cynics who had "been there, done that," and were riding the wave toward retirement. Near the end of my tour with the RSP, one of the recruiting staffers in the battalion headquarters submitted an article to the diversity newsletter. He wrote about me and my diversity training making a big impact on the entire battalion. When we held diversity trainings, I could count on the 1SG to attend, and his enlightenment was powerful. I felt nervously proud to consider that maybe I did make a difference, despite many not liking me.

The commander, who I rarely interacted with, gave me a *highly qualified* rating on my performance evaluation. He wrote, "CW4 Sumner is an exceptional leader and mentor who has proved to be an invaluable asset to the Recruit Sustainment Program." That was about as personal as he ever got. I returned to the JFHQ unit, and no one seemed to notice I was ever gone.

CHAPTER 20

ENLIGHTENMENT GROWING DIM

★ ★ ★

While I was in the Recruit Sustainment Program (RSP), Dr. J.W. Wiley's leadership moments theory had been a major theme throughout our diversity strategies. We first hired him in February 2014, to speak to the top leaders of the Guard. All the generals, colonels, and top enlisted were in the room—all men. My team from the MWP sat against the back wall and watched in awe. He was very comfortable in a roomful of White privileged leaders.

Dr. Wiley used film clips to provoke emotions related to social justice. One scene was from the movie, *42*, about Jackie Robinson, the first Black baseball player in the Major Leagues.[30] The scene depicted Jackie, (played by Chadwick Boseman) going into the baseball stadium's tunnel to scream his frustration over the overt racism he experienced on the field. Another scene was from the movie, *North Country*.[31] The major character, Josey Aimes, (played by Charlize Theron) attempted to address miners in a union meeting. Many of

---
[30] 42, Chadwick Boseman (Warner Bros. Pictures, 2013)
[31] North Country, Charlize Theron (Warner Bros. Pictures, 2005)

the men were spewing sexist comments at her, even when her father was among the miners in the room.

Dr. Wiley used these dramatizations to help make his point to the Guard leaders. "Are you a leader committed to building a new culture here?" he asked. "You and I, we are leaders. We get paid to be leaders. But is that enough for you? It's not for me. If I see an opportunity to step into a leadership moment and make a difference—to energize somebody and keep Jackie out of that tunnel—I'm stepping into it. I don't think Jackie should be in that tunnel, or a woman walk into a room where men are doing that to her. Is it extreme? Yes, but it's out there. That behavior is out there, and we have a front row seat to it. What are you going to do about it?"[32]

He then put up a quote on the screen:

"We don't see things as they are; we see them as we are," a Talmudic principle highlighted by Anaïs Nin in her work *Seduction of the Minotaur.*

"You have to be receptive to seeing things differently," Dr. Wiley said. "You have to take responsibility for building this culture. Each one of you can't pass the buck for somebody else to fix. If you do, you allow those women in the back of the room, who are not engaged allies, to be like that woman— Charlize Theron's character— didn't deserve to be."

I had a lump in my throat—and I was certain the rest of

---

[32] Dr. J.W. Wiley, 2014, Vermont National Guard Leadership seminar

the women did, too—as eyes in the audience turned to us at the back of the room. I silently gasped, cheering on the inside. Somebody was saying it! This was another moment for me. Another glorious moment fueling my purpose.

Dr. Wiley's audacious style and ultimate coolness at the February lecture secured him the keynote spot for an October biannual Professional Development Day. This was a seminar provided to all Vermont officers and senior NCOs. The TF commander wanted to hear from a well known national speaker, Jackson Katz, but our team soon realized his fee exceeded a Guard budget. Dr. Wiley's fraternity loyalty to our Air Guard EO officer favored our ability to benefit from this experienced professional leader in diversity. The TAG himself came to my office and said, "Book him for October."

Some people definitely did not like Dr. Wiley's style or message. But we only heard these opinions through anonymous feedback forms. Since the generals liked him, we accepted the feedback as the pains of cultural change. During the training year, when I and my staff of EO Leaders attempted to integrate Wiley's leadership moment theory into our diversity and EO trainings, the naysayers didn't hold back their disdain. My boss, an Air Guard colonel at the time, introduced the class and insisted on open minds, cooperation, and engagement. Then he left the room. Soon after, one of the senior NCOs persisted in denying examples we presented to demonstrate disparate treatment or the

Life at Camp

disadvantages experienced by underrepresented groups. He became disrespectful and called out the professor from New York as a troublemaker.

The SARC and I were sweating it out, using our tactful facilitation skills, when one colonel in the room shut the person down. He reminded the NCO of the colonel's directive to support the program. The Air Guard EO officer came in and did a great job de-escalating our disgruntled participant. Chadwick Boseman or Charlize Theron did not get much airtime in our future trainings.

When October came, Dr. Wiley was excited and honored to be addressing the leaders of the VTNG. I had kept in close contact with him throughout the year, often venting the struggles I went through being the TAG's Diversity Manager, but always getting the *Rodney Dangerfield attitude,* "*I don't get no respect!*" from the force. I considered Dr. Wiley a great friend and my secret weapon for inspiration to keep going.

For the October event, 500 or more leaders swept into the fairgrounds at the Champlain Valley Expo Center in Essex Junction, Vermont. It was a sea of uniforms. I was extra nervous. I knew several officers who despised the support I was getting for the diversity program. One of these high-ranking officers pulled into the fairground with the bumper sticker on his car: "Annihilate the Liberals."

I took a deep breath and murmured A.A.'s good old Serenity Prayer. A ten foot by ten foot banner stretched across the stage declaring the Task Force's hallmark principles: DIGNITY AND RESPECT. It also held a beautiful quote from our TAG:

> "We will create and sustain an organization that is dedicated to mission effectiveness, valuing diversity, and ensuring each individual has the opportunity and means to reach maximum potential. We understand and embrace diversity as one of our greatest strengths."

Our team had planted a few questions among our friends to ensure Dr. Wiley would have an opportunity to engage with the audience. We knew few would dare to be negative to the General's guest, but few would dare ask important questions, either fearing they'd appear liberal. Dr. Wiley was his truest self as he told a story describing a leadership moment he faced while traveling with his son on a train. Passengers were expressing their disdain for an old woman who had what appeared to be feces on her pants. Rather than be gracious, some passengers moved away in a huff, even giggling. Dr. Wiley felt he had to defend the woman, who was someone's mother, having a hard moment. He could not remain silent if he was to provide an example to his son. He told us the way in which he respectfully enlightened the passengers with his empathetic grace. He had the courage to reveal authentic emotions, and I considered him as brave as a warrior.

In his opening remarks, Dr. Wiley admitted to his desire to help me out. He told the gathering that I was the most passionate diversity facilitator he ever met. His decision to participate was due to my dedication to helping our organization embrace diversity. He allowed himself to be vulnerable so he could make an impact on that room. I watched him invite courageous combat Veterans to be fearless and to *feel*. He reminded them, "Condemning people out of habit is easy. Overcoming deep seated prejudice takes courage."

The generals were authentically grateful to Dr. Wiley. I never heard of any regret there, but the middle management team wouldn't let me contract him again, citing some fiscal law restriction about using the same source more than once. I knew it was bullshit. RRB and the Air Guard had the same old *friend of a friend* people at training events year after year, getting paid big bucks. Their opposition may not have been racism, but J.W.'s presentation was realism, and the real would not be embraced.

The feedback forms from his training held a wide spectrum of responses. Some did not see any relevance to his story or message within our organization. Many wondered why the Generals had brought him in to speak to military leaders. They did not get the implications of his leadership moment theory one bit. Others flattered our crew and top brass for bringing such a thought provoking, engaging speaker to the event. I felt the full range of judgment from my bosses and peers.

My confidence dimmed. I put it all in my imaginary backpack along with all the other lessons learned during battles fought, and I trudged on.

In December, the TAG, the DJS and the two highest enlisted service members of the Air and Army Guard traveled to the NGB's Diversity and Inclusion (D&I) Workshop with me. I used every minute to promote how gender equality was the means to impact the cultural transformation we sought. Their acts of support put just enough gas in my tank to keep me going.

Early the next year, in an email to the Vermont organization, our TAG announced the termination of the Air Guard Wing Commander, stating the general had lost faith in the commander's ability to lead. These two pilot officers had a long history together, so the chatter among colleagues reflected their encouragement that our new TAG was not playing the good old boys' game. At the time, I had no details, but knew one of the good old boys snitched.

I remembered the officer from our trip to Alpena. He was the one who was inebriated at the River Cove bar. He'd been promoted to Wing Commander, and now he was fired. (The true reason for his firing would come to light several years later, in 2018. *VTDigger* published a series of sensational stories entitled "The Flying Fraternity.")[33] I realized, again,

---
[33] https://vtdigger.org/2018/11/26/flying-fraternity-guard-commanders-wings-clipped-secret-rendezvous//

how my experience in Alpena was very different from that of others. While some of us felt like we were making a difference, the dysfunctional pain was still the undercurrent.

Another year rolled on as we submitted our Legislative Report to Vermont lawmakers with little pushback. Our team presented the Gender Report to VTNG senior leaders for the second year without seeing much change. We continued to hear the denials and justifications for the underrepresentation of diverse groups. Each year, we presented to the same audience, even with new faces, the make-up was predominantly white senior ranking men looking at us, bewildered, as if pondering, why does this matter?

Our MWP sought external training materials to incorporate any enlightenment on sexism or gender bias we could find. Dr. Wiley's book enlightened some, but his training series was too deep and intricate for general troop facilitation. In April, 2015, I received a special invitation to D.C. to be part of a training event entitled, Leadership Evolution. It was financed by the Army NGB-EO and Diversity Office. The program manager from NGB invited me and recruiters from around the country to test pilot this format for training. I was open to any avenues that might shift the cultural roadblocks we kept hitting.

I appreciated the instructors, who were Veterans. They were dynamic presenters, yet I was the lone feminist in the room.

I often brought up the gender bias and sexism that I proposed was an obstacle to troop synergy. I always felt like the obvious was missing from the diversity trainings. In groups like this, the initial rejection of gender bias as a real problem always shocked me for a moment, then I let the annoyance rest in my backpack. The few female recruiters in the room were rock stars in their profession, and as I had seen females do before, they bragged about how they managed the sexism. I could tell they had never considered sexism as something to get rid of, but rather a fact to deal with. My ideas about working to achieve gender equality were downplayed, despite the group setting touted as a safe place to open up.

All this solidified once again how warriors were willing to accept sexism as a part of the culture, something to manage rather than something to eradicate. I provided my feedback to NGB, and I presented the training to our hometown diversity team (CDET) and TF as directed, but the program never took off. Like all of the strategies we implemented, they dwindled into the pile of programs, policies, and trainings, all focused on managing diversity. Leaders were much more willing to talk about the problem than about the solutions I presented.

The SARC and I used *The Invisible War* as a means to reach service members. We played the video during a few trainings at the JFHQ level and at the Army Equal Opportunity Leaders Course (EOLC). We witnessed the anger and disappointment of participants watching the film. Story after story exposed the horribly biased, discriminatory reactions toward men and women who were sexually assaulted by their comrades or superiors. Many who reported their assault received punishment themselves, and they experienced severe retaliation.

The executive producer of *The Invisible War*, Jennifer Siebel Newsom, also produced a 2011 documentary entitled, *Miss Representation*.[34] The film explored how mainstream media contributed to the underrepresentation of women in influential positions by circulating limited and often disparaging portrayals of women in our culture. We opted to show this film as a training tool. The level of denial and defensiveness from the audience did not surprise us.

It was always tough to validate experiences for women without offending the majority of the audience, who were men. A year later, we showcased the producers' follow up documentary, *The Mask You Live In*.[35] This second film focused on the challenges boys and men face negotiating America's narrow definition of masculinity.

The tactics we used to make our case to our audiences were uncomfortable, unnerving, and risky. Regardless of the resources used, a breakthrough seemed impossible. My team

---

[34] https://therepproject.org/films/miss-representation/

[35] https://therepproject.org/films/the-maks-you-live-in/

and I struggled to get through to the masculine mind with our message—sexism obstructed establishing the readiness they all touted as their priority. Over and over, I heard, "It will never change, Doris." Some of my friends suggested I move away from diversity work. They cited, "the acceptance of things I cannot change," from the Serenity Prayer. But I could not abandon my quest. Painful realities kept showing up. Two women came to my office fired up about being sexually harassed by their unit's 1SG . As a senior leader of the enlisted members in a unit, the creed of a 1SG is: The job is people—everyone is a first 1SG's business.

I had developed a personal discipline before I allowed clients to vent—I took a deep breath, and assembled some program disclaimers ahead of time. I had to let clients know immediately, they did not have the protection of anonymity when talking to me. Reporting avenues for protected communication regarding sexual assault had to be reported to a SARC, VA, or a healthcare provider, if the victim wanted to protect their right to file a restricted report. Reading the disclaimer gave me time to calm myself, since I continued to be outraged by every story that came to me. I also took the time to put on my armor—I'd rally my weapons of experience and knowledge, anticipating another battle and wanting to do it right. The initial disclaimer conversation between me and the person with a complaint often put a tone of seriousness in the air. These mind-boggling protocols were continuously reiterated during A.T.s, in newsletters, on posters, and when a new leader took command.

In this instance, the two women asserted their situation was not an assault. I listened as they spent time providing me with details. I had developed my counseling techniques, and I was confident I could effectively detail the process to claim, prove, and receive justice for a substantiated case of discrimination. It was not easy to keep my cynicism quiet.

I took their long statements and attached them to the NGB's form for reporting cases of discrimination, checking the box "Informal." They claimed they tried reporting through the chain of command, and it was not working, so they wanted to go on the record. In accordance with regulations, the informal process should be completed within 30 days. Because the alleged offender was in a leadership role, I notified my boss and the unit commander. After that, the case was out of my control, and the rumor mill hit the fan.

Here was another sexual harassment case, this time, submitted by two women. They worked full time for the Guard. By the time they came to see me, they both wanted to quit their jobs and get out of the service. They were both exasperated at the level of unprofessionalism the leader in this unit could get away with.

There were many complicating factors regarding the situation, but mostly, I believe the case against the alleged offender wasn't substantiated because he wasn't outrageous enough. His behavior, language, and leadership style were acceptable to most unit members, but the effect was an incredibly toxic working atmosphere for the women to endure. The case would take the remainder of the year to conclude. It was one of the most infuriating examples of gender bias I had encountered, and I came close to quitting the Guard myself.

I nagged my boss, the DJS, and the JAG about the case missing timelines, noting the clients' growing impatience. They had long given up hope of any positive outcome, even though the alleged offender was reassigned during the investigation. I knew, also, that one of the victims in the case had been investigated for having an improper relationship. That referral was made by the 1SG to the commander, and an investigator was assigned. The client had relayed this information to me when she filed her discrimination claim.

During my discussion with the DJS to find out why there was a delay in appointing an investigator for the sexual harassment case, the DJS suggested the client was just retaliating against the 1SG by filing this case. The delay in appointing an investigator for the sexual harassment claim was due to the DJS waiting for the outcome of the investigation into a possible improper relationship.

In the meantime, the DJS seemed reluctant to accept the sexual harassment claim and follow procedures to appoint an investigator. I felt compelled to inject the requirement for administrative compliance: we could not dismiss a complaint only because a general thought she was retaliating. The DJS revealed some of his personal beliefs about the relationship situation. I held back my anger, stating rather adamantly, "Regardless of whether or not she had an improper relationship, it does not negate her alleged experiences with the 1SG, and there is another victim claiming the same offenses."

Fraternization in the military is prohibited under the UCMJ. It claims such conduct is of a nature to bring discredit upon the armed forces, or is prejudicial to good order and discipline. This rule always irritated me on the surface; I felt it provided command too much of a subjective article to ignore, or to bring action against someone, too much at the whim of the individual in charge. This is no more evident than in the small hometown Guard—the DJS himself was an officer married to an enlisted soldier. My former boss was an officer married to an enlisted member. These were the leaders now judging an enlisted woman who claimed sexual harassment, suggesting her alleged fraternization with an officer invalidated her claim of discrimination in her job.

I pondered the absurdity. Her alleged inappropriate relationship brought discredit, yet the 1SG's alleged sexual harassment was to be dismissed. I was internally screaming. My conversation with the DJS was an attempt to get compliance with the regulation. We were obliged to inquire into an allegation of sexual harassment. If I had not pushed, the case would have been dismissed, but the DJS said, "OK, we'll assign an investigator to look into it, but I still think there was something fishy going on." Another internal scream, as he walked away.

When I read the reports of the investigations and the findings—both unsubstantiated—it was another punch in the gut. I was sick when I thought about telling the two women the outcomes. I wanted to go back in time to the initial meeting and tell them not to bother filing. Just get out now and be free.

My armor and weapons had failed again. Both women were angry, disgusted, saying, "I hate this fucking place." At times, I'd pass them in the halls of the armory. They never made eye contact with me. Moments of frustration, regret, hopelessness, and insecurity gained momentum, even as my retirement date was now posted in the corner of my bulletin board.

I was obsessively determined.

Still pursuing gender equality, the SARC and I were drafting a proposal to meet the 21st recommendation from the list we had published after the 2011 Military Women's Workshop. The 21st recommendation was to follow-up with a gender mixed working conference, so men could be part of the solution strategies for gender equity.

It had been 5 years since that first workshop.

The conference proposal memo identified our target

audience as a diverse group of men and women from the VTNG. Our objective included revitalizing all of the MWW 21 recommendations. The draft outline for the breakout sessions focused on examining the experience of sexism by women, and addressing the challenges for attaining equality. I presented the memo to my new boss, and we received approval in November 2015, for a November 2016, workshop. I did not know what a challenge the next year would be for me. The women who were not making eye contact with me in the halls were exactly what kept me going.

During the 2015 Thanksgiving break, I reflected on my journey. So many events: The Military Women's Workshop, the Lean In groups, Dr. Wiley, *The Invisible War*, *Miss Representation*, the Leadership Evolution training, the SAPR stand-down, the Wing Commander fired, the Legislative Report, the Gender Report, additional sexual harassment and sexual assault cases infused with gender bias. All of it fueled me with a determination to make the most of the 2016 workshop.

Doris J. Sumner

CHAPTER 21

FIGHTING THE NAYSAYERS

★ ★ ★

THE 21ST ITEM IN THE SET OF RECOMMENDATIONS THAT were derived from the MWW was to ensure that a mixed group of warriors would have conversations regarding the sexist culture that the Workshop had identified as a barrier to equality. The approval of this recommendation had excited me, and I looked forward to orchestrating some intense content discussions around sexism. When my new boss let me know that the senior leaders had appointed a female full-bird colonel as the Officer-In-Charge (OIC) of the workshop, I almost got myself fired. My emotions exploded despite the fact that I didn't know my new boss all that well. He reasoned her appointment was because she was the highest-ranking female in the Vermont Army National Guard at the time.

I did not hold back my rejection of the appointment nor calling the colonel out as an opposer to embracing gender diversity. This was a female soldier who I perceived as rejecting any other avenue to success other than assimilation. I was fortunate, though. The boss was kind enough to allow me some flailing, understanding my emotional investment. He asked me to calm down, and he stayed with me until he was certain I'd heard him say, "I got your back. Don't worry."

But this new attention on recommendation #21 was brewing some informal conversations, too. I knew a bit about the woman they appointed as the OIC, and I suspected she was part of the command team that pushed me out of the JFHQ for some field duty, insinuating I was trying to change a culture I didn't know anything about. It was the year I spent in the RRB because they never could find a position for me in the combat units. She was one of the female leaders in a special meeting the TAG called together before the Workshop was approved.

I only heard of that meeting when the CSM let it slip out. He was in my office after one of our enlisted focus groups trying to prove to me that gender wasn't an issue. He said, "The TAG called for a meeting with the highest ranking females in the Guard to find out if another female workshop is even needed."

I responded; "I'm one of the highest ranking women. Why wasn't I invited?"

Soon after the CSM left my office, the TAG called me. A direct call from the 2-star to me rarely happened. He broke into business after his polite greeting and asking about my family.

"Doris, do you have those 21 recommendations on file that you can send me? I planned a meeting with a few women commanders to review them. I want to find out from a command perspective how they see the gender issues." I couldn't argue with that, but I was perturbed he'd tried to do this without me knowing about it.

Surprisingly, that same day, I saw the TAG at the Burlington International Airport. We both were flying to D.C. for business, and I used the time huddled in the hallway at the gate to promote why we needed the workshop. He was polite, but I noticed how anxious he seemed to find his seat, too far from me to carry on the conversation. By that time, the position of the SARC had changed again, with the addition of a new JFHQ full time victim-advocate (VA) position. The Air Guard hired a full time VA as well. Plenty of resources to respond to offenses. I was still operating a one person shop on weekend duty along with my full time job responsibilities.

The new VA at JFHQ was a male lieutenant. He was a smart man who cared about social justice, with experience serving community support centers. At the same time, I was granted a temporary technician slot to fill, and I selected a male staff sergeant. Having men on the team gave the SARC and I a fresh perspective about how men viewed the EO and SHARP programs.

I remember a particular incident where different

perspectives were glaring. I was notified of a Facebook posting by some members of a combat unit. A male SFC posted a picture of an M16 rifle with a penis on the end replacing what normally would be a bayonet. The caption said, "New Sexual Assault Rifle," and the post had a fake Army nomenclature to go with it. Some members of the unit responded with comments about getting these into the supply chain. Even some young women in the Army posted joking comments. The sergeant who made the post was a combat unit VA for the SHARP.

An officer who saw the post ordered him to take it down, and reported it to his commander. When I brought this up with my new employee, not holding back my disgust and disappointment, he said, "Well, I think it is kind of funny." I was shocked. How could he think it was funny? He was a nice guy, a father. After he'd witnessed sexual harassment in his unit and didn't intervene, he felt bad, so he requested additional duty as an EOL. I tried to listen to his honest justification for seeing the post as funny. He said when he first saw it, he laughed, considering it just dumb humor. He confessed that, only after discussing the post with other EO professionals, he could see how it might be offensive. He went on to say he thought he understood why soldiers joined in—most do not think about it after the initial humor.

The new JFHQ male VA took the offense more seriously, and explained the systematic harm the post brought to unit members. He had major concerns that the combat unit's VA was the one who actually posted the assault rifle. The SARC team recommended having his collateral duty assignment stripped. These two lenses on the case were a valuable lesson for me. The VA officer immediately recognized the impact and although my sergeant was a serious and committed EOL, it took some reflection to consider these seemingly lighthearted jokes as having an impact on the culture.

The new SARC was a senior ranking female from the Air Guard. She was one of the leaders who'd been invited to give the TAG a commander's perspective on the need (or lack of it?) for another workshop. We were not close friends yet, but I asked her what they'd said at the meeting, hoping she would be honest with me. She told me the TAG spoke highly of me and let the group know he had complete confidence in me but wanted to get a female commander's perspective. She told me the women in the meeting, not including herself, told the TAG, "Gender isn't the issue." They placed the problem's focus on mentorship, saying women weren't preparing themselves to compete for promotions. As she told me this, my heart was sad and enraged simultaneously.

A new team of us were now tackling the EO, diversity and sexist culture of the Guard, and already, I knew the TAG was skeptical of the proposal to hold another workshop. It was understandable he'd want to get different views, but I was disappointed he sought perspectives from women who were not in the MWP. To my mind, the leaders he asked were the very service members who did not like women's programs or women's events and did not see the need to point out we were women at all.

The tension between myself and the new OIC began during our initial business meeting. She did not work full time; therefore, I was responsible for managing details for the event, but she got to approve them. The first thing she made clear to me was that this workshop would not focus on gender or sexism. The 21st recommendation clearly stated to focus on what our Women's Council concluded was the barrier to equality, the sexist culture. We sparred about this in front of my new boss, but he did not have my back on the issue. This angered me, and it took a lot of my physical fitness runs and attendance at A.A. meetings to get to an acceptance of things I could not change.

She had her own battle scars from the culture, and she let me know how well she felt she shouldered them. That was what you do to be successful. Basically, suck it up and deal with it. She told me the focus on gender was the wrong path and would not bring the organizational change I sought. The resentment and anger I had for her was heavy. I tucked it away and did my job, noting my boss's words—"I got your back"—were insignificant.

I quickly established an agenda of tasks to accomplish the mission of coordinating a workshop—understanding that 11 months preparation time would fly by. The first order of business was to recruit a council of volunteers to help put the workshop together, because we did not have a budget to outsource any tasks. I invited the Vice Wing Commander of the Air Guard to participate, since he was part of the Cultural Transformation Task Force focused on Air Non-Traditional Roles (NTRs). Our TF team, the MWP Program, hounded his team about barriers to recruiting women as fighter pilots. He was a fighter pilot himself, and he'd been active in the TF, earnestly trying to understand our sexism claims.

In addition to inviting the Vice Wing Commander, I also invited an infantry battalion commander to join the committee for the workshop. He was part of the TF focused on Army NTRs, and he was just as earnestly trying to understand sexism. His contributions to promote the integration of women into combat arms were more concrete. His personality and leadership style were the opposite of the SARC and me. It would have been easy for him to hand off the duty, but he didn't. He breathed the hierarchal structure, and he believed in his power to influence troops and make things happen.

I recalled an earlier engagement with him. We must have been talking about the TF, but somehow the conversation turned to power. The SARC rejected his assertion that all leaders had the power to influence behavior change. She argued, "Leaders can influence, but it is a person's individual decision making which factors into behavior change." I could feel his irritation as he stated, "If I tell Private Snuffy to do something, he is going to do it, because I outrank him. His behavior will change." She kept at him, "Private Snuffy can choose not to do it. They may suffer the consequences; however, they still have to choose to follow your order or not." This went back and forth as she tried to convince the battalion commander. "You can't just tell troops to stop sexually assaulting and expect that to be the solution. We must educate individuals and bystanders on why they need to stop or intervene, so they can make a better decision," she said. We witnessed his bruised ego. He did not concede but exited the room.

The OIC and the two highest ranking officers on our committee were people who did not believe the impact sexism had on the culture. I called on junior ranking service members from the Air and Army formations, too. I made sure our team was diverse in rank, gender, age, and occupation. I had been waiting 5 years since the first workshop and I did not realize how high I'd set my expectations.

The first meeting of the committee was tense, as the OIC attempted to steer the workshop theme away from gender issues and more about diluted diversity. I felt she was purposeful in her attempts to humiliate me, asking everybody to describe what diversity meant to them. She stated, "Chief has her agenda. I have mine, but let's allow the group to decide on what the workshop should focus on." A few in that roomful of white Vermonters mentioned gender, no one mentioned race, and most focused on generational diversity and the toxic leaders who spoiled noble efforts. No one took note of the demographics of the "toxic leaders." I disciplined myself to hear everyone out, but my anger toward the OIC was a rolling boil. She suggested and received group consensus of the workshop name: Leadership Inclusion Workshop. Her smirk revealed she was quite proud of herself.

I outwardly surrendered what I really wanted the workshop to be about, but I was determined to highlight the barriers we were certain impacted a cultural change. Our team drafted an excellent memorandum to announce the event. The announcement from the TAG came out in a memorandum in April touting the November event. The memo to the force included a reminder of the 2011 MWW that had taken place five years before. It had a solid overview of the work done in the intervening years. It talked about how the 21 recommendations served as a strategic outline to address numerous issues as they related to gender equality. It highlighted how the Gender Report was created and distributed annually.

The memo added: "While we make progress, gender is just one focus area to consider while fostering an inclusive climate of diversity, dignity, and respect. We recognize diversity is all-inclusive, and will center our efforts on solution strategies to counteract the negative effects of exclusion based on stereotypes."

I made sure to communicate to my boss the workshop was hijacked, that the 21st recommendation was intended to be a continuum of our work in the MWP and the TF to prevent sexual assault. I said the diversion to a diluted diversity program just "kicked the can down the road," as leaders had been doing for years now. I would do my job, but I was angry, sad, and a bit desperate. My boss was calm, and he kept reassuring me the Workshop would meet the objectives I sought.

The responsibilities overwhelmed me. Although an OIC was appointed, I was the staff duty officer doing all the work. I was also an active member of the National Committee for SEEMs and NGB's Joint Diversity Executive Council. I wasn't a feminist in Vermont alone. I was also actively presenting my theory of gender equality to combat sexism at the national levels of the Guard. Fellow EO managers often sought me out for guidance on EO administrative duties and my proactive diversity strategies. In 2012, I received the SEEM of the Year Award. Vermont was selected to receive the 2015 Joint Diversity Award by NGB's D&I Program. There was a conference in March, and the DJS and I planned to attend the conference to accept the award. The year was already full-speed ahead.

Through our first few committee meetings, we set up logistics for our workshop, planning a keynote speaker and four breakout sessions. I used every ounce of wit and intellect I could muster to ensure gender diversity was one of them. The OIC reached out to contract a transgender woman whom she'd befriended and respected. The woman was a former infantry soldier and police officer. Our team was intrigued. I met with her, but the woman wanted four hours for the educational curriculum she had developed, and she was unwilling to do less than her full class, claiming a keynote speech would leave more questions than answers.

I agreed with her and communicated this to the TAG. The OIC was angry with me when her nod for the guest speaker was denied. I found this ironic; the OIC would rather have four hours educating the force about transgender than a workshop focused on sexism. The tension between us was undeniable and escalating. Anything I wanted to inject into the one day event became an exhausting battle for me. In A.A., they encourage us to pray for our enemies, because we can't afford the weight of resentment. This was a hard suggestion for me to follow right then.

With a 2015 endorsement from Secretary of Defense Ash Carter of Sheryl Sandberg's Lean In campaign, our Military Women's council had been facilitating the Lean Ins.[36] Leanin.org

---

[36] https://www.upi.com/Top_News/US/2015/09/22/Defense-Secretary-Ash-Carter-endorses-Lean-In-Circles/4651442946919/

is a nonprofit organization founded by Sandberg. The mission statement is to empower all women to achieve their ambitions, one circle at a time. The Lean In circles provide peer mentorship, skill building and inspiration;

> Leaning in is not a solo sport. In a world where women still face bias and other barriers at work, Circles are a safe space to share your struggles, give and get advice, and celebrate each other's wins. Whether you need help navigating your new normal at work or are looking for support from women who understand what you're going through, your Circle will give you the boost we all need.

Our MWW embraced the proclamations from the book and website. When I first heard of Sandberg's book, I dismissed it. Some of my women friends were excited about the realities she addressed. I clamored (prior to investigating), "We Lean In enough!" When I saw the partnership letter between the DoD and LeanIn.org, I was surprised and delighted. For a decade, I attended annual conferences and trainings, but they rarely focused the discussion on gender bias and the sexism that preceded sex-based offenses. My end of course surveys always let instructors know the service programs were missing the big picture.

The LeanIn.org memo from the DoD provided us permission to talk about gender, and I found a way to use this every chance I got. The memo supported our efforts to get the discussions going on a monthly schedule during the federal work week, and we had conducted two small workshops during drill weekends. We had a collection of examples where gender did impact everyday realities for women in the force. I asked the OIC to give the MWP an hour during the workshop to present selected stories from the Lean In groups.

With approval for one hour, I set out to gather stories. I put out a notice that I was seeking permission from those who shared at the Lean In Circles, or from anyone who wanted their story heard. I asked for examples of where gender bias, sex discrimination, or sexual harassment had impacted someone's career within the last 12 months. I warned people not to identify individuals or submit incidents that included violations of the UCMJ. I said people could submit anonymously, or they had the option to read their example aloud at the upcoming Leadership Inclusion Workshop.

Within a month, I received more than 50 stories. They came in through email or anonymous letters slipped under my door. I was stopped here and there around Camp Johnson many times to listen to the painful humiliations of disparate treatment. I asked two men to be on the team that would facilitate the Lean In session, helping us develop an outline for the precious hour we had. I wanted our content to reach the men who would be in the audience. The two guys gave invaluable insight on how we could structure the hour. They provided their own stories as fathers of little girls, and I welled up with gratitude.

We planned to show a video clip of Sandberg speaking at the Pentagon about why embracing the feminine is important to a cohesive national defense strategy.[37] In her 45 minute video, she highlighted so many of the gender challenges our team had been trying to point out. Things like *performance bias*, demonstrated as a double bind—women cannot be both likable and competent, but the more competent a man is, the more he is liked. And Sandberg talked about those who are oppressed striving to be part of the majority.

We couldn't play the entire video, but we wanted to show a clip where she stated: "The military can take the lead in breaking down the biases against women and people of diverse backgrounds, to create a stronger force and set the path for the nation." Her words were profound.

Was I just a foolish feminist, obsessed? I put high expectations on the 60 minutes given to me to make an impact. I prayed for serenity and went for another long run run.

---

[37] https://www.youtube.com/watch?v=LTZPvLi3Hdc

Doris J. Sumner

CHAPTER 22
BEHIND THE SCENES
★ ★ ★

The Leadership Inclusion Workshop was shaping into a grand event. Our military operational order ensured there was a diverse group of 350 members of the Vermont National Guard, different ages, ranks, units, occupations and gender. We invited special guests from NGB-EO, and the D&I Program. Representatives from Region 1 attended.

Through my contacts, I was able to contract an esteemed diversity professional for our keynote speaker. He was one of the instructors from the training I participated in with the recruiters from across the country. Although I returned to my home base and presented its content to our state leadership, the curriculum hadn't sparked any real buy in, in my state or any others. However, the instructor was a former Marine who was an EOA. He had his own diversity education company, and he wasn't intimidated by stoic service members who wore body armor around their emotions. He would go deep.

The TAG would open the morning session and introduce the keynote speaker, followed by our MWP who had one hour for the Lean In session. After that, the participants would break into four groups to get acquainted with a round robin of diversity topics. We contracted local presenters to facilitate the topics our committee selected: self-awareness-bias, generational communication, building stronger teams, and gender equality. The intensity and attention to detail needed to coordinate the event were enormous, but I was energized and feeling good about the production. I found ways to integrate the topic of gender that the OIC didn't want.

My good friend and mentor from the University of Vermont, Dr. Wanda Heading-Grant, was at the time, Vice President for the Human Resources, Diversity, and Multicultural Affairs Department at the school. She agreed to take on the gender diversity facilitation block. During my tenure, the Guard had contracted Dr. Heading-Grant to speak at Black History Month events, and she knew many Guard members on a personal level. I confided to her my continuous struggles to talk about sexism with Guard leaders. I thought her prestigious background and credibility might shift perspectives in a way our team was unable to do.

After sending out the call for stories regarding experiences of sexism, I'd received a flurry of stories to add to those I had collected in my heart during the past 11 years. These honest confessions made me cry hard. What touched me was the humiliation in their tone, the powerlessness that powerful warriors felt. Their statements expressed resignation, a testament to their futile attempts to be fully recognized, utilized, and respected.

They did not want to file reports. They wanted someone to hear them and to validate their predicament. Women were damned if they reported and damned if they did not. There were few satisfied customers in the EO business. Hope for a positive outcome for a discrimination situation was long gone by the time the person felt fueled enough to officially report and try to create accountability.

I recognized a lack of emotional intelligence in leaders responding to reports of sexual harassment. When deemed unsubstantiated because of technicalities, many leaders didn't thank the reporter for their ambition to make the unit better. Often, they shamed the person reporting for wasting precious time. Much of the damage was being done unconsciously, without intent, yet it was being done. It reminded me of the childish taunting of tattletale, like they were bad to report a misbehavior.

Through personal interactions, training discussions, workshops, feedback forms, and unit climate assessments, I had a plethora of evidence that demonstrated the harmful impact of sexism on the culture of the Guard. Every case was painful for the victim, and I bore the pain of my powerlessness to prevent these acts from happening.

I took advantage of every opportunity to push what I thought was the solution to the problem. On our way to receive the NGB diversity award, I told the DJS about the 50 stories our team was reviewing for use during the Workshop. I was a bit obsessed about gender equality, but I cared about all forms of injustice happening.

We had created an excellent program. There were five categories for the diversity awards: Army Unit, Air Unit, Army Individual, Air Individual, and a special Joint Award. I had written our submission that was approved by all of Vermont's generals. I showcased the efforts of our Cultural Transformation Task Force and the many volunteers who contributed to the events, trainings, and workshops our diversity team had created. We participated at many cultural venues; which took volunteers, innovation, and creativity to integrate into the Guard's overloaded schedules. We held events on Hispanic, Asian, Black, LGBTQ, Individuals with Disabilities, and Native American representation. We created quarterly newsletters, often highlighting local partnerships or unique service member contributions. But, the main focus for the award was our efforts to eradicate sexism.

On the flight to the awards, the bus ride to the conference center, and every chance I got, I talked about those 50 stories and the urgency to take a stand at the upcoming Vermont Workshop.

I am grateful for the graciousness I often received from senior officials, because I realize now that I was very annoying. As a child, one among five siblings with five cousins living next door, I mastered competitive talking to get my voice heard.

The DJS who was a 1-star general was a thoughtful debater and, he often gave me pushback on my own gender bias. He would say things like, "That has nothing to do with gender. That is about confidence."

An example he didn't see as sexism was the "Pink Pen Story." The author was an excellent writer, and I valued her submission. I kept all the original story documents to myself and paraphrased them to certain leaders, wary of reprisal if they read without prefaces. Perhaps my paraphrasing lost the story's strength.

In her words:

> The Color Pink (and Red)
>
> I am a woman, and I am currently undergoing one of the most feminine experiences of my sex: pregnancy, and the pending birth of my little girl. As a man, I envision the singular embodiment of masculinity to be winning a hard-fought contact sport championship. The rougher and more hard-hitting the competition, the better the sentiment of triumph. Conversely, pregnancy has exposed me to legions of all pink related consumer goods. The descriptive colors of pink for girls and blue for boys are expected gender preferences, solidly anticipated within American culture for decades. In my opinion, there is nothing particularly wrong with the color of pink, however my ideal color choice is red. The

Life at Camp

shade of red is strong. It's confident, it's savvy, and it's tough. But manufactures don't usually fabricate little girl baby clothes in red. Instead, they construct them in my gender's supposed symbolic pink hue.

I am an Engineer Officer in the U.S. Army. By virtue of my profession, I principally work for and alongside males. At least 90% of my everyday vocational communication occurs between and with men. Men who are smart, tough, and completely embody my earlier depiction of virility. And men who evidently prefer the color of blue to that of pink.

Approximately six months ago, I was participating in a normal weekly staff meeting. One of my colleagues glanced over, cracked a smile, and uttered a follow-on joke regarding the pink pen another male soldier was using. What followed was a wolf-pack mentality whereby the weakest, most unmanly amongst them was attacked regarding his selection of writing utensils. During this interaction (and the ensuing follow-on exchanges), I said nothing. I was (and still am) the only women in attendance at that routine assembly. I wondered then (as I still do now), how that group of men exhibiting such lemming like behavior didn't see the irony of that incident. I am a woman. Pink is supposed to be my color. They are making fun of pink. Therefore, they are subliminally lessening the importance of my sex, and thus of me.

Being a minority is inherently more challenging. Representing a singular sect of society encompasses a myriad of complexities not immediately recognized at the beginning of a long career. I do not think most competent and strong military women begin their occupations viewing the male dominated field as anything other than a competition. Hearing Sergeant So-and-so can run his two-mile physical fitness test very fast. This meant, I needed to increase my score by 10% to beat him. I don't want to just be close, I want to solidly be faster than him. What is the toughest job, training, or deployment the Army will allow me to do/attend/complete as a woman? Because that's what I want to do. I'll never be considered equal unless I achieve substantially more than the average male soldier.

Thoughts such as these dominated the early portion of my thus far 17-year Army career. At that time, everything was a competition, and I loved every second of it. It is now 2016. After experiencing well over a decade of seemingly small incidents like the pink pen incident, I've developed a somewhat jaded and more hardened outlook regarding our organization because these types of incidents have not necessarily decreased in scope or frequency.

                    Submitted by
                    Army Female Officer

When I told the DJS the story, he immediately said, "That is not sexism. If anyone should be offended, it should be the guy with the pink pen, not her." I know I shortened the story but, I tried to convey how men dissing pink is equal to men dissing feminine. The banter was offensive to the female in the room. She had no recourse in the situation, because if she called them out, she would get what I was getting from the general. I said, "You are denying the harm, because it is unintentional, but downgrading the color pink disparages the feminine and contributes to the perception of feminine as inferior to masculine." He shook his head, "I disagree."

Later, at the conference, I was sitting with several of my counterparts from across the National Guard, and our DJS was sitting with his peers. The 4-star, General Frank J. Grass, Chief of the National Guard Bureau (CNGB), was there to present the diversity awards. Prior to the ceremony, he provided his thoughts on the Guard's Diversity Program. He announced he would take a few questions after his remarks. He began talking about the integration of women into combat arms occupations. Despite the recent repeal of the Combat Exclusion Rule the Guard was making very slow progress at increasing the representation of women attending MOS once barred to them. He predicted the level of representation was going to take some time to rise, but he assured us we'd get there.

I was anxious as I considered whether or not I wanted to ask a question. It's always risky to be called upon, because even if the speaker isn't silently critical of your *foolish* or *irrelevant* question, you wonder if the other 300 people in the room (military senior officers) are thinking it. I was well aware that my general was with me in the room, too. I'd been scribbling my question and editing it for some time, wanting to articulate an intelligent question the 4-star would be able to answer. When he was done speaking, he invited questions.

I raised my hand immediately. He pointed to me and asked, "Is this a planted question?" I said, "No Sir." I walked to the microphone. It was intimidating. I was close to the stage with the audience at my back. I glanced at my written question and said, "Sir, is the National Guard considering integrating Lean In campaign strategies like the DoD had done, with the Sheryl Sandberg small support groups discussing gender barriers for women in male dominated occupations? We can change the policies, but if the culture doesn't change, the representation will not increase at a pace to make a difference." I was proud of my question and my ability to speak so confidently. He looked surprised and gestured to his staff as he said, "I haven't heard of this campaign, but we will certainly look into it."

Like clockwork, he told a story of a woman he deployed with to combat and her remarkable achievements in the toughest situations we can imagine. He considered my comment of culture to mean the culture of war rather than the culture of androcentrism. I returned to my seat and noticed the silent cheering section of my colleagues. During a break before the Awards, Vermont's DJS wandered over to me and said, "Good question." Then he walked away, as I was swarmed by many female colonels and a few generals. The staff officer for the CNGB asked for my card and said she would email me for information. Although we interacted, Lean In never became a national campaign for the Guard.

One female general took me by the hands, looked me in the eyes, and said, "Thank you for asking the question." Others let me know they read Sheryl Sandberg's book. This was another one of those moments that kept me hopeful.

After the break, the awards protocol officer was setting up the room, I asked if I would be called to the stage, and he said, "Who are you?" I said I was from Vermont, and we were informed we would receive the Joint State Award. He stated only the generals or their designees would be on stage. I was a little disappointed, realizing my DJS did not inform me I would be a designee. I returned to my crew of friends. The award recipients were called and Vermont's DJS proudly took the stage. The master of ceremonies read each citation and the CNGB walked over, gave each person a coin, and shook their hands. Vermont's citation was infused with the work we had been doing to combat sexism. At the end, they all stood together, and Vermont's General smiled for the awkward group photo the military PAO always took.

During the entire ceremony, my allies whispered, "You should be up there." I was a little disappointed again when the General left the stage and went directly to lunch with his crew. He never came over to thank me for my leadership in Vermont, although others in the room congratulated me. In the military, receiving a coin from a high-ranking leader is a special way to be recognized. We don't get bonuses, but if you see a showcase of military coins, you know the person had impressed many leaders. I had a collection, including a 3-star coin I received the year before, ironically for asking another great question. I kind of wanted the 4-star coin that General Grass gave each representative, but the DJS planted the coin in his pocket and I never saw that one.

The DJS and I had another opportunity to travel together in late October, two weeks before our Leadership Inclusion Workshop. This time, we would ride in a car for three hours to Hanscom Air Force Base on the planned to show them a video featuring border. I had especially hounded this general about our gender equality problem statement. I wondered what he thought when the regional diversity meeting was scheduled close enough for a joint car ride with me. We had disbanded the Cultural Transformation Task Force earlier in the year due to its redundancy with the long-standing state diversity council I'd been managing.

I advocated strongly to colonels in the Air and Army Guard to continue to focus on Non-Traditional Roles (NTRs), topics taken up by the TF but not the diversity council. The Air NTR was supposed to identify barriers to recruiting, mentoring, and promoting women in those occupations that had a high degree of underrepresentation; like fighter pilots. After all, the 70-year history of the Vermont Air National Guard pilot program hadn't produced a single female fighter pilot to serve in the Vermont unit. If the Air NTRs subcommittee had taken the task seriously, they could have come to our council meetings with recommended strategies to increase the pipeline for women pilots, rather than the claim they often made: "Women just don't want to be fighter pilots."

In the Army Guard, the NTR subcommittee had a lot of work to do enticing women to transfer to combat arms units. Per the Army policy, they needed senior women in the units before recruiters could bring new citizen soldiers into the MOS schools to be assigned to combat units. Some of us feminists thought the integration policy was a deliberate strategy to slow change.[38]

The policy then required two females: an officer and a mid- level NCO, to be assigned to the combat unit before recruiters could recruit women from the community into combat occupations and assign them to the unit. It was nearly impossible to find two woman who had years of experience

---

[38] https://www.army.mil/article/164066/army_sets_leader_first_approach_to_full_gender_integration

in their chosen profession, and wanted to be reassigned to a combat unit. After being reassigned, they would need to reclassify into a combat occupation, and remain in the combat unit until recruiters successfully processed a new recruit through basic training and MOS school. Adding to the challenge, most qualified women were in their childbearing years. The reasoning behind the policy was the thinking junior women needed women as mentors or to ask those "female" questions men could not answer. Our jaded conversations around the bureaucratic details surmised; sure, women can come into the combat arms, but let's not rush into this.

It was a failed policy and after years of stalled increases in representation, especially in the National Guard, the policy has changed. The military has lifted some combat unit requirements and are witnessing the culture changing at a snail's pace. The transition from male only in the combat jobs to qualified warriors in the combat jobs has taken over nine years. The shifts in the culture are promising, but time is still ticking, and the military remains male dominated.

These were tough roadblocks that needed strong leadership and Affirmative Action Plans (AAPs) to make even incremental progress. Our CDET had been a band of activists putting on cultural luncheons and exhibits. We grew into a well organized State Joint Diversity Leadership Council (JDEC–another acronym we pronounced J-DAK). We still did events, but we had a State Strategic Diversity Plan with measured objectives. The colonels running the previous NTR subcommittees in the disbanded TF, didn't attend the JDEC meetings; any work the TF had accomplished faded into the business of readiness training.

In 2021, five years later, Vermont's 86 IBCT became the first combat brigade in the country to have enough females in leadership to be able to recruit women into units directly.[39] This had taken many years and a deliberate effort on the part of Vermont's leaders. It was gratifying to read the VT PAO news article announcing this accomplishment, despite the Guard disbanding the NTR subcommittees.

In that long car ride with the DJS, I wasted no time on small talk. We were headed to a regional JDEC meeting. Each state has a 1-star general representing their council. Our November Leadership Inclusion Workshop was scheduled for two weeks later, and we planned to show them a video featuring our TAG promoting the Workshop. I would provide a briefing on the Lean In sessions that Vermont had done and planned to continue.

I shared more sexism stories with the general during the drive. He was less defensive, but he wasn't confident the Lean

---

[39] https://vt.public.ng.mil/News/News-Article-View/Article/2588545/vermont-army-guard-becomes-first-state-authorized-to-recruit-women-into-all-uni/#:~:text=Women%20may%20now%20join%20any,to%20the%20recruitment%20of%20women

In meetings would affect anything. I continued advocating for the NTR subcommittees to be reengaged, but he seemed to believe all of the things I claimed the subcommittee could do were already happening.

During these regional meetings, I was often boisterous, never intimidated by the senior ranking officers. I continuously challenged the JDEC Chairperson to solicit the NGB Diversity and Inclusion (D&I) Program to implement some national strategies around gender equality. I suggested partnering with the SAPRO Programs, because the link between gender equality and the strategies to minimize sex- based offenses was so very evident to me.

My own general always kept silent. He did not counter me, nor did he support my findings. It was exhausting to have a game plan, but no firepower. The regional chairs were impressed, and many made commitments to come to Vermont's Workshop. When we returned to Camp Johnson, the TAG wanted a final reading of the conference agenda and details of the event. The meeting was set up two days before the Workshop.

For the allotted time the MWP had been given on the agenda, my team planned to read five of the stories we'd collected. Two would be read by men who were sharing their stories of Leaning In—recognizing sexism, and wanting to lean in to combat it. Our team had read all 50 stories collected and chosen the five that would best capture the spectrum of harm sexism caused. We took into consideration the length of each story and the language used to ensure they were impactful but not distracting. I emailed the final conference script, attaching the five stories that would be read. In the final meeting with the TAG, he said, "I read the stories, they are very powerful. I think this will be good."

I spoke up, "Sir, I think you should know, we collected 50 stories and I think you should read all 50, so you can fully assess the enormity of the issues with regard to managing sexism." The TAG nodded and said, "Sure, send them to me and I will read them." As I made eye contact with the TAG, the DJS sat to his right mouthing the words silently, "Send them to me."

I pretended I did not see him, and I quickly left the conference room, my heart beating. I went to my office and retrieved the 50 stories I had printed out and sealed in an envelope. I wrote a short cover memo reminding the General that I'd promised no investigations. I reminded him this was only a small sample from the prior year, and that the intent was for him to comprehend why we can't prevent sexual assaults if we can't address changing the sexist culture.

I said a prayer, took a deep breath, and swiftly walked past the DJS's office to the TAG's office. As I was greeting his assistant, the TAG popped out of his office and reached out for the envelope. He thanked me, and I left. Making it back to the safety of my office, I exhaled. During the last several years,

I had days when I felt I might have pushed these male senior officers too far. More than once, I feared I'd be fired. I had another one of those panic attacks after making this delivery to the TAG, so I went to the gym.

Saturday, November 5th, 2016, the Leadership Inclusion Workshop was all set and took place on the grounds of St. Michael's College, next door to Camp Johnson.

The contentious national presidential election was just three days away. Most people in the Guard kept their political ideology to themselves. I rarely put much thought to whether any of our generals might be Republican or Democrat.

I wasn't thinking about the possible historic event if we elected our first female president on November 8. My heart was full, anxious, and focused on the day right here, and making it the most successful day of the year for the VTNG. My expectations ran wild.

The night prior, we put together a big dinner at a local restaurant for all the generals, VIPs, and volunteers. The OIC relayed that she could not attend, which suited me fine since I was still carrying a resentment toward her. I had purchased gifts for our team of volunteers—day planners with the words "I'm Leaning In" sketched on the covers.

Everyone was excited, looking forward to the day ahead, and we broke bread while cheering on Vermont's reputation for leading the way. Our generals often brought up the famous order given by Major General John Sedgewick at the

Battle of Gettysburg in the Civil War: "Put the Vermonters ahead."[40] I had that glorious feeling of hope again. We were going to make a difference.

---

[40] https://www.govinfo.gov/content/pkg/CREC-2010-07-12/html/CREC-2010-07-12-pt1-PgS5740.htm

Doris J. Sumner

CHAPTER 23

Moving On

★ ★ ★

THE ADJUTANT GENERAL TOOK THE STAGE ON THE MORNING of November 5, 2016. I was standing in the back of the St. Michael's McCarthy Arts Center auditorium. From my vantage point at the top of the sloped room, I had a heightened view of the 350 service members and guests attending. My heart raced a bit. I thought maybe the TAG might get real about the 50 stories, and talk about why he had invested in the day. Although, I considered the upcoming national election made the topic of gender equality comparable to taking a political position.

The general was an impressive speaker, and the troops liked him. He welcomed everyone and touted the team's celebration of their accomplishment the prior evening. He mentioned the 2011 Military Women's Workshop and the 21 recommendations it produced. Like so many leaders I'd heard before, he watered down the synergy problems that existed within the force. He often said, "We are not perfect, but we can strive to be better." He asked everyone to Lean In (using

Life at Camp

the Sheryl Sandberg theme) and invest in the conversations we'd have during the event. Then the day began.

I held back tears, took a deep breath, and remained at the back of the room. Why was I so invested in having someone with power validate the enormous problem existing all around us? I didn't know why I felt it so strongly. I had many happy, successful, fun years in the Army. I'd been a staff sergeant and was now a CW4. The Guard had provided stability to my life, and yet I was in a knot as to why the problem of sexism was so casually tolerated.

In the front row, the full-bird colonel who was the OIC for the event sat with the highest enlisted female in the room, an Army SGM. With them was the first and only female in the VTNG to reach the rank of command chief warrant officer (CCWO).

These three top women did not like me enough to become my allies. I had known the CCWO for decades, but we were never friends. She was the most focused, intelligent, serious woman I knew around Camp. I was intimidated at the thought of engaging with her, so I opted out. I thought of competing for the post of command chief, but I wasn't eligible at the time she applied. When she was selected as the CCWO, I was excited, knowing she was more than worthy and she'd perform circles around the previous chief.

When the CCWO first reviewed the Gender Report, she gave me pushback about gender being a barrier for women. She was another one of those leaders at the TAG's meeting who had questioned whether gender was even an issue. She talked to me after the senior leader briefing. Taking me aside, she let me know that success was about hard work, commitment, and sacrifice. She touted the many challenges she had overcome as a single mom and a successful Guard member. When I asked her if she had worked harder than the men who previously held her position in order to be competitive for the selection, she replied, "Absolutely." I never felt safe enough to keep pushing the idea to her that women should not have to work harder for the same promotions. She served well in the post and then retired.

The female SGM sitting up front on November 5 did become a good friend, but we always saw the Guard and its cultural issues through very different lenses. She was the only female SGM at the time in the VTNG and only the sixth female SGM in the history of the Vermont Army Guard. I had been hammering all the CSM's since I started gender equality strategies about how to fill the pipeline with more women. I could not convince this female SGM to align with me and forge an Affirmative Action Plan. She had her stories, and she shared them with me, but she did not want them included among the 50 stories. She didn't believe it was a gender problem, often citing generational issues that infiltrated good work ethics and accountability. I didn't disagree, and we had many lengthy discussions on how gender bias infused those issues, as well.

Life at Camp

The keynote presenter for the Workshop did a fabulous job opning the event and motivating everyone about diversity. A former Marine who served as an EOA, his presentation was boosted by facts and by his own stage presence. He was the best dressed person there, with his stylish three piece suit and flashy bow tie. He was skilled at working with military audiences, who often attempted to disengage from what they viewed as soft training.

After the TAG's opening and the keynote's energy, though, things went flat. The TAG was called away at the morning break and rumors spilled into the forum that the Vermont Air Guard was being activated. Several of the volunteers were in shock and became distracted.

The Lean In segment was next, and I was a wreck myself. We had technical difficulties screening the video of Sheryl Sandberg speaking at the Pentagon, and this increased the expectation stress I was already experiencing. After the video, one by one, we told the five stories we'd selected. As I read one of the stories, I made eye contact with the top female leaders in the front row. I thought how powerful their truth could have been, if they'd been willing to talk about their experiences. It shook me for a moment as my resentment tingled at the back of my neck, but I carried on. Our two male speakers were powerfully honest about their daughters and about recognizing their own biases. The last presenter, a female sergeant, was shaking as she held a sheet of paper and read her own story. This was by far the largest audience she ever addressed, and she may have found the high- ranking officers and sergeants intimidating. I was grateful for the courage she displayed. She talked about her promotion to staff sergeant and how proud she felt until the guys she worked with—guys she loved liked brothers—made comments suggesting she'd slept her way to the promotion. She expressed her deep disappointment, her pride replaced with distrust. It made her sad. I held back tears.

After our session, the room broke up and we scattered teams to different halls to receive a round robin presentation of various topics on diversity. I heard the mixed chatter, but I held onto hope that the event would be impactful. Our presentation format kept the students in place while the facilitators rotated every 50 minutes until everyone had heard all four presentations. Within each session, we expected the leaders to identify the challenges related to the topic, with participants offering recommendations to counteract the barrier. It was an aggressive agenda.

I was occupied with administrative issues associated with managing the day, so I couldn't observe the class engagements. But I heard bits and pieces, both positive and frightening. Despite the VTANG's Deployment Activation (the rumor was true), the TAG returned and took part in every topic. I spoke to him, and he was very pleased with how the day went. During the wrap up session, the master of ceremonies facilitated summary discussions presented by each group.

I heard nothing new, but I was pleased everyone was hearing the smattering of recommendations our JDEC had been promoting for years. We organized a short unity run to end the day, and the master of ceremonies provided details for anyone who wanted to join in. The TAG made his last comments. I had no expectations, surrendered and exhausted. He challenged everyone to Lean In and make a difference by being inclusive leaders, then he said, "I'll see you at the unity run." This excited me, our TAG willing to join in, even with so much on his agenda.

It was a chaotic scene, as my team stripped the classrooms and loaded equipment in vans to be taken back to Camp. Service members were loading into buses or jumping in their cars headed home. Within 15 minutes, about 20 of us, including the TAG, were in the parking lot doing stretches before we started the unity run. The event was optional and everyone was aware it covered a one mile loop from St. Michael's College past the gates of Camp Johnson and back to the school.

As we stretched, I released the tensions of the day. I tried to disregard my annoyance that only 20 of the 350 attendees took the time to run. Intolerance crept into my thoughts—it wasn't late in the day; it wasn't a hard run; the TAG was there. I shook off the negative thoughts and took comfort in the positive. The TAG spent the entire day at the event despite the Air Guard activation notification. The general was kind, funny, and pumped up to run. Several soldiers in uniform escorted our small squad of runners to the starting line, and we were all chatting happily about the day. One young woman at her third drill in the VTNG couldn't contain her excitement. She said the day was powerful, and she had learned so much. She conveyed her amazement that this is what she got to do for a drill. As we marched to the starting line, I snapped a photo of her walking behind me. She smiled for the picture. The image still brings tears to my eyes. I never saw her again, but her glee was another glory moment I held onto.

Our TAG was a pilot, and he was still in great shape. He must not have remembered the unity run's scope—a slow run, only running as fast as our weakest link. The idea was to symbolize unity. Volunteers carried a banner that read "Lean In and Lead." They fell far behind the pack as the General set a jackrabbit pace. The former SARC ran with me. We had been partners for the 2011 Military Women's Workshop years before. The memory of the General waving our 21 recommendations in front of the male leaders flashed in my mind. She knew my heart and my commitment to do all I could to raise awareness of sexism in our ranks. It felt great to have her there. It was a fast run, and we enjoyed some banter with the General as we cooled down.

I returned to the College foyer where my team had cleared

the rooms with the director of the college campus. The VIPs were escorted back to their hotels, but the keynote presenter (Former EOA, retired Marine) was still chatting with Guard members on my team. I waved for him to join me, and I would take him back to his hotel. When he got in my car, I started to cry. We'd heard an array of feedback regarding the event, and I don't know what I could have heard to feel satisfied with the day, but I supposed these tears were the rush of emotions finally spilling out of me. I felt safe with this diversity colleague, since he'd witnessed my crying before. We had many conversations over the years. He was another ally fired up about the challenges I faced presenting sexism to an all male leadership.

Since he'd retired from the active duty Army, he'd built his own diversity consulting business. Despite presenting as a well fit Marine, he was gentle and his voice calming. He said, "Doris, Doris, Doris. This was a great event. This was successful." He reminded me that, despite the Air Guard being activated for a deployment that very day, our 2-star general returned, took part in every workshop, and got out there for the run. "Take the win, Chief," he said. "Take the win. You did great."

Prior to the run, at the closing ceremony, the TAG had given me his 2-star coin. It took all my intentional discipline not to gloat at those I resented for not standing with me. It was a win. I had many coins. This was the second TAG coin

I'd received and I treasured it, feeling his authentic gratitude when he shook my hand and gave it to me. I somehow knew the 50 stories made him angry, too, but he wasn't sure what else he could do. Today I understand, one person, one administration, one event can't solve a complicated problem. The general intended to be part of the solution, and I am forever grateful for that.

I dropped my keynote speaker off at his hotel and cried all the way home. I called Dr. Heading-Grant and apologized for not being available after the event to thank her for participating. She was gracious and let me know that discussions around gender bias were challenging, but she challenged them right back.

The 2016 Leadership Inclusion Workshop was behind me now. There would be no woman POTUS yet. What a year it had been. We held a standard military After Action Review to go over our impressions and feedback from the event, minus the OIC. I never spoke to her again. There were few constructive insights on the feedback forms we collected after the Workshop. I was out of gas.

There'd be more in the aftermath of the event, though. I had many bosses during my 13 year tenure as Vermont's SEEM. Although the EEOC directs agencies to align EO Officers under the head of the agency, the Guard always positioned the SEEM under the HRO, a few officers down from the top.

Life at Camp

After all the work I did to coordinate the workshop, I received two letters of reprimand a few weeks afterward. In my three decades of service working for the Guard, I only received three letters of reprimand and they all came within the later part of my career. They came to me when I was a senior warrant officer, a GS12 program manager and from the HRO's who managed me.

One prior reprimand was for being rude in an email. Rather than discuss the context and coach me on what my boss deemed as unprofessional conduct, the HRO gave me a letter to be placed in my file. I rolled my eyes in disbelief. Now, my current boss was giving me two reprimands. One for a minor finance infraction, and the other for emailing two women in the Air Guard.

In the emails, which he printed off, I vented my frustration regarding the collapse of the Air Guard NTR subcommittee. In a discussion with one of the women, I told her about sending a letter to Sheryl Sandberg asking for help. The officer asked me, "Does the command want help from Sheryl Sandberg? Are you working for the command or yourself?" The officer didn't like the strategies I was employing without approval from command. As I saw the emails spread out on the table in front of me, I got a lump in my throat. I was a bit humiliated that these women had sent the emails to their commanding officer. It was another cut from women who saw my strategies as improper, contrary to the standing operating procedures.

The HRO now giving me the reprimands and requesting my signature on them, stated he respected my passion and strong work ethic, saying, "If this were early in the 1900s, you would be like an Alice Paul. I mean that." I rolled my eyes, signed the documents, and put the humiliation in my imaginary backpack.

Later, I had an opportunity to apologize to the commanding officer I'd criticized in the email. He served on the TF as the Air Guard NTR leader. Now he was serving the Air Guard as Wing Commander. I thought about the question the female officer had asked me: Was I engaging in strategies the command wanted, or was I engaging in strategies I wanted? It became apparent to me this push for gender equality was mine and not the Commanders'.

I respected and liked the Commander. I felt horrible that he'd read my judgmental statements about him. For instance, I'd written, "The colonel doesn't get it; they did nothing in the NTR to increase opportunities for women to become qualified for pilot programs."

When I talked to him, I held back tears and said, "Sir, I am sorry that someone gave you the personal emails which described my frustrations at running the MWP. I am sorry I made personal judgments about you to women under your command. I am not sorry for trying to stand up the NTR subcommittee, and I'm not sorry for trying to detail the problem statement to women I felt understood the challenges.

I admit my boldness has become somewhat personal, but it is because I am on the front lines.

I engage with women who are experiencing the challenges of everyday sexism. I want to fix the problem, because I believe that is my job. I hope you will forgive me and allow me to continue to work with the Air Guard."

Relaxed and speaking kindly, the Wing Commander said, "First, I forgive you. I know you are passionate about the issues you claim to be a problem. But frankly, Doris, I just don't see them. I talk to females, and they don't describe their challenges as sexism."

I gave him respectful, calm pushback, pointing to the attachment resources I sent in the emails. I did not back down from the problem statement: Underrepresentation of women in the Guard equals sexism. It was another battle lost. I believed the leaders of the Vermont Guard heard my problem statement clearly, but I also was convinced they would not use their power to fix it, because they didn't believe it.

The end was beginning for me. I had two years until retirement, and I wasn't sure I could make it. I considered resigning early, but a friend, the retirement counselor, said, "Hang in there. Don't let them take your benefits."

Doris J. Sumner

CHAPTER 24

GOING NATIONAL

⋆ ★ ⋆

Life at Camp continued. We heard of a bro kicked out of the good old boys' network. The word was, he brought it upon himself, after all he was the one who reported the indiscretions of the 158th Fighter Wing Commander. He broke the code of silence. (The Wing Commander was fired in 2015, however, the details of the falling out would come out later in 2018 to the public in a series of articles about the VTNG.)[41]

When the Wing Commander was fired, some of us considered that accountability. Thus began an underlying reprisal against the snitch. I had little factual information regarding the investigations initiated against the Air Guard member who reported, but it all reinforced the network of power. When the investigations were complete, he was fired. He had been popular in the boy's club and enjoyed his connections at the Wing and Camp Johnson, but they snapped like fishing wire when it gets stuck in the branches below the river's current.

---

[41] https://vtdigger.org/2018/11/25/flying-fraternity-top-gun-culture-pervades-vermont-national-guard/

In addition to news of these investigations on the snitch, I was hearing about a few high profile sexual assault cases with unhappy feedback from survivors trickling through the gossipy airwaves. These tidbits of information I received through watercooler relationships more than professional feedback mechanisms, were always chipping away at my relevance.

One of the teammates within the SAPRO Program resigned, she was experiencing vicarious trauma. It was too much. I didn't know the details of these life impacting offenses, but I witnessed the pain all around. Perhaps I was suffering from vicarious trauma, too, but I soldiered on.

One MST survivor was a friend. She was suffering physically and emotionally from unhealed wounds, and she gave me permission to talk in my book about her pain. She said the real ongoing hurt was not from the sexual assault she experienced, but how the investigation had focused more on her misdeeds and not the actions of the perpetrator. The investigators were digging into her previous relationships and searching her social media post from years earlier. She ended up losing her job and military membership. Depending on who was talking, the gossip characterized her either as a floozy out to manipulate a senior leader to advance her career, or as a victim of the broken, androcentric system that protected the boys.

Whenever this case came up, my thoughts went back to the list of cases I kept in my heart, cases that cast the woman as the problem. My friend had experienced MST on active duty—she was mistreated after reporting a rape. Then she experienced sexual assault in the Guard. The PTSD from that initial experience, coupled with the years she worked to overcome and thrive as a Guard soldier, had been nothing short of heroic.

Her performance in uniform was always rated as excellent, and she ably shouldered responsibilities to her family while off duty, all the while carrying the heavy backpack of MST. Over and over again, I witnessed the compounding damage, and the hard, enduring work of recovery from this sort of pain. Most of the time, women got out, hurt, frustrated, scarred, perhaps angry, but mostly sad. However, some MST survivors opted to remain in the organization. It is tough to quit the military, because we love the good stuff so much. This didn't erase our pain; it only allowed some of us to try to keep fighting through it.

Survivors came to me and shared the long, hard road of re-building trust in the organization that stripped them of innocent aspirations. They donned the emotional body armor with newfound awareness of enemy forces, but they wanted to achieve success with their brothers in arms equally. These stories were from women in Vermont and women across the country.

The continuous stories of pain refueled me to keep trying to combat sexism somehow.

Dr. Wiley was still a prominent mentor, and he encouraged me to write a book about the constant contradictions I found myself in. The Guard hired me to promote an EO program as well as to expand diversity throughout the force. Yet, often I found myself alone on the front lines, with only a few passionate troops holding up the rear. I had no firepower, air support, or even command authority to tackle what I recognized as the enemy—sexism.

I made a commitment to write a book, but first, I had two more years to deal with sexism from inside the Vermont Guard. I knew that I was taking the problem *to* the problem. It was time to shift gears. I focused on elevating our problem statement—which I deemed accurate—to the national levels of the Guard. We had many validations of our analysis in the annual Gender Report generated over several years, but the product was still an internal report focused on Vermont's demographics.

I had a solid reputation among NGB program managers and my counterparts across the country, who often sought my expertise and counsel. The Defense Equal Opportunity Management Institute (DEOMI), requested me to serve as an adjunct instructor many times during the EO proponent training. It was customary for graduates to come back as guest teachers to augment the permanent staff at the school house.

The NGB-EO and D&I program managers recognized my work, appointing me to sit on numerous National Guard panels. My colleagues in New England nominated me year after year to represent us as the Regional Chair for EO and Diversity. When the vacancy for the national Equal Employment Management Advisory Council (EEMAC), came open, all the SEEMs had a vote and appointed me the EEMAC Chair. This responsibility, authorized travel to other states or to the NGB Headquarters located in Arlington, Virginia as needed to support the entire SEEM community. I valued my credibility, but it troubled me that bringing needed change to the culture I joined decades ago was stifled. Too often, we glorified the symbolic firsts without considering why they even existed as firsts. Why hadn't we always seen a continuous flow of diversified talent?

The emotional ride continued as I marked off the months until retirement. I received notice I was to receive another national award. This time it was the Individual Army Award for Excellence in Diversity from the NGB's D&I Program. An annual workshop was scheduled for October at the Professional Education Center (PEC) in Arkansas.[42] I had been there many times, nothing fancy like the big hotels. I circled the event

---

[42] https://www.pec.ng.mil

date on my calendar, determined to make the most of this networking opportunity. I looked forward to perhaps getting my own 4-star general coin.

The Vermont DJS planned to attend the October workshop, and I invited the female lieutenant colonel who had been a battalion commander in the 86 IBCT. She'd been the lone female in the combat arms occupations of artillery way back before there were valid authorizations for women in combat roles. We'd remained friends over the years. She was among the most senior officers who attended the Lean In meetings. She was not fearful of being brutally honest about the sexism she experienced and how it remained pervasive despite her continued professional development.

Another person who came to the awards conference was the new person selected to be the Vermont Air Guard EO Officer. She was a young, passionate, intelligent enlisted who would have to attend officer training before taking on this new role. I intentionally leaned back on any cynicism regarding the Air Guard's EO and Diversity program, instead deciding to let her evaluate for herself. She would have plenty of time.

At the conference, I was in full networking mode. I knew many of the NGB program managers and just about every SEEM. During the first evening social, I introduced myself to a new NGB Joint Diversity Executive Council (JDEC) Chair. The acronyms and levels of JDEC structure can be overwhelming—basically, in addition to State JDEC chairs; each region (there were 7 in the U.S.) appoints a regional JDEC chair; and NGB appoints a head JDEC Chair for the entire Guard. The JDECs meet monthly in their home state, quarterly in the region, and annually at the NGB level. This is a high-level network of influential leaders tasked with carrying out the national strategic diversity objectives.

The new NGB JDEC Chair was the Delaware TAG, and only one of four women who had led a State NG. I'd been practicing my elevator speech to incorporate key points when meeting with influential people, and I spoke to her about Vermont's Task Force. The Non-Traditional Role subcommittee, the MWP, and our Lean In gender focused meetings. She seemed impressed, but I wasn't sure what else I could say because I wasn't sure what I needed to hear back. In retrospect, I was aiming for someone in power to incorporate what we were doing in Vermont into a national strategy.

I also introduced myself to Shirley, the Deputy at NGB D&I. Shirley worked for the 4-star Chief of the NGB, and I spoke to her about the previous NGB Chief's nod to consider Lean In programs for the entire Guard. Intrigued, she talked with me about what Vermont was doing, and I think I mentioned my book idea.

During the social entertainment, I sat with a female brigadier

Life at Camp

general, Region 1 JDEC Chair. She supported all of my female focused strategies and gave me many opportunities at the regional meetings to brief committee members on successes and challenges. The general encouraged me to keep talking with the NGB JDEC Chair or anyone at the NGB level to promote the strategies of Lean In, Gender Reports, and gender diversity trainings.

The next full day of presentations, Vermont's DJS and the two women who accompanied us to the conference were amazed at the national focus on diversity and the impact inclusive leadership could have on readiness. We shared our enthusiasm for the speakers and the strategies they highlighted. The awards ceremony was a separate event hosted by the General Senior Leadership Council (GSLC—pronounced G-Slick) during their dinner and business meeting. I would be attending only with our TAG. My companions at this workshop offered me congratulations as they stayed behind in the dorm rooms. As I entered a small cafeteria style dining room, I recognized few people other than the National JDEC Chair who I'd just met the day before. She was busy chatting it up with several others. I purchased a soda from the bar and spotted Vermont's TAG laughing with the female brigadier general, the New England JDEC Chair.

I waited a moment to insert myself into a group when

Shirley tugged my arm and said, "Sit here, Chief." We were right up front near the podium. She leaned over and said, "Tell me about your book." We had a fabulous talk, and she seemed genuinely interested in pitching the Lean In to the CNGB. I even took a selfie with her.

The awards master of ceremonies called me up to receive my award, and I did receive the 4-star general coin I'd hoped for, given to me by CNGB at the time, General Joseph Lengyel. During my tenure, I met several CNGBs, but I was especially glad to get a coin from this general. I received a coin from the new National JDEC Chair, as well. My TAG had joined Shirley and me up front, and he seemed proud as I took selfies with him, also. Streamed into the recognition narrative was my work fostering gender equality to combat sexism.

My new appointment as Chair of the EEMAC, provided me continued contact with the NGB JDEC Chair and with Shirley. There were always a number of strategies being promoted to improve diversity within the Guard, but no direct focus on gender equality. Competing agencies and levels of responsibility within the military increased the challenge to gain widespread buy in for combating sexism and promoting gender equality as a dominant prevention strategy for discrimination and assault. I often received a quiet pause and a polite nod when I brought up this focus.

I don't think most diversity professionals thought in terms of sexism, despite running the Federal Women's Program (FWP). Most of the focus regarding sex-based offenses was on sexual assault. I rarely got outright enthusiasm to make sexism an overarching theme of any sort, yet I never spoke to a warrior—male or female—who denied there were sexist attitudes throughout the services at every level, from combat to administration. Regardless of where a person served, to women such bias felt humiliating and relentless.

Vermont's JDEC Chair was our DJS, a 1-star general. He attended the regional meetings where I often made the case regarding sexism impeding equality. He was always quiet at those meetings, but he never asked me to stop promoting the problem statement. With the help of Regional 1 JDEC Chair, I gained some outward support from the other state Generals regarding sexism as a major barrier to gender equality, and some of them adopted Lean In Circles in their own states.

During committee meetings, SEEMs from across the country affirmed sexual harassment as the most pressing discrimination issue they dealt with, although racial issues for some states were more profound. Religious discrimination was prominent in states with a large population of Latter-Day Saints. I had never realized this before, and I knew these issues needed to rise to the fore, as well. I respected that there were other forms of discrimination, and I agreed these topics were due attention, but I kept reminding allies: sex crossed all forms of diversity.

There was an intense meeting wherein the EEMAC advised the NGB and service component program managers (Air and Army) of pressing issues in order to determine the agenda and theme at the next annual NGB workshop. My recommendation was to include workshops around gender equality to combat sexism. I stressed this would minimize sexual harassment or sexual assaults.

Guard survey data and several service studies backed my recommendation for training related to gender equality. I provided a study entitled, "Project Diane" that was completed in January 2016, financed by the Army Research Institute.[43] The Project's coordinators, the Women's Foundation of Greater Kansas City, had explored the potential benefits and barriers to gender integration in Special Forces (known as the Green Berets). In addition to studying explicit policies that structure gender inequality, they also investigated the unofficial, everyday activities that continue to exclude women from ascending to leadership roles.

The Project found a great deal of resistance to gender integration throughout the military. It rooted this resistance to traditional gender stereotypes that are pervasive but are too often invisible to military personnel in their daily routines.

---

[43] https://united-we.org/news/project-diane

Authors referred to this invisibility as *gender oblivion*. As I read the Project, my heart pounded. Someone was naming what I witnessed in every story I was told and every case I processed.

Gender oblivion described the covert ways that gender stereotypes influenced everyday practices of individuals and organizations. The Project claimed that, most of the time, gender oblivion is not malicious, nor is it meant to actively exclude or harm women. But the end result is, it does both.

I thought the Guard would capitalize on these validated conditions. Unfortunately, colonels from the service components downplayed the need to center on sexism. I persisted with my contacts, but as the months moved toward the next workshop, I could only secure a 30 minute block of time to present what I entitled, "Combating the Sexism We Tolerate." My goal of a national priority on combating sexism often had me feeling exhausted.

I marked my tenure in the Guard atop my bulletin board.

I boxed the 17 months remaining before retirement, marking a big "X" after completing each month. On a chilly November day, one of my former EOA's, a sergeant, bounced into my office and said, "I got a sexism story for you." This was a continual occurrence for me.

My bright office, with a window looking at Mount

Mansfield, was at the end of a long hallway, on the second floor of the JFHQ building at Camp. The Army Guard Medical Detachment was at the other end of the hall. If you came to Camp, you often walked up our stairs, turning left for the medical unit and right for the HRO. If you stepped into my space, you were treated to the glorious view out my window. I had been in this office for 17 years now, so my nook was a safe space for many to come and chat.

The sergeant was another excited friend on the brink of retirement from the military. She didn't work full time for the Guard, but worked full time for the Post Office. If you attain 20 years of NG service and get out, you do not automatically receive your military retirement. All NG members with 20 years of service begin receiving the retirement at age, 60. Many drilling members remained in the Guard (maintaining the weekend drill pay) until the mandatory retirement age of 60, so they could receive their benefits immediately. She had decided to retire from the Guard even though she had years before reaching 60. A decade ago, she enthusiastically volunteered to be an EOA at the brigade level, volunteering to be the interim SARC.

Her passionate civil rights heart may have stemmed from being a single mother of three children from a biracial marriage. She was another woman who wore her toughness outright, but was as girly as any pink lady. I loved her sense of bold humor, although at times I cringed, because it was borderline inappropriate, especially from an EO professional. She told me her story with the emotional flurry that makes for pleasant storytelling, covering the hurt underneath. She said, "I was at drill last month working the ranges with the supply sergeant. We went to the ammunition point to get some rounds. The small room was full of other supply sergeants getting their units' portions. The room was crowded, about 20 of us, I think. Then some sergeant who had ammo cans in both hands says, 'I need one more can. If my penis was hard, I could grab it.' They all just stopped and looked at me. It felt like a long time, like they were waiting for me to say something. This probably wasn't polite for an EOA, but I stared at his penis area and said, 'It sucks to be you.' They all sort of laughed. I just hated it, you know? I went outside after, embarrassed. I did not want to go back in. I sort of felt sick, like I am so sick of this shit."

Perhaps it was my own vicarious trauma, but I was sick of this shit, too. Because I witnessed her pain as she told the story. I witnessed the humiliation and utter defeat. We were always trying to be "one of the guys," but they never let us forget we were not. I asked her if I could put this in the Gender Report and share with the Joint Senior Leader Council (JSLC). She said, "I don't care. I'm retiring. I am so done."

She was another woman underutilized. A Veteran of

Afghanistan, and upon returning, they delegated her to the supply room as support help. She earned the rank of SFC, but did the work privates do in supply rooms. I wondered, was the State CSM seeking a position to maximize her talent and keep her in the Guard until age 60? I doubted it. This was how we lost powerful women, and men, too.

I read what I called the "Penis Story," at the next gender briefing for the JSLC.

Following the written statement, I said, "This is a 23 year Veteran who is a tough broad, and yet she felt embarrassed and didn't want to go back into the room. What do you think happens to our young recruits, or women who don't want to put up with that crap? What about other terms that are just hurled out there? There were probably men who thought it was a crass comment, but why did they all look at her? You wonder why women aren't applying to be 1SG or platoon sergeant? If a person had said something racist, would they have looked at the Black soldier to say something? Why is it always up to the minority to fix the problem?"

I reminded the senior staff that the majority always claims everyone is equal, yet they often make it clear, we are different, and they treat that as "better" or "worse" instead of just diverse. I gave the analogy: "If this team was in combat and they came under sniper fire, they would each move to a defensive position to eliminate the threat. They wouldn't have looked at one person to do it. The problem is, they don't all recognize the sexist, childish comment, or the awkward look to the female for a response, as a threat to unit readiness. It's not the one insensitive comment, it is the culture—the everyday comments and acts that create a culture most women, and in fact a lot of men, don't want to be a part of.

"Many people think women only make up 14% of military personnel because women don't want to do the tough jobs. But women do want to do tough jobs. They just want to be equals in the fight."

Doris J. Sumner

CHAPTER 25
Let's Get Real
★ ★ ★

Late in 2017, we briefed another Gender Report to the JSLC with the addition of the "Penis Story," submitted from my supply sergeant friend who had since retired. This was the only new area of dialog between the MWP and the leaders. We provided a five-year review of the status since the Reports were initiated and attempted to praise the Vermont Guard's female growth rate of 1%, seeing it as a sign our strategies were having a positive effect. (VTNG female percentage up 1% versus NG remaining the same.

I still harped on the Army CSM's lack of progress getting women into combat arms units, or even assigned as platoon sergeants in any unit. Year after year, we reported 7% of key leaders were women—not enough power to help change the culture. Anything under 20% meant women were often the only female in a room of male colleagues. Since our sole female SGM had retired, we still had no female SGM and few women at all in the pipeline. The State CSM mansplained again the EPMS, ignoring the reasons women accumulated fewer points to compete. It was another exhausting, pointless brief.

The HRO had a new boss. In my job as the SEEM, I had worked for six different HRO's. When we heard who was selected, many of us in HR gained renewed hope. He was a soldier's colonel, friendly, and loved to chat. He was competent and always wore a grin, regardless whether he was pleased or angry.

I had been in the same office for 30 years now. Although I had the longest tenure of any HR employee, several colleagues had been on the island with me a long time. We often had a jovial time, comparing base camp to the CBS show Survivor and gossiping about who would be voted off the island next. We likened getting kicked off more to being saved than to losing a million dollars.

The large bulletin board in my office was always tracking an array of activities as far out as a year and beyond; my retirement month boasted a big star. The first JDEC meeting that year was the best one I'd experienced. It included a presentation on integrating women into combat arms units in the Vermont Army National Guard, 86 IBCT. The presenting officer was a well respected colonel from the brigade. His organized brief described lines of effort and listed the responsible directorates, programs, and leaders. He identified two courses of actions and talked about the challenges or advantages for each. He even detailed the historic bias that left many women lacking in the competitive skills needed to fill the pipeline with qualified candidates.

Since the TF was dismantled and the JDEC unit representation were mid-level leaders, the urgency of strategic diversity initiatives was waning. In my constant efforts to revive the NTR sub-committee, I asked a colonel from the 86 IBCT to take on the Army NTR subcommittee for the JDEC. He was not a fan of mine, and he wasn't all that nice about his response. He said I focused too much on the problem and not enough on the solution. I defended myself with A.A. reasoning: "If you can't admit the problem, you can't fix it."

Despite not committing to taking on an NTR subcommittee, the colonel asked when the next JDEC meeting was scheduled, and I put him on the agenda to speak. Our Assistant Adjutant General attended the council meeting, as well as the DJS. An unusually high number of prominent leaders attended, including several officers from the brigade and the State CSM. I smirked to myself—representation seemed to matter.

As the colonel spoke, I glanced across the U-shaped table we all sat around to check on my Army MWP Manager. She was a rock star warrant officer, and I never had to enlighten her about the culture our program aimed to change. When the colonel validated women were being underutilized and not mentored in the ways men were, our gazes met. If anyone saw us, they would have recognized our eyes enlarging two sizes as we gasped in gleeful disbelief; was he saying the truth? We even noticed several men shifting in their seats to adjust their discomfort. The colonel got some pushback from the CSM and other leaders, but he handled it well since the two generals were asking pointed questions. The dialogue was splendid.

After the meeting, I sent the Assistant Adjutant General my most sincere email. He was the previous TF manager and the general at Fort Drum who had graciously supported our nudges regarding inclusive leadership. My words in the email sent to him:

> I can't express how satisfying the last JDEC meeting was for me personally and for my MWP team. Since 2009, when we first determined our problem statement—that sexism was impeding professional development for women in the National Guard—we understood the issues and barriers for women in the military predominantly differ from women in other types of work cultures, and yet, women in all workplaces have challenges regarding sexism.
>
> Ever since then, I've had many incremental battles to heighten awareness regarding gender barriers in the military for women. To hear the colonel who briefed on the integration of women into combat, candidly talk about bias, and earnestly seek ways to eradicate the potential for bias that impedes fair progression

was amazing, to say the least. My colleagues of the past would be ecstatic.

Vermont is leading the way regarding the topic. I could provide loads of resources to affirm just what a hard subject gender equality is when women take the problem to male leadership. I just want to thank you for your continued leadership and acknowledgment of the barriers which we will continue to work on for the men and women of the Vermont Guard.

The general responded, "Thank you Doris. This is very much appreciated."

Weeks after the meeting, I checked in with the colonel who provided the excellent briefing. I asked him if he was going to take on an official role for the JDEC. He was curt and said, "No. Nobody wants me to, so I am done." Another loss. My thoughts cynically blamed the bros who got to him.

My emotions were always like a cat toy on a string, up and down, piquing my interest and frustrating me at the same time. Disappointed with VTNG and yet hopeful when I found out I was on the agenda for the upcoming NGB training conference. I was also emailing Shirley from the CNGB Office, nudging her about adding sexism and gender equality to the next D&I Workshop later in the year. I was always making noise. I sent her all kinds of reports and articles supporting our problem statement, along with my presentation for the EO training conference. During one conversation, Shirley said, "Make a short video I can show the Chief of the NGB. That will have greater impact than all the articles." My creative brain went into overdrive.

One day out of the blue, I received an email from a general. He was the Special Assistant to the CNGB. His name was Brigadier General (BG) Andrew Salas. General Salas said he'd been given a copy of my research supporting my planned presentation for the upcoming workshop. He wanted to speak to me. In the email, he congratulated me for harnessing my extensive experience to produce a thoughtful presentation and slate of recommendations.

I was excited and called the General right back. We had a great conversation, and he said he would support this presentation at the next D&I Workshop. I had aimed for the national levels of the Guard, and now I had two opportunities to present the connection between sexism and gender equality.

My last year in the uniform seemed to keep getting better. In April 2018, my full time status was changed from title 32, excepted service federal technician to title 5 competitive service (civilian) federal technician. The status change meant that military membership was no longer required to hold the federal job. I would no longer have to wear my uniform to work (Monday through Friday).

It felt weird for many of us in the HRO who transitioned to civilian status while remaining on the job. We laughed about having to buy dress clothes, since our closets were filled with uniforms and running gear. I would remain in the Guard and need the uniform for my final 11 monthly drills. At this point, I aimed my sights at turning 56 on my next birthday and giving it all up in March 2019.

My plans to open a diversity consulting firm and to write my book were in motion. These final months in the Guard were important for networking. Retired friends had let me know—when you are out, you are out. I wanted to make my last year count.

With new hope for progress, I went to the annual NGB's EO training conference. I was not happy that the final agenda had my presentation squeezed in just before lunch, but it was exciting to see "Combating the Sexism We Tolerate" printed in the program guide. In all of my years attending EO and D&I conferences, there were few agenda items focused on the cultural issue of sexism. Now, I would lead the conversation.

Despite the director of the NGB-EO office being female, she was reluctant to embrace my focus on sexism, and we had difficult engagements regarding business strategies. As Chair of the Equal Employment Management Advisory Council (EEMAC), I was the conduit between all the SEEMs and NGB-EO program managers who influenced policy. The EEMAC was revamping the process for handling military and civilian complaints, adding more training for EO managers

Life at Camp

and staff to improve efficiency, and rewriting our committee charter.

Throughout my tenure as the SEEM, I had engaged often with NGB program managers. But many of my close allies who'd worked there had moved on or retired, and morale was dissipating. It made me sad, and the reality of it weakened my ability to influence national priorities. I had two good lady friends who were as frustrated as I was over the inability to prioritize sexism on the agenda.

Two men in the NGB-EO section had downplayed addressing sexism when I tried to get the subject on the schedule for training. One of the men came from the NGB's Sexual Assault Prevention and Response Program (SAPRO). We had many conversations about the topic of sexism, but it was like talking to the Vermont SGM's who always frustrated me. The two men at the NGB-EO office had a major influence on the training agenda. I resented them, but I was aware of my bias and used my A.A. program to keep it in check. My lady friends at NGB and in the SEEM community were the wind behind my audacity to keep talking about sexism.

The official staff didn't introduce me when it was time for my presentation. Stepping onto the stage, I began speaking, getting a bit emotional telling the "Penis Story" to the small group of SEEMs. I started the session out using the term gals instead of guys, intending to spur a reaction. There were a few Black women in the room who did not appreciate it, and I learned why—the word gal is a derogatory term used in the South to demean women of color. Despite being humbled there, I packed my 30 minutes full of real talk about gender bias and acts of sexism, both unconscious and conscious.

The two men who objected to the subject and the Directorate of EO, refrained from taking part in the dialogue. Placing a blank piece of paper in front of the SEEMs, I asked them to write the number one challenge they faced as SEEMs. Inviting their comments on the importance of talking about the link between sexism and sex-based offenses, I asked them, "Do we need to get real?"

Precisely at 1200 hours, the Directorate said, 'Time for lunch. See you all back here in an hour." She did not thank me. Perhaps my insertions ruffled the status quo; she was most likely managing sexism herself. Before I had time to get angry with her rude attitude, many SEEMs surrounded me, offering overwhelming praise. I soaked it in, feeling fantastic. I went to lunch with my friends. We had great conversations and whispered about the wall of resistance to being real at an EO workshop.

As I stepped onto an elevator, headed to my room for a bit of quiet time, one of the SEEMs across the hotel foyer yelled in excitement, "You rock Chief Sumner! That was some awesome realness." As the elevator door closed and

I pushed the button for floor number five, I teared up with gratitude.

Fully 80% of the comments the SEEMs wrote following my presentation said sexual harassment was the number one issue they had to deal with. There were positive comments about the talk. Over and over again, I received validation from the troops; they recognized the status gap between feminine and masculine. Yet many leaders denied it.

The idea of making the video was still stirring in my head. Shirley wanted to show the CNGB my problem statement. I learned later than most staff officers that it was best to be brief. I also never was brief. But I knew if you wanted a busy commander to listen to you, you had to say something quickly and hold their attention long enough for them to ponder what you said. A quality video could be the attention getter we needed.

The NGB-EO budget did not allocate enough funds to contract a professional agency to produce a video. I would have to find an inexpensive way to develop a quality product. With my new boss's approval, I contacted the Vermont PAO which had the talent and equipment to produce such a video. I wanted the video ready to bring to a Region 1 JDEC meeting where I'd have another chance to present my sexism brief. Shirley told me she'd be at the next venue, and I wanted to impress her.

Our DJS approved the video project. The DJS general and

I had gained a level of respect for what we each wanted to accomplish before retirement. He was scheduled to retire in the coming months and my retirement date was six months after. Over the course of the last year together, I recognized his progress in understanding the unique challenges women face in the tough jobs of the U.S. military. He began helping our team in the MWP develop key talking points to make a greater impact to the leaders.

We'd talked a lot over the years, given his position of leadership with the JDEC. We spent one road trip talking about white privilege for hours. It was a great place to risk raising subjects. Trapped in the car, neither of us would stop talking. I had the faint feeling he was actually getting it.

Now, he seemed to have softened. He accepted that I understood—men work hard to become distinguished officers, earning rank like general or SGM. Men work hard to survive combat, command troops, and make decisions that are life and death matters to so many service men and women. Now, he seemed to understand that women did all these things too, along with managing minority status and sexism.

Since our first contact with the PAO, we'd met a frustrating bureaucratic wall of resistance to creating a video focused on the point we wanted to make. I submitted a letter of intent to the PAO outlining our objective and a rough script. The male lieutenant responded with a resounding rejection, citing policies and misunderstandings on our aim. I was very reactive and emotional in my response. The PAO and I went back and forth, and I included the DJS in some of the conversation. The PAO questioned just about every claim I made about sexism, demanding I prove each point with some data source. The DJS knew my temperament well. One of his direct emails to me cautioned that getting frustrated with the PAO for doing his job would not help us get the project done. I had support for the video, but PAO's were trained to glorify the military, not expose the dysfunction behind our "Mission Accomplished" banner.

The DJS was all in on the project and its intention but, he took a more cautious approach to making the point than I did. He knew Shirley would be in Connecticut at the next Region 1 JDEC meeting. He wanted Vermont to look good there, and he may have even wanted the Chief of the NGB to recognize what we were doing to combat sexism.

A group of young talented service members put together a first draft script we called, "Packing Sexism in the Rucksack." I'd invited them to help out, since hiring a media company was not an option. We specifically made it real and used everyday language to make our case. The scene included two women and two men, all of them National Guard members taking a hike on their day off. They talk about a Guard member who was sexually assaulted by another person in their unit. The conversation included how the offender had a reputation as a sexist but too many people overlooked it because he was a top gun. One actor stated that the SHARP training was not working.

The conversation went on to cover a number of topics, including how sexist words are used every day, leaving many warriors feeling offended, but how it's not safe to speak up. There was talk about how men are harassed for trying to intervene when they observe sexist behavior.

The PAO would have none of it. We argued over scripts for weeks. I had to take in extra Alcoholics Anonymous meetings to manage the huge resentment and anger I built up. If those in power do not buy in to what you are trying to accomplish, it takes energy, resilience, and tenacity to keep trying to sell it. I thought of the Air Guard EO Officer in Alpena convincing the Wing Commander to let the conversations flow. My battle scars were mounting, and I was tired of trying to sell sexism as the problem the military had to solve if it was ever going to get rid of sexual harassment and sexual assault.

If you have rank or power, it's easier to accomplish something. I outranked the PAO, but he had more power. It was infuriating. The generals put the Guard's reputation in the hands of this young, white, male, privileged officer who did not believe we had a sexist organization. The DJS did his best to support the vision I had, but in the end, the final product was amateurish and mundane. The junior team I'd asked to help me put together the video, changed the script as directed. In the short scene, a young female soldier is talking to a male soldier at the base gym. She expresses the challenges she faces maintaining the respect of her unit members. He quips, perhaps an unconscious misunderstanding, "Just be competent."

The TAG followed up the scene with: "Too many women are having these conversations within our organization. Sexism isn't just sexual in nature. It is the underutilization and lack of respect for a person based on their gender identity. Most of the time, sexism is targeted toward women, however, men are treated unfairly based on gender as well. We recognize this as gender bias, and it is affecting our readiness. When a service member doesn't feel respected or valued, they may underperform or leave. We can't afford to lose talent."

I assumed the TAG half-heartedly believed the words written by me in his script. He truly wanted a culture change, but I was not confident he believed gender equality would change it.

Next in the video, two MWP Managers made statements regarding countermeasures to sexism, followed by what I considered an embarrassing finish from the CSM. The DJS directed the CSM take part in the brainstorming meetings to put the script together. I suspected his intent was to hover over our conversations and rein them in. After scrapping many scripts and changing the format several times, often based on the PAO's feedback, we created a draft that didn't include the CSM on camera.

The CSM said, "You are being gender biased right now. You are excluding me." Perhaps my annoyance was visible when I said, "OK, let's work something in." The CSM said, "Never mind," and stormed out of the conference room. He returned to the doorway and said, "Chief, can I see you a minute?" Out in the hall, he chastised me for my gender bias. I was defending myself and the aim of our video when he said, "I don't want to bug you now. You are in a meeting." Completely annoyed, I said, "You came and took me from the meeting, but you don't want to hash this out now?"

In the end, our team used the CSM's own words in the script. He'd shared his own gender bias story, and he retold that. He spoke directly to the camera in a stiff take that looked to me like he was a hostage. He said:

> "I was raised to respect women. I often look at the female in the room after using a cuss word and say, 'Excuse me.' One day, a respected female master sergeant informed me that each time I did, I was treating her different, and not equal to everyone else in the room. She told me if I was going to apologize for cussing, I should apologize to every service member and not just her. This opened my eyes and made me consider what other words or terms I used that may exclude other people."

Life at Camp

The PAO handed me the final floppy disk the day before we were to leave for Connecticut. After watching the video, I had an overwhelming feeling of failure, I wanted to scream, but I laughed instead, and showed a few friends, who had similar responses. Even the DJS smirked, but we took it with us.

Doris J. Sumner

CHAPTER 26
RIGHT ON THE MONEY
★ ★ ★

Senior officers and enlisted attended the Connecticut Region 1 Joint Diversity Executive Council workshop. All attendees were members of their State JDECs, but not all of them worked on diversity or EO as a part of their official daily activities. The Connecticut SEEM was new to the job, but he was highly motivated to build his own JDEC and volunteered to host the meeting. He contracted with a well renowned businesswoman, speaker, life coach, and television host, Liz Nead to provide a gender diversity block of instruction. When I first read the meeting agenda, it impressed me that their state invested in such a national talent.

The SEEM put me on the agenda in late afternoon. I was disappointed that Ms. Nead would leave after her morning presentation and wouldn't be there to hear me. I reached out to her before the scheduled event, and we had a great conversation, including a review of our talking points to avoid mixed messaging. I felt like the country tomboy engaging with the gorgeous entrepreneur. Ms. Nead laid out her argument well, supporting her premise that everyday gender bias impedes equality. She used humor, facts, and her personal experience. She was entertaining, and it was hard for me not to be jealous of her beauty. I liked her and her message. I was excited to see the audience respond to her presentation with significant questions and validations. It made me more eager to do a good job when it came my turn, and the thought of playing our amateur Vermont video was stressing me out.

I worked with the Connecticut team to trim the video. We only played the first scene and the TAG's message. Shirley's flight had been delayed, but she arrived at the meeting just before my presentation, easing my anxiety. Several other SEEMs who had also been at the national workshop were in the audience. I did not do the *gals* loop again. And I skipped the "Penis Story," but was just as emotional when I recounted another example of everyday sexism:

"A young female lieutenant was at A.T. camp conversing with several administrative colleagues near the Headquarters tent. A young enlisted soldier walked by and shouted out to her, 'Hey, there is the best XO [Executive Officer] I ever had.' She said it made her proud as she waved and turned back to her team. One of the other male officers said, 'He just said that because he wants to sleep with you.' She described how this colleague stripped her moment of pride. It was replaced with that pit of annoyance, thinking to herself, 'He can't just let me have the moment.'"

I followed on, "This happens too often for women in the ranks, and it rids us of self-confidence and trust. We have to work harder, smarter, and longer to achieve what men take for granted. Sure, men banter and tease, but it's their cultural lingo, and it brings them closer. The same banter to women from men, often wedges distrust between us. This is the sexism I speak of. The lack of cultural acknowledgment. When we go to war around the globe, we are expected to respect the variety of cultures we encounter. Our understanding of different cultures helps us navigate effectively and gain the respect of our allies. If we are to be inclusive leaders, we must respect gender as a culture."

Vermont's DJS sat quietly as the audience engaged with me. There were smart questions, and I encouraged other states to invest in conversations about gender bias and perhaps try some Lean In groups. One of the SEEMs spoke to me in private. He was at the prior SEEM training where I presented on the same topic. He encouraged me to take my emotions out of the presentation. He said, "You look too emotional, and it is unprofessional, but good job."

Shirley grabbed me and we had a pleasant discussion. I apologized for the video, but she said it was fine. She reminded me how impressed General Salas was with my material. Shirley reassured me I would be a presenter in October, at the next national diversity training event. "I'll be in touch," she said.

It was the end of the day. The organizers had coordinated a group outing tour at the Pequot Museum and Research Center in Mashantucket, Connecticut. It gave all of us time to network with each other, as well as learn about the Pequot Tribal Nation, which many of us had never heard of before this. The Center was an impressive collection of real life scenes of Indigenous people and interactive exhibits. A special cultural meal was provided by the Museum staff, many of whom were Pequot tribal members.

I had an amazing time with great conversations. A few senior officers I'd never met before thanked me for my presentation. One senior female officer sat with me on the bus and told me her personal stories regarding sexism. This always reinforced to me that idea that the issue of sexism needed a safe place to land. She didn't know me, but she appreciated the space and opportunity to share such personal pain. These moments were the emotions I carried, and although some bubbled to the surface when I presented, I didn't want to stow them away just to look more professional.

I met a young lieutenant from New Hampshire, who was the first female to qualify as an infantry officer in NH. She told Vermont's DJS and me about her experience with bias during the application process and throughout her qualification training. She confessed her annoyance at the competitiveness her brothers in arms so often overplayed. If she beat them in any type of competition, they glared their annoyance or made excuses. Her husband was supportive of her accomplishment, but they were both discouraged at the continued cultural barriers women had to overcome. She had such an honest and reflective style. The DJS turned to me after she walked away and said, "You need to get her to come to Vermont and speak to the infantry brigade." My creative mind was sparking.

The next day of the Region 1 workshop was filled with business meetings and the exchange of ideas and working on a cohesive regional strategy to increase and capitalize on diversity.

As soon as I returned to Vermont, I began coordinating an event for Women's Equality Day later that summer. I wanted to bring over the infantry lieutenant from New Hampshire, and I was eager to get a panel of other interesting women. I worked with my MWP Program managers, and we came up with a four-day series of events to celebrate Women's Equality Day 2018.

I had enough experience to know that getting my boss's buy in was crucial to any expectations for success that I had regarding diversity venues. The new HRO was all in and said he would ensure participation. The marketing announcements for our event, to include an impressive lineup of panel guests and presentations, were in our diversity newsletter and blasted on the diversity boards.

Life at Camp

I popped into the Vermont Air Guard PAO one day to pick up some printed material and met a stunning woman officer. I was discussing the September women's event, and somehow, she let me know she was an F-16 pilot. I was instantly starstruck. We walked over to the base clubhouse, and I asked her to tell me everything. I'd met many F-16 pilots before and had worked for and with F-16 pilots over the years, but I never met a female fighter pilot.

For almost two hours, she told me her career story in vivid detail. Pilots from the Vermont Air Guard flight line began entering the club for lunch. One of them was her husband. She blushed and waved. She wasn't from Vermont and hadn't been here long, but I wondered why I never heard about her before. She wasn't currently flying. She told me that her father inspired her to be a pilot, and the movie Top Gun steered her toward being a fighter pilot. She admitted some challenges with being the anomaly—a woman—but she said she'd never experienced outright sexism. She was the first female Viper Pilot at Mountain Home Air Force Base in Idaho.

I listened in awe, waiting to hear how she had ended up here in Vermont, sitting in front of me, without a flight suit on. She had met her husband in an academic course following her F-16 training, but their respective tours separated them. Eventually, they found themselves stationed in Nevada together. They got married and started a family. She left the

F-16 flying program and began flying the MQ-9 Reapers, a remote Piloted Aircraft, some of the most advanced combat aircraft in the world. My heart raced as she told me about saving lives in Afghanistan from a Las Vegas control center. She loved flying, but she was exceptionally happy being able to fly remotely while carrying her children, and then continuing to serve while raising two toddlers. Her husband left active duty and took an F-16 pilot slot at the Vermont Air Guard. She transferred to the 158th Fighter Wing in a non-flying position, and she was enjoying their new life being with the Green Mountain Boys.

Our two hour talk seemed like minutes, and I didn't want to leave. We exchanged contact information. She liked what our MWP was doing, although she'd never heard of the Air Guard MWP Manager. I kept my cynicism discreet. I asked if she'd be interested in participating on a panel at the September Women's Equality Day (Women's Equality Day is August 26 annually, VTNG MWP event held in September 2018). I felt like I'd hit the jackpot. She was eager to support me, but my hope sank when she said, "Let me check with the leadership." She didn't know of their daunting rebuke of strategies I attempted to enact with the Air Guard. I worried that leaders would keep her away from the MWP.

After my letter of reprimand, I was hesitant to recruit an Air Guard female to be a MWP representative. I was cautiously waiting for the right person when a good life a friend, and member of the 158th Fighter Wing, began working at Camp Johnson in a full time position. She was serving on drill weekends as a 1SG, had experience working on the flight line, and had been on deployments with the Wing. She knew the culture well, and she excitedly accepted the collateral duty to be the Wing leader for the MWP. Through her leadership, we secured approval for the fighter pilot to join the panel, and she would be a panelist herself.

Soon after this, my friend Shirley from CNGB office called and surprised me with the news that I'd been accepted as a panelist for the Defense Advisory Committee on Women in the Services (DACOWITS). This was a separate opportunity from being a presenter at the October D&I Workshop. Shirley had been engaging with DACOWITS to ensure they had a better understanding of the differences between Guard issues and warriors serving in the active duty military. I'd heard of the Committee and read many of their successful policy pushes, such as the repeal of the Combat Exclusion Policy, but I'd never engaged with them before. Their website states:

> DACOWITS is one of the oldest DoD federal advisory committees. The Secretary of Defense composed a committee of civilian women and men to provide recommendations on matters and policies relating to the recruitment, retention, employment,

integration, well being, and treatment of service women in the armed forces. Since 1951, the committee has submitted over 1,000 recommendations to the Secretary of Defense for consideration.

Shirley outlined the parameters for my role on the panel. I would be one of five National Guard women testifying for the Committee. My topic was "Sexism in the National Guard." Each member had a maximum of ten minutes to speak. Shirley reiterated the maximum time. She knew I could say nothing in less than ten minutes. I was jumping up and down with equal measures of excitement and terror.

My longtime friends from the NGB were excited to hear of this opportunity. They had a lot of experience with DACOWITS and called to give me support. I notified my boss and the senior leaders. Then I prepared to craft the most important message of my career into a ten-minute speech. I was very nervous about the opportunity, and I reached out to my friend Jacqui. She had worked at the NGB for decades, navigating the leadership, functional, and cultural changes. Jacqui was now in the D&I Program, and she knew Shirley well.

Since this was a special trip to D.C., I was on my own making travel arrangements. The Committee meeting would be held in a fancy hotel, but all the rooms were completely booked up. Finding a hotel that meets the federal per diem requirement can be tricky in Washington. I ended up at some run-down motel that was under renovation. Being a soldier, and considering it was for one night only, I didn't care. The surrounding area didn't look very safe for an evening run, so I called Jacqui. When I told her where I was and sent her a picture, she said, "Oh, no! You won't stay there. Give me 30 minutes, and stay in your room."

I wound up checking out, and I took an Uber to an address Jacqui gave me. It was a beautiful hotel within the per diem rates. When I opened my door, I found an apartment with many luxuries, plus a complimentary dinner pass. I called Jacqui and she told me, "This is where you need to be. Enjoy your evening, girlfriend."

I took a long run on a safe bike path, showered, and ate my free dinner. Then I practiced my speech over and over before sinking into a very comfortable bed.

Thank you, Jacqui.

"Combating the Sexism We Tolerate" was a six slide presentation. I practiced my talking points, filling every second of the ten minutes they'd given me. After thanking the Committee for inviting me, I jumped right into my opening statement: "The 2017 DACOWITS Annual Report solidifies much of what we identify as a problem statement. Women are underrepresented throughout occupations and grades within the armed forces.[44] The objective of this brief is

---

[44] https://dacowits.defense.gov/Portals/48/Documents/Reports/2017/Annual%20Report/DACOWITS%202017%20Annual%20Report_FINAL.PDF?ver=2018-02-28-222504-937

to suggest the reason for the underrepresentation and a bold call to action."

I used only one demographic slide. It highlighted the national representation of women in senior ranks or command positions versus the Vermont numbers for those posts that I'd been showing my local leaders. When requesting the national data, I found myself in another battle to get numbers from the Air Directorate of the NGB. The female colonel I contacted there argued with me about the need to know clause. She had me defending our problem statement, and she had concerns about my presentation. I was running short on patience and wondered why I was the only one looking for this data.

My contacts prevailed on my behalf at the NGB and I got the Air and Army Guard numbers. It did not surprise me to learn the macro picture wasn't much different from the situation in Vermont. The Army National Guard senior representation of women in 2018 was 7%, with a total representation of 17%. The Air National Guard senior representation of women in 2018 was 13%, with a total representation of 21%. Regarding women in command positions, the ARNG was between 3-10% and the ANG was between 5-19%. There was a lot to unpack regarding the overall picture, but to me, it spoke loud and clear.

After highlighting the disparate representation, I went right into what VTNG MWP called the "Gender Gap

Analysis." I spoke clearly and confidently. "We proclaim the culture as the primary reason for the underrepresentation. The secondary reasons, such as lack of interest in joining, having babies, historical institutional barriers, and minimized opportunities for networking and mentoring, are all secondary. Women can do anything they want to do, but if they do not feel valued, heard, respected, or see potential, they opt out. Because, frankly, we have a lot to do." I reminded the audience of research done in 1997, after the Aberdeen Scandal, and how a follow-on study concluded that 26% of women and 7% of men were experiencing sexual harassment during their tenure in the military. I reminded them that the 2017 DoD SAPRO Report had identified the same prevalence.

I called out sexism as a readiness issue.

My heart raced as I hammered our proclamation: "I have hundreds of sad, sometimes tragic stories where women underperform, stop injecting their ideas, and eventually leave the service. Centuries of overvaluing masculine traits and oppressing feminine traits continues. We are not embracing what women bring to the team the way so many corporate organizations and teams have. We can't recruit a general or SGM—we must grow them. Retention is our bottom line. Would you apply for a job with an organization if a third of its employees were experiencing sexual harassment? And decade after decade, the numbers are not changing."

I finished up: "Men and women are not opposites. We are on a gender spectrum. It is time we value the full spectrum of our human resources. The military has been the leader for cultural change in our country. We believe if we change the culture, women will come, they will stay, they will lead. We need to hold our military accountable for a gender balanced power dynamic, because we know diversity makes all things better. It is our time."

The back of the room had a dozen guests, including Jacqui, Shirley, and the NGB JDEC Chair. There were representatives from the Service Women's Action Network (SWAN)[45] and other organizations interested in these topics. The 17 Committee members didn't applaud, but the back of the room broke into applause upon my final words.

Preceding me on the agenda was a brigadier general from New Hampshire, who spoke about the Mothers of Military Service Leave (MOMS Leave) Act[46], a push for all armed services reserve members to receive maternity leave, just as active duty women did. Following me, a warrant officer spoke about lactation support policies that lacked enforcement, and about maternity uniform distribution needed in time to be of benefit to service women. I appreciated these topics, but my gender bias kept thinking about who was still in charge of all this.

---

[45] https://www.servicewomensactionnetwork.org

[46] https://www.congress.gov/bill/117th-congress/house-bill/3688

Another member spoke about the path for women in the NG to reach general officer rank, stating that the secret sauce for promotion was having mentors, champions, and advocates. I kept a straight face, but my mind went to thoughts about all the men and women who do not mentor, champion, or advocate for women, and their reasons more often than not amount to sexism. The woman ended with: "Success is a matter of fitness—mental, physical, social, and spiritual, a message one must live and demonstrate for others, as well."

The final young enlisted presenter spoke of the need for mentorship early on, and she described the isolation many women encounter. I caught the sadness in her subject, as I always did, and I tucked it away.

My presentation was the only session that received applause. I recognized the Committee members' detached stares. They thanked us and sent everyone on a break. The panel thanked each other, as participants came up to engage with us. A mathematician approached me and tried to correct my "third of its employees" statement regarding harassment, but we ended in mutual agreement that the prevalence was too high.

One woman from the Service Women's Action Network (SWAN) handed me her card and said, "I was the one who started clapping. I loved your presentation." An older woman handed me a piece of paper with an author's name and book title on it—*A Vindication of the Rights of Woman: with Strictures and Political and Moral Subject by Mary Wollstonecraft*—and said, "Great job, keep at it."

Then one of the DACOWITS members, John Boggs, came over. He was a tall, handsomely fit man with a confident face. He looked me straight in the eye as he reached out to shake my hand, bending over me a bit where I sat. He said very precisely, "Right on the money."

I was taken aback, and thanked him. He told me he was a retired Marine infantry commander. My presentation had impressed him. He said he started his own consulting firm, doing a lot of training for organizations, focusing on gender bias and other diversity challenges. There were others in line behind him, so he thanked me again and left, but I certainly wanted to keep talking to him.

During my presentation, I'd been asked about NG leaders' responses to my findings. I probably answered too honestly. I admitted conversations were not being held on the topics of sexism and gender equality. As I spoke, Shirley quietly walked up front and handed me a piece of paper, then returned to her seat. On the paper, she'd written, "The NGB JDEC implementing unconscious bias training." When I saw her approach and set the note down, I half feared it would say "You're fired." I found a way to inject the welcomed information back into the conversation, and give a plug to the NGB JDEC. At the end of the event, Jacqui gave me a warm hug and said, "Let's meet for dinner. I'll pick you up." The Committee went back into session, and I stood in the hall of a grand hotel all by myself. I caught sight of a mirror, staring at myself in my Army service uniform, with my hair too short for my liking. Did I do good? I did the best I could.

I went out and enjoyed a long afternoon run, and I was ready when it was time for a good celebration dinner. Jacqui picked me up in her beautiful car, consulting her OnStar service provider to get us to a very nice restaurant. We always jumped into conversations like we lived next-door to each other. No matter the subject, it was engaging to talk to her.

Then she got serious and said, "Doris, your topic will not go anywhere."

My heart sank. What? I couldn't believe it. She told me Shirley was pleased with the presentation, and had even noticed that I was the only panelist who received applause. But Shirley had added I focused too much on gender and not enough on the other wide array of diversity characteristics that the D&I Program needed to work on with the Guard.

Throughout the year, Shirley had brought up my singular focus on gender, but I always defended the significance. What we make right for gender, we make right for every other diversity characteristic, I argued. Gender crosses all forms of diversity. I thought she had accepted and was championing the strategies I laid bare. After that, no matter what else

Jacqui and I talked about as we splurged over dessert, my heart was low.

I got back to my room to pack for an early flight back home. I looked at myself in the mirror again and asked, "Did I do good?"

Not good enough.

CHAPTER 27
FINAL YEAR AT CAMP

★ ★ ★

My final full year at Camp was proving to be the most emotional ride of my life. I had been in A.A. for 29 years. Phil and I raised two children, and we had three grandchildren. Phil, survived active duty Army deployments, two Guard deployments, and was feeling the physical challenges that come from life as a combat soldier. I was a seasoned warrant officer and had spent my adult life at Camp Johnson in the JFHQ.

Just outside the security gates of Camp, they stationed a giant minuteman statue standing on a large piece of Vermont granite. I loved this statue. I saw a warrior and not a man.

The minuteman's long ponytail and physical features didn't define a gender for me. The words etched into the granite read: "Dedicated to all Vermonters throughout our History who served in Defense of the Green Mountain State and our Great Nation." They were inclusive, and I was so glad they didn't include the term "*boys.*"

The Camp Johnson base sat back from the main route linking the towns of Essex Junction and Winooski, though

LIFE AT CAMP

officially on Colchester land. Many could drive by on Route 15 daily and never notice the Headquarters of the Vermont National Guard positioned there. Bland brick buildings scatter the grounds, scarcely any tailored landscaping. The only decorative features are the historic old tanks and planes identifying the place as military.

Right next door to Camp Johnson, sitting picturesquely north of the roadway, is what locals call "The Fort" or Fort Ethan Allen, named after the eponymous American Revolutionary War figure. An 80-foot watchtower made of Vermont granite, sits timelessly at the far east corner of the Fort. The old, colonial brick officer quarters, with tall oak trees in between each building, line the road opposite the parade field. Late in the 1800s, the busy installation was filled with cavalry troops and their horses. Now the area is used for housing, businesses, town garages, and a lovely path through the parade field used by joggers.

Once inside the security gates of Camp Johnson, you pass the Fallen Heroes Memorial for the Global War on Terrorism, installed in the middle of a grassy field. (The Memorial has since been moved outside the security gate, so the public can have easier access). A half wall, built of brick and granite, gently curves around a bronze sculpture of a soldier kneeling in reflection over the boots, rifle, and helmet of a fallen soldier. Plaques anchored into the stone wall list the names of Vermont Guard members who perished in Operation Iraqi Freedom/

Operation Enduring Freedom. The walkway leading up to the Memorial is paved with bricks, etched with dedications to the fallen comrades from fellow service men and women, family, and grateful citizens. The only really beautiful place on the base, in my opinion. I was proud there had been a group of people who made the effort to build and maintain the Memorial. As my retirement grew nearer, I did not take these sights for granted. I took extra time to etch them in my memory. I felt the undercurrent of my emotions—did my service matter?

Many friends I made over the years had retired and, although I missed them, they were out of my circles. Every interaction this final year seemed to bring more intensity to the relationships that remained. I felt like I was always in reaction mode.

During this period, the DACOWITS circulated an email with an attachment that I thought was a copy of minutes from the meeting at which I presented my "Combating the Sexism We Tolerate" speech. There was no mention of the National Guard panel in the document. I called Jacqui and bemoaned the situation to her, criticizing myself for thinking I could make a difference.

I was frantic and desperate, and I turned to the internet to find John Boggs, the Marine infantry commander who had validated my message at the meeting. He graciously responded, and we had a friendly conversation. John Boggs said he would check with the Committee to see why the National Guard panel topics were not included in the minutes. It turned out that the email attachment was not the minutes from June.

I got a serious phone call from a DACOWITS staff member telling me my direct contact with Mr. Boggs had been inappropriate.

The minutes from the meeting did eventually arrive, and a summary of the National Guard panel was conveyed. It included actions for the Committee to follow up on, but no objectives aimed at my call to action around gender equality to combat sexism. I felt a ping of failure again, despite Mr. Boggs emailing me, "Keep pushing the topic."

The fourth Sexual Assault Response Coordinator (SARC) in eight years was selected. He had served as a full time VA and was ready for managerial duties. I respected his intelligence, which matched his compassion for the warriors who sought the SARC's services. We did not have the sisterhood bond I had enjoyed with previous SARCs, which became evident when a man came to us seeking some understanding.

A male officer who sexually harassed a coworker stopped by my office. After the incident was substantiated, and the offender submitted his resignation papers, leaders directed him to serve out his term isolated to a small office, upstairs near the HRO. He had served on the base for decades. During his visit to me, he asked if the SARC and I would meet with him, so he could tell us his side of the story. I had known the officer for many years, and we had a friendly relationship. But after reading the statement from the victim, I lost respect for the officer. I had to maintain my professional demeanor with anyone I had privileged information about, but I agreed to the meeting. I expected he would set up a time for us to listen to him.

I mentioned the invite to the SARC, and he said the man came to him, too, asking for us to get together. The busyness of the days went by. I walked past the downstairs office where the offender had previously worked and saw him back at his old desk. A new female employee sat where the victim of his sexual harassment had worked. I was shocked and went up to the SARC's office. My temperament and tendency to react was always at the tip of my tongue. Emotionally charged, I vehemently complained to him about what I witnessed.

His reply was curt. "Oh, Doris, the guy is resigning. He said he is sorry. He told me his side. What do you want to do, hang him in the foyer?" His defense of the man surprised me, but his defense of the leaders who allowed it bothered me more. I caught the words *his side*, and responded, "Well, I haven't heard his side. Although I was asked to hear his side of the story, apparently, I was not called when he came to talk to you. Regardless of his side, the leaders of this organization have a responsibility to protect employees from men who have sexually harassed women." He defended the officer again, almost sounding like he felt bad for him, saying, "He's losing his career. Isn't that enough?" I had no fight left for the situation, so I walked away, not even asking what his side of the story was.

In the lead up to my retirement, I watched colleagues take over many of my council positions, and it was a relief to have less to do, but I also felt the loss of relevance. Although I kept at my boss to hire my replacement so we'd have transition time before I left, he just barked at me to make a continuity book. I checked off the months on my bulletin board and purged the 13 years of files from my space.

The Director Joint Staff—a man I worked for over many years—retired, and there was no final goodbye for me. Whatever ceremonies they held, I was not there. My respect for him had grown, though, despite the damage some of his early learning curves had cost.

The new colonel taking over as DJS was a well liked officer. He'd made the respective rounds of assignments that propelled him into the DJS slot. I felt a sense of calm about the new power, thinking the learning curves would be shorter.

I took my last Army Physical Fitness Test, maintaining my score above 280, which I had done for decades. Our JFHQ Unit conducted a unity hike climbing Mt. Philo, a peak from the town of Charlotte provided a magnificent view of the Lake Champlain Valley. I was in good enough shape to run up and down the trail, taking photos of unit members to seize these rare moments among playful soldiers.

Some of us ladies would take occasional afternoons off for spectacular day hikes. The hike coordinator, my friend Karin, called them "Women Empowering Women" time. She had coordinated the hikes for years, inviting women to enjoy the opportunity to network and bond. She created a logo and T-shirts. Some of her brother coworkers in the RRB gave her shameful pushback, sending out emails in jest that called for some male bonding time. One senior sergeant even created a logo, calling it "Men Making Men More Powerful."

It was a busy summer, and I was enthusiastic about coordinating the four-day event for the Women's Equality Day 2018. I was grateful the fighter pilot and the infantry officer agreed to be on the panel. Attendance at diversity events normally was comprised of the warriors who didn't need any cultural enlightenment. I could always count on my women warriors to show up for support. I conveyed to my boss and the DJS the need to direct employees who really needed enlightenment to attend. They nodded, suggesting to me that they agreed. This was the final hoorah, and I felt like I had found a voice that could expand people's understanding.

Just before the event in September, I was off to Cape Canaveral for my last gig as an adjunct instructor for the Defense Equal Opportunity Management Institute (DEOMI). I loved DEOMI, and its location didn't hurt. This year, I finally gained a permanent sergeant in the EO office who would drill

Life at Camp

with me. She and two other Army soldiers would also attend the EOA Course at DEOMI.

My good friend, and the former 1SG from the Recruit Sustainment Program, had retired to Cocoa Beach and lived right there on Patrick Air Force Base. It thrilled me to have the opportunity to instruct, assist Vermont soldiers in the course, and visit my friend again.

I was working with other instructors, fellow SEEMs. We bonded over the hard work of managing the program we had no power over. When venting frustrations over a particular case and my strategies to solicit accountability from commanders, one fellow SEEM said, "You like to fight." At the time, I couldn't see the enormity of my journey, going from a tomboy to a truck driver in the Army and on to becoming a feminist activist. I didn't recognize how I used my personal pain or regrets to relate when responding to the pain shared with me. I took every case personally, and perhaps my bias interfered with just being an advocate of a process.

I embraced being beside the Atlantic Ocean and savored every sip of my favorite coffee as I walked the beach before reporting to work. I knew I would never be here again in uniform, and I wept a bit when I thought of the long road since I'd first attended a course at the school house ten years before. Somehow, reenergized, I returned to Vermont, back at Camp, geared up to make the upcoming Women's Event the best ever.

My new boss and I had several hyperemotional meetings. I pushed for more support during the Lean Ins, more unconscious bias training, improved engagement for the NTR subcommittee, and we were refining a policy for reporting incidents of sexism outside the formal process to track the prevalence of events and the command response. I liked the new boss, because he was chatty and challenged me. But I often felt he was a chameleon and patronized me when he was tired of bantering.

All summer, as the Women's Equality Day approached, I engaged with my boss and the DJS about the event. I felt like I was being especially assertive, attempting to get 86 IBCT leaders to attend the event.

The diversity events I scheduled over the years were primarily during the technician workweek, not interfering with the hardened training schedules of the military. This four-day event would be during the workweek, Tuesday through Friday. I used every marketable asset available to me. Sending out emails, pinning up posters on the diversity boards, announcing at our quarterly meetings, and including the information in the biannual diversity newsletter. I asked the TAG to send out an email encouraging support of the Women's Equality Day schedule, but instead of the TAG sending it, my boss sent out a standard announcement. The effort to get leaders as enthused as I was about the venue was exhausting.

LIFE AT CAMP

I was proud of the all-female lineup for the event. Beginning on Tuesday, September 11, we would have an esteemed panel of female guests, including the fighter pilot, Mary, the local CEO of Vermont's largest power company, the battalion commander in the brigade who first served in artillery combat units, the first infantry branched officer from New Hampshire, an Army platoon sergeant (the only one we had), and an Air Guard 1SG (who were few and far between).

I contracted a facilitation team to present a one day workshop on Wednesday. A member of the team was a local feminist, Jan Reynolds. She had done a few gender diversity sessions for us over the past year. She was an adventurer, athlete, author, and diversity facilitator. Her book, *High Altitude Woman*, was about her experience as one of the first female mountain climbers to embark on treacherous journeys.[47] She had also competed as a biathlete in the early days of the sport. Since the Vermont Guard had a robust Mountain Warfare School, and a Biathlon Program, I hoped to lure interest from members of the unit.

Thursday would be movie day. One movie in the morning, and one in the afternoon. I selected *North Country* for the morning. The movie was dated, but who doesn't want to see Charlize Theron? We chose another dated movie, *Iron Jawed Angels* for the afternoon. These were movies to evoke

---

[47] High-Altitude Woman: From Extreme Sports to Indigenous Cultures--Discovering the Power of the Feminine by Jan Reynolds (Inner Traditions, 2013)

conversations about the historical challenges women endured and how stereotypes developed.

The final day, I would give my presentation, "Combating the Sexism We Tolerate." With the Marine commander's comment—"Right on the money!"—still bouncing in my consciousness, I felt confident that I could appeal to those in the organization who had shrugged off my gender diversity strategies. I was ready for pushback from the most defiant antifeminists. My alcoholism and codependency too often drove the incessant expectation that I could make things happen, if I only tried hard enough. My ego had been bruised many times. The lesson, of course: my serenity is inversely proportional to my expectations.

Recovering alcoholics are taught through painful lessons, one day at a time—honest work done for the right reasons would always benefit our higher power and not our own inflated ego. This recipe could have brought me more peace, but I could not see it clearly.

CHAPTER 28

Go Fuck Yourself

★ ★ ★

I WENT ALL OUT FOR THE WOMEN'S EQUALITY DAY 2018 event. I lugged over every poster, banner, handout, or pictorial display I'd put together in the last decade. The Army Aviation Support Facility (AASF) cclassroom we used was on the third floor of the expansive flight facility, a mile from Camp Johnson on the way to the Air Guard, with the Wing and the Burlington International Airport's busy runway in view. The large sunny classroom could seat sixty. I hung the huge ten-foot banner we'd used at the 2011 Workshop—"Pursuing Excellence Through Diversity"—inside the room, filling the whole expanse of one white wall. Just inside the entrance doors of the facility and in the halls, I marked the venue with signs directing any participants to the classroom.

I had conducted many classes in this room in my tenure as the SEEM, and I'd always stressed over the technical task of connecting the overhead projector to my laptop. Each instructor who used the room had to hook this up and sign into the system to get their presentation to work through the

Life at Camp

projector. I had trouble with it again, and I was close to losing emotional control. My expectations were stealing my serenity. A technical person came over and fixed the problem. I was already exhausted as I lugged fruit bowls, water bottles, bags of hard candy, and individual snack items up three flights. Finally, dressing up each table with fun facts about women's suffrage, the barren military classroom was transformed into a Women's Military Museum.

I stood in my power pose, looking around the room, my confidence wavering. What else could I possibly do to convince the force that sexism was the hideous parasite oppressing talent and impacting real synergy? "I wish I was better" was the thought always whispering to my ego. The start time approached, and a few employees made their way to the classroom. Mary, our speaker from the power company, texted me that she was trying to find the entrance. Saying a prayer, I went outside to wait for her. I didn't have an official partner for this event, so I asked my friend Karin to engage with people in the classroom until I welcomed Mary and escorted her upstairs.

Mary arrived right at start time, so we skipped our normal social greeting. I'd known Mary for decades, and we had many friends in common. I was proud of her success at becoming CEO of a large business. She had been the keynote speaker for our 2011 Military Women's Workshop. I'd attended several events she took part in, and I'd witnessed her professional success. I was grateful when she accepted our request to speak at this event, donating her time. We hugged and quickly went upstairs.

We arrived in the room to find 17 seats filled. No senior leader from the VTNG was there. Three men sat up front, one of them a senior grade officer, but he wasn't in the leadership command structure. The other two men were friends of mine who worked at the aviation facility. Karin and a few others from our Women Empowering Women group sat with attentive stares. I sat my guest in the front row of tables, facing the Guard employees.

Empty seats scattered about in the large room were painful reminders of another failure. I thanked our guests for their participation in the event, and transitioned to the opening session. The women would introduce themselves and discuss the gender challenges they faced in their careers. And they would talk about some ways they navigated within their male dominated occupations in order to be successful.

Mary spoke first. Her words were soft and deliberate. She said, "First, thank you for asking me to speak to the National Guard and attempt to make a positive difference on such a solemn day. I am from New York City, so September 11 is personal to me. I would do anything the Guard asked me to do to help."

Holding my professional posture, I shifted in my chair up front so no one could see me holding back tears. Each woman was exceptionally powerful, and they allowed themselves to be vulnerable. The participants made thoughtful, appreciative comments about the gender bias the women experienced, and the grit needed to overcome sexism. One man who had served as a 1SG in combat was emotional, professing his respect for women who endure the unnecessary bullcrap.

There were only two Air Guard women in the audience to hear the fighter pilot speak. She talked more about the overall lack of female pilot representation then of personal experience with blatant sexism. Her story demonstrated the enormous commitment and personal sacrifice needed for anyone to pursue such a career. Her talk was smart and inspiring, and it embarrassed me that the Air Guard lacked enough respect to come and listen to her experience.

The lieutenant colonel from the 86 IBCT was as blunt as she ever was, but no men from the combat units came to listen to her, or to the infantry officer from New Hampshire. The Air Guard 1SG spoke about her role and about her experience losing out twice before finally being selected as a 1SG. She explained her strategy of reaching out to the successful men and asking them bold questions: "What do I have to do to make rank?" Much of the feedback she received from men indicated she'd have to work outside of her comfort zone and her culture zone. She understood she'd need to push, but the way to achieve success from the men's perspective felt more like a maneuver than a privileged place to strive for.

The panel event ended, and small friendly conversations ensued. Saying goodbye to Mary, I couldn't help but apologize for the TAG's absence, but she knew the deal and said, "I was here for you." Cleaning up the room, I was steaming mad. I couldn't wait to change into my physical fitness gear and run. My boss texted me: "How did today go?" I responded, "I am angrier than I have ever been at the senior leaders of the Vermont National Guard." He did not respond.

I went for a run and reviewed in my head all the preparation I put into this day. Where did I go wrong? Why was participation less than the gathering for the Black History Month luncheon? I was so sick of trying to make this topic important to men with power. I knew the women on the panel had enjoyed the opportunity, but they were painfully aware that few were interested in their experience."

"Maybe tomorrow will be better."

I went to my office Wednesday morning prior to the second workshop scheduled in the aviation classroom. I went to see my boss and asked him where were all the employees who were supposed to attend the first presentation? Hadn't he or the DJS directed members of the brigade or the wing to be there? He was cavalier with his response, almost asking for pity, halfheartedly apologizing, claiming he couldn't be there since he was in a painful budget meeting. I was emotionally charged, reminding him that we had Mary there, and it was frankly embarrassing that no representative from the Adjutant

Life at Camp

General's office came to thank her. It was September 11! I reminded him of the fighter pilot, and the guest from New Hampshire. My emphasis grew as I spoke about the lieutenant colonel from brigade speaking about the women serving in combat arms units, and no combat leaders were there to hear her.

He still had a grin on his face and was hardly defensive when I said, "Do you know, if I was your wife, I would slam the cupboard doors right now? I am furious."

I left the HRO and headed to the AASF for day two of the Women's Equality Day 2018. I had contracted local author Jan and her co-facilitator Bob for a lot of money to conduct a one day interactive diversity workshop. It was expensive, but I had sufficient diversity funds to cover the cost. I told my boss and the DJS we needed 40 employees to make it worth the presenters' time. I arrived at the classroom, greeted the instructors, and nine students attended. I was boiling inside again, and I had to use every ounce of professionalism not to let it show.

The material and interaction during the workshop were worth the money. The instructors complimented each other. A few of the same friends attended day two, but some new people were there, and the feedback cards were positive. But I left day two still angry, sad, and disappointed. I surrendered to the noise in my head, shaming myself and blaming the Guard for their willful ignorance. It was their loss. My boss didn't even check in.

Day three, movie day was another disappointment. Two guests for the morning show and one for the afternoon. My warrior ladies already saw the movies, so I had no friends attending. One of my former bosses watched *Iron Jawed Angels* with me. He had a daughter, and he asked if he could borrow the movie. He was apologetic to me about the lack of leader support, and he encouraged me not to give up. Now, as a retired civilian working for the Guard, he knew of my long, painful journey, and I appreciated his kind support.

I saw both movies before, but I still cried watching Alice Paul have a tube shoved down her throat. I still cried at the scene of the union meeting when Josey Aimes addressed a room of sexist assholes.

As I went for another long run, I wondered who would attend the sessions on the final day. I had no energy to attempt more solicitation calls, and none for sending another email I was sure most employees would delete without reading. Somehow, I resolved—I would present to whoever came, and I would be just as passionate as I was in front of the DACOWITS or a room of SEEMs. On the last day, three of my women warriors returned to support me. These intelligent, successful women of the Guard believed in my message, but why not men? There were a few new faces, including my husband, for a total of seven participants.

I loved Phil's thoughtful comments and questions. He had a great way of pointing out the obvious sexism that many of us

Life at Camp

didn't even recognize. His long history of serving in combat units, in combat zones where he led troops, was the type of lens needed to add value to the conversation. I wished we could have had a dozen men like him there. My allies in the room made me feel grateful that I had coordinated these four-days of training, regardless of the outcome. Thirty-five employees in all, from a local base with over 900 employees, attended the event. My friend Karin was famous for her fun Facebook posts, so we posted pictures making them look joyful. She helped me clean up the room, and as I packed stuff into boxes, I grieved, knowing my time to retirement was short, and I would never unpack them again.

I felt anger, and it took a lot of recovery tools to push the emotions aside and be present for life. I returned to work the following Monday, marking the days off on my calendar—197 to go. I had a poor attitude, and I was certain to make sure people knew.

I asked my boss about the advertisement for my job, but he kept giving me the brush-off. I inquired about it with the ladies from HRO staffing section. They held the same cynicism I did. The leaders always left us in the dark until they finally flicked on the light and said, "Hurry it up." I knew if they were going to advertise for my replacement within the USAJOBS system for federal employees, it could take up to three months to select a candidate. I figured they'd hire someone after I left, so expecting a transition was pointless. I diligently worked on the continuity book for my replacement to use, and I purged my office.

We did monthly Lean In sessions all year, and in September, we held a review of the topics we had covered over the last six months. Our topics came from the Lean In website. We'd held sessions on the imposter syndrome, about women plagued with self-doubt, especially in male dominated environments. We held a session on the challenges of finding and maintaining a mentor. Men were hesitant to mentor women, fearing someone might falsely accuse them of sexual harassment, or their partner would become jealous. We talked about the double bind syndrome—when a man helps a colleague, the recipient feels indebted to him and is highly likely to return the favor, but when a woman helps a colleague, the recipient's feeling of indebtedness is weaker. She's a communal resource, right? Women are supposed to help people. When men help, it's considered an imposition and he is compensated. When women help, they often get unfavorable remarks on their performance for not remaining focused on their own job.

We talked about the challenges and reprisal that follows if someone intervenes when they witness gender bias or flat-out sexism. These session topics were powerful. Men confessed to their biases and showed empathy for the predicament minority status individuals dealt with in the organization. One male lieutenant colonel from my office admitted that, if he had earnestly intervened whenever he witnessed sexism, he would not *be* a lieutenant colonel.

September's Lean In was approaching in a few days. I got an email from the TAG. He told me he planned to attend. I surmised it was because he heard how angry I was about the Women's Equality Day. I assumed some of the top leaders would be embarrassed that such a well known professional as Mary might be very honest in the Vermont business community. Maybe they feared she'd discuss the lack of leader support at the National Guard women's event that she took part in. After reading the general's email, I responded in my head, "If you really want to impress me, why don't you email the entire organization and tell them you're attending the Lean In session, and not just sneak over to appease me." Step ten of the A.A. 12 steps reminds us to pause, use restraint of pen and tongue, rather than react. Many of us added words to that phrase: restraint of pen and tongue, *email, or text*. I did not respond to the TAG.

I wore civilian clothes now that I was a title 5 civilian federal technician nearing retirement, but most full timers knew I was an Army CW4. I arrived early at the AASF for the 1500-hour Lean In session. An alarm was blasting and about a dozen soldiers who worked at the building were standing outside. I parked my car and approached a group to ask what was going on. No one had any information, so we just stood there waiting for the all-clear. I recognized an Army senior officer who was in charge of a small, special unit based out of this large facility. He knew who I was. A couple years before, we'd argued about the definition of sexual harassment. He was the commander in charge of the sergeant who'd posted the "sexual assault rifle" on Facebook as a joke. His unit members had chimed in with jokes about the Army nomenclature, and about getting the "rifles" into the supply chain. He wasn't happy that his soldier's collateral duty assignment had been withdrawn as a consequence of that post, and he had let the SARC and me know it. In the parking lot, the commander's small crew along with others from various aviation units were dispersed among the cars, but they were close enough to hear some of the banter between various unit members. The commander was joking with his executive officer (XO). She was a young 2nd lieutenant. I knew her because she attended the EOLC to support her unit. Their chatter had something to do with World War II, and she said to him, "You would know. You were there." I think she was teasing because he was a good deal older than she was. He quickly responded with, "Go fuck yourself."

I saw several of the young soldiers nearby smirk, but the lieutenant laughed, amused that she had roasted him. I felt a leadership moment of a kind that Dr. J.W. Wiley had warned me about. He told me I would encounter them often in an environment where verbal sensitivity is seen as a weakness. I chose not to say anything at that moment, because I knew

Life at Camp

it would undermine the commander in front of his troops.

The blasting alarm went silent. We all went about our business. The commander and his crew went to their unit area, and I made my way to the Lean In classroom, still pondering the "Go fuck yourself" comment. The classroom filled up quickly, more than the usual crowd because our TAG was there along with the DJS. The State CSM and a few other senior officers came. I was facilitating the meeting, and the generals sat very close to me.

I opened the session by detailing the topics we would review. We were discussing "intervening when we see or hear a sexist comment." I asked the participants what I should do about witnessing a senior officer telling his XO to go fuck herself? I felt the entire room freeze, and I saw the TAG's face drop. I had to solicit responses. "What do we do?"

I stated, "The XO did not seem offended. She laughed. The young soldiers did not seem offended. What was the harm? The commander and XO probably know each other very well, and this is just every day banter, right?" Participants were delaying feedback, perhaps intimidated by the rank present. The TAG contributed to the conversation, affirming that the language was not professional, and he said that I should confront the officer in private. Others agreed. The rest of the hour was full of honest conversation about the enlightenment that these meetings brought. Many employees confessed they did not consider such phrases, or the lack of intervention, as demonstrating *exclusivity*—excluding someone as a means of discrimination. These interactions of unprofessional banter were the culture; you either joined in or remained out of the circle. The TAG thanked me for holding the Lean Ins and said, "Let's continue to have these important conversations."

A friend came up to me after the meeting and said, "I know the commander you were talking about. He talks like that all the time, but it won't do you any good to confront him. He is famous for saying, 'If you don't feed me, fuck me, or rate me, I don't give a fuck.'" It did not surprise me that he could be so crass, but it definitely made me reconsider my approach for a leadership moment.

Back at my office the next day, I told my boss about the commander's comment. As usual, he maintained a hokey grin and said, "I'll talk to him." Of course, he knew the guy—they deployed together. I suggested he call him right then, with me in the room, but he brushed that off and assured me they would have a serious talk. I wish I had pushed him, but my fight was weakening. I knew there could be reprisal for someone. Once my boss gave him the talk, the commander would tell his XO that someone complained, and he'd jokingly say, "Gee, why can't we pal around? I was just kidding, right?" And the XO wouldn't have the power to be real and respond that she doesn't like being talked to like that. So, the XO would put the comment in her imaginary backpack and drive on, allowing the commander to set the command climate to his comfort. Or more realistically, she didn't even consider it sexism.

I saw the DJS in the hall and engaged with him about the Lean In and the commander's comment. I asked him if something should be done, and he said to let the HRO talk to him. He was a very kind, soft spoken general. He had less of an ego than most of the senior officers I'd worked with over the years. Although I respected him, I still thought his reaction to this situation was weak. I thought to myself, why wasn't anyone angry about sexism? Why couldn't someone in power call the commander to the carpet and reprimand him for such unprofessional language? I was a senior officer, and this leader had no problem talking like that in front of me. Would he have said, "Go fuck yourself" if the General was present? The tip given to me by my friend was no secret—my husband and several other friends confirmed, the commander's favorite comeback when confronted was "I don't give a fuck." I let it go. And I did not run into that commander again, not giving a fuck myself

Doris J. Sumner

CHAPTER 29
THE ISSUE WITH ISMS

★ ★ ★

During October, the National Guard Bureau's Diversity and Inclusion Program held its annual conference at the National Guard's Professional Education Center (PEC). My boss wanted to attend the conference, and I invited the new Air Guard EO officer along. She hadn't completed her certification training yet, but she was still motivated to serve the command in EO. I also invited the female Army battalion commander from the 86 IBCT. The four of us sat together in a room of 300 service men and women from across the country. Many of the participants were EO, special emphasis, and diversity managers. There were also high-ranking service members who sat on State JDECs, and yet many of them had no background in topics being covered at the conference, my boss included.

As General Salas and Shirley had promised, they fit me into the conference schedule as one of four panel members speaking on a diversity topic. Our time slot was at the end of the second day. Each panel member had five minutes to speak. After our presentations, we'd take questions. I met the rest of the panel during a conference social event on the first evening. Each of them had an impressive bio included in the program guide.

Colonel (Retired) Victoria Bowens. a Black woman, with 30 years of Navy experience in Human Resources, Manpower Training and Development. Her topic was racism within the ranks. She was a certified diversity professional, and she held certification as a "Game Changer" within the Office of Personnel Management's New Inclusion Quotient (NEW IQ). She had an impressive list of medals and awards.

Mr. Danny Garceau is an Anishinaabe tribal member serving as Director of the Society of American Indian Government Employees (SAIGE). He spent thirty years on active duty in the U.S. Army and Army National Guard and retired as a SGM. He would share about Indigenous people and the continued oppression against their proud culture.

Chaplain Colonel Larry Bazer was serving as Deputy Director in the Office of the Joint Chaplain for the NGB. Chaplain Bazer was in charge of the development of joint policies, guidance, and programs for the 2,200 National Guard members in the Chaplain Corps. His topic was religious diversity and continued discrimination based on religion, which is often not reported.

The team of panelists were friendly and enthusiastic, eager to learn from each other. I was intimidated. My bio had no professional degree listed. The paragraphs instead detailed the years of work I had been doing in Vermont to bring gender equality to the forefront as a means to combat sexism. I appreciated General Salas and Shirley for including me in this group of established professionals.

At the social, we each talked about the focus of our five minutes, and we determined the order in which we'd speak. I couldn't relax, so I left the event early. In a barren barracks room overlooking the parking lot that stretched across to the social hall, I watched the traffic of conference attendees coming and going. I kept scribbling notes for my talk, trying to maximize my five minutes. My insecurity consumed me.

The quality of the working group topics and conference speakers impressed my boss and the female officers. A top leader from the Office of Personnel Management, Mr. Clarence Johnson, spoke about the pillars of diversity. I'd heard these things before, but I was glad exposure to these ideas continued. He and his team filled his presentation with confirmed facts regarding the lack of growth in diversity within the most diverse organization of our country.

We were all privileged to hear from one of the surviving members of the Little Rock Nine, Ms. Elizabeth Eckford. She was one of the African-American students who, in 1957, were the first Black students ever to attend classes at the previously all white Little Rock Central High School in Little Rock, Arkansas. After being denied entrance by protesters against the Brown v. Board of Education of Topeka decision, a picture of her showed an angry mob following her, threatening and yelling at her. The elderly Ms. Eckford made the trip to the base and sat in her wheelchair on stage. She conveyed such grace and reverence for the National Guard, despite the racism she had to be protected from decades ago.

An executive advisor from the Defense Advisory Committee on Women in the Services (DACOWITS) gave a powerful presentation demonstrating the need for the Committee. My resentment bubbled up over what I perceived as ignoring the obvious—she didn't use the words *sexism* or *gender equality* in her presentation. I had an inner attitude—I was intolerant, hearing about pregnancy and family care plans as barriers for women within the military. I knew these were valid problems, but they were issues *because* the organization, as a whole, was androcentric.

At one point, the executive advisor asked us to note on a three by five card what we considered the most pressing problem for women in the Armed Services. She said she'd give the cards to the DACOWITS President. She called on several participants to share what they had written. My confident boss stood up with his grin, proud of his comment and his question. He shared how sexism is a problem for the command culture and we need to fix it. Then he said, "If you are in denial about it, ask yourself how many of you in here would feel confident recruiting your daughters." I gave him a slight nod of approval for raising the issue. I wrote sexism on my three by five card, and I wondered how many of the 300 cards matched mine.

During the presentations, I continued scribbling notes for my time on the panel. It was the undercurrent of my mood all day. My boss had to leave early, so he wasn't present for the panel. I shrugged off another rejection, always taking things personally and assuming Vermont leaders were not interested in me. I listened as the first two panelists spoke. Each of their messages highlighted the lack of an empathetic culture among leaders, their actions and reactions often revictimizing warriors who brought issues of exclusion to them.

I knew I lacked understanding regarding racial issues. During my certification training for the EOAC in 2008 at the Defense Equal Opportunity Management Institute (DEOMI), the class on white privilege made me cry. It was an emotional breakthrough, and though I still lacked true understanding, I gained compassion. I had little knowledge of the Indigenous cultures many service members represented, as well. SAIGE was an entity I paid little attention to. Not that I didn't care, but these types of issues did not occur for me in my daily life in the Vermont Guard. I felt pride and compassion for Mr. Garceau.

It was my turn.

"Sexism is the readiness issue of our time. In order to eradicate sex-based harm from our force, we must rid our force of the attitude of sexism. Sexism is not just about sex.

Sexism is an attitude that one sex is superior to another. In a male dominated environment, the effects for women are more devastating, but sexism affects all genders.

"The acts and effects of sexism are often unseen and difficult to pinpoint. A lack of confidence is the prominent goal of sexism, much like bullying. The goal is to weaken others to boost your own insecurities. Sexism erodes trust; if you can't trust your battle buddy, you can't be an effective force.

"A sexist culture is the camouflage that predators seek, because the spectrum of behavior isn't interrupted. In the military, sexism is tolerated—if you can't take a joke, you shouldn't be in the military. Often, the jokes in a unit are sexist, because historically we have linked masculine as the 'superior' sex related to being an effective combat warrior. Often, men express their sexuality by objectifying women.

"I'm going to give you two examples of sexism having a devastating impact on retaining talented women in our force. These stories are not meant to revictimize the women who have given me permission to share their pain. I tell these stories so we may spare other women pain."

I knew that military members often expected, when the idea of sexism was discussed, that they'd hear about sexual harassment in the forms of quid pro quo or nasty comments being hurled at women. I had shared these stories before, and I felt compelled to use them in that setting as prominent examples of sexism without the sexual innuendos. I told the story of the female battalion commander speaking at a brigade level operation meeting and the brigade commander's snarky remark, "You don't have to be the smartest person in the room." I also included the "Best XO I ever had Story" and how often, perhaps unconsciously, men chip away at any confidence women attempt to build up. I continued, "Comments like 'Pussy,' 'Bitch,' 'Sissy,' 'You throw like a girl,' 'You let a girl beat you,' 'Women have easier physical fitness standards,' 'She must have slept with the commander to get that promotion,' 'You need to smile more,' and other sexist remarks impact the synergy among our gender mixed teams. These are going unchecked.

"Most of the time, these types of comments are not malicious or done to actively exclude or harm women. But the end result is that they do both. If we as an organization will not invest in understanding the cultural biases regarding gender, we will not change the culture and we therefore continue to camouflage the space for sex-based harms to occur.

"The gender diversity of our force has been stagnant for decades, because most women do not want to manage sexism, and they get out. In order to change the culture, the current leaders must recognize the impact of sexism and hold warriors accountable to an increased level of professionalism rather than tolerate sexism.

"In Vermont, we have integrated Lean In Circles to provide space to talk about gender bias. These small, interactive sessions are a tool to explore our biases and support the countermeasures each of us can do to combat the sexism we often, unconsciously tolerate."

The last speaker was Chaplain Blazer, and our points were amazingly similar. He spoke about often unconscious religious biases showing up in everyday language. But there is risk in calling it out—there is retaliation. Often leaders do not know how to manage the conflict, and the chaplain said many members of the pastoral staff use exclusionary words, also.

It was a powerful 20 minutes chock-full of talk about the cultural challenges facing 430,000 Guard members. The room was silent for a long pause. All the panelists were asked questions, but my topic had the most validations. I was sorry my boss was not there to hear women speak about the reality they felt. They expressed feeling helpless to change the culture and keep doing the jobs they loved. More and more, I was certain that not everyone experiences blatant sexual harassment, but most service members have experienced or witnessed the damaging impact of sexism.

At the break, many came to thank me for bringing the topic up in such a bold way. My fellow panelists seemed impressed with my delivery, and I felt grateful to be among a group of such professional activists. The break provided an opportunity for General Salas and the newest chairperson for the NGB, Joint Diversity Executive Council (NGB-JDEC) to come and talk with me. The new Chairperson, Major General (MG) Richard Hayes, remembered me from a workshop the year before. He said, "I remember you, Chief. I remember because I never forgot that line: *'Sexism is not just about sex. It is an attitude that one sex is superior to another.'* I never heard it explained like that before."

I was invited back the following week for the NGB-JDEC quarterly meeting to give a presentation.

I was pleased.

Back at Camp, I let my bosses know about the invitation and made arrangements to attend. The Vermont TAG was a member of the NGB-JDEC. He let me know he wouldn't be there for the council meeting, but would be at the Professional Education Center that evening for the General Senior Leadership Council (GSLC) dinner, and he'd be at the TAG council meeting the following day. The GSLC was an opportunity for all the State TAGs to meet with the CNGB to discuss Guard issues.

Here was another national presentation I was invited to give, and the leaders from Vermont would not be there. Again, I always took these situations too personally, like the leaders didn't care rather than they were busy people. My expectations on others were often out of bounds. In A.A., we use step six & seven to recognize the character defects which cause us unnecessary humiliations. Although I consistently prayed for relief from my expectation management issues, this continued to bruise my ego. I took comfort the generals were not advising me I was wrong. During email and phone exchanges with General Salas and Shirley, I learned I would have 45 minutes to present on sexism. Finally, I found someone with influence and power who respected the perspective I was trying to shine a light on. Feeling elated—almost not believing it—I sent an email to my husband, to Jacqui, and to other SEEM allies posing them the question: Who gets 45 minutes on any topic with generals, much less sexism?

I would use the same presentation—"Combating the Sexism We Tolerate"—but I planned to tell different tales from the emotional stack of the stories I carried within me. I always asked women for permission to use their accounts to make valid points in my presentations, and I always maintained as much anonymity as I could. But too many were never told. These were personal, painful experiences, and I held each story with humility. I hoped I could use these experiences to make a positive difference for future warriors.

I traveled back to Little Rock alone and met Jacqui there for dinner. She was proud of my persistence. I filled up every second of the 45 minutes they gave me. The NGB-JDEC included 1-star generals and alternates from each of the seven regions across the country. NGB D&I Program Managers and representatives from the service proponents were also part of the council.

The 4-star general, CNGB, General Joseph Lengyel would

arrive in the afternoon. The diversity council used the morning for presentations and to prepare a synchronized summary of events that each state was conducting. I had to keep reminding myself to manage my expectations, but my expectations were 4-star high.

Jacqui and Tina, from the D&I Program sat next to me in the meeting room. They knew I was nervous, and they gave me their sister love and support to boost my confidence. General Hayes introduced me, and he boasted about how moving my five minute presentation had been the week before. I thanked the council for their investment on the topic and provided a brief background of my service. I said, "I speak on behalf of the State Equal Employment Managers from across the country and the thousands of service members who manage discrimination."

I provided a disclaimer, letting them know I may use offensive language in my attempt to provide the reality of the reality. "Discussing sexually-based offenses and acts of gender bias may be crude and make us uncomfortable. We, as leaders of change, have a duty to take on the uncomfortable work. Our discussions, although difficult, do not compare to the acts our service members endure. We must honor the pain they carry and heal from, if we are to prevent others from enduring the same. This has everything to do with readiness and the lethality of our force."

I went through each slide just as I had at the NGB-EO

training conference, the Region 1 JDEC meeting, and the DACOWITS, except this time, I didn't show emotions. Maintaining my professionalism, my words landed with impactful tones. I paused and allowed the officers to reflect on the information I gave them, because I knew most of them had not heard the crude boldness of sexism in a room full of colleagues before.

I provided another story from my stack. A woman warrior said, "I was training with several male colleagues, and I was speaking about a newly promoted 1st lieutenant female. One of the guys said, 'We all know how she got that don't we?' He laughed and nudged a guy next to him, and all of them laughed. I said, 'That's totally inappropriate.' They said, 'Oh, what are you, the Equal Opportunity officer?'"

I told them about the young female officer alone with a male senior sergeant in an armory the Friday before drill. She was on a step stool writing on a grease board when the sergeant said, "Ma'am, you're making me feel a certain kind of way." She explained to me that her first thought was fear, not that she outranked him. Often these situations put humans in survival mode—they don't feel safe. She didn't feel safe to give him a command to come to the position of attention and then admonish his remark, so she responded in jest, "Clean up your mind." Then she sent messages to staff to find out when they would arrive at the armory.

I spoke about the Project Diane, the official DoD studies,

which revealed little progress had been made since the Tailhook or Aberdeen Scandals. I pointed to the military academies' continued high prevalence of sexual assaults, and to Lieutenant General Jay Silverias' viral YouTube video.[48] In the video, the Lt. Gen. ordered all 5,000 students and staff to the hangar where he made a fiery speech denouncing racism. I applauded his leadership, but I made the point that no general ever got that angry about sexual assault incidents at the academies or anywhere else.

I continued, "We've all accepted sexual harassment and sexual assault as part of the military life. We put our efforts into managing the sexism and the effects of sexism. A captain friend once told me he heard two Afghan Sheikhs talking about Improvised Explosive Devices (IEDs). One sheikh said the devices were a normal operation of the village, but the other argued against that attitude, saying they needed to reject IEDs as normal. The second sheikh professed, 'We must not accept this as a way of life. We must defeat the problem.'

"I believe we must stop managing sexism and combat sexism. The military should be the beacon of unity, the model employer. Women and men shouldn't need protection from their brothers in arms.

"They socialize military members to wear their pride

---

[48] www.youtube.com/watch?v=WfjZ1otkS3o

Life at Camp

externally and keep their disdain internal. I take no pride in claiming sexism as a readiness issue. Yet, the citizens of our country are well aware of the sexism problem in the military; our Veterans with MST are telling them. Just google 'military sexism' and you will see the word 'phenomenon.'

"It is because of my love for the National Guard, I implore you to consider sexism as part of the diversity and inclusion efforts. I've attended EO and D&I workshops, trainings, and conferences for over 13 years, and the topic of sexism has been minimally addressed, even at the school houses. We often dilute the problem. What I speak of is not fun, uplifting, or easy. The topic is uncomfortable; however, I believe the military needs to take on the uncomfortable and be the change we seek for our country. We have a unique opportunity to embolden a shift from responding to sexual offenses to preventing them. We know all sexual offenses last forever; they cannot be erased or forgotten. It is imperative we prevent them from occurring."

That was it. The room was quiet for a few reflective moments, and then General Hayes asked if anyone had questions or comments. Major General Laurie Hummel, who was the Adjutant General for Alaska, spoke first. She thanked me and said to General Hayes, "This presentation should be recorded. In all my 31 years in the military, I have never heard a better presentation explaining the challenges regarding sexism. Chief explained the readiness issues commanders face, and

I think every commander should hear this presentation. I want to bring her to Alaska."

I glanced at Jacqui and Tina, and we gave each other the silent high five stare. Several others provided positive support for the presentation. It was another high. A gratifying moment, and I was glad to have finished my mission. As always, I was not oblivious to the discomfort of several people in the room. Lunch went fast, and we settled in the conference room to make final preparations before the CNGB arrived. Vermont's TAG came into the room and nodded my way. He was well known and greeted several officers, so we had no time to talk before the meeting was called to attention. General Lengyel was a soft spoken man who made those around him relax, but they never dismissed the respect they had for his authority, competence, and focus on the National Guard.

Each general from the 7 regions across the country greeted General Lengyel and briefed us on the streamlined diversity strategies listed on the screen. It surprised me how casual generals were, and nervous at the same. Some were horrible at presenting and making key points, and others were impressive. The brigadier general from our Region was a fantastic presenter. Yet, Vermont's activities were rolled up into unconscious bias training, and I don't think the phrase Lean In was said. She never mentioned the Gender Report.

Life at Camp

The meeting was about to be wrapped up, and I found myself hyper-emotional. I was scribbling on a pad of paper and elbowing Jacqui—"What about my presentation?" As I glanced at Jacqui and Tina, General Hayes told the CNGB they'd heard an excellent presentation from Chief Sumner during the morning. General Hayes paused as he stumbled over the title, indicating that I should say it out loud.

He started, "The Chief did a presentation on...." And I said, "Combating the Sexism We Tolerate." The Chief smiled at me as General Hayes finished. "It was powerful." General Lengyel thanked the diversity council members for their hard work and leadership on important strategies to diversify and strengthen the Guard. As he stood, they called the room to attention. He waved and said, "Carry on."

I was holding back tears that surprised me. They were pushing to leak out of my eyes as my throat tightened. I made my way through a swarm of networking people to the nearest ladies' room, and Jacqui and Tina followed me. I had an embarrassing cry in the lounge space while my allies consoled me. A couple of female leaders took notice as they passed us by.

My mind raced, and I was feeling sad and dismayed. What had I accomplished? The topic and the work Vermont had done were just folded into all the other activities, none of them astonishing the CNGB. What were my expectations? Tina assured me the generals were pleased, and they said the message was not lost. I excused myself and said I just need a few minutes alone.

In all of my years of sobriety, my expectation management skills were still a mess. I went to a stall to isolate, and I prayed to my God: "What am I doing?" I just sat there and cried. Tina came into the lounge again and called my name, saying General Salas was looking for me. I went out to the busy hallway, still bustling with oak leaves, eagles, and stars. BG Salas approached me with his kind face and said, "You did a fantastic job. I want to introduce you to General Lengyel, because I think he should recognize you for your presentation."

General Lengyel was surrounded with many people seeking his attention. General Hayes heard about the request to introduce me, and he told General Salas, "No, let's not do it here. Let's bring her to the dinner." Tina told me to show up for the military dining-in at the PEC Officers' Club at 1700 hours, and they'd have a ticket there for me. Because I was a civilian federal technician now, I didn't have an Army service uniform with me. Trying to escape the invite, I said, "I have nothing to wear." Tina said not to worry. I should show up in my business casual attire. Feeling uncomfortable, I said it was all unnecessary, I didn't need to be recognized. Murmuring softly, I said, "I'd rather go back to my room and eat Ben & Jerry's."

Jacqui was shaking her head *no*. She said, "You are going.

Go back to your room, freshen up, and show up at the dining-in. You can eat ice cream later."

Back in my barren room, I was free to cry some more. It seemed impossible to breakthrough with what I saw as a huge problem. I could not understand how the world was not angry at the constant sexism battle. I thought about Shirley and her pushback, recognizing my white privilege. Racism was a battle just as often diluted, downplayed, and ignored. People of color suffered the effects of racial bias every day in every category of diversity. I had many Black friends who diligently worked for civil rights, but I never stepped into their marches. Growing up in Vermont, I never had to confront racism nor ableism, classism, heterosexism, or all the other forms of oppression. Now I sat on the bed trying to accept the vast amount of people who never considered sexism.

Doris J. Sumner

CHAPTER 30
VERMONT DIGGER'S DIG
★ ★ ★

I made my way across that small, lonely base post in Arkansas, wishing I still smoked so I could pause for a purpose, but I kept moving. I went into the post exchange (PX) and bought an evening snack and Diet Pepsi, knowing the PX would be closed by the time the dining-in was over. Diet Pepsi was my drug of choice.

Dressed in casual clothes and carrying a plastic bag, I approached the mess hall where ticket takers sat at a small table near the entrance. They didn't see my name on the list, so they sent someone in to check my status. I recognized a few generals as they passed me by and provided their credentials confidently. Then Lieutenant General (LtGen) Scott Rice approached with his aide.

LtGen Rice was the director of the Air National Guard. He was a 3-star now. I knew him when he was the Assistant Adjutant General for the Massachusetts National Guard, a 1- star at the time. I didn't tell many people the reason I had received his 1-star coin, but every time I saw him at Guard venues, I contemplated reminding him. In 2010, I was working the registration desk for an early diversity seminar. When the Guard's diversity program began, (before the JDEC's were formed) representatives from each state diversity council assisted NGB to plan, contract, and execute the diversity conferences.

At the national level they had diversity program budgets and staff, however in the state, no authorizations for any diversity positions. Many of us were dual-hatted as SEEMs and assigned in collateral duty positions as the Diversity Managers for our state. We went to EO trainings, conferences, and meetings, and then to diversity trainings, conferences, and meetings.

This was a transitional time, as National Guard leaders admitted that Equal Opportunity, Special Emphasis, or Affirmative Action policies weren't bringing about diversity goals, so they stood up a separate program. I recognized the duplicated efforts right off. Some of the SEEMs refused to take on collateral duty for the diversity program. I opposed the dual programs, complaining if commanders really respected EO and all of the programs under that umbrella, there would be no need for a separate diversity program. But I was attracted to the mission of highlighting diverse talent.

It would take many years before the NGB streamlined the programs of EO and Diversity, and yet there are still few authorized diversity managers within the various State National Guards. Corporations separate the two, but the Guard enmeshed the resources together. So, to support a state diversity program, volunteerism was paramount. I jumped in.

Our volunteer team at the registration table back in 2010 was ill prepared, and several officers were frustrated with an array of payment options for a variety of breakout sessions. LtGen Rice had been somewhat curt and impatient, and, although we didn't take offense, a fellow commander did let the CNGB know about it. The next morning, LtGen Rice apologized to the entire registration team, saying he had no excuse for his rudeness. He gave us each a coin.

Now he greeted me warmly, he stepped right up to me, shaking my hand, almost pulling me in. He said, "Chief Sumner, I want to know what you said to the JDEC. General Hayes said you blew them away with your presentation. I'm sorry I missed it." Perhaps it was my casual wear, my upcoming retirement, or the coin from him I kept, but I felt empowered to express in short how important the message of combating sexism should be for the generals who want to increase the relevancy of the Guard within the DoD.

When I spoke the word sexism, LtGen Rice responded casually, telling me how he is a feminist, and his wife was not afraid to point out his unconscious bias when he slips up. I had to make it more serious, so I said, "Sir, what does a female officer do at an outpost when a service man comes up from behind and whispers in her ear, 'You make me horny?' She has to manage the moment, because they happen, and they shouldn't." He handled the comment with grace and said, "What are you doing out here?" He escorted me right past the ticket takers. In the busy dining hall, I found my TAG. He was very pleasant and glad to see me. The dinner was less formal than I expected, with a buffet arrangement.

A *grog bowl* was being passed around. This is an old military custom, where service members put various alcoholic drinks into one bowl, and a senior official can name who has to drink from it. There are many ways to play the event out, and although I'd never witnessed a grog bowl before, I imagined this one to be very tame. It still didn't seem very mature, and it surprised me that my TAG drank from the bowl.

I kept thinking of my Diet Pepsi getting warm in the bag I had with me. I wanted to go back to my room. One of the female colonels, who was an aide to a general, started talking to me. She'd heard about my presentation, and she confirmed the reality I laid out. She told me about a couple of her experiences and nonchalantly bragged about her management skills. The CCWO from the NGB was sitting close enough to hear our conversation. She had been at my presentation and kept very quiet. Now, she nodded and handed me her Chief coin. She thanked me for my presentation.

The room got quiet and General Lengyel, General Hayes, and a few others stood at the front of the room. General Hayes had less hesitation to speak about me here. He said in all seriousness, "Right now, I want to recognize someone who brought a very serious topic to our Joint Diversity Executive Council today. Chief Sumner from Vermont provided us a thorough presentation regarding the issues of sexism in our force. Her research and recommendations are vital to the readiness of our National Guard. I recommend you learn from Vermont what they are doing to combat sexism and promote equality. Chief Sumner, come on up here."

General Lengyel shook my hand, thanking me for the presentation saying, "I appreciate your work, Chief."

Someone handed me a clear glass rectangular trophy with the National Guard minutemen etched within. The generic statues were used throughout the Guard. We had a case of them in Vermont, and I handed them out for commendable service. Although this was generic, I took it as a treasure, considering the reason I received it. I shook General Hayes and General Salas's hands and returned to my seat, placing the statue next to the Chief coin I received earlier.

After I sat down, a young enlisted man was recognized. He had an amazing story about overcoming obstacles to join the National Guard. The soldier had become successful at recruiting many others into the Guard. He seemed very smitten to be among all the generals. The spectrum of our experience was vast, but we exchanged congratulations with pride.

I grabbed a dinner plate and sat to eat beside my TAG. He turned to me and asked, "Doris, have you heard of a reporter who is doing a story on sexual assaults in the Vermont Guard?" I hadn't heard about it. "No," I said. The TAG was soft spoken, and he told me he had concerns about the reporter reaching out to a victim of sexual assault because of where the reporter was getting the information. As the general spoke, I didn't think he was accusing me of being that source, but I felt uneasy. Was he insinuating the story should not get published? "Anyone could talk to the reporter about the sexual assault," I responded. "A bystander, the victim's family, or anyone they talked to about the incident. If they aren't happy with how the Guard responded, they need a place to go." He said, "I know, but I still did not appreciate the reporter reaching out to the victim." I was glad it was time to leave, and I scurried back to my room with my Diet Pepsi. An early flight would take me back to Camp Johnson.

Two weeks later, I was in my office when my Air Guard MWP came in and asked if I'd seen a *VTDigger* article. *VTDigger* had featured many articles about issues involving the Vermont Air Guard basing the new F-35 jets. We clicked on the link and gazed at the headline: "The flying fraternity: A 'Top Gun' culture pervades the Vermont National Guard."[49] Journalists Jasper Craven, Mark Johnson, and editor Anne Galloway, wrote it. The

---

[49] https://vtdigger.org/2018/11/25/flying-fraternity-top-gun-culture-pervades-vermont-national-guard/

story announced a series of articles to come about the good old boys' club at the Guard.

The authors wrote that they'd uncovered many allegations that the Guard has created a toxic environment for women. They also interviewed a whistleblower who alleged he'd been retaliated against when he reported the misconduct of a top leader in the organization. The article claimed the authors had read hundreds of emails and official documents and had interviewed more than 20 current and former VTNG members for a series of stories to be published in the upcoming week. The sources had requested anonymity for fear of reprisal, because the organization did not authorize them to speak with the press. The article said the journalists had requested an interview with the TAG on October 31, but their request had been denied because the general was out of town. I realized the general was with me in Little Rock, Arkansas, and I felt a new rush of anger as I asked myself, did he think I spoke to *VTDigger*? Is that why he asked me about it?

We continued to read.

The journalists had requested another interview with the TAG, but that was denied, also. Instead, the Vermont National Guard PAO requested all questions be submitted in writing. Officials always claimed the Guard treated all of its members with dignity and respect. The PAO rejected the idea of a drinking culture and stated that the organization had a process to hold all members accountable for substantiated offenses that violate the UCMJ. As I read these canned remarks, it made me sick. I amused myself with the question and answer: if the Guard treats everyone with dignity and respect, then why do we need a process to deal with a failure to do that? Because there's a culture of androcentrism that keeps chipping away at the team we tout as one team, one fight.

The reporters summarized their findings and referred to the 2013 stories about the Adjutant General's race. The *VTDigger* story held us glued to the screen, and we continued reading about how, after the general's withdrawal, a law was passed in May 2013 that mandated annual reports from the Vermont National Guard accounting for all instances of sexual assaults, sexual harassment, and discrimination based on sexual orientation.

The article mentioned Representative Jean O'Sullivan's support of that bill, yet she cautioned that the annual report was not capturing the daily culture where sexual harassment happens.

The article included Rep. O'Sullivan's push for another bill, which passed in the House yet was stalled in the Senate. The new bill would require the Guard to report on recruitment, retention and promotion of women, as well. That bill included language to bring more oversight and accountability to the election process of the Adjutant General. The 2018 Senate rejected her efforts. General Cray told reporters, "Change will take time."

My colleague and I gasped.

I did not know of any service people who spoke to these reporters, and I had not been approached. I didn't know what was coming, but somehow, I knew they had a story to tell.

The very next day, another story hit the *VTDigger* site with the headline, "The flying fraternity: Guard commander's wings clipped after secret rendezvous."

A picture showed a ceremony from 2014, when the old Wing Commander transferred the flag to the new Commander, Colonel Thomas Jackman. I knew Colonel Jackman pretty well. His fighter pilot call sign was *Snatch*. Our first Sexual Assault Response Coordinator (SARC) couldn't convince the leadership that this call sign was sexist. The colonel defended it, saying he'd *snatched* up all the beer to earn the nickname.

Colonel Jackman had made a fuss over our attempts to conduct Lean In sessions at the Air Base. He interrupted one of my facilitators (the temporary male sergeant who worked for me) with a sexist comment during one group. I can't recall what the colonel said, but it was blatant enough to disrupt the facilitation. The young male sergeant, not realizing he was addressing the Wing Commander, spoke to the colonel after the session, calling him out. Once the commander identified himself, my employee came to me. "I am probably so fired," he said. "I couldn't help myself. That colonel was so sexist."

I knew two more articles were coming from *VTDigger*, and the Camp was buzzing with rumors. I felt a need to email the generals and my boss. On November 27, 2018, I wrote, "I did not contribute to any of the *VTDigger* articles; however, I suspect the stories to come will validate what my team has been stating for years: sexism is a problem. You can't have sexual harassment or sexual assault if you don't have a climate of sexism." I further stated I was available to discuss the organization's response to the articles.

Day three of the series produced: "The flying fraternity: Africa, alcohol and the Afterburner Club."[50] Jasper Craven was thorough as he detailed incidents of pilot privileges. A culture of hard partying was described. The Vermont PAO's canned remarks painting the organization as above reproach enraged me. Every time I read those canned responses; they reaffirmed the position the organization took toward any challenges to its culture. I didn't care for the PAO after the disastrous video he'd produced for the JDEC. I recognized his privileged status and loyalty to his job, and his typical response to a challenge: downplay any suggestion of unprofessionalism. It angered me he was the person in place to influence the TAG's response to these stories. I was emotional and taking these stories to heart. I vented to my husband, friends, and God: "Why isn't our Adjutant General responding?"

---

[50] https://vtdigger.org/2018/11/27/flying-fraternity-africa-alcohol-afterburner-club/

I found out he was still of town and had opted to rely on his PAO team, waiting until the series was completed before he'd make any statement.

Day four, November 28, 2018, another article: "The flying fraternity: Ghost soldiers of the Vermont National Guard."[51] This story included the first criticism of the Army Guard, claiming delayed discharges were providing a false sense of readiness. One comment from a survey read, "Stop hiding ghosts." The system in which service members separated from the Guard under special circumstances—for medical reasons, for instance—could take some time, with some individuals remaining on inactive service and delaying their benefits, resulting in some complaints that they were "ghosts." Sources told the reporter that unfair hiring and promotion practices were the actual issues with recruiting and retention. My bias always saw these two issues as a cultural problem of good old boys taking care of each other.

The series kept coming (seven parts in all), and it surprised me that so many Guard members reached out to Jasper Craven. It was shocking how horrible the culture was for women who had never spoken to me nor filed any complaints. It was worse than I had been claiming. My lack of understanding, not recognizing the extent of the experiences, was embarrassing. I worked in my corner office at Camp, with my view of Mount

---

[51] https://vtdigger.org/2018/11/28/flying-fraternity-ghost-soldiers-vermont-national-guard/

Mansfield. I stood at diversity meetings touting the MWP and our great Lean In sessions. My day to day experiences were frustrating, but they didn't involve the blatant, harmful, humiliating sexism described in these articles. As I read the fifth piece, November 29, 2018, "The flying fraternity: Female Guard members claim a barrage of harassment," I wept so hard I could barely breathe.

The reporter had spoken to women from the Air Guard who experienced offenses at Alpena, Michigan. This was the A.T. I attended in 2013 with the Air Guard. Reading the article through my tears, I read women's descriptions of a toxic culture, validating the idea that sexism is based on entrenched androcentrism. On and on, the article confirmed that I had been hearing only a fraction of the impact. I always wondered how such an esteemed organization, with thousands of expert professionals, could allow such a culture of unprofessionalism to erode our readiness. We got tons of shit done, we performed, we left on planes to defend freedom, but we kept managing the sexism instead of eradicating it.

My alcoholism, codependency, and ego internalized the journalism as my own failure. What a dope I was. General Hayes recommending the Adjutant Generals consider what Vermont was doing to combat sexism was banging around in my head. It crushed me to consider: I was the lead Equal Opportunity and Diversity Manager for the Vermont Guard, receiving awards and recognition for the very organization being described here.

Jasper Craven was thorough, and I appreciated the *"Digger"* name as I read his summary of Representative O'Sullivan's hard work to legislate some kind of accountability. Maybe the 2013 bill on reporting harassment, assault, and discrimination incidents to the Vermont Legislature had helped hold Guard leaders accountable to process cases. But hiring a full time SARC and a full time VA had not changed the culture of the base.

How could my blood not boil as I kept reading the PAO's remarks that rejected any real accountability?

Many friends and colleagues agreed with my criticism, my outright disgust, for the PAO's continued inflammatory response to the press. His denial of sexism, favoritism, privilege, unethical—even unconscious—biases was the epitome of the exact dysfunction I had been trying to highlight. The canned remark our TAG used too often echoed in my head: "We are not perfect." I had to use every bit of A.A.'s step ten—self-restraint—to avoid calling the PAO.

CHAPTER 31

WE ARE NOT PERFECT

★ ★ ★

VTDigger did not produce a Friday or Saturday article. It gave many of us time to breathe, but it also kept us in suspense as rumors floated that more was coming. Saturday morning at the JFHQ drill, the Operations Sergeant Major felt a need to address the unit. JFHQ formation was held in front of the main armory at Camp Johnson, and it often included the highest-ranking members of the Guard. The unit itself was made up of mostly "old-timers" who had completed their field experience. The Director Joint Staff (DJS) was in attendance along with other senior staff.

The SGM said in a very casual tone, "Some of you may have been reading the *VTDigger* stories or social media posts about them. There is a lot of crap out there. I am warning you not to comment on social media. You don't want to get yourself in trouble."

The DJS moved up front and added something like, "We are an elite organization, with great people. Although we are not perfect, we follow the policies, we investigate, and we hold personnel accountable for violations. Understand that the articles do not disclose the entire story."

I was standing at parade rest, and although it was chilly, I was not shaking from the cold. I could feel eyes on me despite most heads facing front. I was furious at the call to discount the news articles. There was zero ownership from these two senior leaders. Their message dismissed the risk women took to voice the challenges they managed every day. These were our sisters; they were warriors, just like those in the formation.

The DJS told the unit if anyone had questions, his door was open. We were dismissed, and I could not walk fast enough to the front office. I stood off the main foyer at parade rest outside the DJS's office. Unit members passed me by, and I suspected they knew why I was standing there. I got a few consoling nods from allies. The highest ranking female in the Guard (since the female OIC I'd worked for in 2016 was now retired)—who had intentionally distanced herself from me—passed me and entered the administrative office of the DJS. We had previously conversed in short hallway interactions, but she was not an ally, nor did she ever contribute to the MWP events. Her husband was a combat arms officer who'd served with me on the Cultural Transformation Task Force. As a couple, they were the *A-Team* of the Guard. She was another woman who could really have helped. I chose not to let her intimidate me, but she often ignored me and that could deplete my energy. The DJS came in from the formation, and I asked if we could talk. He was always respectful and kind, both in his tone and words. As soon as the door shut, I felt out of control emotionally. I maintained some professional demeanor, but certainly was on the edge. My voice was loud enough for the female colonel out front to hear me. The general listened to me as I voiced my strong dissatisfaction at the call to dismiss the news stories.

He defended some of their stance by claiming the Guard followed regulations, and I interrupted, "No, we don't." I reminded him of the disparate treatment of soldiers depending on their rank and who they knew. I reminded him of the phenomenon of bias we all have. I added the reality that we had walking wounded carrying MST, and they were often revictimized by a broken system. I railed against the PAO's canned remarks that we treated everybody with dignity and respect. I claimed these patronizing statements only dismissed the reality for those who felt so disrespected that they had put their pain out in public.

Grace afforded me another kind general—he asked me to calm down. I asked why I had been ignored all week, while the two male PAO's were being consulted on the Guard's response to the articles. He told me the TAG had been out of the country when the stories first broke, and he was allowing the PAO to respond until he could take a measured

Life at Camp

approach, wanting to address the force before he addressed the public. The general said, "I know the Adjutant General respects you and your input," adding that he would talk to the TAG about my concerns. Thanking him for listening to me, I walked out of the office, passing the female colonel who kept her head down. I was so sick of bystanders.

In the safety of my own office, I shut the door, fell on the floor, and sobbed, profusely. I curled into a ball hugging my knees, feeling very wounded myself. My heart hurt so bad thinking about all the crap—the workshops, the briefings, the cases, the research, and the women who had shared their pain with me without expectation that I could ease any of it. All they wanted was to be heard. I thought about the officer whose horrific case was substantiated, and still she left the Guard. Or my old boss, who didn't want to think about the Guard, because it was too painful. I thought of all the women who left too soon, without the organization benefiting from their extraordinary skill sets.

What a complete failure. The question the female Air Guard Officer asked me a year ago pounded in my head: "Are you doing what the leaders want you to do, or what you want to do?" I answered myself: The leaders were fine with the sacrifices made. Sexual harassment and sexual assault were just part of the culture we had to manage.

I composed myself enough to check my email, and I found a message from Mary, the CEO, the lady who spoke on

September 11 to the 11 Guard members who cared enough to attend our Women's Equality Day event. She expressed her sorrow for the articles and wrote, "You must be horrified." I found comfort in responding to her, venting how I was not part of the response team. She wrote back, "Just because they did not ask you, doesn't mean you can't provide your input."

This comment returned me to sanity, and I wrote what I would say if I was the Adjutant General. As I was hastily typing, the kind DJS opened my office door and peeked in.

"Chief, the TAG wants you to come join him," he said. "He is putting together his message to the force and wants your input." I said, "Now?" I asked him to give me five minutes. I went down the hall to the psychological health nurse, who was a kind friend. She gave me some lavender to sniff and helped me release the bubble of emotions trapping my voice.

I went to the foyer outside the TAG's office. The female colonel focused on her computer, opting out of any pleasantries. I saw the two male PAOs and the JAG standing quietly by. The TAG was always calm, but today he was especially solemn. He explained he had wanted all of the news articles to come out before responding to the troops with his statement. He thanked all of us for being there and said he wanted our collective thoughts on what should be in the message he was preparing to deliver to the field.

The smell of lavender was still in my nose as I silently repeated my mantra: *I am worthy*. I maintained my composure, but I had a feeling the TAG knew I had been crying. When invited to speak, I explained that validating the concerns of those who spoke to the reporter was extremely important. Regardless if those service members did not know all the decision making factors, their willingness to put their perception in the public view was something we should acknowledge with gratitude rather than contempt

I suggested the TAG acknowledge sexism was an issue we had been tackling using the Military Women's Program, the Task Force, and the Joint Diversity Executive Council. I encouraged us to highlight the proactive strategies we employed to chip away at the toxic culture described in the articles. The TAG's nods and note taking were comforting. He listened to the others as well. I felt their approach was much of the same self-protecting boilerplate bullcrap: we follow all the regulations; there are privacy rights that need to be followed; we are not perfect. I had to interject: "Can we please say, 'We strive to treat all people with dignity and respect?' Because, not all service members are treated with dignity and respect, and it's insulting to suggest this occurs."

I left the room with a bit of a resentment that if I had not fallen apart in front of the DJS, I most likely would not have been invited to this meeting. The TAG responded through an organizational email regarding the *VTDigger* stories, and I recognized some of my words. I had valuable insights, and what I contributed to the meeting was value added, but I still felt angry with my perception that I had to fight to matter; I always took everything personally.

At drill that day, I emailed the female battalion commander who supported the Lean Ins often. I rambled off how I was so done with the Vermont Guard and how the sexism was playing out against me. Top leaders saw me as "Doris, the passionate feminist." Though they might respect me, they did not respect what I recommended they do. Leaders were doing what they wanted to do. It was their call, they were the commanders, but it sucked.

On Sunday of the December drill, it was customary to have a unit holiday party. The JFHQ unit was to meet at the local bowling alley. I had three drills left. I always felt alone at unit parties, despite knowing everyone and being in the unit for decades. I was an extravert, friendly, and funny, but in the unit I felt disconnected. The new master sergeant who worked with me brought her children and was busy chasing them around. I was not bowling, and I stood alone most of the time. I took a selfie with a friend who had four drills left. A colonel interrupted us and asked to speak to me. He was a male colonel who took part in the Lean Ins and was a person I had spoken to about some challenges when he worked in the HRO, but I didn't know him that well.

He had a kind face with sorrowful eyes when he said, "Chief, I got an email from you yesterday, but I think you meant to send it to someone else." Their last names were

Life at Camp

spelled alike, and I hadn't been careful before hitting send. I was shocked and fearful, trying to remember what I had written to the person I intended to email. The colonel reached out, touched my arm, and said, "Don't worry. I understand. I read it, and it made me sad thinking about all you have gone through. Thank you for the many years you have kept up the fight. You made a difference, even if you can't see it." I almost cried right there, but I made a joke about it and thanked him. I went to the bathroom and cried.

The career end was coming, and my years of trudging left me far from the mountaintop where I had felt so empowered a few short years ago. Fondly remembering the first SARC and how we had rolled up our sleeves with a plan to combat sexism, coordinating the Military Women's Program. It was hard not to feel I was headed back down that mountain, surrendering.

That same day, *VTDigger* published another article for the series. I wasn't sure the TAG knew there was more to come. December 2, 2018, the headline shocked many of us: "The flying fraternity: Chaplain's female assistant claims coercion."[52]

The story revealed that she had filed a sexual assault unrestricted report in 2013, the same time I went to Alpena, Michigan, to support the Sexual Assault Prevention and

---

[52] https://vtdigger.org/2018/12/02/flying-fraternity-chaplain-female-assistant-claims-coercion/

Response Program (SAPR) stand-down. As I read the article and reflected where I'd been when she endured such agony, it made me ill. I had worked with her every summer for eight years on the employee picnic committee, working side by side, planning a party for 500 employees. We enjoyed the hard volunteer work together. She was a professional and dedicated to every detail of the party. These memories reinforced how invisible the pain of MST is. This detailed story from a woman I knew well broke my heart. When she was retiring from the Air Guard, she'd hinted to me she was working with the SARC. I remember seeing sorrow in her eyes, but I never considered the Air Guard Chaplain had caused it.

It was another story of leaders in denial. This chaplain sat at the table during monthly SAPR Program meetings. Part of his job was to comfort service personnel when they wanted to file a restricted report. His contact information was all over the training posters. "Tell the SARC, medical personnel, or the Chaplain, and get the support you need." Now, his disgraced behavior was laid out in black and white. When the Air Guard Chaplain retired with his benefits intact, no one in the force had known why—no one except the staff of the SARC, the leaders of the Vermont Guard, and another wounded Veteran who carried the weight of MST.

When the articles first came out, I emailed my boss, who I did not run into very often. He was out of the office a

Life at Camp

good deal of the time. Rumors were springing up that the Adjutant General was retiring, and the names came out of a few leaders vying for a nomination to replace him. Now we understood the boss's frequent trips to the State House in Montpelier. He planned a run to be the next TAG. The other prominent contender for the job was the former Wing Commander. My only solid memory of him was how smug he'd been in Alpena.

In the email I wrote to my boss, I was rude. I wrote,

> I've had eight HROs since I've been the SEEM, and you talk to me the least." The stories in *VTDigger* are about the sexist climate in the VTNG, and yet my consultation was not sought out by the senior staff. Instead, the leaders are relying on young male officers who have not studied the command culture regarding sexism. This is hurtful. I have something to offer. I emailed yesterday and not one of you responded, even to validate you received my thoughts and thank me. The IG saw me in the hall, and she asked for my thoughts. I understand the defensive posture regarding reporters who want to paint a negative picture of the Guard. I understand the Guard response must be measured. But perhaps my thoughts are relevant to consider. I think going on the defensive only continues the negative morale,

> and is why people are talking to a reporter. Saying we are not perfect is getting old.
>
> Saying we are transparent, or all cases are processed strictly by the book, is not true. We don't have to say it is a good ol' boy system, but we should be void of comments which put angry Veterans on the defense. It doesn't help our cause. Changing a culture doesn't take time, it takes leadership. I don't pretend to know everything, but to be dismissed is insulting. This is why I am starting my Empowering Gender Opportunities, LLC (EGO) business, because egos are in the way of making the culture better.

He did not respond. Looking back now, I see my emotions were controlling my reactions. A junior officer might have been written up for a message like that, but I was pushing my short-timer status. We knew each other very well. When we did speak, my boss apologized for his hectic schedule. He explained that the two captains advising the TAG were PAOs, trained in media messaging. I understood this, but my resentment against the PAOs kept me feeling defensive.

The last day of the series came on Monday, December 3 2018. "The flying fraternity: Whistleblower says Guard retaliated against him."[53] A picture of Jeff Rector appeared on the screen. Of all the articles, this one seemed to garner

---

[53] https://vtdigger.org/2018/12/03/flying-fraternity-whistleblower-says-guard-retaliated/

the most anger. Anger from Guard members against Jeff, for what they perceived as disloyalty, and anger from the public against the Guard for what Jeff described as retaliation for telling the truth about behaviors within the boys' club. I am certain they saved it for last for this reason. I knew Jeff well. He was the Air Guard SARC, also the OIC of the employee picnic committee I had been on all those years. The connections in the story pinged like a pinball machine. When the Wing Commander was relieved in 2015, and many of us thought the TAG was not favoring the boys, it was because Jeff Rector had reported the Wing Commander's rendezvous plans. The TAG had no option but to fire the Wing Commander.

Now, reading the *VTDigger* articles, we recognized Jeff was the staffer who had warned a pilot about going off base in Djibouti, and received a "Stop the fucking drama" response from the top pilot. Jeff was not perfect—according to the article, he had contacted the offender in a sexual assault case. The offender had been moved just feet away from Jeff's SARC office. The article claimed a notarized statement from the offender agreed that his relocation was likely made to entrap Jeff. The lengthy article was infused with what Jeff described as retaliation. Jeff used the phrase, "I'm no longer inside the fence." Within months of the Wing Commander being fired, Jeff felt the target on his back. He'd been one of the good old boys for decades. He knew everyone, and he had enjoyed his life on base. But as many in the article validated, once you are out of the circle, you're out.

I was emotionally in Jeff's corner, and I was surprised by several friends who attacked him. Some members felt his decision to report the popular Wing Commander's behavior was dishonorable, and others described his interference with the sexual assault case as creepy and counterproductive, given his position as the SARC. I didn't know about the cases at the Air Guard, despite sexual harassment being entangled within the investigation. Jeff came to me early in 2016, panicked over an investigation the Air Guard had started against him. I referred his reprisal claim to the IG, because he had no previous EO connection. I heard his fear, and when I read this story, I immediately recognized that he had been targeted.

The news story spoke of a sexual harassment charge brought against Jeff after they fired him and escorted him off the base. Their investigations had brought up three charges, and Jeff hired a lawyer, claiming they were trumped up. After Jeff was gone, I remembered the colonel who brought over a young female, and it appeared to me that he was almost pushing her to file a sexual harassment claim. Despite the alleged infraction happening a year prior, Jeff no longer being an employee, the colonel wanted her statement on a discrimination form.

In her statement, she said Jeff had asked her about her

personal life and if she wanted to go to lunch. Her only remedy; to never work with him again. I felt sad for her, since she had been in the Guard less than three months when the events occurred. Even at the time of the report, I wasn't sure if she was pushed to submit the claim, or if she was supported in making the statement. She didn't have to worry about seeing Jeff again—the Air Guard leaders had pushed him out.

What an emotional week. I wanted to call the reporter or write to him. Jasper had worked over a year to compile these stories, but I couldn't help feel he missed the big picture I was aware servicemember free speech rights are not the same as civilian counterparts. When we join the armed forces, There were 16 employees rights are diminished to align with the good order and discipline of the military.[54]

I had worried when I was speaking to the Vermont Legislature about the Gender Report Bill, so I looked up the details regarding free speech rights for military members. Limits to a military member's free speech that could result in disciplinary action included acting disrespectfully to a superior officer, insubordinate conduct, willful disobedience, conduct unbecoming an officer, and conduct prejudicial to good order (including bringing disrepute onto themselves and the service), and more.

The rules are more accurately described as codes of conduct

---

[54] www.afjag.af.mil/LinkClick.aspx?fileticket=x9OMCddZNbM%3D&portalid=77

than limits to free speech, but most service members knew that, if commanders didn't like what you said on social media or to the news outlets, it wasn't difficult to bring charges against you. Feeling powerless, I sent an anonymous letter to Jasper. In the letter I complained that he'd focused too much on the Air Guard. The Army was worse regarding sexism. I acknowledged his hard work and thanked him for giving voice to the many who carry grievances. But I told him the missing theme was the androcentric culture, which perpetuated the tolerance of sexism and the Guard leaders' response to reports of disparate treatment. The series accurately described a boys' club, thus Jasper's choice of the series title: "The flying fraternity."

The rules dictated that I remain anonymous. Until you get the retirement check, the organization can punish you for conduct violations. Many friends affirmed this to me, time and time again. I noted in my letter to Jasper, "After I retire, you will know my name."

As the Guard was preparing to respond to the articles, the DJS included me on an email regarding a meeting with the TAG to discuss the planned press conference. Governor Phil Scott's spokesperson and a few staff members from the Vermont Legislature were in the room. It was an intense meeting, with everyone carefully choosing their words. I held back, intimidated by and respectful of the position the TAG was in.

Life at Camp

The accusation of such a pervasive problem seriously hurt the TAG, and the recent announcement of his retirement was an untimely event. It was feared some would think his leaving was connected to the circumstances and the media attention. It was entirely sad to me—he ran to become the Adjutant General to fix the sexism problem, and he ended his term with a media series detailing the problem he couldn't fix. I respected the way he opened himself up to the room of professionals who were there to help him. He wanted to put an honest response out to the media, but he was smart enough to understand how things can get twisted.

I reiterated the work we had done as an agency to eradicate sexism. I still had a sick feeling in the pit of my stomach. All that work, and yet this crap had been happening. I remember suggesting that we admit we are a sexist organization working on combating the sexism through our diversity initiatives. The JAG said, "Thanks, Chief. I hear you," but then looked at the TAG, saying, "Sir, I don't think you want to go down that road." This didn't offend me, though. I knew my thought was too bold. And I could see the blind spot the TAG had regarding the culture of the Guard. He enjoyed much comradery and success. The general knew that horrible things happened, he had reviewed previous sexual assault cases. Perhaps his blind spot was that these were bad apples, not a result of the climate.

The press conference was scheduled for Thursday.

Late Tuesday evening, I got a call from a friend who was in and also worked as a civilian contractor for the Guard. She was upset and needed to talk. She explained that she recently taught a class for soldiers, and one student left a voice message on her work number about obtaining the certificate for taking the course. He thought he'd hung up the phone, but she heard him begin talking to a male coworker, another Guard member, describing the instructor (her) in a sexually demeaning way. The fellow coworker did not reject the comments, and the conversation carried on for seven minutes. The objectification of her as a fellow Guard person and woman was disgusting. My friend was trying to forget about it as she lay in bed that evening. She told me, "I just can't shake it, Doris. I feel dirty." She cried. She'd had a favorable opinion of the student and appreciated his dialogue during the class, thinking he could be an excellent instructor. I was as supportive and comforting as I could be while my blood boiled. We were in the middle of a media crisis over the sexist Guard, and this joker left a voice message like this.

I asked my friend if she was going to Camp the next day, and she said yes. I asked her to meet me so that I could hear the voice message and we could discuss the next step. I comforted her until she felt calm enough to hang up. We met in her office, and I listened to the disgusting voicemail. She appeared calmer, but still emotional. She knew me well

Life at Camp

and was an active member of our MWP. I asked her if she would tell the Director Joint Staff about the voice message and how it made her feel. I thought, since we were preparing to face the press the very next day, perhaps the DJS was a leader who could convey to the group the type of sexism we were attempting to eradicate from our force.

I wanted the working press response group to comprehend why service members were talking to reporters. Each event was personal and painful, and often leaders didn't adequately respond to service members who reported such personal, private, hurtful offenses. My friend wanted to forget this ever happened, but she felt obligated to report the offense. I knew there were many who put these offenses deep in their invisible backpack and carried on. I wanted the team to understand that the agency needed a consistent, strategic, and synchronized effort that would never fully prevent all offenses, but was needed to work in that direction. This case was unintentional, yet the damage was deep. Despite the Guard's response programs or policies, there was a cultural problem if two soldiers had such blatant disrespect for a fellow warrior.

It was easy to see why—sexism was rarely punished.

She agreed to meet with the DJS, but added, "I don't want to punish this one guy—to make him an example of anything—but sure, I think telling the General directly may increase their dedication to the fight."

I called the DJS and explained what happened, asking if he would come up and meet with her. The General listened as she detailed the incident. He apologized on behalf of the organization for what she experienced. He nodded to me saying, "I am certain Chief Sumner can assist you in filing an official report and allow the commander to set things straight." She thanked him and he left. The generals always believed that commanders set things straight.

Why wasn't the General furious? Why wouldn't he call the soldier's commander and demand the soldier be fired immediately? The evidence was clear. Civilian friends always agreed these sorts of incidents meant instant dismissal from their workplaces. The delayed actions in the Guard always bothered me, but I was just an advocate of an ineffective process.

During the press conference preparation meeting, the DJS never said a word about a new sexual harassment case. I don't know if he told the TAG about the incident. I don't know what I was expecting, but I wanted this group of people to validate the reality that the *VTDigger* reporters had documented in the seven part series.

After the press conference, my friend met with the commander of the soldier who had left the voice message. The unit's EOL was in the room. The woman wanted to confront the soldier as part of her "make whole" resolution in the informal sexual harassment discrimination case she

Life at Camp

filed. Then the command would be responsible for further accountability. The meeting was uncomfortable, but the woman was brave as she expressed her hurt at hearing his disgusting objectification of her. She also scolded the other soldier for not shutting it down. She asked, "Do you know what you would have heard, if I left you a voice message and forgot to hang up? I would have said you were an outstanding student and perhaps should be recruited to be a unit representative for the training."

The two soldiers were forced to eat crow, but the commander did not end the offender's Active Duty for Operational Support (ADOS) tour. The soldier who left the voice mail was an instructor for another class that was in the middle of training, and the commander told me, "I can't fire him. I have no one else to take his place." The commander promised to end his tour after the class was through, but we heard otherwise. Another unsatisfied customer.

I read the entire series again. It was true to me: Guard personnel did sexually harass other Guard members; Guard personnel did sexually assault other Guard members. Many of these warriors did not trust the reporting process.

I personally agreed with the news articles' summations of the cases reported. I believed a married Wing Commander took an F-16 jet to rendezvous with a married military member. I believed pilots went off base to unauthorized locations in Africa. I believed the allegations that several service members were kept on the rolls long after their terms in service ended, and not getting the official discharge papers delayed their benefits. I was certain there was some unprofessional behavior in Alpena, Michigan, including the drunk Vice Wing Commander needing to be escorted back to his room. I believed the survivors story that a chaplain sexually assaulted her, and the chaplain received no punishment. And I believed the Air Guard member who felt he had suffered reprisal and was losing benefits due to early separation from the Guard.

I did not have all of the information—few people did—but I formed an awful regret for touting our program nationally.

They held the press conference in the foyer of the Green Mountain Armory, Camp Johnson. Our response team was told to stand behind the TAG and Governor Scott. We were advised not to make facial expressions, the PAO warning us that many cameras would be aimed at us. The Governor greeted members of the press and assured them he had total trust and confidence in the TAG. He validated the need to stand with the Guard leaders and hear their response to the recent stories as an act of transparency.

The TAG followed the Governor. I stood behind him at parade rest. The foyer was full of reporters and they did aim many cameras right at us. I had heard the speech in the pre-read, and I didn't like it much. I liked the TAG, but his defensive tone disappointed me. He appeared angry

Life at Camp

that the stories were written, instead of furious that the events happened. I had no frame of reference, no expertise in responding for an entire organization about sensitive information. I tried to understand and have compassion for him, because I knew he loved the Guard. Still, I couldn't help but feel he missed an opportunity to show empathy at the prospect of ongoing sexism and the challenges involved in trying to fix the problem. I worked so hard to expose the problem and suggest ways to address it during the last five years. As he spoke, I grew sad for us all.

One of the first things he said was, "I vehemently reject the characterization of our organization." He said, "We are not perfect. We make mistakes, and this is an opportunity to learn." A reporter asked him if his rejection was on the facts or the tone of the reporting? They followed with another question: What facts did you dispute? The TAG said he had issues perhaps with the number of cases cited, but he would get back to answer what facts he disputed. In the end, there were few facts to dispute, only the characterization of the Air Guard as a "Flying Fraternity" with a Top Gun culture. The reporters pressed the General on a decision to ban *VTDigger* from receiving press releases for a short time, taking it as retaliation for seeking a valid story. The general admitted he had wanted to send a message—he didn't appreciate the reporters contacting a survivor. The ban against *VTDigger* receiving releases was removed.

The General claimed pilots did not enjoy special privileges. He defended what was described in the article as an "Afterburner Club," an exclusive partying place for pilots. He described the essential need for after-action reviews by teams, to gather and discuss their performance, to bond and improve synergy, but he dismissed the suggestion that there was any exclusionary behavior toward others in the force.

The Governor and the TAG insisted that they investigated all inappropriate behavior. They said they followed processes in accordance with regulatory procedures, and they administered appropriate accountability. Nothing to admit here, except, "We are not perfect."

CHAPTER 32

THE FINAL BLOWS

★ ★ ★

THE JOB AD TO BACK-FILL THE VERMONT SEEM WAS posted to the USAJOBS website. HRO employees tended to stick around a long time. There were 16 employees. Our HRO staffer held the second longest tenure in the department after me. She had seen a lot of crap over the years and, like me, she liked to run as a stress reliever, except she ran marathons, a lot of them. Her office was adorned with shiny medals and colorful bands. I felt envious of her commitment, but I chose the shorter runs, just long enough to sweat out enough of my frustration so that I could jump back into the thick of it. She told me the new ad was coming out, and only Army Guard officers were eligible to apply.

I was furious, which wasn't unusual these days. I marched down the hall into my boss's office and asked why they were limiting the pool of applicants to military personnel. My boss said, "I think we'll get applications." I spoke with contempt. "No, there has been no Army Guard personnel wanting to do my job. We had to plead for years to fill the weekend EO job.

Life at Camp

We don't even have Air Guard personnel who want the job."

I had been around long enough to know that the way the HRO advertises the jobs has a lot to do with who they want to apply. You didn't have to be a staffer to recognize this. The year prior to my retirement, the Guard mandated eligibility for many positions—including positions in the HRO—to title 5 civilian federal technicians. Many of us didn't want to give up wearing our uniforms every day, however the need for a replacement for me was looming. Since the job had no military commitment tied to it, this meant a wider net of candidates could apply through the federal USAJOBS application process. But they'd just shut out any civilian applicants.

I was so frustrated with my boss's answer that I requested to meet with the DJS. He listened to my reasoning for holding onto the civilian status. I pointed out the media attention on the command climate, and issues with service members distrusting the EO process. "If leaders of the Guard are dedicated to improving trust, why are we limiting the candidates who could take over the job?" I asked. He nodded.

A few days later the staffer told me they pulled the ad for the SEEM and added Air as well as Army Officers. I scratched my head—how does this help? There was a cap on how many positions could be coded as civilian. She told me this civilian asset was given to the security program. The window to get additional civilian assets from NGB had closed.

I threw my hands in the air and slumped in my chair. My disillusionment grew. They did not care about the SEEM, the Military Women's Program, or the JDEC. It appeared they used the same shortsighted playbook with blinders on. The leaders primary aim in this game of musical chairs in hiring was to take care of a guy in the security program. He was reaching his maximum age of 60 and would need to retire militarily, but he did not want to give up his high-paying title 32 federal technician job. If the agency allowed him to work security as a title 5 civilian federal technician, he could continue after his military retirement.

Several of us sat together venting over the situation, mocking their reasoning. Witnessing the boys' playbook could be annoying at times. "After all, he had to put his kids through college. They couldn't just turn him out to the unemployment line at his age." They had turned a previous female security SGM out, but she had no family to support, right? My colleague made a valid point. "We know someone with a security job is better suited to be a uniformed person than a specialized EO officer. But, hey, got to take care of the boys." We sighed together, and I enjoyed another vent fest with the circle of women who were excited for me that I would leave the island soon. We loved our ongoing *Survivor* joke.

The current SARC anticipated that he'd be the only qualified applicant among those applying for my job. This made me question how the leaders had decided to advertise

LIFE AT CAMP

my backfill, since the SARC who would apply was an Army officer. I didn't even know he was interested in the SEEM job, which didn't include a promotion with the reassignment. My insecurities played havoc with me. I didn't trust that leaders cared who took over the SEEM job, but I was powerless. The SARC suggested that if he got the job, he would expect the female VA to manage the Joint Diversity Executive Council. He said, "I can't do it, I'm a white male." I had little fight to persuade him that he should lead the JDEC.

I was ultrasensitive and concerned that the many strategies I had put into place would be dismantled. The SARC assured me that he supported the MWP and what the JDEC mission was all about. It was a blow to my ego that not everyone was 100% behind my strategies. I enjoyed a solid partnership with other SARCs, but I had to accept that it did not make this guy bad because he didn't want to tackle the job the way I did. I realized I was more distraught at letting go than I thought I'd be. At the time, it felt like the path I had been trudging was for nothing, and those still around to march on would never know I was there at all.

I prayed to accept that my tireless effort, my trudge, mattered somehow. The SARC applied and, at my retirement party, he told me he got my job.

The usual team was preparing to head to Montpelier in 2019 to testify regarding our annual Legislative Report. This year, the Vermont House Committee on General Housing and

Military Affairs (Military Affairs Committee) had requested to see the Gender Report despite Rep. O'Sullivan's bill not ever getting out of committee. Our TAG asked the new male SARC and me to clean up the Gender Report for public viewing.

The SARC, who was a qualified PAO, and I obliged, going over sensitive information before releasing the Gender Report for the Legislators and the public to see. The TAG admitted he did not want to send the Gender Report to the Legislature, but the Military Affairs Committee chair insisted on it after the *VTDigger* series came out. The SARCs suggestions were valuable, and he helped minimize some of the harsher accusations regarding sexism. It annoyed me that we had to desensitize any talk of sexism that we wanted men to read.

We sent the annual Legislative Report to the Military Affairs Committee as usual. As in the past six years, the Committee planned a day for the TAG to brief them on the content. Prior to his testifying, his staffers developed a script to explain the data. Although we were reporting in January 2019, the data was for the Fiscal Year 2018 (October 1, 2017-September 30, 2018). We reported eight sexual assaults, with four of them involving members of the Vermont Guard as the accused.

For the sexual harassment portion, I had to discuss six cases. Details about processing the cases were not included—instead our glowing response was touted. This year, during pre-testimony conversations among our staff, I sensed the TAG was adamant that we give as little detail as possible

Life at Camp

and get it over with. Many times, over the past five years, the TAG complained about the Vermont Guard being required to report this data, when other State agencies, such as the Agency of Transportation, Vermont Department of Health etc. didn't have to. I inserted my observation: We had a higher calling then other agencies, and we had a terrible track record.

The TAG was on his way out the door, and the election of his successor was scheduled within weeks. The TAG wanted to send our cleaned up Gender Report[55] as an addendum to our full Legislative Report, but the Vermont Women's Caucus wanted a separate review. They planned another day for our testimony. I couldn't help but have high expectations. The Gender Report was finally a product the outside world could see.

The TAG, the SARC, and I met with the Women's Caucus to discuss it, but they had only received the 48 page Report one day prior to our meeting. Some only got it when they sat down. They hadn't had time to consider the information or ask questions. We touted the work that went into capturing and narrating the data. We bragged about the strategies we were employing to create a more inclusive culture for women in the Guard. Perhaps our strategies were not solving the problem, but I was proud we were trying. In a future retrospective time, I saw Vermont had been doing a lot to shift the culture.

---

[55] https://legislature.vermont.gov/Documents/2020/WorkGroups/House%20General/Military%20Affairs/National%20Guard/W-Steven%20Cray-Vemont%20National%20Guard%20-%20Military%20Women%27s%20Program%20Annual%20Gender%20Report%20-%202018-1-22-2019.pdf

Our testimony in Montpelier was another blow for me, though. The entire Report was too overwhelming, too much, too complicated. Dedicated lawmakers did not know what to do with all that information. They scanned details of the sexist culture that was still limiting opportunities for women and still maintaining a climate for sex-based harm to occur. Their faces blank, they gave minimal nods, and I could see their thoughts in a bubble above their head: What were we supposed to do about it?

As the three of us drove to Camp afterward, I sat in the back seat of the car. The SARC drove, with the general beside him. Their conversation was a blur to me as the thought bounced around in my head: What could the Legislators do?

I tried to shake off these continuous disappointments. My A.A. program taught me to flip the moments with gratitude. The Gender Report was in the hands of Vermont Legislators.

Although I had frustrations, I was considered a fun person who had many connections. My friend Karin was an ally who visited me often. Four years before, three of us on the staff in the Recruit Sustainment Program (RSP) bunked at the recruit barracks, telling stories of survival and laughing our way through weekends. Both of these hard charging soldiers carried the weight of experienced sexism in their backpacks.

I enjoyed hiking with the Women Empowering Women group. I had many friends who supported my efforts and inspired me to keep trudging along, claiming I was making a difference.

I always admired the RRB, but it was an intimidating arena. Karin had witnessed many gender based offenses and she wasn't afraid to step into leadership moments, but the male recruiters treated it like banter and not setting boundaries. Women from recruiting always had to prove themselves among the boys. It is essentially a sales job, and sales can be a brutal occupation, highly competitive. One has to be combative to sell the Army.

The first female recruiter I met helped me put together the Women's Exhibit at the Air Show in 2006. She was a confident, outgoing soldier. She managed her connections like an entrepreneur. I was starstruck with her, but somehow, I let her down regarding a sexual harassment case she filed in my office. She left the National Guard, taking her talent and her pain with her.

Another female recruiter shared with me her horrific experience after I retired. I had seen her from time to time—again, starstruck with her confidence, outgoing attitude and the way she commanded any room she walked into. When she left the Guard, she asked me to visit her and hear her story. She gave me permission to share in my book that she had been sexually assaulted by a fellow recruiter. Although I had heard the rumors when it happened, I did not have the details, and I did not realize what a painful process she endured. She told me the civilian authorities took six months to investigate the incident in question, and in the end, they could not press charges. The Guard began an investigation and that took 18 months to complete. The charges of sexual assault were substantiated, and the offender was given punishment. The lengthy time it took to complete these investigations, however, gave the offender time to earn pay and credit toward his retirement.

My friend filed for an early medical retirement related to her Military Sexual Trauma (MST).[56] The process to apply and receive the medical retirement based on MST is a bureaucratic and emotional roller coaster. She endured all of this while continuing to work as a pregnant soldier. During this time, she alleged retaliation in the form of HIPPA violations and harassment. I had no idea she was going through all of this as I was focused on my own battles, but when I sat with her during our visit, we cried together. I would ask for her support the following year when I made the case for the Vermont Legislature to pass the 2018 Gender Equality Bill, which never made it out of committee. This is the statement she submitted: "I was the perfect recruiter to bring females into the Guard; strong, beautiful, positive, funny, and intelligent. The Army Guard will continue to derail competent woman until there is accountability not to do so." The sexual trauma led to another

---

[56] www.benefits.va.gov/benefits/factsheets/serviceconnected.mst.pdf MST Fact Sheet March 2022 (va.gov)

immeasurable loss to the organization and another otherwise dedicated service member.

There were others in the battalion who suffered from MST, their stories will never be told. These women always impressed me with their tenacity. Over the years, not one of them denied the hyper-competitive culture of sexism they had to manage. My relationships with each one of them was special, but we were never a band of sisters. I've imagined what a force we could have been.

Now the end was near for me. I thought about each one of these women and the battle scars they carried. What did we have to show for all our grit? Often, when service members retire, they receive a shadow box. These come in all different sizes, shapes, and content. The box tells the story of your service. Neatly affixed to velvet inside the box are the different ranks you wore, patches from units you served in, medals and awards earned, coins, or flags. I attended many retirement parties by now, and each shadow box I saw, I envied.

I wasn't sure how or who puts together shadow boxes, but I was fortunate to meet a professional sergeant when I was asked to assist the Honor Guard. An Honor Guard unit provides ceremonial services for fallen comrades. The team typically consists of two or more uniformed service members who fold and present a U.S. burial flag to the family, and who play "Taps." I had only done this duty a few times in my career. I was coached in those duties—I would present the folded American flag to the next of kin. We did an excellent job. After the services, I told the sergeant I would retire in six months. He said he put together many shadow boxes as part of his job, and he would make one for me.

Karin and I talked about the shadow box. Her retirement was months after mine, but she didn't know if she wanted a shadow box or a retirement party at all. Over the years, she had watched several Guard officers she'd known in Reserve Officers' Training Corps (ROTC) at the University of Vermont build a career, become colonels, and retire with honors. After she and two other females completed their ROTC, they were put into Inactive Reserve, because there were no available slots for female officers, who were shut out of many jobs due to their gender.

Karin applied to become a helicopter pilot, attaining the highest score on the written exam and maxing her Army Physical Fitness Test (APFT), her vision scoring 20/20. She never got a call about any slots for flight training. Unable to keep her commission without a job, she resigned her commission and continued her career as an enlisted soldier. She held many roles during her 38 years, ending with the respectful rank of master sergeant. We pondered together: If she'd been given an opportunity to attend flight school, what might her career have looked like? If we did not have to manage sexism, what would our shadow boxes look like?

We were grateful to serve, and we were proud of our accomplishments, yet we knew our trudge included an invisible

Life at Camp

force working us harder, adding drag to our forward momentum.

I had the gift of writing poems, and I wrote many over the years. My favorites were for friends who left Camp, off to the next adventures in their lives. Karin and I started scribbling a poem about the shadow box. We knew many survivors, and we dedicated our collective thoughts in this poem:

> A Light on my Shadow Box
> Pride, confidence, accomplishment,
> Memories flood my heart.
> I'm mesmerized at the medals,
> My mind drifts back to the start.
> A military career spanning decades,
> The ladder displayed by rank,
> Yet, between the memorabilia,
> A piece of my heart sank.
> I could see it between the patches,
> The dark corners of the trail,
> The hurt and shame and anger,
> The shadow of betrayal,
> The pain rose up within me,
> And tears filled my eyes,
> Mixed in with the glory,
> The suppressed pressure of lies.
> I told myself I survived,
> I succeeded despite your damning,
> I overcame the obstacles,
> Often the last one standing.

Doris J. Sumner

I proved over and over,
Your rebuke of me wouldn't win,
I worked harder, stronger and smarter,
Much to your chagrin.
As I gaze upon my career,
Displayed inside this box,
A voice stirs within,
What status quo tries to block.
I will not let this shame lurk,
In the shadow of my pride,
I shed the light on sexism,
And reject what altered my guide.
Sadness swells on what would be,
And how the box would look,
If my faith and trust in the structure,
You had not so arrogantly took.
Gender bias hurt enough,
But sex-based trauma more,
The scars may be invisible,
But they remain within my core.
I shed light on the shadow box,
Which depicts my military esteem,
And encourage survivors to do the same,
And change the stories' theme.
Whether unwittingly or not,

Life at Camp

My score was less than from the start,
You claimed one team, one fight,
Yet I often felt apart.
Because I was not equal to you,
You objectified my being.
Often, I was jealous
Of those who were just fleeing.
Yet my will to be a patriot,
Surpassed your haughty contempt,
I obtained glories for my own,
There was nothing I wouldn't attempt.
The guide for a career path,
Should be free from oppressing talent,
So the light may cast out shadows,
And beam on the truly valiant.
I shine the light on my Shadow Box,
I embrace the glory I deserve,
I reject the sexism which remains,
So, equality may be preserved.

When the sergeant showed me my shadow box, I was very emotional. It was beautiful, better than I could have imagined. It had my enlisted rank from private to staff sergeant and then my warrant officer rank from warrant one to chief warrant officer four. He found the patch from my active duty tour at Aberdeen Proving Ground. There were no sharpshooter rifle badges, but the collection of ribbons and unit crests made the black felt look majestic. I thanked him profusely.

While I was still moving closer to retirement, my boss, a colonel at the time, Gregory C. Knight, was elected to be the next Adjutant General for the State of Vermont. Of the candidates, he was the one many of us thought would be the most authentic leader. He was extremely proud and excited. He and I had a good relationship despite the brassy way I engaged with him as a short-timer. I was pleased he was the new TAG, but I knew he had some of the same blind spots his predecessor had.

At the last Joint Diversity Executive Council (JDEC) meeting, the outgoing TAG came to give me a special letter, telling the group, "She already has my coin." It was a heartfelt letter, and I appreciated his words. I couldn't help feeling sad remembering him peeking his head into the Air Staff office five years before, asking my colleague and me to be on his task force to reduce sexual assaults in the Vermont Guard.

Sexism sucked.

The Director Joint Staff, gave me his coin at the JDEC meeting and promised the work would continue. The Army recruiters were there, and I snatched up one last resentment, finding out they had blown off a special seminar targeted for men at the University of Vermont just days before. I had secured 20 seats for Guard members. My 1SG and I went to the event, and we kept looking for uniforms among the 600

Life at Camp

local businessmen in attendance. The keynote speaker had spoken about redefining masculinity, and about calling men to action to change the culture. The RRB SGM made some excuse for not getting his team there.

Although I believed the DJS who told me the work would continue, I was ready to be done with the work. The last weeks of my time in service, I was on orders to oversee a 60 hour EOLC. We had a full class and a cadre of EOA's to teach. The female master sergeant who took on the EO Sergeant's job was soaking in all she could, knowing that when the next class came along, she would be the lead instructor.

It was a bittersweet experience, and I tried not to tear up like a sappy old warrant officer. The bright soldiers were outstanding leaders. We had lively presentations from class teams on various topics—racism, white privilege, sexism, transgender, and diversity. One young soldier broke out his guitar and played a beautiful song tying into the lesson of resisting a rush to judgment. He said, "You may have thought I was just some dumb infantry dude, but I am much more." He told us he wrote songs, and he played his guitar and sang the Luke Combs song, "Beautiful Crazy." I let the tears fall.

During the EOLC, the *Burlington Free Press* ran a picture of the next Adjutant General on their front page with the headline:

---

[57] https://www.vermontpublic.org/vpr-news/2019-02-21/lawmakers-elect-col-greg-knight-as-new-leader-for-vermont-national-guard

"This is a conversation that everybody needs to have."[57] The article stated, "New Adjutant General says sexism in Guard's culture must be addressed." I read his statement to the class, declaring that he needed more women to join. He had previously served as the Recruiting Commander, and he was always recruiting.

Texting my old boss, now the new TAG, I wrote, "Sir, we are talking about sexism today at the EO class and reading the newspaper. I think the young soldiers would love to hear what you have to say." I felt confident this would get him over to the training institute. He showed up and spent an hour with the 30 students. I watched some hesitation from the class, but the new Adjutant General got some good honest feedback from them about their view of the challenges they would face. I was hesitantly hopeful.

Getting ready to leave Camp for good, I cleared my computer of files I had been saving since 2005. It felt surreal. I'd been crossing out the blocks of time on my whiteboard for the past 15 months. I finished purging my filing cabinets and desk drawers. My continuity book was complete for whomever followed after.

I had gathered binders of articles, stories, research, and reports about sexism. I had large binders from the 2005 Program Evaluation visit, documents and meeting minutes from the creation of the CDET/JDEC, tokens and posters from the diversity venues and the Military Women's Workshops we worked so hard to coordinate. My office walls had been covered with social justice posters and pictures of civil rights activists. I had a large framed copy of the Declaration of Independence. I brought all of it to my car.

Several years before, one of my nieces had bought me a beaded curtain, the colored beads forming the image of Rosie the Riveter. My niece had texted me a picture of it, taken at her job at Goodwill, wondering if I'd like the $20 item. Rosie was proudly displayed on the wall in my office. Many friends who stopped by took a selfie with me, pumping our fists, with Rosie behind us. It was one of the last items I took from my office.

I reflected back to 1981, the year I joined the Army. What a tomboy I was, with limited confidence in what I could become. My alcoholism had derailed some possibilities, but the sexism was insidious, even if much of it happened to me without my realizing it. As I embarked on my journey in the Army, I had not considered those who cleared the path before me. My time as the SEEM had been more than a job. It was a journey. Despite the challenges and too many feelings of failure, I was still proud of my accomplishments, proud of my service, and grateful for every experience. I had made something out of this Army life.

I attended my final drill at the JFHQ in March 2019. The 1SG did an outstanding job of putting together a myriad of certificates. They presented one to Phil as the supporting spouse. The new Land Component Commander gave me his coin. The Director Joint Staff and the CCWO addressed the formation. They all used words like *passionate* and *dedicated*. Karin arrived and snapped her famous Facebook photos.

I had prepared a speech, and Karin switched to video mode. Watching the recording later, I cried. I told the gathering I would never apologize for being a feminist and pushing all of them to consider gender bias. I said again, "It is real, and the pain from it is real."

I told them the master sergeant in the military Equal Opportunity section needed a senior officer to fill the HREO job. The office had never been staffed in compliance with regulations. I said, "I don't understand why many of you are not stepping up to volunteer to help the TAG. The last two TAGs have run on a platform to combat sexism and improve the culture, and why wouldn't someone want that job?" I thanked my allies, and I also thanked those who didn't like me at all, because they pushed me to work harder.

The pride I felt contradicted my sense of failure to combat sexism. Many of us accept the culture as the price for that final shadow box. You survive, hang your plaques, and move out.

I knew I couldn't just let go.

CHAPTER 33

Not Letting Go

★ ★ ★

The question kept ringing in my head: what could the legislatures do with the Gender Report?

The first workday after my retirement, I got busy. I registered my business name: Empowering Gender Opportunities, LLC (EGO).

My family came up with the name through a brainstorming session based on my mission: "To empower men and women to embrace their own gender identity and respect each other's unique gender qualities. To motivate everyone to counteract sexism through effective enlightenment strategies."

Phil liked the acronym, EGO, and we locked in a website name; *www.itsallaboutego.com* just seemed right. I often slammed the egomaniacs who would not take my problem statement seriously, because they knew they would have to change.

I developed a business plan to serve as a diversity consultant focused on gender. I hired a marketing company to help establish my logo, website, social media platforms. I planned to write my book, as Dr. J.W. Wiley had encouraged me to do.

Life at Camp

I told many friends I was going to write a book about how the military hired me to be an SEEM and then fended off equal opportunity from happening. Many cheered me on, and some were halfhearted as they laughed and said, "OK, you do that."

At my HRO good-bye party, the assembled friends and colleagues touched my heart with a beautiful plaque, Rosie the Riveter etched into the Green Mountain Boys' Flag. Rosie memorabilia from friends and family became my sweetest tokens. My longtime coworker, the staffer, and I laughed and teared up thinking of the life we had put together since we first arrived in 1988.

There were many fresh faces sitting around the table. I'd witnessed a lot of changes over the years at the HRO. My first boss often visited Phil and me, and he told us it was all worth it for the retirement check and freedom.

The new TAG, Major General (MG) Gregory C. Knight came to say goodbye, and although he did not have his own TAG coins yet, he gave me a special coin from a deployment of his, Task Force Saber from Operation Iraqi Freedom, 2005 Army, Ramadi, Iraq. He had served as the battle captain for the 1st Battalion, 172nd Armor of the 86 IBCT. My heart was full of gratitude, because I knew this coin was special. Vermont lost six souls in that horrible conflict.

The coins reinforced my shaky confidence—I made a difference.

I was very grateful for the coin from General Knight. I asked myself, who was I to add this coin to my collection? It made me want to fight harder somehow to accomplish the impossible.

My husband and I retired at the same time, and I was relishing the celebrations. After turning 18, we both had joined the Army, and we were both ready to retire at age 56. The local Eagles Club was a great place to throw a party, and we hung up a ten-foot banner congratulating ourselves. We pulled out all our memorabilia from 38 years and made exhibit boards of old photos, laying our trophies, coins, and ribbons on tables. Our daughter Joanna put together a slide show of photos, including the life we'd built with our children, family, and friends.

Troy, our son, was master of ceremonies for the event, and I was proud the party got to see him and hear his humor. Joanna and sweet granddaughter, Rayya, swarmed around like butterflies, making everything brighter. Family and A.A. friends filled the tables between Guard members who came to wish us farewell.

Members from the Region 1 JDEC team stood up to give me accolades for always pushing the team to tackle the uncomfortable work we did. The Region 1 General presented us with his coin for excellence. It was the first general coin my husband ever received, and Phil was appreciative of the recognition.

Life at Camp

The Director Joint Staff presented me with the Legion of Merit, an illustrious award. He was sincere when he promised me the JDEC would carry on.

It pleasantly surprised me to hear the State CSM speak fondly of me, poking fun at our differences. He and Phil had served in the 86 IBCT together and enjoyed a brotherly hug. My husband was never a bro, and he served outside the circle comfortably. I fought for women to be on an equal playing field with men, but I was well aware of men who were outcasts, too, their incredible talents untapped.

Dr. Wiley addressed the crowd and spoke eloquently about our shared passion for social justice. He let the gathering know that he knew many people in our business, and he never met a person so passionate about making things better for people than I was. These accolades could have had me bawling—I was always an emotional person, dropping tears over Hallmark commercials. But, for some reason I was impassive but for a smile.

For all my speeches over the years, my last one was mundane. Of all the people I should have honored, I didn't mention my mother. Her strength, independence, and support fueled the tenacity I held throughout my career. For years, I prepared my presentations and practiced to be sure to make my point, but for this one, I thought my words would flow. As it turned out, my emotions seemed locked up.

Phil, who did not do public speaking very often, took the

time to share his heart. He acknowledged his parents and shared his heartfelt gratitude to serve as a 1SG, bringing a company of soldiers to Afghanistan and bringing them all back home. When he was growing up, Phil wanted to be a superhero, and choosing to be a soldier was as close as he could imagine. His talk teared people up.

It all went by so fast, but we captured loads of pictures, plus one big group photo that we mounted, centered now, in a matte with signatures. Then the time was up, the party ended, the room emptied, and Phil and I left overwhelmed with gratitude.

After the retirement events were over, I spent a lot of time trying to introduce myself to the civilian community as a diversity consultant focused on sexism. I contracted with a book writing coach, Paula Diaco, and developed my book plan. I sent EGO introductory letters to a long list of small businesses in Vermont. I reached out to every police and fire station in the state.

I was not seeing returns.

I met with the leaders of a local women's organization "Change the Story." The group appreciated my candid talk about the sexist environment I endured, and the work I did to change the culture of the Guard. They seemed interested to engage with me at future workshops. I coordinated a small workshop at my local community room entitled, "Check Your EGO: A Bold Conversation about Sexism in the Workplace."

Life at Camp

A few friends showed up, along with the police chief, whose office was in the building.

The slim participation did not deter me.

The *Burlington Free Press* article, February 2019 highlighted the new TAG's claim that he was committed to combating sexism in the ranks. The article quoted me giving examples of women who endured everyday sexism in the Guard, noting my skepticism about change.

Soon after, I was interviewed by my hometown paper, the *Milton Independent*.[58] On May 2 2019, the story on me came out. The paper put my picture on their front page with a prominent headline: "Combatting Sexism" by Michael Frett. The story carried a bold subhead: "Former Guard member to consult with companies." The piece quoted me saying, "If we can't combat sexism in the military, we can't combat sexism in the United States of America."

Retired now, I was home to meet the Post Office delivery driver. Grabbing the paper, I ran into the house to read. I was over the moon. Feeling like I was on the mountaintop again, ready to take off and fly, to actually make that change and combat sexism.

Planning a long vacation with my husband was a pleasant distraction. In early May, we left on a cross-country road trip to visit Phil's brother in San Diego, California, stopping to see family and friends along the way. Our first stop was at

---

[58] https://issuu.com/miltonindependent/docs/2019_0502_forweb

Fort Belvoir, Virginia. Phil had never been to the District of Columbia, and he wanted to see the Capitol that he'd been defending for 38 years.

I let my friend Jacqui know we'd be in town, and we ended up crashing a party where many members from the old NGB-EO Office were gathered. The mood of the group was festive, celebrating a doctorate degree conferred on one of the retired EO Program Managers. It felt like family.

Phil had fun with the group and made a joke when we took a group photo. "Someone someday is going to say, 'Who is the white couple?'"

We all laughed.

All along the trip, we embraced the road, the scenery, the friends and family, and we had the time of our lives.

When we returned, Jasper Craven contacted me. He's the lead reporter who wrote the series on the Guard in *VTDigger*. I met with him several times, and we had long conversations while he attempted to put together another series. In these conversations, I cried, I cried a lot. My emotions were still trapped within me because I was still waiting for a mission accomplished-feeling. Jasper had been in touch with some of the women I served with and with other women who reached out to him after the sensational series ran in November 2018. He wanted to hold the Adjutant General's feet to the fire now regarding the Guard's public proclamations to combat sexism.

Life at Camp

Although he worked hard for over a year, Jasper never managed to publish additional stories on the topic. There were challenges of timing, the emerging urgency of COVID-19, and some of the women he was speaking to had mixed feelings about putting their pain in the public eye. The topic is hard. The book *She Said: Breaking the Sexual Harassment Story That Helped Ignite a Movement*, written by Jodi Kantor and Megan Twohey, is all a person needs to validate this fact.

Jasper eventually left *VTDigger* and went to work for another local media outlet. This circumstance reinforced for me how hard it was for Veterans to get their stories told.

Vermont State Representative Jean O'Sullivan and I remained in touch. My immediate goal was to speak at the annual Women's Economic Opportunity Conference that Senator Patrick Leahy and his wife Marcelle hosted. Over the years, I had attended the conference many times. Speakers and breakout sessions were always informative, but *why there was a need* for the Conference was lacking. We all knew there was an underrepresentation of women in business, but why was that so?

I wanted to scream, Sexism!

Jean set up a meeting for me to meet with Senator Leahy's office.

I was excited and enjoyed talking to Sen. Leahy's State Director, John Tracy. He was a Vietnam Veteran, and he seemed engaged with the culture I described and with the challenges the TAG had minimizing the prevalence of sex-based offenses. At one point he made a remark similar to the Army JAG officer, saying that eradicating sexism was impossible given the nature of the business. We all agreed more needed to be done. I left the meeting feeling hopeful that I would be invited to the September conference.

I was not offered an opportunity to present at the Conference. I was still undeterred.

The week following my meeting at Senator Leahy's office, I met with the TAG, General Knight. I brought a two-page list of recommendations for him to consider in efforts to combat sexism. We had a friendly conversation, being sure to snap a selfie and post it on Facebook.

In his initial interview after being elected, General Knight promised to hold a series of meetings with every woman in the Guard. I found out he planned to accomplish this by coordinating an all-woman conference in November. I urged him not to make it all-female and to include men, opening up mixed gender conversations. He said simply, "I promised I would speak to all the women, and that is what I am going to do."

I left feeling his strategies were redundant, but after all, it was his command.

He also promised an external assessment of the Guard culture. I was curious to hear the results of that. An investigative team came from the NGB, and the Vermont Guard leadership provided the names of people to be interviewed. Despite the assessment done in the summer of 2019, the 2020 pandemic delayed the results, and the unflattering report came out in 2021 with little attention paid.[59]

The workshop the TAG promised included contracting with Major General (Retired) Martha T. Rainville as one of the speakers, and I reached out to her. I remember being on the road driving when she called, and I pulled into a store parking lot to take the call. We talked for over an hour. I cried to her, telling her the challenges I had faced in my job as SEEM. I explained to her how difficult it was to watch leaders of the process, be unable to "make whole" those who came to me broken by the offense of gender bias, sexual harassment or sexual assault.

The General was empathetic, understanding, and very supportive of my desire to write a book. And Rep. O'Sullivan was still trying to get the Gender Bill passed. General Rainville suggested we talk again and perhaps meet later during the year when she visited Vermont. She validated my experience, and she wanted to learn from me so she could provide General Knight the best possible presentation at the workshop in November.

As the summer rolled on, a few contacts from the Guard reached out to me to let me know—sexism was alive and kicking. Many liked the new TAG and appreciated his

---

[59] https://vt.public.ng.mil/Portals/19/Documents/Organizational_Assessment/VTNG_Organizational_Assessment.pdf

openness, but several of my friends said, "He hasn't changed a thing." I felt very gone.

In October, I met General Rainville at a coffee shop. We spent another hour together talking about the proposed bill. Besides information about the demographics of women in the Guard, Jean and I were attempting to add a Chief Diversity Officer to the bill, someone who would work at the pleasure of the governor. We wanted to provide the governor with an asset who could reflect the nonfiltered command culture of the Guard to lawmakers and help recommend sound strategies to increase the representation of women in uniform.

I suspected General Knight would not want, nor see the need, for a Chief Diversity Officer who worked for the governor overseeing the Guard's diversity program. There were many cultural barriers for equality in the organization I had served, but I had not been able to talk frankly about them to Legislators or the public while serving for the TAG. As service members, we were expected to shine a light on the positive and not the negative.

I thought an external position was needed to more accurately describe the culture than having the Guard write its own report.

Senator Kirsten Gillibrand, representing New York's congressional district had been working to pass the Military Justice Improvement and Increasing Prevention Act since 2013. Since then, the bill has been updated. The Senator has

Life at Camp

been a fierce advocate for survivors of MST, and continues to seek ways to decrease the high prevalence of sex-based offenses. She focused on accountability for the perpetrators as one means of deterrence. Senator Gillibrand's bill moves the decision over whether to prosecute serious crimes out of the chain of command and over to independent, trained, professional military prosecutors. Uniquely military crimes would be left within the chain of command.

Those opposed to the bill provided congressionally mandated studies of the military justice system that supported leaving the prosecutorial decision making process alone. They vehemently opposed the bill for a variety of complicated reasons, but all I heard from the top generals at the hearing was, "We got this."

Senator Gillibrand's fiery response: "General, the numbers are going the wrong way. You keep telling me you've got this, but you don't have it."[60]

The fight for the MJIA reinforced how hard any change would be for the U.S. Military. They kept writing their own report card and deciding what they were going to do to solve their problems of sexual harassment and assault. It reminded me of the A.A. saying, "My best thinking got me here, and my stinking thinking will keep me here."

---

[60] https://www.gillibrand.senate.gov/news/press/release/video-gillibrand-grills-top-army-leader-and-demands-taking-problem-of-sexual-assaults-seriously-after-dod-releases-shocking-new-report-showing-that-sexual-assaults-in-the-military-have-dramatically-increased

The military's continued high prevalence of sex-based harm remains unchecked and unaddressed as I write this, except for annual hearings re-stating the problem. Year after year, the reports load up with new strategies, but the harm keeps occurring. I submitted comment after comment on Senator Gillibrand's website recommending gender-equity accountability, to no avail.

General Rainville and I discussed and agreed that installing an external asset to advise the governor would provide assurance to service members that someone was hearing the real deal. A trained diversity consultant could review the relative data from the Air and Army Guard, comparing the overall data with the organization's own assessment.

The position could also provide access to confidential consultation for service members who didn't trust the chain of command or the administrative processes that historically had let them down.

We wanted to make it clear that a diversity consultant would not have any command authority to make decisions, initiate investigations, or process discrimination cases, but would provide truth telling and recommendations for legislation. I did not see it as a threat to the TAG and leaders, but General Rainville understood the wariness of commanders who were concerned about a chink in their chain of command. Her support would be crucial for the proposed bill.

It was a remarkable feeling to have her understand what

Life at Camp

I was trying to accomplish. Our coffee shop conversation moved between the bill and the TAG's November Women's Conference. I was almost desperate, encouraging her to use this opportunity to validate the reality of sexism for women in the Guard. She told me that she did not encounter overt sexism during her tenure, although she was well aware it existed.

We spoke about former Senator Martha McSally, who served Arizona's second Congressional district. Her emotional Congressional hearing in March 2019 in Washington was further confirmation of the insidiousness of MST. During the hearing, Senator McSally had revealed to being raped by her commander. She stated she did not immediately report the rape, distrusting the system. In her testimony she recalled the attack and then described how she was horrified at how her attempt to share her experience was handled. Her sad yet powerful statement: "I felt like the system was raping me all over again."[61]

The story only heightened my urgency to keep fighting. I was emotionally attached to the new team at the Guard preparing the upcoming Women's Conference, although I did not know many of them. I felt the TAG was just repeating the cycle.

What was the purpose of another Women's Conference? Again and again, I wondered: how much evidence do they need to see sexism is the problem?

---

[61] https://www.nytimes.com/2019/03/06/us/politics/martha-mcsally-sexual-assault.html

I had produced the Gender Report for six years. After speaking with General Rainville several times, I was confident she understood how denial dominated the service culture, with the dogged refusal to recognize sexism as a prominent barrier to synergy. Her understanding would be an invaluable contribution to the redundant event.

All of this could still infuriate me, and the thought did not escape me—"if I let go, none of these events can bother me anymore."

In November, the Guard held the Women's Conference. At a retirement party the day before, I saw General Rainville and the TAG, and I could not stop myself from reminding them to validate sexism.

While the Conference was going on, I attended a spiritual retreat with women from A.A. I tried to be present for the weekend with these women, but my heart was with the VTNG women.

Someone sent me a link to a live feed from the event, and I isolated in my room to watch it. I tried to make out the identities of staff members from the small screen on my phone. Some women I recognized who had not been active with the women's group during my tenure, and there were some new service members I didn't recognize.

General Knight speaking style was more casual than General Cray's had been, but he still downplayed establishing an agenda to combat sexism. I knew my expectations were super high, but his opening remarks didn't move me.

General Rainville was eloquent. Her voice was never booming, always gentle, with deliberate tones. The focus of her presentation was to reinforce confidence, competence, taking on tough jobs to create opportunities for professional development. Her time as Adjutant General had provided her opportunities to tackle the issues of sexual harassment, but she admitted her disappointment that there was still so much work left to do.

Just as a recovering alcoholic in a restaurant might notice how many alcoholic drinks a nearby table orders, I picked up on the term *Green Mountain Boys*. I counted it eight times in her 20 minute talk. This saddened me, but I knew it was her identity.

Jessica Nordhaus, from Change the Story, had the most relevant message. Speaking to this group of 300 women, she shared facts regarding the disparity of opportunity and achievement for women in the workplace, disparities caused by gender bias. She opened up the floor for comments, and there were some combative remarks offered denying the problem within the Guard.

One woman, though, made a valid point, asking, "Shouldn't men be here rather than us? We know the problem; the men need to hear it, because only they can solve it."

I clicked off the site on my phone. I cried and cried, still carrying pain in my invisible backpack. The rest of the Conference would include break out groups discussing various solutions. It was a repeat of 2011 in 2019. I knew they felt like they were doing something, but I felt like they were helping to maintain the status quo.

The Guard's focus disappointed me again, and I could not shake the feeling of failure. This is why I did not cry giving my retirement speech. But for the grace of God, my spiritual sisters hugged me and brought me back to the present.

CHAPTER 34
KEEP FIGHTING
★ ★ ★

"When you put your hand to the plow, you can't put it down until you get to the end of the row."
—Tacie Parry Paul, *Alice Pauls' mother*

I had a framed picture of Alice Paul above my desk at home. She was raising a glass, toasting a victory; the ratification of the 19th Amendment. Her face was soft, a small grin, but not gloating. Some days, I'd look at her serious face thinking, "OK Alice, I'm on it."

Representative O'Sullivan and I had conversations about how to get the Military Affairs Committee interested in hearing about the bill. With the help of Major General (Retired) Martha T. Rainville, we revised the original (H.771) to include a Chief Diversity Officer (H.401).

Each January for the past seven years, the Committee had received a Sexual Assault and Sexual Harassment; Report from the Guard under 20 V.S.A. § 427. Although the Gender Report was not mandated in that statute, the previous TAG promised to include it, as well.

Life at Camp

Because I was not letting go of the Guard, I was eager to see the 2019 Report.

The Legislative Report published in early 2020 contained the standard content that was called for, but I could not find any public record of a Gender Report. A friend sent me a seven-page slide detailing the demographics and statistics regarding women in the Vermont Guard. This was billed as the Gender Report 2019. It didn't surprise me, but it discouraged me.

I heard the Army officer who was hired for my SEEM job had resigned, and the brass returned the civilian asset that had been moved to security, putting it back into HRO. The waste of a year insulted me.

Jean thought it was a good time for me to visit the Vermont Women's Caucus at the State House, to provide my perspective as a retiree. I visited the Caucus twice, armed with short quotes from my contacts at the Guard confirming that the fight for equality was still on. A *VTDigger* reporter was always present in meetings, taking notes.

These interactions gave me a sense of empowerment, and I was hopeful we could attract some support regarding sexism as a major readiness issue for the Guard.

My continuous networking wasn't netting me business contracts, but minor victories fueled my days. I was set up to work at small events, speaking about gender bias issues in the workforce, and I began writing my book.

Periodically, the national news began mentioning a new

coronavirus causing illness they called COVID-19. The news alarmed me, but I did not know the danger our country and the world were in. I was invited by the Military Affairs Committee to testify at a hearing for bill H. 401 on March 11 2020.

The TAG of the VTNG, General Knight, would also be there. I met up with Jean in the crowded halls of the Vermont Capitol Building. I had a written speech prepared, and I agonized over the best arguments to convince the Committee on the need for oversight.

The TAG and his deputy greeted me. The committee room was small and overcrowded. The conference table took up most of the space in the room with extra seating lining the wall. Representative O'Sullivan wished me well and left me alone, sitting on the sidelines, awaiting my turn. When it came around, I shuffled to the end of the table for a seat. I spoke methodically, using the best lines, all of them, from years of campaigning for gender equality accountability.

"I take no pleasure in pointing out what remains dysfunctional in the Guard or the military," I said. "Let me be clear, there is a lot commendable about the Vermont National Guard. Not everyone is having a bad time—in fact, most people love their experience. This does not dismiss the issue we are here to discuss today. I salute authentic efforts to improve the command climates and solidify the Sexual Harassment/Assault Response and Prevention Programs. However, neither the strategies nor the priorities are happening at a pace to cement the lasting change needed to prevent sex-based harm from happening. I could enjoy the benefits of retirement and let the new generation continue on. However, I joined in 1981, when sexism was a documented problem for the military, and despite valiant efforts to diminish the issues, sexism remains a problem.

"The purpose of the bill is to give VTNG the tools necessary to make progress diversifying the power core of our force and thus shifting the cultural landscape, which has a documented history of a sexist culture affecting the lives of our service members. We cannot deny the effects of sex-based harm right here in Vermont. The last two Adjutant Generals ran on platforms to defeat sexism. Vermont has the historic recognition of appointing the first ever female Adjutant General after 361 years since the birth of the National Guard. Major General Martha Rainville (Retired) brought a fresh cultural shift needed, after a long tenure with Major General Edwards' authoritarian style."

I spoke about the NGB policy and program for diversity running with insufficient staffing. "There is a second staffing challenge—that of hiring an internal Diversity Manager. The status of working for the Adjutant General may inhibit an employee from being brutally honest, or perhaps their research might not be incorporated into permanent records. I was the Diversity Manager, and I provided reports to my superiors based on collective research, including data that

I could assemble. They respected me in my field. I received many accolades.

Yet, year after year, my recommendations have not been taken seriously enough to enact Affirmative Action. I am concerned that the reason for this includes the very gender bias I am attempting to point out, that is to say, If I were a man, would they recognize my insight and take action? Even if the Diversity Manager is male, the recommendations require men to give up the cultural power in order to equalize the playing field."

I detailed the lack of adequate staffing for the Army military EO program. Reading it now, I see I was too detailed, but I wanted to point out the long, persistent fight to get the respect the program deserved, if we wanted the results the program could offer. Good intentions stood up the EO program but bias diminished its effectiveness.

I spoke about the reality of unconscious bias, stating: "Reports confirm, there is an increase of gender bias in male dominated environments. Assimilation is the survival tool." A current member of the Guard provided me a letter to read supporting the bill H.401 and the need for change. She described her decades of experience and the continued uphill battles she faced: "Why do I still attend meetings, 29 years after joining, where I am the only female in the room? I have reached the point during some meetings where I stop talking, because no one is listening."

Life at Camp

Another part of her letter read: "I have watched other senior female officers get ignored when explaining things, even when they are the subject matter experts (SMEs). However, when a man says the same things just after, it is like the heavens parted and God spoke. I love this organization, or I would not take the time to write. I believe we can be better, and everyone should have the tremendous opportunity to join and lead, if they choose. We need to eliminate the sexism, or we continue the predatory landscape where there continues to be sanctuary for those who do women harm."

I provided an example of the everyday sexism experienced by Guard women who felt trapped, opting for the, "Woman on the Ladder Story." I made the point that reporting the incident meant reprisal for the woman; holding it in meant shame. The change in Guard leadership was not changing the circumstances for women. The Legislators hired new TAGs but the culture remained the same. The woman who provided me the story about being on the ladder was agonizing over her choices, to get out of the Guard and give up all she had endured over the last decade, or just carry on. I was compelled to talk about her dilemma.

"In closing," I said, "The H.401 bill will give the Vermont Adjutant General an asset to manage the diversity needed in the Guard to combat sexism for all."

When my testimony was over, General Knight took his seat at the table as I went back to the sideline. He had no prepared speech, and he looked like he was sitting down with friends at a dinner table. He acknowledged my perspective and thanked me, but then stated, "I don't necessarily agree with everything Doris said." He did a good job boasting of his plans to make a difference like no other general had before. I maintained a stoic pose as I listened. I knew the terms he used, the staffing he spoke about, and the organizational barriers for the proposals he planned. Faces around the table looked impressed. It filled my mind with counterarguments, but my voice was quieted.

One of the Representatives, a Navy Veteran, asked the general a question. I had spoken to the Veteran prior to the hearing, and he'd expressed his sorrow over the tragedy of sexual-based harm. He had pain in his eyes. When he spoke to General Knight, he spoke with the same intense emotion: "What are you going to do about the woman on the ladder?" The General had no specific answer for building her trust, except to say he'd sent an agreement letter out to be signed by every leader in the Guard.

My silent retort; She feared harm in the moment. She feared reprisal if she reported the incident. She feared exclusion, if she didn't go along with the culture. She lacked power, despite her rank, and a letter would not change that.

The room broke up, and a Representative who knew me well leaned over to say, "Good job." I left Montpelier that day, and I have not returned. The world stopped moving. COVID-19

Life at Camp

was serious, and many shifted gears but me. I woke up the next day and wrote out my rebuttal to the TAG's plan. I pointed out the barriers to achieving what he talked about in his testimony. I could recognize them because I worked in the arena. My email:

> "I did not include in my testimony that in 2016, I collected 50 stories like the incident I described of the woman on the ladder. These are women who experience everyday sexism as described in *Project Diane*. These realities impact confidence, security, and retention. In the, Workplace for Women Report by the Vermont Commission on Women, 80% of women who are sexually harassed change jobs.[62] Women in the Guard cannot leave—they must stick it out until their term ends.
>
> "I gave these 50 stories to General Cray in November 2016, and also to Major General Knight before I retired, in my desperation to convince them of the magnitude of the cultural problem. Although both of these generals acknowledge sexually based offenses are a valid problem, neither of them has validated the cause. Major General Knight claims he will bring NG women to the Women's Caucus who will report the command climate. He doesn't comprehend his power and influence. Of course, they are going to give positive reviews. He still claims

---

[62] https://changethestoryvt.org/wp-content/uploads/2019/12/WomenWorkWages2019.pdf

he will talk to every female, somehow believing this will help, and not considering how personal sex-based offenses are.

"I was a soldier for 22 years before I realized I was operating in a sexist environment. My privilege never considered I was being oppressed, or kept from accomplishing my goals based on my gender. I assimilated to the dominant culture. I managed sexist jokes, harassment, and even the nonviolent sexual assault from my first company commander in active duty. It was not until I was a collector of pain from women who trusted me—and who often regretted trying to hold the offenders accountable through the biased process—that I fought for change.

"The Guard is sexist. The all male leadership is in denial of the impact their bias is having on the recruitment, retention, and promotion of our force. Without measured accountability, the status quo will continue and every three years, *VTDigger* will publish the pain a new leader promises he can change."

I emailed Jean and the other committee members, the only response came from Jean, assuring me the bill was not dead, and we would work over the summer on reintroducing it. Her focus was on the shutdowns now, unemployment, rising COVID-19 cases, and preparing response teams for the pandemic.

I understood, and I took my foot off the gas pedal. I felt depleted, like I'd climbed a mountain and did not want to trudge back down.

Like so many other events, my speaking opportunities were canceled. I used my time to write as much of my book as I could, honing my vocabulary, and shaping my story.

I tried to keep up momentum, posting to my Facebook page, LinkedIn, and my EGO blog when anything related to the ugliness of sexual harassment, sexual assault, or the military made the news. I spent hours trying to create a one minute promotion video for EGO services.

Troy and I laughed at the outtakes. I posted my own testimonials and YouTube videos promoting the need for bill H.401.

I was still sensing my mission, and I thought these intervals of action could come to fruition.

Grace Elletson, a reporter from *VTDigger* called me and asked what I thought about the TAG getting his bill, H.750, passed, but the H.401 bill nixed. The news shocked me, and I was angry all over again. H.750 would create a provost marshal position for the Guard, a person who would serve as a liaison between civilian law enforcement and Guard officials when crimes were committed by Guard members.[63] The general had spoken about H.750 at the hearing on March 11.

---

[63] https://legislature.vermont.gov/bill/status/2020/H.750

I rolled my eyes at creating another after the offense resource rather than preventing offenses from occurring.

During the phone interview with the reporter, I was in reactionary mode, not considering any fallout. It made me super angry to realize the general had been maneuvering his networks with the Legislators to get his bill passed, while I had taken my foot off the gas, respecting the State's COVID-19 priorities. After I got off the phone, I was full steam ahead to find more Guard personnel supporting the need for bill H.401. Within a few days, I had 23 statements specifically citing why oversight was essential, but my outreach triggered outrage with some MST survivors. Open wounds remained among women fed up with downplaying sexism as a problem, as well as the lack of focus on prevention. Six women, some still in the Guard, agreed to join on a Zoom call with Representative O'Sullivan and General Rainville. On July 10, we had a heartbreaking exchange through video screens, where women were brutally honest about their experiences with sexism. The mutual support fired us up and solidified the urgency to get something done and stop the dysfunction and harm from continuing.

Grace Elletson spoke to Representative O'Sullivan about the bill being passed over. Jean had the experience, tact, and forethought to respond to the reporter with less combative language than I had. She said that, although the TAG authentically was addressing sexism, she differed with him on an approach. In the final article published in *VTDiggers*, July 2020, "*Independent oversight of the Guard sexual misconduct nixed,*" the TAG restated his opinion that the Chief Diversity Officer was redundant; he already had an EO manager shouldering those duties. He did not think an independent reporting channel to the governor was necessary. He admitted there could be a clash within Guard leadership if the Diversity Officer reported to the governor and the EO manager reported to the TAG. I read this with frustration and thought: of course, there will be a clash if there are two different narratives.[64]

The annual reports, the assessments, the media stories have always been in retrospect. Year after year, decade after decade, the military continues to fail at preventing sexual harassment and sexual assault. The numbers are getting worse, the damage is still being done, and I ask myself why we should allow them to keep trying without oversight? I couldn't speak to the reporter with tact or forethought. When she asked me what thought, I said, "The general doesn't want oversight."

I am certain I vented my position. The reporter wrote about the general testifying and rejecting the need for oversight, then she quoted me as saying, "He just blew a bunch of smoke up their butts." This comment came from my bruised ego and frustration.

One survivor I contacted suggested holding a rally to draw attention to the issue and the proposed bill. I talked with Jean

---

[64] https://vtdigger.org/2020/07/20/independent-oversight-of-guard-sexual-misconduct-nixed/

and General Rainville, weighing the risk, but also listening to the group of women seeking a means to have their outrage heard. We had large print signs—"Reject Sexism." "Check Your Bias." "Pass H.401." "Predators Retire-Victims Harassed." My husband, Phil joined us. His sign read, "Diversity Improves Everything."

It was the military drill weekend, and plenty of traffic moved in and around the gates of the Camp Johnson roadway. It was the hardest demonstration I ever participated in as part of the fight for equality. Reflecting on centuries of suffragettes and feminists, I swallowed my privilege hard. I loved the Guard, and I still wanted the Guard to love me. I did not like the feeling of opposition with the Guard, and yet I felt the need to fight.

To my knowledge, there had been no amount of public pushback against the Guard regarding sex-based issues. The F-35 basing was the only other major bad press the Guard received in a long time. Guard members kept their eyes forward coming through the gates past pickets with signs. Civilian traffic beeped in support, with a small percentage of drivers giving us middle fingers. My women allies were there in solidarity. Two MST survivors were from the Army Recruiting and Retention Battalion, and both of them were outspoken about their pain, humiliation, and mistreatment. The exchanges triggered these women. They were hurt. They had tucked their battle scars away to meet the daily task of carrying on the jobs in uniform. But this was a time to be heard. One survivor brought her baby, still nursing the child. The scorching sun beat down, and we set up a shaded area to watch her baby and give her a turn at waving the signs. *VTDigger* snapped a few photos and talked about the event in an article submitted by Grace Elletson.

I sent the 23 statements I'd gathered from women in support of H. 401 to Jean and Martha, hoping the painful messages might spark another shot to get the bill considered. I emailed Senator Leahy, too, pleading with him to consider the urgency to act. Stories and activism related to Vanessa Guillen, a female soldier stationed at Fort Hood, Texas who claimed sexual harassment and was murdered in the spring of 2020, were flooding the airways.

The Secretary of the Army, Ryan McCarthy, tweeted, "I am directing an independent & comprehensive review of the command climate and culture. We have to listen in order to create enduring change."[65]

Among the 23 statements, one woman put the call to action so clearly. I was certain someone would listen.

In part, she said,

> I had the honor of working within the Vermont National Guard for five and a half years as a civilian contractor. It was the most gratifying job I've ever

---

[65] https://twitter.com/SecArmy/status/1281641910327824386.

done in my life, to this day. It was also the job where I witnessed more sexism and toxic masculinity than I could have ever even fathomed. These issues were pervasive, from cadets all the way to colonels. There were many upstanding and respectful soldiers I worked with and helped, but the sexism and toxic masculinity embedded in the culture deterred their journey. It's my experience that if there is going to be real, meaningful change to abolish sexism from a male dominated organization, then the culture needs to be addressed on every front and in a sweeping fashion. I petition you to make the Vermont National Guard take all the women soldiers who have experienced sexism over the years seriously, and use an external Diversity Manager.

Other statements were pages long, detailing rape, sexual assault, being ostracized, disrespected, avoided, or set up to fail. One Guard officer wrote:

As a woman and an officer in the VTNG, I can confirm that sexism is still a reality for those serving. Sexism is something that drove me from full time service doing a job I loved and excelled at. It was not the pay, it was not the technical difficulty of the job, nor the burden of responsibility. The reason I left was the inability to be effective in my job, because I was ignored, excluded, told to be quiet, to be submissive, to accept the behavior in order to move up. I did not sit by and allow this to happen. I met with my leadership, I followed my chain, I went to the highest-ranking commander. In the end I felt I had to solve the issue myself. I had no other choice but to leave my full time job. There has still been no change. I dread going to drill each month, and I am disheartened by the lack of accountability. Unfortunately, I have 7 years left as a traditional Guardsman before I can retire, making filing a formal complaint unwise—just making this statement is a risk in and of itself. Only after leaving the full time force, I grasped how toxic the environment was. I was broken; physically, mentally, and emotionally. It has taken almost six months to feel normal again. I see this same thing happening to other women in the Guard—both Air and Army. We need your help. We need you to hold our leadership accountable. Help us make the VTNG a place where all are welcome. Help us be heard.

Only Senator Leahy responded to my email. His statement was respectful and honest. He said he could not comment on bills before the Vermont Legislature and encouraged me to contact my local representatives.

The fallout from my comments in the *VTDigger* article, the rally at Camp Johnson, and some of my personal Facebook posts where I vented about military sexism, were painful. They reinforced the complications of combating sexism. There would not be a person, policy, law, speech, or rally to pin a "Mission Accomplished" banner anywhere. I was sorrowful reading my anger in the article. "Blowing smoke up their butts." Ouch. I knew it would displease General Knight and others. Three women friends from the Guard private messaged me to express their disappointment. One friend told me, "Some think you want to be the Diversity Manager for the governor. Your message is getting lost."

These comments shook me, because I did not want the job we were pushing to establish. And I did not like being disliked. Friends knew my heart was in the fight for the right reasons, but many people didn't know me. Humbled, because I had not been tactful with the reporter, I chalked it up as a lesson learned, but selfishly, I still wanted to be understood.

Opposing the National Guard made me uncomfortable. I felt a sense of urgency to apologize to the TAG. I emailed and called, but I received no response from him. In hindsight, I wish I had sought to collaborate with General Knight on the oversight we were seeking to impact changes. We may never agree on tactics, yet I know we agree on the mission for gender equality. His newly hired Air Guard Diversity Manager contacted me though, and we had a pleasant conversation. Her position was a military drilling position and not a full time technician position. She was a senior officer who understood the military culture. Years before, she had filed an EEO

Life at Camp

discrimination case based on gender against her home state and won. She'd been ready to retire before she was called back and asked to do this job for Vermont.

During our conversation, I conveyed my intentions regarding the bill, the rally, and my book. Regretful for not being more careful with my words, I wanted General Knight to hear my apology. She listened and respectfully validated my experience, understanding my desire to push for change and accountability. Before she hung up, she said, "No more bad press, please."

I could not refrain from saying, "If the Guard treats everybody with dignity and respect, there will not be bad press."

I took refuge in my beautiful gardens, playing with our granddaughter Rayya, and hosting our daughter Joanna's wedding at our home. These were the important pieces of my life. My husband, family, and friends knew my heart was breaking as I met each minor success with a daunting new challenge. I prayed to my God, I spoke to my sponsor, support team and my patient husband. They all encouraged me to keep going, to keep fighting, and to keep writing my book.

Doris J. Sumner

CHAPTER 35

God's Taps

★ ★ ★

I WAS SAD AND DESPERATE DURING THIS TIME. THE SADNESS did not consume me, but it lingered beneath the gratitude I felt to be a retired veteran. I had my wonderful family and the opportunity to play with sweet Rayya during her school break. We challenged each other to cross the monkey bars, climb big rocks, and catch frogs. I was not busy with my business, Empowering Gender Opportunities, LLC (EGO), because I wasn't savvy enough to sell myself. I obsessed with my mission.

I emailed the group of women who had provided statements for the State Legislators, joined the rally at Camp Johnson, and took part in the Zoom call with Representative O'Sullivan and General Rainville.

To them, I confessed my mistake of not measuring my words when talking to the *VTDigger* reporter, Grace Elletson, and how this cost us some measure of support. The TAG didn't return my calls; however, the one I received from the Air Guard Diversity Manager was effective in defending the intent of our strategies.

Life at Camp

I let the women know their statements supporting Jean's bill, H.401, were sent to the legislators. I wondered: how loud could I scream? Who could I tell? What could help make a difference? After each of these minibattles, I wanted to shut down. There were many times I had to deploy the steps of my A.A. program to keep me sane. My character defect of self-centeredness had me wanting the world to understand me. I had to balance my agenda with God's agenda for me.

Each day I got up and said the Serenity Prayer. Then I rolled up my sleeves. Jean's calls and emails always fired me up, and I raised my coffee cup to Alice Paul's picture. Jean included me on some communications with the president of the fourth largest federal labor union—The Association of Civilian Technicians (ACT)—who represented Title 32 and Title 5 members of the National Guard full time workforce. Someone brought H.401 to his attention via the *VTDigger* article about the bill being nixed. He was very interested in the proposed language and accountability regarding the treatment of women in the Guard. In his email to her, he included a link to a report from the Service Women's Action Network (SWAN), citing a recent post on the ACT's Facebook page, and wrote to Jean, "It is amazing what women have endured in the military over the years."

The report entitled, "Where We Stand" was the 10th edition. The data only made me angry.[66] SWAN had done

---

[66] https://www.servicewomensactionnetwork.org/swan-research

so many instrumental things to improve the lives of women in the services, but no one was talking about equal respect based on gender. The statistics seem to tout success, claiming a dramatic increase in recruitment. I did not agree. The percentage representation of women being 1.6% in 1973 grew less than 1/3% each year. It has taken 45 years to reach 16.3%. How was this a dramatic increase?

The percentage for women in senior positions or positions of authority was dramatically lower than their overall percentage. The report boasted about the representation of minority women, women officers, and the representation of women admirals or general officers. I saw no reason to cheer. I looked at Alice Paul's solemn face in the picture above my desk. She knew.

The problem was so plain to me. I often thought about Alice's quote: "I never doubted that equal rights was the right direction. Most reforms, most problems are complicated. But to me, there is nothing complicated about ordinary equality."

The email traffic with ACT went dead, and so did my correspondence with Jean. She lost her reelection bid for the Burlington, Vermont, Chittenden-6-2 District. I knew she was hurting, and I resisted any nagging. Then, like God tapping me to keep on the mission, I received an email from Vermont Public Radio (VPR) inviting me to talk about the Vermont National Guard's efforts to address and combat sexual assault

Life at Camp

misconduct.[67] Within two days, I was being interviewed on the local news program, "Vermont Edition." Jane Lindholm's voice on the phone line had me starstruck, and I was instantly comfortable. I had no prepared remarks, but her questions led me to respond with such clarity. I sat up straight, although no one could see me. It was a 25 minute interview, and Jane told me offline, "I could have gone on for an hour. Thank you."

I spoke about the pride Veterans carry. It is a big deal to serve, and our military has great, competent, dedicated professionals. I pointed out the sexism not to disrespect the greatness, but to develop that greatness. I reminded the audience that most people are having a great time, but one in 16 women are not.[68] They are being sexually assaulted. Despite the great effort and resources DoD applies to eliminate sex-based problems, sexual harassment and sexual assault remain prevalent. I spoke openly about being sexually assaulted by my first company commander, and about not realizing I was in a sexist organization until I was in my 40s.

My call to action was to increase representation of women boldly. Jane asked, "But how do you increase representation of women in an organization that is sexist?" "Right!" I exclaimed. "We need the leaders of today to be held accountable for bold

---

[67] https://www.vermontpublic.org/programs/2020-10-27/former-national-guard-member-to-end-sexual-misconduct-culture-must-change

[68] https://www.rand.org/pubs/research_reports/RRA1318-1.html#:~:text=Without%20bold%20action%2C%20sexual%20assault%20and%20sexual%20harassment,and%20one%20in%20 29%20men%20experience%20sexual%20assault.

changes. They have no sense of urgency to change a culture they benefit from. Their blind spot is thinking if you are competent and work hard, you can achieve success. I did."

I was proud of the interview. The Guard's Diversity Manager texted me. "Great job today." I sent a link to Senator Kirsten Gillibrand, Senator Patrick Leahy, Jean, and others. Senator Leahy, as always, responded with his faith in Major General Knight and support for women in the military.

In November 2020, Jean responded to my emails. She was engaging with the Women's Caucus again and was resending our testimonials reminding the Military Affairs Committee our work was not a referendum on General Knight but on their obligation to the citizens of Vermont for a safe working environment. She heard my VPR interview, and asked if I was going to watch Norah O'Donnell? CBS was advertising the 4-part series on Military Sexual Assault. Jean sent me the link of a news article from Variety.com about O'Donnell's extensive investigation, calling the military's efforts to combat sexual assaults a consequential failure.[69]

I watched the series, keeping track of how much airtime the story got. I jumped on my computer and sent CBS a message, along with a YouTube video I made: "Military MeToo, Let's Do This." In my video, I thanked Norah O'Donnell for taking 18 months and spending the resources to uncover the tragedies of

---

[69] https://www.variety.com/2020/tv/news/norah-odonnell-military-sexual-assault-cbs-evening-news-1234833602/

a handful of women in the U.S. military. All four episodes took about 15 minutes to tell. The stories were heart wrenching. I had listened as the Sexual Assault Response Coordinators (SARCs) validated the lack of urgency by commanders when the SARCs took cases to them. In my video, I spoke cynically about the Secretary of the Army coming out after the story and claiming the DoD takes these cases seriously. He made a commitment to do something by December 8. "What are you going to do?" I asked. My cynicism was growing ugly.

I ranted in the video about the other 50 States and territories where units were silenced, because the victims could not find a reporter to tell their story. I restated the problem: the lack of gender equality. And without accountability, equality would continue to evade us.

"Women in the military must be competent, competitive, and manage sexism in order to become successful," I said. It was possible, at a rate of 16-19% representation and holding steady, but the damage was still being done. I added, "Men suffer too. Men who do not fit the masculine identity structure cemented in the 400 plus year history of the U.S. military. The defense of our nation is not a man's job. It is an American's job."

My last line in the video was, "I hope someone is listening."

It was another hyper emotional ride which leveled off as they always did.

Phil and I love the Christmas season. We begin the day

after Thanksgiving, decorating, shopping, and preparing for Christmas morning. Joanna's marriage brought us a wonderful son-in-law, Kory and two step-grandkids, Lily and Silas. The time together was extremely special. It was an easy distraction from the yearlong failure to get bill H.401 passed, finish my book, or gain any interest in the services I could provide through EGO.

COVID-19 just added misery to the mix of negative emotions I kept at bay through conscious gratitude. The only thing I accomplished was to lose Major General Knights' respect. Many of my Guard friends were losing interest in my sexism posts. They were too tired to write anything. I was tired too. I thought of Alice Paul's quote when she was asked why she never married, and she spent her life crusading for women's rights. Strong women bestowing their strength, her mother, Tacie Parry Paul told her this: "When you put your hand to the plow, you can't put it down until you get to the end of the row." Perhaps my plow had met the end of the row. My mother was proud of me and the success I achieved. She did not embrace feminism, yet she revered strong women. Her generation often romanticized defined roles—men being men and women being women.

My book writing was my focus now, and I tried not to get distracted by the everyday sexism stories in my newsfeed. One day, Jean called and said she had a fresh approach to getting the bill passed. She had added language in an effort to address what commanders didn't like about oversight. It seemed good to me. I loved it. I started feeling excited again. This roller coaster was an emotional ride, and I could not help but get excited when a new strategy provided hope. I hung on loosely to the thought we'd be invited back to the State House, but we never were.

Another tap on my shoulder arrived in early 2021. The Vermont Commission on Women (VCW) invited me to speak at a Commission meeting. They referred to an article in *Seven Days*. The large picture of the TAG grinning, standing beside a Representative at the State House. The article: "New Policies Target Sexual Misconduct in the Vermont National Guard."[70] Written by Jasper Craven, the reporter who had written the series in *VTDigger*. The tone of this piece was more positive, giving the General's strategies time with an optimistic view. Still, Major General Knight admitted that sexual assault numbers haven't meaningfully budged on his watch, with six cases of abusive sexual contact reported so far for Fiscal Year 2020. The General said it must stop.

The only cynicism in the article was from me:

> Doris Sumner, who retired in 2019 after a long Guard career that included 13 years as the organization's equal employment and diversity manager, believes the misconduct will keep occurring

---

[70] https://www.sevendaysvt.com/vermont/new-policies-target-sexual-misconduct-in-the-vermont-national-guard-content?oid=31476375

unless systemic changes are made that go well beyond what Knight has put in place. Sumner oversaw many discrimination and retaliation cases in her Guard work. She also served as an informal den mother to mistreated members. In her mind, any policy, no matter how aspirational, can be exploited or ignored without accompanying independent oversight. The issues in the Vermont National Guard are beyond complex and require experienced professionals, in and out of the system, in order to continue the organization's focus on defense, strength and mission readiness.

In a VCW email, they stated they planned to invite General Knight to their meeting, but they wanted to hear from me first: "The members would appreciate having the perspective of a woman who was on the inside and to learn some ideas you have to make change." The Air Guard Diversity Manager called, asking if she could listen in on the VCW meeting. There was nothing to hide, so I agreed.

I read a quote from a woman in the Guard: "I live in a misogynistic world, where they don't blatantly discount women. It's much more subtle and pervasive. I can't just tell them something and have it accepted. I must justify it. They all think somehow, they can fix it because it's them. Their egos allow them to believe it."

It was another speech, another plea, another push to help

this group understand the grueling operating climate Guard women had to manage. They could not just quit. I ended my comments with: "Any organization unwilling to provide access to the command climate can maintain the command climate tolerable to them. Are the numbers not budging tolerable to us?" (Referring to the article citing the TAG admitting the numbers not budging)

The Council members asked meaningful questions. They provided accolades for the work Representative O'Sullivan had done. A few suggested they could engage with the Vermont Legislature to readdress the need for H.401. It gave me a small spark of hope. Over the course of the next six weeks, there were many local and national articles and newsfeeds regarding the blatant sexual misconduct of our society, both in the military and out. I came across an article written in *The Washington Post*, July 13, 2020. The title: "What can stop harassment in the U.S. military: Here's what my research suggests."[71] Written by Stephanie Bonnes, Ph.D.

The professor's approach to the research impressed me, but even more her attitude about the findings. The term she developed, *bureaucratic harassment*, flabbergasted me. The definition was all-consuming, it described the totality of the problem I had been trying to scream about all along. Bureaucratic harassment is the active manipulation of rules

---

[71] https://www.washingtonpost.com/politics/2020/07/13/what-can-stop-sexual-harassment-us-military/

and policies to undermine women's careers, reduce women's power in the workplace, retaliate against women for rejecting sexual advances, and prevent them from reporting sexual abuse.

I contacted Professor Bonnes hoping to exchange ideas on how to leverage our ideas on improving the culture in the military.

Professor Bonnes was friendly and open as we exchanged talk of our collective challenges regarding military sexism. I applauded the term, bureaucratic harassment, and her suggested solution; a cultural change in the warrior masculinity that denigrates the feminine. She expressed frustration with the military's stall tactics—the continuous need for studies or surveys to identify a problem they know is present. One military base asked her to conduct a survey, denying they had the same statistics the DoD and every other research institute was publishing regarding the prevalence of sex-based harm.

Her article sparked little interest in tackling the culture. She had no fresh ideas for how to get through to anyone, or suggestions for any entity who could elevate the idea of culture change and apply accountability for dismantling the masculine warrior identity. We agreed we needed a bold and powerful campaign to replace the old paradigm with a gender neutral warrior identity. It was proven time and time again—humans can fight, not just men. Professor Bonnes was writing a book, too. We promised to keep in touch. It was a gratifying connection, yet another dead end.

Guard friends were detaching from me more and more. I had Veteran buddies, and we enjoyed lighthearted posts on Facebook about our daily lives as retirees. I started to let my interest in Guard activities go a little. My heart was set on finishing my book and seeing where God wanted me to go. Maybe I could get a job.

Another tap from God. An encrypted message came to me on Facebook. The service member still in the Guard wrote: "Chief, I apologize for not seeing the culture of this organization as clear as you did."

It took my breath away because I knew the person had been quietly struggling with the command culture. The person never wanted to be quoted. She had a lot of fear.

I responded: "Well, it takes time, doesn't it? I worry about all of you and the survival techniques you have to use."

She responded: "I'm worried about me. I thought about just quitting today. But then I have to feed my family. I'm just going to do my job and put my head down until I finish school and then leave."

Rolling up my sleeves again. I wrote a letter with the salutation: "To anyone who cares about our U.S. military personnel." How many times could I send out these pleas with little response? Like many times before, I posted my outcry to my weblog and sent emails to the contacts I had collected. Signing on to LinkedIn, Twitter, and Facebook, I posted a link to the letter. I wanted to start a movement, a rallying cry, a collective voice to combat sexism. How could I help this friend and the many others who were stuffing the pain in their invisible backpacks and trudging along? I heard nothing back.

The taps from God kept coming, and I was just annoyed with it all. Each day a new article or newsflash glared like neon lights—the problem nothing was fixing. The former POTUS sex scandals, New York Governor Andrew Cuomo's sexual harassment allegations, the Marine TikTok video going viral. Each one discouraged me. I ranted: nobody cares.[72]

I was notified the VTNG TAG was set to speak to the Vermont Commission on Women (VCW) over Zoom on March 10 2021—364 days after our last engagement together. The team invited me to listen in. Feeling defeated, I didn't care, I didn't really want to listen, but I said yes. I had an attitude of surrender. My ego did not want the general looking at me. I imagined he had disdain for me. I specifically wore the red Women Empowering Women shirt my friend Karin had given each of us in the group. As I clicked on and saw myself among the group of Commissioners, I felt small.

---

[72] www.independent.co.uk/news/world/americas/us-politics/trump-sexual-assault-allegations-all-list-misconduct-karen-johnson-how-many-a9149216.html

www.pewresearch.org/short-reads/2021/08/06/fast-facts-on-views-of-workplace-harassment-amid-allegations-against-new-york-gov-cuomo/

www.wnct.com/news/military/camp-lejeune-marine-says-marine-corps-failed-her/

Life at Camp

I looked around the Zoom room and noticed General Knight had brought along a large squad of troops to meet the moment. I felt it was overkill meant to demonstrate to the Commission that he had a handle on the issues women faced in the Guard. I could see the new SEEM Zooming in from my old office.

I listened, nodding, taking notes, pursing my lips, letting every proclamation sink in. The TAG mentioned an app the VTNG instituted whereby service members could send in anonymous tips to a group of internal professionals who would collect the statements and steer advocacy, support, or policies to respond as warranted. This piqued my interest, and I wondered how the app would work.

Another woman on the virtual meeting was one of my MWP Managers. We had been in the trenches together. She helped me coordinate the 2016 Military Women's Workshop. She texted me during the call, saying she was glad to see my face. Her bicep emoji on the text warmed my heart.

The Commission chairperson thanked the general and his team for their report and then directed a quick break. I clicked off and went for a walk. A woman from the Guard sent me a message saying some leaders in the Guard got the impression from my media posts that I believed the Vermont Guard couldn't do anything right. The collection of articles quoting me eroded trust, and people backed away when that happened. She seemed to be trying to justify the enormous amount of silence from Guard members in regard to my media messages. She added: "Doris, you'd be happy with the changes being made. It takes growth and time, but the culture is truly evolving."

Later, the Air National Guard diversity officer called me. Although my granddaughter was with me, I took the call, curious about what she wanted. She touted everything their team was doing. She encouraged me to tell anyone feeling defeated to trust the system. I complimented the array of strategies and policies, and the quarterly reports being sent to the National Guard Caucus at the Vermont Legislature. I commended General Knight for claiming Diversity and Inclusion (D&I) as a priority.

These women wanted validation from me, almost eager to convince me that all was good. The diversity officer was excited as she said, "They are even considering retiring the term *Green Mountain Boys*." She thanked me and said my energy, my leadership, and the focus I put on sexism throughout my tenure is a part of why they have an established strategy. I was tearing up. My granddaughter was waving to me to come play.

I said, "Goodbye."

CHAPTER 36

PUTTING THE PLOW DOWN

★ ★ ★

The encrypted message—"I apologize for not seeing the culture...I'm worried about me...I have to feed my family...."—floated in my head. Was I abandoning her? Perhaps she would find the app the team talked about, the anonymous way to submit your honest fears regarding inclusion.

I thought about the women not on the Zoom call, the women not standing with Major General Knight. Was I abandoning them? The Guard made a compelling case that progress was being made. Women were not reaching out to me personally as often with discouraging messages. Perhaps my plow was at the end of the row.

In a surrendered mood, I wrote an email to the Vermont Commission of Women (VCW) thanking them for focusing on women of the Guard. I conceded that the General had the team and focus right. The Vermont Legislature's National Guard Caucus' quarterly updates reassured me that some oversight would continue. Determined to effect closure, I emailed former Representative Jean O'Sullivan and a member of the Military Affairs Committee, Representative Thomas Stevens. My message included: "Despite some still feeling trapped, the anonymous app the general spoke about, as a means for members to report offenses and avoid systems they still fear, is a big step and is what I have been seeking. I provided many of these issues to the leadership during my tenure, and it felt like they fell on deaf ears. But new personnel and new leadership has refreshed the energy, and I salute them all. Therefore, unless I hear more, I am withdrawing the pursuit of H.401." Representative Stevens wrote back, thanking me for my perseverance and energy. He added: "I know advocates for H.401 will be watching."

On March 11, 2021, I posted a memory on Facebook. A year before, I'd gone to the State House in Montpelier, unaware of the turbulent year that would come. I thought I could make a difference in combating the sexism everybody seemed to tolerate. My post was meant to bring some sort of closure. After a few days, my cynicism returned. He won. The general won. He'd brought his team to that Zoom meeting to convince me to stand down. There were women not on the call who, I knew, still suffered. The general knew wounded Veterans, but he never invited them to his office for a healing session. The insecurity that I did not do enough always tempted me to feel like a failure.

I did not deny Major General Knight believed he was doing

all the right things. The service men and women standing with him believed it, too. They had to believe. I gave them all credit for the changes being made. But progress was still too painfully slow in coming.

When you are a part of something, the dysfunction within it can be a blind spot. I was aware of my bias, my own sexist attitudes. Sometimes, my husband, Phil, would accuse me of hating men. "I don't hate men," I'd say. I dislike that somewhere along the evolutionary path of humanity, masculine became superior to feminine in many societies. Some believe it was the Divine's intent. I did not and do not believe that at all.

During the final days of writing my book, the Veteran who gave me the "Penis Story" sent me an article. *Seven Days* had published a piece titled, "Sergeant Accused of Sexual Assaults Remains in Vermont Guard Despite Criminal Record."[73] The author—Jasper Craven. In spite of being instantly angry, I smiled thinking Jasper would continue to shine a light on places where the Guard might fail to eradicate sexism in the force.

The story caused an uproar on social media, as angry local Veterans posted their disgust with the guy being protected. According to the article, the offender had a long rap sheet that included at least eight misdemeanor criminal

---

[73] www.sevendaysvt.com/vermont/sergeant-accused-of-sexual-assaults-remains-in-vermont-guard-despite-criminal-records/Content?oid=32612688

convictions, the latest being a sexual assault. Still carrying my resentment toward the PAOs, I read their canned responses. The Vermont Guard officials added that they never had a complete accounting of the individual's record, in large part because the Guard relies on members to self-report their own criminal charges. The TAG now touted the new positions his bill, H750, authorized, enabling a provost marshal to notify Guard leaders when service members get arrested. This was progress.

Reading the article, anger boiled within me. Wasn't I done with this work, Alice? I thought my plow had reached the end of the row. The Guard's excuses disgusted me. It was clear the sergeant—the alleged predator—was able to camouflage himself and his behavior for 15 years within the Guard. Despite all the charges against him, unit members helped their guy out and downplayed the warnings from females who had to deal with him.

I tended to take these stories personally. This was the Guard I was in—this was the SEEM job I failed at.

In the article, a woman from the Guard tells Jasper Craven how she tried to warn the organization about the offender. I knew the woman. I knew that she left the Guard before earning her 20 year retirement benefit because of the sexism she endured. That's a considerable loss for a Guard member, but it was the Guard's loss too, because she had talent, tenacity, and a high degree of competency. She wrote a post on Facebook about the *Seven Days* article that giving her first name was painful, and it was difficult for her to resist posting as people made statements.

The woman talked about denial among military supervisors who refused to see the monster the sergeant was. But she claimed she had hope for the new administration, and believed in the possibility that necessary changes might be made. Many had hope that things were going to change. My clenched fist loosened. I had to believe this scenario would never happen again. Leaders would listen more intentionally and denial would be weaker. I had to respect where current warriors were on their journeys. They were trudging the same path I had been on. It was an unrealistic expectation to think we could all be in fight mode at the same time.

These finals days, I was in a reflection period. After our rally at the entrance to Camp Johnson, several women Veterans had posted their support. A lieutenant colonel from Kentucky was a Veteran who always rooted for me. We met at a diversity conference and became instant soul sisters. We got each other like combat Veterans get each other. We held shared experiences that remain deep within you, unexplainable. You recognize the invisible battle scars, and you each know when to laugh at the pain and when to be quiet. She understood how warriors compartmentalized their pain to stay in the fight. The Kentucky National Guard had hired her as a Diversity Manager, but they didn't take her seriously. She posted on my personal Facebook site:

> I served 32 years in the military, but had blinders on, blinders that allowed me to focus on my own civilian and military education and achievement. I did not think of all I witnessed and experienced until I was assigned to the Kentucky SAPRO and worked in Equal Opportunity and Diversity. As I attempted to coordinate events, I was told these were hen parties. I began to notice the women leaving and why. I identified the lack of emotional intelligence in the masculine power core. As I aspired to make rank, my respect for the system, not the military, dwindled. I was then haunted by all that I had not noticed, and all that I had not championed. My thanks to the brave women of the VT Guard who share their stories. My admiration and salute to Doris, who has tried and tried to bring awareness and now will be publishing a book.

The whisper, "Let go" was getting louder. I was sad about letting go. I thought there was so much more fighting to do. Do I like to fight? I never liked to fight, but I did fight when it was needed. I was proud of that now. I accepted it would take many more cultural battles before this fight was done. As a friend had put it—growth and time. I could feel it. I was out of time. My plow was at the end of the row.

I thought back when, in the midst of my battles to combat sexism while I was in uniform, I would sometimes ask to meet with a survivor whose case I had processed. It was her circumstance that often fueled my determination to keep fighting. I would discuss my strategies with her. She listened, understood, and asked: "What do you want your legacy to be about?" I told her then, point blank, I wanted to combat sexism in the Guard. I see today, my answer was an unrealistic expectation. A.A.'s infamous line, "Progress not perfection," pinged my heart.

I met this woman a few more times over the years, always feeling guilty for hanging on to an event she would prefer to put in the past. But she supported my efforts, and she agreed to let me write about her case in my book. She told me she had a new life now, and her wound had healed. My wound was still open at the time.

Over the course of the last few occasions when I had high hopes, I heard the voice inside telling me to let go and allow the struggle to pass to new warriors. The battle *hand-off* was necessary. I felt a sense of calm coming to me. I thought about what I learned: It will not be an aha moment or victory. A documentary like *The Invisible War* did not defeat systemic dysfunction. Like the Military Justice Improvement Act, the I am Vanessa Guillén Act of 2021 (MIJA), and all the other actions taken during this struggle, including the Nineteenth amendment, they were moments in time, fleeting celebrations on the spectrum of change. Alice Paul's slight smile in my photograph reflected her insight—she knew there would be more battles. Progress was being made; the TAG's squad of activists proclaimed their hope and vigor, their determination to extend privilege to all. I'd been waiting for a general to say, "Oh, we get it, Chief," and actually implement the H.401 bill for gender equality—and that this action would minimize offenses from that time forward.

I could see clearly now, there would be no such scene. I accepted that the United States military will always be evolving, just like humanity. I learned that I did make a difference. I learned to be grateful for being a part of the solution, and I didn't need to *be* the solution. I learned that men are trapped, too, in the warrior masculine identity. I learned that I had found a place to put the pain of sexual offenses—rolling it into the actions I could never let go of. Without this pain, I might have done less. The struggle was my purpose, and I felt proud, slightly smiling like Alice.

I was in a small State, a small National Guard unit, but my view of the problem and the solution was big. My respect for all Veterans: past, current, and future warriors, grew immensely. I could feel my gratitude to all of the leaders who tried hard with me. I learned that combating sexism will continue, and I learned to be OK with that, too. Perhaps my book will enlighten activists, encourage them to consider actions needed in male dominated organizations that cling to hyper masculine identity. The cultural power needs to shift. Perhaps someone will help redefine our United States military, so when we think of freedom fighters, we do not see gender.

Phil had built a tree house in the corner of our property. It was my favorite place to be when I took a break from life's mission. Today, I thought about the long, hard journey. I had broken branches that blocked me on my trudge. I wore the path down, making the direction easier to see for others who may follow. I stood on the platform and pondered: what was it all for? Not for the "Mission Accomplished" banner. The journey was progress, like the many before me had accomplished, and those who will follow me will accomplish. I nodded. I had to let go of the plow for now. Perhaps my book would inspire someone or some action. I could feel the grip on my expectations loosening.

The world was better today. In my tree house, I took off the imaginary backpack. I took out the pain, sorrow, regrets, expectations, and all the stories entrusted to me. I laid them down, and I asked God to take them, heal me. I asked God to let warriors know—I was not abandoning them; I was entrusting them to a power greater than myself.

We were never really tolerating sexism. We were fighting sexism. Women joining the United States military are joining an evolving entity, just as I did in 1981. Their grit, competence, courage, and talent will battle on. Men, too, will embrace the diversity.

Life at Camp

I was suddenly lighter. I had a calm sense of energy. I wasn't reluctant to continue on whatever journey lay ahead. I could put the plow away, Alice. I could play now with my granddaughter, trusting the world was a better place for her.

If my granddaughter told me one day, "I'm joining the Army," I would not gasp. I would salute her.

The End, for now.

DIAGRAM 1
FULL TIME FORCE STRUCTURE VS. DRILL STATUS STRUCTURE

General diagram of a State NG workforce structure. All States are different, however, all have a force of personnel who work full time (Monday through Friday) in varying employment statuses to support those in uniform who come in one weekend a month to train. It is important to note the power of the full time personnel, who establish and maintain the strategic objectives and coordinate with the State Legislatures on the readiness of the force.

Joint Force Headquarters Unit located at the Headquarters of the State located at the HQ of the State National Guard. Air and Army personnel work here. This is where the Adjutant General and other top officers work full-time and are militarily assigned to a unit, where they serve on drill weekends.

A Wing of the Air National Guard Wings are typically all contained in one loWings are in one location. A Wing Commander, Vice Wing Commander and staff in the HQ unit. Depending on mission, several or more Groups (Large Units) such as Operations, Logistics, Maintenance, Information Operations, Security. In each group, there are Squadrons, in each Squadron, there are Flights. The number of personnel assigned depends on the mission of the Wing.

Each **Army Brigade** (State size, two to five Brigades) each has a HQ unit and a team of full time staff work during the week to prepare for drill weekends. # of personnel assigned depends on mission

Each Brigade will have several **Battalions (BN)** Army BN HQ, same as Brigade-has full time staff preparing for drill weekends.

Each BN will have several **Companies**, Staffed with full timers

Maintenance Shops supporting BN's are staffed with full timers

All of these units have drilling members who are assigned to positions and come once a month to conduct the training or exercises set up and supported by the full time staff. Generally, 1/3 of the total force works full time or civilian resources (federal technicians) are hired to conduct the business. Most States use a State Military Department to maintain the buildings and grounds of the bases.

Many States have a **Regiment School House** with a full time staff and instructors on orders cycling through Army soldiers from across the U.S. between drills for Army Service Component Leadership schools.

Vermont has a **Training Site Facility** and unit which maintain the Ethan Allen Firing Range used by units for weapons qualification.

Vermont has a **Mountain Warfare School** with full time staff and soldiers on orders conducting training for DoD students from Vt or around the Globe.

Vermont is considered a small State. In 2019 the approximate strength was 2,400 Army soldiers drilling and 950 Air Guard drilling at one Wing. A full-time staff of approximately 500 Federal Technicians and 400 Active Guard Reserve members.

Both workforces gender representation has remained consistent between 13-19% for the last decade, with a representation of women in key leader positions between 5-10%.

Reference; https://legislature.vermont.gov/Documents/2020/WorkGroups/House%20General/Military%20Affairs/National%20Guard/W~Steven%20Cray~Vermont%20National%20Guard%20-%20Military%20Women's%20Program%20Annual%20Gender%20Report%20-%202018~1-22-2019.pdf

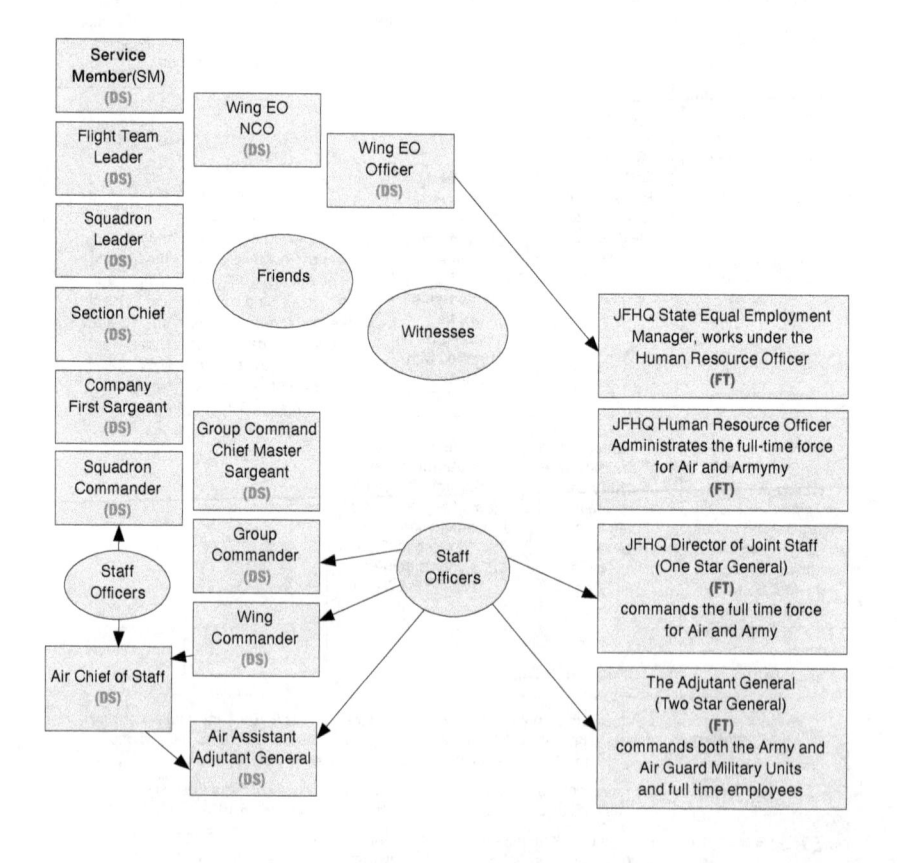

DIAGRAM 2A
AIR CHAIN OF COMMAND AND EO PROCESS

General diagram of Air Guard unit chain of command positions for military and EO Process

Air Units: Flight, Squadron, Group, Wing

Commander Rank: Captain-Flight, Major/Lt Col-Squadron, Mid-grade Colonel-Group. Senior Colonel or Brigadier General-Wing

Equal Opportunity titles in Air Guard: Equal Opportunity Non-Commissioned Officer (NCO), Equal Opportunity Officer for the Wing Works Monday through Friday as Federal Technicians or Active Guard Reserve employees **(FT)**

Works one weekend a month and two weeks a year, drill status employee **(DS)**

- Service Member (SM) (DS)
- Flight Team Leader (DS)
- Squadron Leader (DS)
- Section Chief (DS)
- Company First Sargeant (DS)
- Squadron Commander (DS)
- Staff Officers
- Air Chief of Staff (DS)
- Wing EO NCO (DS)
- Wing EO Officer (DS)
- Friends
- Witnesses
- Group Command Chief Master Sargeant (DS)
- Group Commander (DS)
- Wing Commander (DS)
- Staff Officers
- Air Assistant Adjutant General (DS)
- JFHQ State Equal Employment Manager, works under the Human Resource Officer (FT)
- JFHQ Human Resource Officer Administrates the full-time force for Air and Armymy (FT)
- JFHQ Director of Joint Staff (One Star General) (FT) commands the full time force for Air and Army
- The Adjutant General (Two Star General) (FT) commands both the Army and Air Guard Military Units and full time employees

DIAGRAM 2B
ARMY CHAIN OF COMMAND AND EO PROCESS

General diagram of Army Guard unit chain of command positions for military and EO

Army Units: Team, Squad, Platoon, Company, Battalion, Brigade, Division/Installation

Commander Rank: Captain-Company, Lieutenant Colonel-Battalion, Colonel-Brigade, General-Division or Installation

Equal Opportunity titles in Army Guard: Equal Opportunity Leader (EOL)-Company & Battalion, Equal Opportunity Advisor (EOA)-Brigade, Human Resource Equal Opportunity Officer (HREO), Installation

Works Monday through Friday as Federal Technicians or Active Guard Reserve employees **(FT)**

Works one weekend a month and two weeks a year, drill status employee **(DS)**

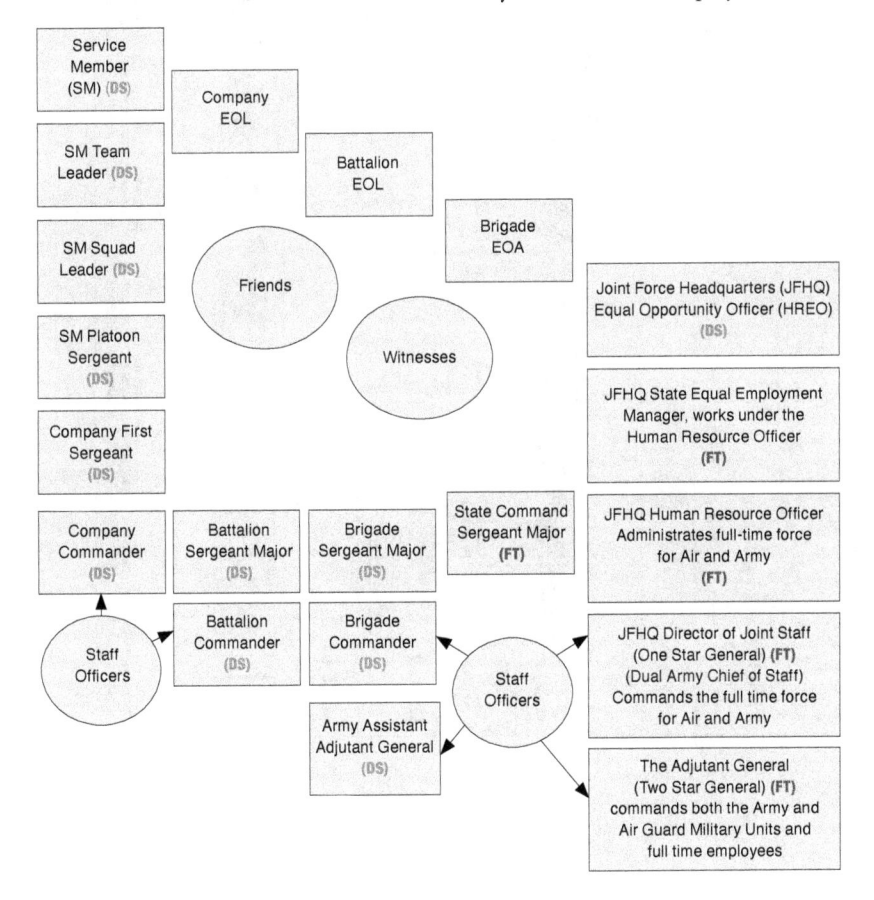

- Service Member (SM) (DS)
- Company EOL
- SM Team Leader (DS)
- Battalion EOL
- SM Squad Leader (DS)
- Brigade EOA
- Friends
- Joint Force Headquarters (JFHQ) Equal Opportunity Officer (HREO) (DS)
- SM Platoon Sergeant (DS)
- Witnesses
- JFHQ State Equal Employment Manager, works under the Human Resource Officer (FT)
- Company First Sergeant (DS)
- Company Commander (DS)
- Battalion Sergeant Major (DS)
- Brigade Sergeant Major (DS)
- State Command Sergeant Major (FT)
- JFHQ Human Resource Officer Administrates full-time force for Air and Army (FT)
- Staff Officers
- Battalion Commander (DS)
- Brigade Commander (DS)
- Staff Officers
- JFHQ Director of Joint Staff (One Star General) (FT) (Dual Army Chief of Staff) Commands the full time force for Air and Army
- Army Assistant Adjutant General (DS)
- The Adjutant General (Two Star General) (FT) commands both the Army and Air Guard Military Units and full time employees

DIAGRAM 3A
AIR FORCE RANK

Enlisted

	E-1	E-2	E-3	E-4	E-5	E-6	E-7	E-8	E-9	E-9
Air Force	No Insignia									
	Airman Basic (AB)	Airman (Amn)	Airman First Class (A1C)	Senior Airman (SrA)	Staff Sergeant (SSgt)	Technical Sergeant (TSgt)	Master Sergeant (MSgt) / First Sergeant (E-7)	Senior Master Sergeant (SMSgt) / First Sergeant (E-8)	Chief Master Sergeant (CMSgt) / First Sergeant (E-9) / Command Chief Master Sergeant (CCMSgt)	Chief Master Sergeant of the Air Force (CMSgt)

Officer

	O-1	O-2	O-3	O-4	O-5	O-6	O-7	O-8	O-9	O-10	
Air Force	2nd Lieutenant (2nd Lt.)	1st Lieutenant (1st Lt.)	Captain (Capt.)	Major (Maj.)	Lieutenant Colonel (Lt. Col.)	Colonel (Col.)	Brigadier General (Brig. Gen.)	Major General (Maj. Gen.)	Lieutenant General (Lt. Gen.)	General (Gen.)	General of the Air Force (reserved for wartime only.)

DIAGRAM 3B
ARMY RANK

INSIGNIA OF THE UNITED STATES ARMY

ENLISTED (Green and Gold)

E-1	E-2	E-3	E-4	E-4	E-5	E-6
No Insignia Private	Private	Private 1st Class	Corporal	Specialist	Sargeant	Staff Sargeant

E-7	E-8	E-8	E-9	E-9	E-9
Sargeant 1st Class	Master Sargeant	1st Sargeant	Sargeant Major	Command Sargeant Major	Staff Sargeant

WARRANT OFFICER (Silver and Black)

W-1	W-2	W-3	W-4	W-5
Sargeant 1st Class	Chief Warrant Officer	Chief Warrant Officer	Chief Warrant Officer	Master Warrant Officer

COMPANY AND FIELD GRADE OFFICER (Gold and Silver)

O-1	O-2	O-3	O-4	O-5	O-6
(Gold) 2nd Lieutenant	(Silver) 1st Lieutenant	(Silver) Captain	(Gold) Major	(Silver) Lieutenant Colonel	(Silver) Colonel

GENERAL OFFICER (Silver)

O-7	O-8	O-9	O-10	O-11
Brigadier General	Major General	Lieutenant General	General	General of the Army

577

DIAGRAM 4
ACRONYMS AND TERMS TABLE

AAP	Affirmative Action Plan	An Equal Opportunity report identifying underrepresented groups of employees and how the agency plans to diversify representation.
AASF	Army Aviation Support Facility	A large building located near the national airport where Army aviation units are maintained.
ACFT	Army Combat Fitness Test	The Army Combat Fitness Test is the assessment for the physical domain of the Army's Holistic Health and Fitness System. As a general physical fitness test, an age and gender performance-normed scoring scale will be used to evaluate a Soldier's physical fitness.
AG or TAG	Adjutant General, The Adjutant General	Indivdiual in charge of the federally recognized National Guard and any other organizations or components of the organized militia as may be created by the governor pursuant to federal or state law in each state. In the majority of states, the adjutant general is appointed by the governor. Sometimes the acronym AG is used as well as TAG.
AAG	Assistant Adjutant General	The Assistant Adjutant General an officer to assist the TAG in the discharge and performance of his or her duties.
AGR	Active Guard Reserve	Active Guard Reserve Service members that serve full time on Active Duty in the National Guard units and directly support the NG.
ALICE	All-Purpose Lightweight Carrying Equipment	A military backpack, load-carrying Individual Carrying equipment for Army soldiers.
ANG	Air National Guard	A federal military reserve force of the United States Air Force.
APFT	Army Physical Fitness Test	The Army Combat Fitness Test is the assessment for the physical domain of

		the Army's Holistic Health and Fitness System. As a general physical fitness test, an age and gender performance-normed scoring scale will be used to evaluate a Soldier's physical fitness.
ARNG	Army National Guard	A federal military reserve force of the United States Army.
ASLC	Army Senior Leader Council	An Army council made up of top enlisted advisors and senior level commanders.
A.T.	Annual Training	The field duty event for drilling members of the National Guard, generally lasting 14 days.
CDET	Cultural Diversity Enhancement Team	A diversity council helping with the agencies strategic diversity goals.
CDET	Cultural Diversity Enhancement Team	A diversity council helping with the agencies strategic diversity goals.
CDET	CDET Representative	A VTNG specific collateral (part-time) service position on the agency's diversity council. Volunteers had responsibilities to update diversity bulletin boards, print out diversity flyer events, add events to unit newsletters and attend diversity meeting to provide updates
Challenge Coin	Challenge Coin	Historically, challenge coins are presented by commanders in recognition of special achievement.
Chief	A warrant officer grade	An officer in the armed forces holding rank by virtue of a warrant and ranking above a noncommissioned officer and below a commissioned officer.
Cmdr	Commander	An officer in charge of a military operation or organization.
CMSgt	Chief Master Sergeant	An Air Force rank, senior enlisted E9.

CNGB	Chief of the National Guard Bureau	An officer who is a member of the Joint Chiefs of Staff. In this capacity, serves as a military adviser to the President, Secretary of Defense, National Security Council and is the DoD's official channel of communication to the Governors and State TAGs on all matters pertaining to the NG. Is responsible for ensuring the more than 453,000 Army and Air National Guard personnel are accessible, capable and ready to protect the homeland and provide combat ready resources to the Army and Air Force.
Competitive service Title 5	Competitive service employment	Positions subject to the civil service laws passed by Congress to ensure that applicants and employees receive fair and equal treatment in the hiring process. Individuals must go through a competitive hiring process before being appointed which is open to all applicants. This process may consist of a written test, an evaluation of the individual's education and experience, and/or an evaluation of other attributes necessary for successful performance in the position to be filled.
CSM	Command Sergeant Major	An Army rank, senior enlisted E9 with command authority.
DACOWITS	Defense Advisory Committee on Women in the Services	Committee composed of civilian women and men appointed by the Secretary of Defense to provide advice and recommendations on matters and policies relating to the recruitment, retention, employment, integration, well-being, and treatment of women in the Armed Forces of the United States.
DJS	Director Joint Staff	A position in the National Guard Headquarters, the rank of general 1-star who oversees the full time employees of both services.
DoD	Department of Defense	The Department of Defense provides the

		military forces needed to deter war and ensure our nation's security.
EEMAC	Equal Employment Management Advisory Council	The council made up of representatives from Management Advisory each regional State Equal Employment Council Manager in the National Guard. 8 regions and one SEEM nominated as the EEMAC Chair. The EEMAC Chair represents all SEEMs and is the conduit between the SEEM community and the NGB Equal Opportunity director.
EEO	Equal Employment Opportunity	Equal Employment Opportunity is the federal program managing discrimination cases.
ENFJ	Extroverted Intuitive Feeling Judging	One of the 16 types of personalities identified by the Myers Briggs Type Indicator.
EO	Equal Opportunity	Equal Opportunity is used for the Military program managing discrimination cases.
EOA	Equal Opportunity Advisor	An army position title to depict the person who assist commanders of brigades in managing the Equal Opportunity program.
EOL	Equal Opportunity Leader	An army position title to depict the person who assist commanders of companies or battalions in managing the Equal Opportunity program.
EOLC	Equal Opportunity Leaders Course	The Army proponent course to train soldiers who have been appointed with the additional duty of Equal Opportunity Leader.
EPMS	Enlisted Personnel Management System	The management of enlisted soldiers, who represent the majority of the force, drives personnel readiness in all components of the Army. The Enlisted Personnel Management System (EPMS) is the total

		process that supports personnel readiness and the soldier's professional development and personal welfare.
ESGR	Employer Support for the Guard Reserve	ESGR, a Department of Defense office, is comprised of trained volunteers and staff. They work to promote employer support for Guard and Reserve service by advocating relevant initiatives, recognizing outstanding support, increasing awareness of applicable laws, and resolving conflict between employers and Service members.
Excepted service	Excepted service employment	EXCEPTED SERVICE positions in the National Guard Technician Program that require military membership in the National Guard as a condition of technician employment are in the excepted service under the provisions of 32 USC 709. This status means you are excepted from the rules that govern civil service employees in the areas of tenure and competitive requirements for appointments. Employment as a NG military technician does not result in competitive civil service status. Loss of military membership for any reason will cause termination of technician employment.
First Sergeant	Sometimes referred to as 1SG, First Shirt, Top	The first sergeant serves as the commander's advisor on all enlisted matters of the unit. The first sergeant is the highest-ranking non-commissioned officer that still performs hands-on leadership. Although equal in grade to rank of master sergeant (MSG), personnel at these two ranks typically have very different responsibilities. The first sergeant ensures the force understands the commander's policies, goals and objectives, and also ensures support agencies are responsive to the needs of all assigned unit personnel and their families.

GAO	General Accounting Office	GAO provides Congress, the heads of executive agencies, and the public with timely, fact-based, non-partisan information that can be used to improve government and save taxpayers billions of dollars.
GSLC	General Senior Leader Council (GSLC)	In the National Guard, the GSLC was a council made up of Adjutant Generals from the States and Territories.
HMMWV	High Mobility Multipurpose Wheeled Vehicle also spelled out humvee	A four-wheel drive, military truck and utility vehicle produced by AM General.
HQ	Headquarters	The main administrative function of a unit.
HR	Human Resources	The short version for Human Resources Office.
HREO	Human Resources Equal Opportunity Officer	A position in the National Guard Headquarters, which manages the military Equal Opportunity program for the Adjutant General.
HRO	Human Resources Office or Officer	A function of the National Guard which handles hiring, benefits, retirement and other administrative needs for employees. The head of the department title.
IG	Inspector General	Leads an organization charged with examining the actions of a government agency, military organization, or military contractor as a general auditor of their operations to ensure they are operating in compliance with generally established policies of the government, to audit the effectiveness of security procedures, or to discover the possibility of misconduct, waste, fraud, theft, or certain types of criminal activity by individuals or groups related to the agency's operation, usually involving some misuse of the organization's funds or credit.

JAG	Judge Advocate General	Judge advocates are commissioned officers in one of the U.S. Armed Forces that serve as legal advisors to the command in which they are assigned.
JDEC	Joint Diversity Executive Council	A diversity council with senior level members overseeing the agencies strategic diversity goals.
JDEC Chair	Joint Diversity Executive Council Chair	"Each State National Guard has a JDEC with a 1-star Brigadier General who represents the JDEC. Each Region (8 in the U.S.) represents a Regional JDEC Chair. The Chief of the National Guard Bureau appoints an overall NGB JDEC Chair. The JDEC's meet monthly in State, quarterly in regions and annually with the CNGB."
JSLC	Joint Senior Leader Council	A military council made up of senior leaders who discuss strategic objectives and determine mission priorities. Generally led by a 2-Star General and the Brigade or Wing Commanders as well as the top Enlisted Advisors of the force represented.
MBTI	Myers Briggs Type Indicator	A introspective self-report questionnaire indicating differing psychological preferences in how people perceive the world and make decisions.
MEPS	Military Entrance Processing Station	A joint service organization that determines an applicants physical qualifications, aptitude, and moral standards.
MOS	Military Occupational Specialty	Used by the U.S. military to identify a specific job.
MST	Military Sexual Trauma	A term used by the military to refer to experiences of sexual assault or sexual harassment experienced during military service.

MWC	Military Women's Council	Vermont Guard council made of members supporting the Military Women's Program.
MWP	Military Women's Program	Vermont specific acronym for the Vermont National Guard women's council focused on improving the unit-level experience for women in the Guard.
NCO	Non-Commissioned Officer	A non-commissioned officer (NCO) is a military officer who has yet to earn a rank or commission. These individuals hold leadership positions within their units, but they rank lower than commissioned officers.
NGB	National Guard Bureau	A federal instrument responsible for the administration of the National Guard established by the United States Congress as a joint bureau of the Department of the Army and the Department of the Air Force.
NG	National Guard	A special part of the U.S. military that answers to both state governors and the president.
NGB-EO	National Guard Bureau Equal Opportunity	The National Guard Bureau's Equal Opportunity program.
OD	olive drab	In the military, od green stands for olive drab, which is a color that is commonly used in camouflage.
OIC	Officer In Charge	A military title for the officer commanding a specific mission.
OPM	Office of Personnel Management	Function to serve as the chief human resources agency and personnel policy manager for the Federal Government.
P.T.	Physical Training	The military acronym for exercising. Short for APFT.
PAO	Public Affairs Officer or Officer	Public Affairs Officers research, plan, budget, execute, and evaluate operations involving the public. They liaise with the

		news media and provide guidance to senior leaders on decisions that impact mission success. They also collect and present information to internal staff on current operations and matters affecting the military community.
PEC	Professional Education Center	The Lavern E. Weber Professional Education Center, located at Camp Robinson in North Little Rock, Arkansas, is the national training center for the Army National Guard. The Professional Education Center (PEC) has been a full-service training and conferencing facility since 1974.
PSC	Personnel Service Company	A unit designation once used in the Vermont National Guard. The unit's garrison purpose was to review personnel records for other units in the organization and submit for updates as necessary.
PX	Post Exchange	It is basically a retail store, typically set up like a department store or a strip mall, with smaller shops and service vendors nearby. Many installations have an exchange, some with uniform shops, barbershops, laundry and dry cleaning, gas stations and convenience stores, fast food outlets and lawn and garden shops. Every service branch has its own exchange system either a PX (post exchange), or a BX (base exchange)? and they're all operated separately.
RRB	Army Recruiting and Retention Battalion	The unit in the Army National Guard that recruits citizens into the force and conducts administrative actions to retain service members.
SAIGE	Society of American Indian Government Employees	National non-profit organization representing American Indian and Alaska Native Federal, Tribal, State, and local government employees.

SAPR	Sexual Assault Prevention and Response	The title of the Air Guard Sexual Assault program.
SAPRO	Sexual Assault Prevention and Response Office	A function which represents the Secretary of Defense as the central authority charged with preventing sexual assault in the military and facilitating recovery for survivors.
SARC	Sexual Assault Response Coordinator	A program manager of the Sexual Assault Prevention and Response Office.
SEEM	State Equal Employment Manager	The Manager of Equal Employment Opportunity (EEO) will oversee and implement the company equal employment opportunity and affirmative action policies and plans and will provide management with guidance related to equal employment opportunity and affirmative action requirements.
SEPM	Special Emphasis Program Manager	Special Emphasis Programs (SEP) were established in the Federal Government to remove barriers to equal employment opportunity for groups that were traditionally not represented or subjected to discrimination in the workforce. SEPMs are the Program Managers of these programs.
SGM	Sergeant Major	An Army rank, senior enlisted E9.
SHARP	Sexual Harassment/ Assault Response and Prevention	The Army's integrated program to provide a proactive effort to end sexual harassment and sexual assault.
SME	Subject Matter Expert	The military uses the term for an individual(s) who exhibits the highest level of expertise in performing a specialized job, task, or skill within the organization.
SPMO	Support Personnel Management Office	Old name for the full time federal office managing title 32 federal technicians and active-guard-reserve employees of the

		State National Guard. Changed to Human Resources Office (HRO) in the 90s.
TAG	The Adjutant General	The adjutant general is the individual in charge of the federally recognized National Guard and any other organizations or components of the organized militia as may be created by the governor pursuant to federal or state law in each state. In the majority of states, the adjutant general is appointed by the governor.
Technician	Title 32 federal technician/ title 5 civilian federal technician/	Title 32 federal technicians are in the excepted service under the provisions of 32 USC 709. The employee serves in a civilian position (M-F) in the administration and training of the NG or in the maintenance and repair of supplies or equipment issued to the NG or the Armed Forces. Title 32 excepted positions require military membership as a condition of technician employment. This status means you are "excepted" from the rules that govern civil service employees in the areas of tenure and competitive requirements for appointments. Loss of military membership for any reason will cause termination of technician employment. Title 5 competitive (civilian) federal technicians are those employees that fall under the civil service requirements. The NG has a percentage of the full time force in excepted and competitive positions.
TDY	Temporary Duty Travel	A TDY trip is pre-authorized official travel to a location, usually of a short-term duration to conduct official business or training."
TF	Task Force	A unit specially organized for a task.

Training stand-down	Training stand-down	A training stand-down is an organized cessation of normal duties until a specific training is accomplished.
UCMJ	Uniformed Code of Military Justice	The UCMJ is federal law, enacted by Congress which applies to all active duty members as well as activated National Guard and Reserve members and military academy students. Some civilians serving in support of the military during wartime are also subject to the UCMJ.
VA	Victim Advocate (The acronym is also used for Veteran's Administration, however, not in the context of *Life at Camp*.)	A person who provides immediate and ongoing support to victims of sexual offenses by providing resources and information. They work under the direction of the unit SARC.
VTANG	Vermont Air National Guard	The Vermont Air National Guard, we pronounced it like V-TANG.
VTARNG	Vermont Army National Guard	The designation given to the National Guard Army unit in the State of Vermont.
VTNG	Vermont National Guard	The designation given to the National Guard units of the Air Force and Army in the State of Vermont.
Wing	Short for Air Base flying unit	The Vermont Air National Guard is officially the 158th Fighter Wing. Airmen refer to the base in short as the Wing.
XO	Executive Officer	The XO is the second-in-command, reporting to the commanding officer. The XO is typically responsible for the management of day-to-day activities, freeing the commander to concentrate on strategy and planning the unit's next move.

ADDENDUM 1

★ ★ ★

Original submission May 14, 2018 and updated November 1, 2018: Recommendations to Combat Sexism in the National Guard from Vermont State Equal Employment and Diversity Manager, CW4 Doris Sumner.

National Level;
1. Make Combating Sexism a theme and priority for National inclusion message and or the next CNGB Diversity and Inclusion Workshop.

2. Create a PSA regarding sexism in the NG Military and our commitment to combat it and not just tolerate it. Use real service members in the ads who have been managing the sexism and are seeking a change in tolerance and how we are holding ourselves accountab to call it out, report without reprisal and respectfu and responsibly respond.

3. Institute a policy to ensure all sexually based offenses are reported at the lowest level regardless if a service member wishes to file a resolution request IAW

Complaints Management Regulations. Sexually based incidents include informal incidents which include crude offensive behavior. Unit Equal Opportunity Leaders and Victim Advocates advise lowest level leadership on response. Incident reports are channeled through the Equal Opportunity lanes to State Equal Employment Manager and shared with Sexual Harassment Assault Response Program Coordinators. The incident reports are used to identify offense trends as well as responses.

4. Request research be developed and reported on the prevalence of sexually based offenses and the representation of women within the command.

5. Advise Leader Development Schools to incorporate additional training on the phenomenon of unconscious bias training and how this impacts the decision-making process. Specifically, gender oblivion as described in the Army Research Institute studies in integration of women into combat roles (Project Diane[74]). Also, Professor Stephanie Bonnes article[75], 'What can stop sexual harassment in the U.S. Military.'

---

[74] https://united-we.org/news/project-diane
[75] www.washingtonpost.com/politics/2020/07/13/what-can-stop-sexual-harassment-us-military

6. Advise DEOMI and other Proponent School Houses to develop course curriculum for EO, Diversity, HRA practitioners to learn the history of the women's movement for equality. To understand the negative impacts the entrenched outdated gender stereotypes are having within the organization. Course content should include the practical counter-measures being adopted as best practices in corporate climates and how to employ those at the operational levels of the National Guard.

7. Direct both Air and Army NGB Equal Opportunity, Diversity, Human Relations, SHARP/SAPR Programs to coordinate National/Regional workshop on the topic of unconscious bias training focusing on gender (sexism) and include counter-measures to disrupt the negative impacts.

8. Ensure Program Directorates from all wellness programs, EO, EEO, Diversity and Inclusion, ANG Human Relations Advisors, SHARP/SAPR, Suicide Prevention, Drug/Alcohol Prevention, Family Readiness, Veteran Outreach and Resiliency Programs have opportunities to participate in workshop on the topic of unconscious bias training focusing on gender (sexism) to better understand how gender covertly shapes the nature of daily practices.

9. National Guard Bureau adopt a support directive for Military Lean In Circles as originally done by 2015 Secretary of Defense Ash Carter.
10. Solicit gender demographics from each state and Territory annually to review recruiting, retention, promotion rates and progress integrating women into non-traditional occupations comparing to the prevalence of sexism measurements.

State Level:
1. Make Combating Sexism a theme and priority for State readiness message.
2. Nest State policy from NGB on the Reporting of Sexually Based Offenses (incident reporting).
3. Direct both Air and Army State Equal Opportunity, Diversity, Human Relations, SHAPR/SAPR Programs to coordinate state workshops on the topic of unconscious bias training focusing on gender (sexism) and include counter-measures to disrupt the negative impacts.
4. Ensure program directorates from state wellness programs, EO, EEO, Diversity and Inclusion, ANG Human Relations Advisors, SHARP/SAPR, Suicide Prevention, Drug/Alcohol Prevention, Family Readiness, Veteran Outreach and Resiliency Programs have opportunities to participate in workshops on the topic of unconscious bias training focusing on

gender (sexism) to better understand how gender covertly shapes the nature of daily practices.
5. Conduct Lean In Circles as encouraged by NGB support directive.
6. Create gender demographics report annually to review recruiting, retention, promotion rates and progress integrating women into non-traditional occupations comparing to the prevalence of sexism measurements.

Commander Level;
1. Make Combating Sexism a theme and priority for ACOM readiness message.
2. Nest Command policy from State on the Reporting of Sexually Based Offenses (incident reporting).
3. Support training allowance for workshops on the topic of unconscious bias training focusing on gender (sexism) and include counter-measures to disrupt the negative impacts.
4. Conduct Lean In Circles as encouraged by State support directive.
5. Ensure performance measures accurately reflect support for gender equality. Measurable items include attendance at training on the topic of unconscious bias focusing on gender (sexism). Other measures include attendance or support of Lean

In Circles at unit level, maintenance of valid mentoring relationships, leadership moments which include intervening early when witnessing offensive, subordinates accountable for sexist comments, acts or policy violations of substantiated sexual harassment and UCMJ violations.

Individual Level;
1. Attend and participate as required training on the topic of unconscious bias training focusing on gender (sexism).
2. Participate as mission allows in Lean In Circles.
3. Ensure your performance reflects support for gender equality. Measurable items include attendance at training on the topic of unconscious bias focusing on gender (sexism). Other measures include attendance or support of Lean In Circles at unit level, maintenance of valid mentoring relationships, leadership moments which include intervening early when witnessing offensive, sexist or objectifying language or acts. Holding subordinates accountable for sexist comments, acts or policy violations of substantiated sexual harassment and UCMJ violations.

NOTE:

Vermont Statutes Annotated, Title 20 § 427.[76] Requires the Adjutant General to Report to the Vermont Legislative body annually the number of sexual harassments, sexual assault and sexual orientation harassment cases. The report must provide the policies in support of prevention and the disposition of substantiated cases. In 2018 the Vermont Statute was amended to also include the annual Gender Representation Report depicting the overall percent of women and the representation of women in command positions. The agency will report efforts to increase recruiting, retention and promotion of women.

The Vermont National Guard Reporting of Sexual Harassment Incident Policy was created in 2014 to measure the prevalence of sexually based offenses. These incidents are situations in which the aggrieved does not wish to submit a discrimination case, however the actions meet the criteria within the policy of sexually based offenses on the spectrum of harm. The policy requires the lowest level command to seek advice from the SJA, EO or SHARP personnel in how to best respond to the incident to eradicate the continuance of sexist behavior while respectfully validating aggrieved service members.

---

[76] https://legislature.vermont.gov/statutes/section/20/023/00427

ACKNOWLEDGMENTS

★ ★ ★

First and foremost, I thank my higher power who never abandoned me even when I abandoned thee. This source of love, acceptance and energy cannot be denied; I know I would have missed my purposed filled life without tapping into this awesome fountain. I thank my husband Phil who always accepted who I needed to be. I thank my children for teaching me about unconditional love and the many forms of powerlessness as a parent. I learned from them, we don't control the outcome, the universe does. All we could do was our best. I would not have written a book if it was not for Paul Diaco who I met through her sign making business. She coached me into becoming an author and introduced me to her sister Pat Goudy OBrien my editor. Thank you, Pat, for so many hours and emails to form this memoir from my heart. Finding the professionals who assisted the publishing process were God moments. I thank Stephen Russell Payne who mentored me and provided guidance on how to become a published author. Carrie Cook for her artistry and emotional cheerleading to endure the challenges of bringing this project to the public. Thank you, Lara Bessette, for proofreading all the acronyms and titles and your enthusiasm for the project. Thank you Karin, for being my Lucy. My alcoholic anonymous support systems who kept me sane and sober. All the Veterans in my social newsfeed that liked my *Life at Camp* updates and sent me messages to keep up the fight. My family who believed I could do this, thank you all.